THE BIG BOOK OF CANADIAN GHOST STORIES

Other Books of Canadian Mysteries by J.R. Colombo

"They are the best collections of their kind being produced by anyone, anywhere, as far as I can see." (Hilary Evans)

Strange but True (Hounslow / Dundurn, 2007)
More True Canadian Ghost Stories (Prospero, 2005)
Terrors of the Night (Hounslow / Dundurn, 2005)
The Monster Book of Canadian Monsters (BSDB, 2004)
True Canadian UFO Stories (Prospero, 2004)
The Midnight Hour (Hounslow / Dundurn, 2004)
True Canadian Ghost Stories (Prospero, 2003)
Many Mysteries (C&C, 2001)
Ghost Stories of Canada (Hounslow / Dundurn, 2000)
Ghosts in Our Past (C&C, 2000)
Weird Stories (C&C, 1999)
The UFO Quote Book (C&C, 1999)
Mysteries of Ontario (Hounslow / Dundurn, 1999)
Singular Stories (C&C, 1999)
Three Mysteries of Nova Scotia (C&C, 1999)
The UFO Quote Book (C&C, 1999)
Closer than You Think (C&C, 1998)
Marvellous Stories (C&C, 1998)
Haunted Toronto (Hounslow / Dundurn, 1996)
Ghost Stories of Ontario (Hounslow / Dundurn, 1995)
Strange Stories (C&C, 1994)
Singular Stories (C&C, 1994)
Ghosts Galore! (C&C, 1994)
Close Encounters of the Canadian Kind (C&C, 1994)
Voices of Rama (C&C, 1994)
The Mystery of the Shaking Tent (C&C, 1993)
Dark Visions (Hounslow / Dundurn, 1992)
The Little Book of UFOs (Pulp Press, 1992)
UFOs over Canada (Hounslow / Dundurn, 1991)
Mackenzie King's Ghost (Hounslow / Dundurn, 1991)
Mysterious Encounters (Hounslow / Dundurn, 1990)
Extraordinary Experiences (Hounslow / Dundurn, 1989)
Mysterious Canada (Doubleday, 1988)
Windigo (Western Producer Prairie Books, 1982)
Colombo's Book of Marvels (NC Press, 1979)

THE BIG BOOK OF CANADIAN GHOST STORIES

John Robert Colombo

DUNDURN PRESS
TORONTO

Copy-editor: Allison Hirst
Proofreader: Jason Karp
Designer: Erin Mallory
Printer: Transcontinental

Library and Archives Canada Cataloguing in Publication

Colombo, John Robert, 1936-

The big book of Canadian ghost stories / John Robert Colombo.

ISBN 978-1-55002-844-7

1. Ghosts--Canada. 2. Haunted places--Canada. I. Title.

BF1472.C3C575 2008 133.1'0971 C2008-903780-4

1 2 3 4 5 12 11 10 09 08

Conseil des Arts du Canada Canada Council for the Arts

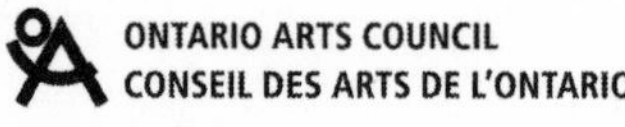

We acknowledge the support of the **Canada Council for the Arts** and the **Ontario Arts Council** for our publishing program. We also acknowledge the financial support of the **Government of Canada** through the **Book Publishing Industry Development Program** and **The Association for the Export of Canadian Books**, and the **Government of Ontario** through the **Ontario Book Publishers Tax Credit program** and the **Ontario Media Development Corporation**.

Care has been taken to trace the ownership of copyright material used in this book. The author and the publisher welcome any information enabling them to rectify any references or credits in subsequent editions.

J. Kirk Howard, President

Printed and bound in Canada
www.dundurn.com

Dundurn Press
3 Church Street, Suite 500
Toronto, Ontario, Canada
M5E 1M2

Gazelle Book Services Limited
White Cross Mills
High Town, Lancaster, England
LA1 4XS

Dundurn Press
2250 Military Road
Tonawanda, NY
U.S.A. 14150

Our formulations of the regularities of nature are surely dependent on how the brain is built, but also, and to a significant degree, on how the universe is built.

For myself, I like a universe that includes much that is unknown and, at the same time, much that is knowable. A universe in which everything is known would be static and dull, as boring as the heaven of some weak-minded theologians. A universe that is unknowable is no fit place for a thinking being. The ideal universe for us is one very much like the universe we inhabit. And I would guess that this is not really much of a coincidence.

Carl Sagan, astronomer and author,
"Can We Know the Universe? Reflections on a Grain of Salt,"
— *Broca's Brain* (1979)

CONTENTS

INTRODUCTION

The Big Book of Canadian Ghost Stories is the most extensive collection ever published of accounts of encounters with ghosts and spirits in this country. As such it is a weighty and a creepy collection!

In these pages you will find close to two hundred narratives — most of them frightening, all of them perplexing — of the supernatural, the psychical, and the paranormal. Many of these accounts are reprinted from the columns of old newspapers and magazines; many of them appear in the words of the witnesses themselves and have never before been reprinted. The stories contributed by journalists excel in atmosphere and are meant to frighten readers. The stories related in the first-person singular by eyewitnesses to the events themselves offer readers a particular sense of verisimilitude: "These things happened to me!" All of them are gripping to read.

These accounts of strange events come from the archives that I have been maintaining now for more than thirty years. The items that I have collected originate in a number of sources, including wide reading of the periodical press; nineteenth-century newspapers and journals; popular books and scholarly texts; websites devoted to such subjects as superstitions, psychical research, and parapsychology; personal correspondence, originally in the form of letters, now mainly email; and, finally, face-to-face encounters and on-site investigation. Later on I will discuss some of the characteristics of these stories, these narratives. Here I will add but a few words on the sources of the present narratives and the principles behind their organization.

About two-thirds of the stories in this jumbo collection are the most popular ones that originally appeared in the earlier collections that I complied over two decades. The first compilation was *Extraordinary Experiences* and it appeared in the year 1989; thirty-odd collections later, there appeared *Strange but True* in 2007. I have selected the most vivid of these ghost stories from these collections, reluctantly excluding eyewitness sightings of lake monsters, sea serpents, and creatures of the woodlands, not to mention descriptions of eerie happenings, peculiar coincidences, strange powers, and seemingly miraculous cures. (Maybe I will be able to publish accounts of these in another Big Book in the future.) Also excluded for good measure are sightings of flying saucers or unidentified flying objects, of alien beings from other planets in our solar system, in our galaxy, or in other dimensions of time and space. Still, at the same time, I have included a dozen or so stories which, while not specifically ghost stories, nonetheless are accounts that will be of interest to readers of such stories, for they retain the creepy atmosphere and leave the reader in a state of puzzlement. What remains are very human accounts of the reactions of men and women to inexplicable visions of ghosts and spirits.

The organization of the host of ghost stories in this collection is simple in the extreme. The earliest stories appear in the first section, "Ghosts of the Past"; the latest stories appear in the second section, "Ghosts of the Present." Within these sections there are subdivisions based on types of stories, but as ghost stories elude classification, these are no more than indicative. The turn of the twentieth century is a practical division between the Past and Present. The popular press becomes more demanding and the public becomes more critical of reports of psychical matters. As well, the Great War created a new wave of interest in psychical phenomena, specifically communication with the War Dead. It was still a gentlemanly period. The word of a witness of good character was accepted without argument, so it was an uncritical period, one concerned with telling a good story, relating an oft-repeated tale that is sometimes marked by a merging of fact and folklore.

Psychical research, begun in earnest in Britain and the United States in the 1880s, took a new turn in the 1930s. A cold eye was cast on superstition. Psychical research, formerly conducted in the parlour or on the stage, was directed into experimental laboratories like those at Duke University in Durham, North Carolina, where the study of psychical phenomena became known as parapsychology. It was conducted by research psychologists with an interest in double-blind experiments and statistical studies. Parapsychologists may be more scientific and technically sophisticated than psychical researchers, but nonetheless they have their blind spots too.

The modern period merges into the contemporary period which is one marked by a hypercritical spirit, reflecting the scholarly and scientific rebuttal of "claims of the paranormal" identified with a semi-scholarly, semi-popular publication like *Skeptical Inquirer*, launched in Winter 1976 by the Buffalo-based Committee for the Scientific Investigation of Claims of the Paranormal (since renamed Committee for Skeptical Inquiry). It looks askance at the phenomena in two ways: critically and psychologically. There has been a parallel rise in academic interest in the subject of the psychical and the paranormal, coupled with a sceptical sense, on one hand, and a continuing public interest in trance mediumship, demonic possession, facilitated powers, and enhanced abilities, on the other.

For thousands of years men and women of all ages and backgrounds, all cultures and climes, have continued to report the existence and appearances of ghosts and spirits — what might be called "unreal presences"— and while some periods are more credulous and some more critical, accounts of spirit phenomena continue to be recalled and reported. They also continue to be read, avidly, by the general public.

Organizing ghost stories is like herding a clutter of cats: the phenomenon resists organization and classification. One commentator who reviewed a selection of accounts of paranormal experiences came to the conclusion that the accounts could be separated into three classes of experiences. The first class is *fact*: the occurrences happened as described. The second class is *fancy*: the account is frivolous or insubstantial and not to be taken seriously. The third class is *falsehood*: it is an attempt to deceive someone for some form of gain. While there is something to be said for such a classification, this approach to human nature and personal motivation fails to take into account human motivation and expectation and the variety of paranormal experience through the ages.

So far I have been describing these texts as stories, narratives, or accounts, and I will continue to do so, though it is useful to attempt to distinguish these terms. The word *texts* implies written statements that are oral in origin; scholars like the word *text* which sounds scientific or at least scholarly. The word *stories* implies works of fiction which belong in an anthology of short stories, not in as told-as-true collections of memoirs or non-fiction; it suggests a still point between legend and folklore. As well the word is used by reporters to refer to newspaper *articles;* that is occasional *reports* and serious *studies*. The word *narratives* stresses continuity and an objective perspective of public events and subjective experiences. The word *accounts* recalls an impersonal recital of deeds with attendant descriptions of psychological states. The words *tales* and *yarns* are also possible, but they suggest the light-heartedness of the *folktale* — *folklore* and *urban lore* — which are irrelevant considerations here. As mentioned, the preferred term for scholars is *texts*, which suggests an order of words originally oral, but it will not be used here because it has failed (for good reason!) to catch on with the reading public. So while we have here all these texts, they will simply and conveniently be described as stories, narratives, or accounts of ghosts and spirits.

There, I used the words *ghosts* and *spirits*. The words trip off the tongue and when this happens there is generally a reason for it, a "rightness" of expression. A thumbnail distinction between the two words is that *ghosts* are immaterial or semi-material likenesses of familiar people, whereas as *spirits* are energies or forces that may or may not resemble human beings. It is currently fashionable to describe both ghosts and spirits as *entities*, that is as presences, creatures, or characters that are powerful to some degree and seem to have lives or drives of their own, a form of existence different from that of living beings. Hence the use of the following phrase by research psychologist Michael Persinger: "the entity experience." On occasion he uses the phrase "the sense of presence."

Whether ghosts and spirits exist is a question that is repeatedly asked and never responsibly answered. It may safely be said that if these entities exist at all, their existence is unlike that of human beings, animals, plants, or objects: that is, objectively. They might exist subjectively, the way dreams, nightmares, sensations, impressions, and thoughts exist. Yet the distinction between objective and subjective is not all that differentiated: thoughts and feelings may be shared and are often collectively experienced. This is taken for granted by scientists. We inhabit a universe mainly composed of "dark matter" which astrophysicists argue we cannot yet detect. We have harnessed the power of electricity, a force that cannot be seen, and scientists have made striking gains in the worlds of atomic and particle physics, not to mention the worlds of DNA and the genome. No alchemists or prophet of old ever described such forces and powers though they may have imagined them. Psychologists talk of "drives" in the human psyche which are not directly observable, except as they are made manifest in mood or behaviour. Even so, the psychologist C.G. Jung has hypothesized that it is possible to "exteriorize" inner feelings and project them tangibly onto and into the outer world to change objects and influence minds at a distance.

The words *ghosts* and *spirits* are not the only ones that will be found in these pages. There are synonyms for them that come readily to mind. Some of these are arranged in alphabetical order and the reader is invited to add favourites of his or her own not included in this inventory: *angels, apparitions, demons, devils, doppelgangers, fiends, ghosts, ghouls, goblins, gremlins, imps, monsters, phantasms, phantoms, poltergeists, presences, revenants, shades, shadows, spectres, spirits, sprites, visions, wraiths*.

Whether you want to refer to them as ghosts or spirits — the broadest and most inclusive terms — there is no shortage of these entities in the Canada of the past, or of the present. As I mentioned earlier, I gave my first collection of such accounts the title *Extraordinary Experiences*, on the assumption that accounts of such experiences are relatively rare. But over time I changed my mind about this because I have come to appreciate the fact that, far from being rare and unusual, they are quite common and quite prevalent in the population. At the present time there are 33 million Canadians, and at times I fear there may be as many as three million ghosts in the country!

Let me explain.

"Have you ever seen a ghost? Have you ever felt that you are in the presence of a spirit?"

These are questions that I regularly ask people when I meet them at parties or receptions. Most people answer with a firm "No!" and leave it at that.

Then I ask my supplementary question: "Do you know somebody — a relative or a friend — who claims to have seen a ghost or spirit?"

There is generally a pause here, before even the die-hard sceptic replies, "Yes, as a matter of fact, my mother / cousin / neighbour / friend says he saw a ghost."

"Do you believe that he or she is telling the truth as it is perceived?"

"Yes, I do."

Try asking these questions of yourself and then for yourself. If you have yet to experience a ghost or spirit, do you know someone you respect who has claimed just such an experience? I am willing to bet that you, the reader of this book, has experienced a ghostly encounter, or that you know someone who has. But even if you have never seen a ghost, sensed a spirit, or witnessed the effects of a poltergeist (a noisy, unseen spirit); even if you have yet to witness a feat of levitation, experienced the thoughts of other people, had a premonition of the future; even so, this book is for you.

You may remain sceptical or incredulous — and there is good reason to do so — yet there are good reasons to take the contents of this book seriously. Experiences of all kinds are recorded in the pages of this book and they tell us a lot about human nature. People like to be frightened, and this is a collection of spooky stories. The stories are eerie and creepy in that they will cause you "to pause to wonder." Some of them will leave you shaking your head in disbelief — or wonderment.

Not many of us will ever enter "an old dark house" at "the midnight hour" in search of "entities of evil." But most of us may wish to do so vicariously, or virtually, through the medium of the printed page. Do not complain to me if on turning these pages your hair stands on end, goosebumps run up and down your spine, your stomach turns over producing a queasy feeling, your eyes water, your hands shake … and you think you will never recover!

Perhaps I am exaggerating a little, but I myself have felt such sensations and been moved by such feelings as I heard or read these accounts for the first time.

Lurking behind the symptoms of fear and dread is this arresting thought: "Can such things be?"

Let me now turn to the "reality question."

The events and the experiences described in the accounts that appear here are records of encounters that have occurred in Canada or to Canadians over the last two centuries, though the majority of them have occurred in the last half-century. While they are reported to have occurred in this country, they could also have been reported to have occurred in other countries in the anglosphere and in other countries in non-English-speaking parts of the world. The characteristics that set them apart as specifically Canadian are related to geography and topography more than to demography or culture. Let us travel from east to west to north to identify a few of the characteristics of these accounts. The Atlantic Provinces are rich, as you might guess, in mysteries of the sea: phantom ships, grey ladies, etc. Quebec has ancestral spirits that linger and recall the haunted heritage of its *terroir* and *paysage*. Ontario will not easily be severed from its poltergeists in isolated farmhouses. The Prairies claim no end of *Windigos* and spirits of the plains and woodlands. The West Coast is enlivened with Sasquatches and Ogopogos and other sea-born mysteries. Even the Far North maintains an entitlement of spirits; indeed, more than most regions, it has named spirits, like Sedna, the Inuit goddess of the waters whose fingertips resemble the waves. Canadians are heirs to a haunted heritage, but only now are we discovering the riches and treasures of the land.

All countries have legacies of spirits. In fact, the earliest records of mankind are rich in the acceptance of ghosts and spirits, the existence of other supernatural or supernormal beings, and accounts of their interaction with men and women on earth. Indeed, the "ghost story" is probably the oldest of all stories.

Yet there is a difference between earlier narratives and modern narratives. The earlier ones assume a supernatural setting — these things happened regularly; the later ones assume a rationalistic setting — these things do not really happen at all but only seem to happen. The earlier ones are often described in terms of folkloric motifs, whereas the later ones became data for studies of psychological states. The earlier stories are lacking in psychology; the later stories may perhaps be about little more than psychology.

By *psychology* I mean what used to be called "abnormal psychology," the study of delusions, illusions, fixed ideas, obsessions, etc. But these days, psychologists take a wider view of such matters than they did in the recent past: they talk about "emergent powers," "facilitated abilities," "trance states," "intuition," "creative imagination," "the subconscious" or "the unconscious," even real and virtual realities. The standard polarity that exists is between worlds that are "real" and those that are "imaginary."

More contemporary is the three-fold division: *real, imaginary, imaginal.* The first term refers to "consensus reality"; the second term refers to "fictitious" constructs; the third term, which begs more consideration, refers to "collective" experiences rooted in expectation rather than in the physical world or psychological states *per se.* The word *imaginal* is less well known than the other two terms. It was coined in the 1950s by Henry Corbin, the French scholar of Persian literature, to brook the difference between the real and the unreal. Hence an *imaginal state* shares the features of a social construct and the characteristics of a work of the imagination, being allied with Plato's Ideal Forms and Jung's Archetypes. One thinks of "collective" states shared by the "faith-based" beliefs, practices, and behaviors of "faith-based" adherents, role-players, etc. The USS *Enterprise* is the still centre of a virtual cosmos in the future. Hogwarts School of Witchcraft and Wizardry is the still centre of a world parallel with ours. "UFO Land" of the Raëlians of Valcourt, Quebec, is a "real" one! Psychologists may dismiss these as "fabrications" but individually or as a group they offer insights into our *human nature* as well as *inhuman nature.*

The truth is that most of us in our everyday lives combine reality and imaginal worlds without necessarily noticing any difference. The conventional structures and trimmings of our shared world vanish for a second or two, to be replaced by forms and functions that are deeply odd and sometimes acutely disturbing. When one of these "shifts" occurs, we may prefer to regard it as a fugue state or ignore it and then try to forget it. Sometimes we do notice it, and strive to remember it through repeated retelling of what happened, or what we think happened, and this is where these narratives of the supernatural and the paranormal command our attention. Such at least is the view of the psychological dynamics of *anomalous experiences*, to adopt the phrase coined by the late Graham Reed. He was a Professor of Psychology at York University, Toronto, and the author of a standard study *The Psychology of Anomalous Experience* (1972). In his phrase the present book is a collection of accounts of anomalous experiences.

This book is also a collection of *memorates.* The term *memorate* is useful to refer to a truthful, first-person account of an anomalous experience. The term, not used by Reed, may be found in folkloric studies. It was used by folklore specialist Edith Fowke who noted it was introduced in 1934 by the theorist Carl Wilhelm von Sydow to describe the characteristics of a short, first-person account of an experience that is meant to be shared with a circle of friends or like-minded listeners or readers. By that definition, this book is a collection of memorates that are not widely told because they describe the anomalous experiences of individual men and women.

Over the years I have observed the structural characteristics of the memorate of the anomalous experience in action. There are three characteristics that are present or implied in all such stories. The account begins with a warning or an admission: "You will not believe what I have to tell you," or "You will find it hard to believe what has happened to me," or "I find it hard to believe what I am about to tell you." That is the first characteristic. The second characteristic is the sharing of the account itself, which is usually baldly but boldly recalled, almost in outline, with the addition of some sketching in of atmosphere and psychological interpretation: "It was a dark night," "I felt like I was going mad," "Maybe I am going crazy," etc. The third characteristic is the disclaimer: "You may not know what to make of what I have told you; I hardly know what to make of it myself!" Most informants are willing to share the ambivalence they feel about what they have experienced. They do not really require that anyone believe in any one explanation of what they recall of what had happened to them.

So admission, sharing, and disclaimer are the three characteristics of the well-formed memorate. What I find particularly intriguing are two other observations about the attitude of the narrators or witnesses to the events or experiences. The first observation is that the witness does not know what to make of the episode. The experience is bizarre; it is suggestive but inconclusive. It is suggestive of other levels of reality but inconclusive about their real nature or causation. If the experiencer is at a loss for an explanation, what about the listener or reader? So the experiencer does not necessarily *believe* in the existence of ghosts or spirits. After all, if you believed that they existed and could interact with us, the experiences would seem to be unexceptional.

The second observation is of equal moment, for it has to do with the fact that an experience is being recalled that took place years if not decades in the past. A middle-aged informant will begin, "When I was ten years old I had a terrible experience," or "It must have been ten years ago that it happened." Over time memory plays tricks but such anomalous experiences are seldom forgotten. They may be traumatic but they are seldom successfully suppressed, despite the fabled "false memory syndrome." What are being recalled are episodes of a psychological nature that took place in the past, often in the distant past, that lasted at the most a few minutes but usually for a few seconds. It would be interesting to know why people are so deeply moved by their anomalous experiences.

I have long felt that when we entertain thoughts like ones that involve ghosts and spirits and energies and powers — especially "powers that are not ours"— we are led to give at least residual meaning to such words as *fate*, *destiny*, *afterlife*, *entity*, *experience*, *special gifts*, etc. The supernatural, the psychical, and the paranormal are popular ways of encountering the notion of entities with great energies that are inexplicable by nature. We might regard such concerns as vestiges of superstitious beliefs and practices, yet we might also regard them as speculative probes, attempts to come to grips with the mysteries and puzzles of life and the world. An aphorism that I frequently recall runs like this: "Ghosts are good for us." They are good for us in the sense that they cause us to question what we always assume to be the nature of reality as we know it.

When I mention to casual acquaintances that I am interested in ghost stories, I am always asked the following question: "Do *you* believe in ghosts?" Whenever I publish a collection of Canadian quotations, nobody ever asks me if I "believe in" Canada or if I "believe in" quotations, though both of these are abstractions. How do you define Canada? How do you define a quotation? Yet the question that is asked of me is a reasonable one in the circumstances. My standard reply is the following: "I do not believe in ghosts. I do not disbelieve in ghosts. I am *interested* in ghosts." If the questioner wants to pursue the subject of my attitude further, I may add the following complexity: "I do not *believe in* ghosts because ghosts belong to the category of experience, not belief."

The word *belief* is indeed a slippery one. People will believe all sorts of things: the sun will rise in the morning; if I switch on a desk lamp it will light up; poverty is the root of social problems; subatomic particles exist; evolution is a scientific theory; there is intelligent life in the universe; there is a loving and merciful God; reincarnation is a fact; etc. Some of these beliefs are warranted, others are unwarranted except on the basis of faith, an emotional predisposition to accept the proposition. Belief in ghosts and spirits is unwarranted on the basis of physics but probably warranted on the basis of psychological needs and drives.

As well as being asked if I *believe in* ghosts, from time to time I am asked if I have ever encountered a ghost. The question is usually expressed in the following manner: "Have you ever *seen* a ghost?" The English idiom is *to see a ghost;* despite the fact that, in a ghostly encounter, nothing much is seen. Something is sensed or felt (a breeze, an odour, a cold spot, a tingling sensation, goosebumps, etc.). The most general reaction is a sense of uneasiness, unhinging, fear, sweat or chill, plus sounds, interior or exterior. I always admit the truth: I have yet to see a ghost. Yet from time to time I have experienced many of these sensations and feelings, in given locations (especially old and creaky buildings, sanctuaries, churches, shrines, etc.). Such reactions are widely reported by members of the general public, who may or may not be interested in the paranormal, but taken in stride. Such reactions are quite common, shared by sceptic or believer alike.

While I have yet to see a ghost or sense the presence of a spirit, I have met and conversed with many men and women who feel and believe that they have done so. I have encouraged them to write out factual accounts of their experiences and then send them to me so that I may share them with my readers. About five hundred people have done so, and because many people report not just one or two but three or four such experiences, I have been party to publishing close to two thousand such stories over the years.

Another good question is the following: "Why do people love to read or hear stories about ghosts and spirits?" This is a variation of the question, "Why do we enjoy being frightened?" If the latter question could be answered with ease, horror-fiction writers like Stephen King and horror-movie directors like David Cronenberg would be even more effective and famous than they are today!

A good question to ask is, "Why do people tell such incredible stories?" I have given a lot of thought to the different ways this question may be answered. I can tie myself up in knots coming up with plausible reasons, a few of which have already been mentioned. Instead of wrestling with the question, let me suggest it is related to the following question: "Why do people love to read and hear such incredible stories?"

The simple answer to these questions is that many people are fascinated with the unknown and wish to experience it or, once they have experienced it, wish to share it with other people not so lucky — or unlucky.

ACKNOWLEDGEMENTS

I am pleased to acknowledge the contributions made by those correspondents who generously contributed their experiences to the pages of this collection. Without their altruism with respect to their sharing of recollections there would be no book at all. So I am indebted to them as well as to fellow researchers Dwight Whalen, W. Ritchie Benedict, and Ed Butts, who pooled with me the published accounts of eerie events and odd experiences that they have encountered in their life and work.

As in the past, I have discussed many of the components of these experiences with Dr. Edith Fowke, Dr. Cyril Greenland, Dr. David Gotlib, and Dr. Daniel Burston — a folklorist, a psychiatric social worker, a psychiatrist, and a psychologist. My sense of the whole is that while it may be an entertaining experience for the reader of this book to encounter these stories, it is also worthwhile for the contributors, the witnesses and experiencers, to recount them and to share them in forms that "fix" them in time and place, as memory is malleable over time. Stories have a habit of "wandering" from their moorings through repeated recitals. Print has many limitations, but one of its strengths is its permanency. Thus, committing an account of an event or an experience to print helps to objectify it: at the same time as the reader is drawn close, the narrator is able to withdraw from the engagement. So the telling of stories that are real or unreal has a therapeutic effect: vicarious for the reader, beneficial for the narrator.

Over the decades the compilation of this material would not have proceeded as expeditiously as it did without the contributions of my late research assistant Mary Alice Neal and friend and research librarian Philip Singer of "Metro Central" or the

Metropolitan Toronto Reference Library. I am also indebted to two documentary television producers, Sean C. Karow and Christian R. Page. I am grateful to the lively spirits of the Dundurn Group — including publisher Kirk Howard, Tony Hawke, Beth Bruder, Barry Jowett, editor Allison Hirst — for their belief in the possibilities of this book and offering the opportunity of making the dream come true. Fans, students, and aficionados of ghost stories are indebted to two British writers for the form and content of their favourite tales. The Anglo-Scottish scholar and author Andrew Lang (1844–1912) devoted much of his literary life to preserving and presenting the traditional tales of myth and legend. He is identified with the "coloured" series: *The Red Ghost Book*, *The Green Ghost Book*, etc. There are one dozen of these books, and well-thumbed copies of them may still be found in nurseries, in closets, in summer cottages, etc. The Anglo-Irish writer and lecturer Elliott O'Donnell (1872–1965) became known in his day as a leading "ghost hunter" and gave readers of his books the thrill of encounters with ghosts and spirits throughout the British Isles and the British Empire. Lang focused on the supernatural (traditional, irrational) and O'Donnell on the paranormal (psychical, parapsychological).

I am pleased to say that two Canadians have walked, Indian file, in the footsteps of Lang and O'Donnell. I am thinking now of the psychical researcher R.S. Lambert (1894–1981) and the parapsychologist A.R.G. Owen (1919–2003) — along with his wife Iris M. Owen (b. 1916) — who have published landmark studies of, respectively, the supernatural and the paranormal in this country. Overall, it is to Lang and O'Donnell that we are most indebted for the ready availability and widespread popularity of tales of imagination and weird stories that are told-as-true. So in a sense the present collection of ghost stories is dedicated to the memories of these scholars of the mysterious. The spirits of Andrew Lang and Elliott O'Donnell, of R.S. Lambert and A.R.G. Owen, haunt these pages!

GHOSTS OF THE PAST

We enjoy reading ghost stories for reasons that have to do with pleasure and pain. We enjoy a thrill and a chill. The blood in our veins heats up with fear; it cools down with terror. We cherish the sensations, at least vicariously, as we take pleasure in having our preconceptions about this world and the next challenged or confirmed; in having our assumptions about life and death questioned and perhaps even answered.

Here are accounts of ghosts and spirits that bring us tidings and warnings from other worlds. Do these beings exist in some fashion? Are they figments of our imaginations? Are there half-human beings, harbingers of dimensions of existence beyond our ken and beyond death itself? If such entities exist, does this mean that there is life after death?

The ghost stories of the last century and a half that we know and love the best are short works of imaginative fiction like Rudyard Kipling's tale "The Phantom Rickshaw" and Oscar Wilde's satire "The Canterville Ghost." These are short stories, works of the imagination rather than of experience. The first story is an engaging tale of a grim haunting in India that leads to a strange but inevitable death; the second story is an amusing account of how difficult it is to continue to haunt England's Canterville Chase after a brash, fun-loving American family has taken up residence there. These stories were written around the turn of the nineteenth century; they and hundreds like them have continued to enchant readers to this day. These are literary works and hence products of the imagination.

The imaginative English ghost story reached its apogee of popularity in the early decades of the twentieth century. In the capable hands of such practitioners as M.R. James and Algernon Blackwood, traditional tales involving ghosts and spirits that haunt peculiar people or inhabit abandoned buildings and crumbling chapels in remote locales were more often than not viewed in the light of abnormal psychology or discerned in the darkness of psychical research and occult studies. Added to the traditional tale, with its elements of attraction and repulsion — pity and terror — was a scientific explanation or a pseudo-scientific interpretation.

It is interesting to note that there are many "ghost stories" but only a handful of "ghost novels." A ghost story is about a haunting, whereas a novel, being so much longer than a short story, needs to offer repeated hauntings as well as psychological character analysis and development. Henry James's novelette *The Turn of the Screw* is a good instance of a longer work that is principally a presentation of character analysis. After reading it one may argue for years about whether or not the dead Quilp haunts the living as a ghost, or the memory of Quilp haunts the living as a memory or obsession.

The true ghost story, as distinct from the literary ghost story, emerged on the scene about the same time as the literary ghost story appeared, that is, in the late nineteenth and early twentieth century. Folklorist Andrew Lang collected popular traditions of the past, and writer Elliott O'Donnell collected popular traditions of the present. Lang blew the dust off the old parish records and O'Donnell interviewed witnesses and descendants of witnesses, travelling to locales reputed to be haunted. Working independently they filled innumerable books with exciting, traditional or told-as-true ghost stories. Their stories reflected the popular beliefs that were held at the time throughout the British Isles.

Canadian readers grew accustomed to reading about the ghosts and spirits of England, Scotland, Ireland, and Wales as described in the pages of collections like Lang's *The Blue Fairy Book* (1889) and O'Donnell's *Scottish Ghost Stories* (1912). The success of these books resulted in the publication of many successor collections. The genre of ghostly collections reached its apogee in *Lord Halifax's Ghost Book* (1936), a widely read collection that retold the by now familiar tales of haunted country homes and castles. With only one tale did Lord Halifax venture farther afield. He included an account of the Mackenzie River Ghost, the most famous ghost story of the Canadian Northwest. That story also appears in the pages of the present collection.

Evidence of the continuation of popular interest in ghosts and spirits may be attested by the fact that The Ghost Club opened its doors in London in 1862 and as a luncheon club it continues to function to this day, its most noted member being the ghost-hunter and writer Peter Underhill. Further evidence of popular interest in the subject is supplied by the founding of the Society for Psychical Research in Britain as well as its U.S. counterpart, the American Society for Psychical Research. In both Britain and America in the 1880s, scientists and scholars banded together to inquire into the status of ghosts and spirits. They examined the claims of mediums and spiritualists and considered the nature of trance and hallucinatory states. Both societies continue in their inquiries to this day.

The study of ghosts and spirits is not a scientific discipline. These spirits cannot be invoked at will. But it does seem possible to discuss them "second hand," so to speak, by means of the anecdotal evidence that we have in the form of true ghost stories.

The words "true ghost story" imply that the ghost story or narrative is true to life. Yet the essence of a good ghost story is that it is not true but false to life in selected particulars. Spectres and spooks do not abound in real life; they do not interfere in our ordinary lives, at least routinely. We do not normally enter houses that have reputations for being haunted unless we regard ourselves as ghost-hunters. Such experiences are anomalous, spontaneous, irreproducible, irregular, and rich for being so rare. Anomalous experiences are reported from time to time, but rarer than such subjective experiences are anomalous events. Anomalous events are not subjective but objective occurrences, witnessed by two or more people at the same time. We have reason to wonder about the sanity or sobriety of people who report such events. (The French phrase *folie à deux* comes readily to mind.) After all, textbooks of psychology group such accounts into a chapter usually headed "Abnormal Psychology." Page after page in the psychiatrist's handbook, *Diagnostic and Statistical Manual*, is devoted to the disorientation experienced by human beings who present anomalous symptoms. It is interesting to note that the words "anomalous experience" were coined by a Canadian psychologist, Graham Reed in 1988.

George Bernard Shaw is justly celebrated for the ridicule he heaped on popular attitudes. Reviewing a book of ghost stories, he referred to "the classic — therefore untrue — ghost story." He had in mind the accounts of hauntings and encounters with ghosts and spirits that have come down to us in collections by Lang and O'Donnell. The truth is that there is no way to prove or disprove that Borley Rectory in Sussex was once haunted by the spectre of a headless nun, or that Edinburgh Castle continues to be haunted by the Ghost of the Headless Drummer. Nor is there any way to determine with ease the mingling of fact, fantasy, or falsehood to be found in any single ghostly account. It is probably true that every account of an encounter with a ghost adds irrelevant information and subtracts relevant information, and so it might be considered a confabulation rather than a direct report. People convince themselves of the truth of what they want to believe. Over the years their experiences tend to conform to their new beliefs.

There are two types of told-as-true ghost stories. They are not mutually distinct because they have much in common. The first type is the supernatural tale, a traditional tale associated with a person or a place. It is traditional because it is old, it is told in different ways at different times, and there are no living witnesses to vouch for its authenticity. Its mark of authenticity lies in its antiquity.

The second type of told-as-true ghost story may be called the paranormal account. It is not a traditional tale because it is a novel experience associated with a single person at a given place on a stated day. There is a living witness, and the account takes the form the folklorist knows as the memorate. The memorate is characterized by an air of wonder and disbelief. The witness begins the told-as-true account in words like these: "You won't believe me when I tell you what happened to me last night." The witness concludes, "That's what happened to me; I don't know what to make of it." Between the opening and the closing is the first-person description of an experience or event that is paranormal in nature and truly anomalous.

Most of the stories in this section are supernatural stories but some of them are paranormal accounts. Other stories are hard to categorize, as if the writer of the account is undecided, whether he is retelling a traditional tale, with its attendant lore and atmosphere, or telling for the first time the story of one person's actual experience. Both types of tales are intriguing and well worth reading.

These stories first appeared in the columns of more than one dozen daily and weekly newspapers published in Canada in the nineteenth century. Such stories were popular in their day (as they are in ours). Quite often they appeared in the late fall or early winter of the year, as it was the custom of editors to run lengthy ghost stories or accounts of ghostly lore in Christmas or New Year's editions of newspapers, just as editors today commission articles on spectres and witches or Wicca in late October to coincide with Halloween. Such stories were much appreciated and widely read.

So far no mention has been made of the earliest of tales of ghosts told in this country: the traditional lore of the Native Peoples. The Indians and the Inuit have a rich heritage of stories that admit of the existence of spirit-beings and their presence in the everyday lives of the aboriginal peoples of the past and perhaps also of the present. Many of the powerful myths and legends of the native peoples have been recorded, but when they are repeated by Europeans they are treated as little more than stories for children. Imagine the effect if the mythology of Europe was reduced to such tales as "Jack and the Beanstalk" or "Little Red Riding Hood," and such superstitious rhymes as "Sun at night, sailor's delight; / Sun in the morning, sailors take warning." The native traditions are embedded in a worldview and a narrative cycle that is adult and neither childish, primitive, nor savage. It pays to ponder the native tales, both Indian and Inuit, for the purposes of the tale telling: cautionary, explanatory, anticipatory, etc.

The population of Canada in 1867, the year of Confederation, was about 3.3 million, which is the approximate population of the Greater Toronto Area in 2008. The newspaper readers of the day were less demanding than are readers these days. They did not have available to them the wide range of newspapers and tabloids, not to mention magazines and television, that we take for granted. For their thrills and chills, they may have been less demanding than contemporary readers of the *Globe and Mail*, but they were far less credulous than are the readers of a supermarket tabloid like *National Enquirer*. The population of the country in 1867 was rural, and it was the Victorian period with all the earmarks of colonialism and imperial sentiment. A social gulf separated the classes — working, non-working, respectable professional, etc. The stories in this collection may be said to go from one military engagement to another: from the Rebellions of 1837–38 in Upper and Lower Canada to the South African or Boer War of 1899–1902. The first readers of these stories may no longer to be counted to be among the living. Whether they have joined the ghosts and spirits described in these pages and entered into the realm of the spirits is another matter entirely.

The editorial standards of the papers were variable. Generally the standards were higher in the larger cities, lower in the smaller communities. Local editors and reporters wrote many of their feature stories, but not all of them. Throughout most of the century there were no newspaper syndicates and papers were not yet links in chains; syndicates and chains came with the twentieth century. But there were exchanges of newspapers, and editors frequently picked up stories from other publications and reprinted them, usually with credit. A number of the stories included here are reprints of stories that were written for and published by other newspapers. An attempt has been made to locate the first appearance of a news story, but it has not always been possible or worth the effort to do this. Editors of the day were not much concerned with matters that contemporary Canadians take for granted: matters like ethnicity and multiculturalism, political correctness, native peoples, science, etc.

The texts of these stories have been freshly keyboarded based on photostatic prints of reels of microfilms of the original newspapers. It is interesting to note that whereas the microfilm images are in black and white and the original newspapers were printed in black and white, over the last century the newsprint itself has acquired colour, a dull brown or a drab yellow. The pages are brittle in the extreme. We are lucky they were microfilmed when they were, otherwise their contents would not survive into the twenty-first century. It would be a shame to have these columns of type with their ghostly accounts crumble into dust.

Early on I resolved to reprint the texts of the stories verbatim, adding nothing, subtracting nothing. Little by little my resolve weakened, as I faced texts that were riddled with misprints, misspellings, inconsistencies, irregularities, irrelevancies, and inaccuracies. By the end, I compromised and edited ever so lightly or slightly the stories that needed such treatment, leaving the others as I found them. I have retained the rhetorical style of punctuation, so unlike the grammatical style of punctuation taught in today's schools (when punctuation is taught at all). For each story I retained the full title and subtitle, but I deleted all subheadings within the body of the text, for in most instances these were introduced to assist the compositor to complete the layout of the page rather than to assist the reader to recognize the internal divisions of the story. I organized the stories quite loosely by theme and then ordered them by year. There are stories for most regions of the country, but it should be borne in mind that representation is largely a function of population. In other words, regions with more people are regions with more stories.

There are three reasons why I feel it is interesting to reprint nineteenth-century newspaper stories on the threshold of the twenty-first century. The first reason is that the accounts read well, some of them surprisingly well. They offer the reader the thrills and chills that are so characteristic of good ghost stories, whether the stories are literary or true-to-life. Over all, I have favoured longer accounts over shorter accounts, and complete tales rather than instances of spot reporting of current events.

The second reason is that these stories reflect the concerns and interests of readers in the past. It turns out that these concerns and interests are largely those of readers today. There are accounts of newspapermen visiting haunted sites, of reporters attending seances, and of journalists interviewing fortune-tellers. Such reports were being written in the nineteenth century, often in a manner best described as tongue-in-cheek, and they are being written in the twenty-first century, often tongue-in-cheek!

The third reason is that the appearance of these stories in newspaper columns in the past establishes for a fact that there were "ghosts in our past." We Canadians have a "haunted heritage." These stories attest to our continuing concern and speculation about "the beyond"— what Stephen Leacock amusingly referred to as "back of the beyond"!

It is surprising to realize that many of these nineteenth-century stories are critical in spirit. Their writers pose the most difficult question of all: "Can such things be?" One senses that their answer is the following: "No, such things cannot be." The Committee for the Scientific Investigation of Claims of the Paranormal (CSICOPS) was not founded until 1976 but even then there were sceptics and scoffers aplenty. While I hold no particular views with regard to the existence of ghosts and spirits, I adhere strongly to the belief that a good ghost story, a told-as-true story of the strange and the mysterious, whether supernatural or paranormal in origin, is worth its weight in gold. The veridicality of a weird story turns on one's estimate of the character and personality of the informant. Is the witness someone you would trust? Is the account being related faithfully by a journalist acting in good faith?

I should stress that these tales are essentially incredible, unbelievable, so it is not surprising that reporters and even participants are of "two minds" about what they maintain is being recalled and reported. They are of "two minds" because human nature is divided about the nature of the inexplicable. In the 1770s, Samuel Johnson and James Boswell discussed the possibility of the existence of ghosts. Dr. Johnson said, intriguingly, that all experience is in favour of them, whereas all argument is against them. The appeal of the true ghost story — the spell it casts upon the reader or listener — derives from the certain knowledge that these things are impossible. Yet as long as one considers even the possibility that something impossible has occurred, the spell holds. The spell should hold for the duration of the tale … and then some. In other words, we should be haunted by the possibility that "such things can be."

These stories offer us some insights into life in nineteenth-century Canada, but I believe that they tell us more about our ancestors and about ourselves than they do about the realm of the spirits. What they tell us for sure is how in the past and in the present we have handled and continue to handle the convention of the ghostly visitation and the spiritual intervention in human affairs. As communications theorist Marshall McLuhan once said about technology, "The most human thing about man is his technology." His insight might be applied to ghosts and spirits: "The most human thing about man is his spirits." We are distinguished in the way we deal with the puzzles of preconception and perception and the grand mystery of existence itself.

Canadians in the past have been disinclined to deal with the supernatural, a psychological fact recognized by the novelist Robertson Davies. He wrote that we suffer "the rational rickets" because we are unwilling even to entertain the notion that we are not alone in the world and in the universe. In his essays, stories, and novels he presented us with the ghosts and spirits — the hopes and fears — to be found in our collective past and in our private pasts, and he dramatized how they will not stay still until recognized and seen and felt and heard and heeded.

Here, then, are the ghosts in our past.

1

FIRST PEOPLES

At first glance the words "ghost stories" do not seem to refer to the stories told by Canada's Native Peoples. But upon reflection — especially if the order of the words is reversed, so that instead of "ghost stories" we have "stories of ghosts"— the description does apply to the traditional tales of the Indians and the Inuit. Indeed, here are ancient, tribal stories which have been passed from one generation to another, as they appeared in newspaper columns in the late nineteenth century. No doubt much is lost in the bald retelling of these stories; but much is present too. They relate experiences which might have begun with actual experiences. Here are notes on these contributions to this collection.

"Spirit Lake." The tales included in the column "Spirit Lake," reprinted from the *Quebec Morning Chronicle*, 28 May 1847, were randomly collected and selected. As the Aborigines of Australia had their "songlines," which told the traditional tales of the features of the landscape and revealed the inner natures of the forces that met there, so the Indians of Canada had their tales of the lakes and rivers, mounds and hollows, and of the land. The writer of the article suggests that these "idle legends" give us "an insight into the Indian mind." What he should say is that they give us insights into the human mind and into mind-sets quite unlike our own. It is not known what lake the writer was describing, but he might have meant "Mille Lac" rather than "Mill Lac." For some reason quotation marks introduce the second and subsequent paragraphs. As there is no indication of the source of the copy, if it is indeed quoted, these have been discarded.

"Esquimaux Superstition." This tale appeared in the *Montreal Star*, 23 August 1890. Where the information included in this long paragraph originated is not immediately apparent, as it predates Fifth Thule Expedition mounted by the explorer Dane Knud Rasmussen by at least thirty years. Europeans are ready and willing to point to the beliefs and practices of other peoples and then dismiss them as superstitious lore, failing to examine their own belief systems and traditional practices and finding in them remarkable superstitions as well. This article exemplifies this habit, as does the one that follows.

"Tribal Romance." This item appeared in the columns of *The Globe* (Toronto), 8 December 1894.

SPIRIT LAKE

Spirit Lake — This lake, which the French have named Mill Lac, and certain ignorant Yankees, Rum Lake, was originally called by the Chippeways, Minsisagaigoming, which signifies the dwelling place of the Mysterious Spirit. In form it is almost round, and about twenty across in the widest part. The shores are rather low, but covered with a luxuriant growth of oak, hard maple and tamarack. It is shallow, but clear and cold: has a sandy bottom, and yields a variety of fish; and contains only three islands, which are small and rocky.

The Mysterious Spirit alluded to above has acquired a great notoriety on account of his frequently taking away into the spirit land certain people whom he loved.

A little boy was once lost upon the margin of this lake. The only trace of him that ever could be discovered, was one of his arrows found lodged in a tree. And the Indians believe, too, that the aged mother of Hole-in-the-day (the great chief) was also carried away by the Mysterious Spirit. One thing is certain, say they, she disappeared in the twinkling of an eye from the party with whom she was travelling many years ago. These are indeed idle legends, but give us an insight into the Indian mind.

The ruling chief of Spirit Lake, at the present time, is Naguanabic, or Outside Feather. A son of this old Indian, while hunting once pursued a deer to a very great distance, which he finally captured.

Out of revenge for the improper conduct of the animal, the cruel Indian tortured it in a variety of ways, and came home boasting of what he had done. At the feast usually given on such occasions, the old chief addressed his son in the following words: "We are thankful to the Great Spirit for furnishing us with food. But my son has acted wrong in torturing that animal, and if the laws of the Great Spirit are not changed from what they were in times past, that boy shall not be privileged to kill another deer during the whole winter." And I was told that he did not, and that no cruel-hearted man ever can, under similar circumstances.

It was from the lips of this aged Indian that I obtained the following legend:

"A thousand winters ago, the Great Spirit caused the sun to be fastened in the heavens, for the purpose of destroying the world on account of an enormous sin which had been committed. The men of that time assembled together in council, but could devise no means to avert the calamity. The animals of the earth also held a council, and they were about to give up all hopes of a release, when a small animal stept forth and avowed its intention of gnawing off the string that held the sun. He entered the earth, and after travelling a long time, finally reached the desired planet and accomplished his purpose. The heat of the sun, however, was so great, that the sight of the heroic little animal was impaired, and it returned to the earth — a poor blind mole."

ESQUIMAUX SUPERSTITION

Esquimaux are believers in ghosts. They also believe in the transmigration of the soul, and spirits return in animals, winds, rocks, ice and water, that are evil, angry or good as the elements may be favourable or unfavourable, and that they can be appeased by hoodoo rites if the performer is sufficiently versed in occult sciences. To change the wind, for instance, they chant, drum and howl against it, build fires, shoot against it, and, as a last resort, fire the graves of the dead. Tribes put hoodoos on each other by ceremonial dances, and howling. The hoodoo of total destruction upon neighbours is the building of a fire within sight of those coming under their displeasure. Tribal relations are severed by making a fire outside and burning all ornaments or disguises used in ceremonial dances, such as raven skins, eagles' tails, deer horns and masks. Tribes that are hoodooed answer by a return hoodoo, but with families and individuals it is different. Outlawed by their tribe or relations, they become discouraged, hopeless and gloomy, and "go off and die." Eclipses of the moon create the greatest consternation, and almost paralyze the people with fear. Arctic earthquakes having been coincident with eclipses of the moon, they say that an eclipse is the shadow of the earth being piled up and shaken. All the unutkoots in a village will howl and drum till it is passed, claiming that they have driven the thing away. Among the Nooatkos all hands rally around a pair of buckhorns, form a circle and march around to the music of drums and wild chants till the eclipse is off.

TRIBAL ROMANCE

Totem Story of Gi-a-wak, the Bird God — The Sea God's Command — Adventures of a Disobedient Kit-Kat-La Youth — Curiosity Satisfied — Saved by a Beautiful Maiden — As in Modern Romances the Course of Their Love — Does Not Run Smoothly — A Typical Legend from the West Coast —

(Special Correspondence of The Globe)

Victoria, B.C., December 1. — Away back in the misty past a mighty sea god dominated the inlet which penetrates the territory of the Kit-Kat-La tribe on the west coast. On one occasion he issued an order forbidding, under pain of his extreme displeasure, anyone throwing clam shells into the water. The chief of the tribe was the unhappy possessor of two sons, who were continually in trouble because they refused to listen to the advice of their elders, and who were a source of great anxiety to their parents. One fine day, as they sat upon the shore of the inlet they decided for lack of other diversion to stir up the sea god and find out what manner of deity he might be. Procuring a canoe they loaded it with clam shells, and the elder of the lads paddled to the middle of the inlet, while the younger took his position in the bow of the little craft and awaited developments. The big brother then proceeded to throw his cargo of shells overboard, but the first handful had scarcely touched the water when a tremendous commotion took place. The canoe was overturned, and the youth who had so wantonly offended the sea god was overwhelmed and sank to the bottom of the inlet. After a time he recovered consciousness, and when he opened his eyes he found bending over him a tall and beautiful maiden, who regarded him with tender compassion for a moment, and then in gentle tones asked him why he had allowed himself to commit such an indiscretion as that which had placed him in the position in which she had found him. The gentleness of her speech served to allay his fears, and when he had recovered his self-possession she told him that she was the sea god's daughter, and that the only reason that his life had been spared was that her father was absent attending a great potlatch amongst the minor celebrities of that part of the world. When she had heard the commotion which had been the result of the foolish young man's disobedience she hastened forth to ascertain the cause. She took him by the hand and led him away across the bottom of the inlet, where he was enabled to live by the magic power of the nok-nok.

They came to an immense stone house. In front of it was a tremendous totem pole, on which were carved a crest and story that no mortal man would dare to attempt to interpret. They entered the house and found that during the absence of the daughter the sea god had returned. Before the fire he sat, an old man, with penetrating eyes and an expression of indescribable ferocity on his wrinkled countenance. As he turned his head in the direction of the newcomers the poor young man's blood froze in his veins. Not a word was spoken. The girl placed the young man near the fire and brought him food. When he had partaken of it he fell into a profound slumber. He awoke, only to have his fears excited by the terrible visage of the old man, who sat silently as before. The maiden again brought him food, and again he slept. Four times did he sleep and awake, and to him it appeared that four days had thus been consumed. Finally the sea god spoke. Addressing himself to the young man he said:

"Your disobedience of my command merits death, but my daughter has pleased for you because she loves you. There is one way that you may be spared your life and restored to your home and friends, and that is by making her your wife. Bear in mind that she is not to be treated as a being of earthly origin, but as the child of the sea god. Fail not to honour, to respect, and to love her, for if there be any lack of fidelity or affection it will result not only in her loss, but in the visitation of vengeance upon you."

The sea god, having thus delivered himself, relapsed into silence, and the young man again slept. When he awoke he found himself on the shore of the inlet at the exact spot where he and his brother had planned the adventure. Beside him was the sea god's daughter. He was unable to recognize the surroundings, for since his departure to the realm of the sea god a great change had come over the land. The maiden explained to him that each of the seeming days that he had slept had in reality been a period of ten years, and that forty years had passed away since he had disappeared beneath the waters of the inlet.

Together they proceeded to the home of his tribe, where the young man, for his was a perennial youth, told of his strange adventure. He was received with great rejoicing, and elevated to the chieftainship. Time went on, and the pair settled down to the enjoyment of domestic life. He fished and hunted and discharged the duties of his chieftainship, while she twisted his fish lines, made his nets, built the fires, and prepared the food.

But there was one thing that she refused to do. She never would bring the water from the spring. Every day the husband brought home a bucket of water, and on its arrival the wife stirred it with her forefinger. He questioned her as to the reason of this proceeding, but every time he introduced the subject she gave him a look that reminded him of the sea god, and he finally dropped it. He was a handsome fellow, as the maiden of the sea had long ago discovered, and he fell prey to feminine charms other than those of his wife. On the day that he had forgotten the charge of the sea god he took the water from the spring as usual to his home. His wife stirred it with her finger; but no sooner had she touched it than it turned an inky black.

"Time will dull the keenest weapon; the sea god's warning has been blotted out." Thus spoke the sea god's daughter. Then she darted towards the shore of the inlet. He called to her to come back, and ran after her, but she sped on with the fleetness of the gazelle, and upon reaching the water leaped in and disappeared from view. He tried to follow her, but the waves dashed him back upon the shore and left him in helpless despair. Now that she was gone he discovered that he loved her more than any of the Kit-Kat-La maidens, whose seductive smiles had lulled his recollection of the sea god's admonition, and he felt that he was the most wretched man in the world.

He launched his canoe and paddled out upon the inlet, calling and calling to his wife, but the echo of his voice was his only answer. Finally, when he was about to give up the search a large bird flew down to the edge of the canoe and made inquiry of the poor man as to the cause of his trouble. When he had related his story the bird said:

"I have need of a servant in my house, and if you will serve me faithfully and perform the task I have for you I will restore your wife to you."

At the end of the period of the man's service he reminded the bird of its promise and called for a fulfillment of the obligation. When the bird, by many questions, had assured himself that his love for his lost wife had remained true despite his troubles, it revealed itself, and the husband was astonished and overjoyed to find that he had been serving his wife, who had taken on the form of Gi-a-Wak, the bird-god. Together they returned home, lived happily and founded the family of Gi-a-Wak.

This is the tale related by Mr. J.F. Bledsoe, now of Victoria, upon whom was conferred the honor of the family name and the totem story by the Kit-Kaw-La tribe of Indians, among whom he sojourned for a time.

A CERTAIN PAGAN POW-WOW

Peter Jones's major written work is, as mentioned, *History of the Ojibway Indians with Especial Reference to their Conversion to Christianity … With a Brief Memoir of the Writer and Introductory Notice by the Rev. G. Osborn, D.D., Secretary of the Wesleyan Methodist Missionary Society* (1861, 1970). It preserves much Ojibwa lore and has revealing passages about the spiritual traditions of his people. With respect to the latter, Jones describes his attendance at "a certain pagan pow-wow." He was not much impressed with this "pow-wow"; a performance of the rite of the Shaking Tent, as is apparent in the passage that follows.

Yet Jones might well have been more impressed. The conjuror, or *jessuhkon*, seemed to be a knowledgeable and honest person. By consulting the "familiar spirits," or *munedoos*, or by listening carefully to a concealed confederate, he ascertained the fact that there were native Christian observers among the rite's pagan participants. As well, the conjuror gave Jones a careful account of what the "spirits" had conveyed to him about the wisdom of the Indian people embracing Christianity. On this issue the voices of the "spirits" were divided.

> On the 9th of August, 1828, I was engaged in preaching to the Indians at Lake Simcoe, at which time the Great Spirit began in a very powerful manner to convert them from paganism to Christianity. During the day some of the Christian Indians informed me that a certain pagan pow-wow had intimated his intention of consulting his munedoos, to ascertain from them whether it was right for Indians to forsake the religion of their fathers, and to take hold of the white man's religion. I requested them to let me know when he would begin his performance, as I wished to go and hear him for myself. Shortly after dark they brought me word that the pow-wow had gone towards the pine-grove to commence his incantations. I immediately accompanied them in that direction, and we soon heard the rattling of his conjuring wigwam, called in Ojebway jessukhon; which is made by putting seven poles in the ground at the depth of about a cubit, in a circle of about three or four feet in diameter, and about six feet high, with one or more hoops tied fast to the poles, to keep them in a circle. The sides were covered with birch bark, but the top was left open. Into this the pow-wow had entered, and was chaunting a song to the spirit with whom he wished to converse. The jessuhkon began to shake as if filled with wind. Wishing to see and hear his performance without his knowing we were present, we proceeded towards him as softly as we could, and placed ourselves around the jessuhkon. On our approach we heard the muttering talk of one of the familiar spirits, in answer to questions he had put to him. This spirit told him that it was right for Indians to become Christians, and that he ought to go to the

meetings and hear for himself. The next spirit he invoked spoke decidedly against Indians becoming Christians, and exhorted him to adhere to the religion of his fathers. The third spirit spoke nearly as the first; with this addition — that he, the conjuror, was quite wrong in supposing the Christian Indians to be crazy, as if they were under the effects of the fire-waters; that they were not as they appeared to be, but that all the time they were crying and praying, they were in their right minds and worshiping the Great Spirit in their hearts, and according to His will. The fourth spirit informed him that shortly one of his children would be taken from him by death. One of the Christian Indians standing near whispered to me, saying, "If we kneel down and begin to pray to the Great Spirit, his enchantment will be broken, and all his devils will have to fly." I replied, "We had better not disturb him," as I wished to hear the end of it. My friend then in a low whisper prayed that the Great Spirit would have mercy on this poor deluded Indian. That very instant the jessuhkon ceased shaking, and the muttering talk stopped, as if the evil spirits had all been put to flight.

The juggler then spoke to himself: "I suppose the Christian Indians are praying at my wigwam?" He then began to sing with all his might, and presently his jeesuhkon was filled with wind, and began again to shake as if it would fall to pieces. Then a grumbling voice spoke and said, "The Christian Indians are standing all around you." Upon this the conjuror came out of his jessuhkon. We then asked him what news the spirits had communicated to him? He replied, "Some have forbidden me to become a Christian, and encourage me to live as my forefathers have done; but others inform me that it is perfectly right to be a Christian, and that I ought to go and hear the missionaries for myself; this I shall now do, and to-morrow I shall go and hear you at your meetings."

I have now stated what came under my own observation in this one instance, and I leave the reader to form his own judgment as to the power by which these deluded Indians perform their incantations. This Indian, according to promise, attended worship the next day.

INDIAN INCANTATIONS

Sickness is a part of life, not just the converse of health. One of the functions of the "medicine-man" or shaman was healing or curing. "Indian Incantations" appeared in *The Nor'Wester* (Winnipeg, Red River Settlement), 14 June 1860. The European observer of this healing ceremony writes with an odd and unidiomatic style but displays no reportorial interest or ability. For instance, he did not bother to mention whether or not the "sick boy" recovered.

> An incantation-service for the recovery of a sick boy was performed by some of the Indians in this neighbourhood on Sunday the 3rd inst. The "medicine-men" had been all possessed by the diseases and the "powers of the air" had been invoked to no purpose. The airy spirits summoned in these emergencies are supposed to club together in some tranquil grotto, and, as they are an uncommonly sleepy set, the child's relatives sat up several nights in succession, crooning a wild monotonous chant and beating their drums with a vigour and persistency which sadly disturbed the slumbers of some of the pale faces within earshot. But the spirits could not be drummed-up. Notwithstanding all the pother, the invalid grew worse; and, as a dernier resort, public worship and a dog feast were resolved on: the flesh of the canine quadruped being held to be peculiarly pleasing to the spirits aforesaid — as it undoubtedly is to those who partake of the savoury dish for them. Eight or nine dogs were slaughtered to furnish the feast on this occasion.
>
> The ceremonies of the day were conducted by the chief, Grands Oreilles, and three of the most ancient of the tribe. Those taking part in the proceedings assembled on the prairie, within an oblong enclosure, partly shaded by the branches of which it was composed. The performances were prefaced by speechifying and a race through the enclosure by two of the men — one beating the drum and the other keeping time with a kind of rattle (cee-ce-quin). More speeches, chanting and running around followed. The youth in whose behalf the rites were gone through was present all the time, wearing a bunch of many-coloured ribbons depending from his head and being otherwise fantastically tricked out. To prevent his faith being shaken by their prior ineffectual

efforts to cure him, they flourished their medicine-bags at the noses of the devotees present — coughed in chorus — grimaced hideously — swallowed wampum-beads and again expectorated them in token of the Great Spirit's approval. And to still further convince him of the potency of the medicine, they obligingly fell down as if overpowered, when the sick youth made a pass at them with his medicine-bag. In this way the red men prolonged their curious worship far into the afternoon.

In the evening, when the feasting was over, the young men turned out to ball-play and the old folks looked on, applauding and betting by turns. The young fellows taking part in the games were naked, with the exception of a girdle round the loins, and in their attempts to drive the ball to either goal, they ran with amazing swiftness. Their dusky forms, flitting over the prairie in the dying sunset, looked more like shadows than aught human.

AN INDIAN LEGEND

Over the centuries the Manitou and trickster motifs of the native peoples have often been blended with the stories of the Old and New Testaments so that the two threads are tightly intertwined, as in the following legend. "An Indian Legend as Told by a Blackfoot Chief" appeared in the *Fort Macleod Gazette* (Fort Macleod, Alta.), 24 August 1892. The account is signed "Vex." The writer might be a newspaperman, a trapper, a hunter, a surveyor … he is certainly someone who keeps a diary and sees himself as a writer and a preserver of Native lore. He writes:

"While sojourning among the Blackfoot, I chanced to hear many of their old legends, and, thinking that most of your readers would be delighted with an extract from my diary, I will take the liberty of writing you one in particular, as related to me by one of the principal chiefs of the Blackfoot nation."

A little chief from the country beyond the rising sun paid a visit to my camp and expressed his pleasure at meeting his red friends of the West, and also at the remarkable improvement we are making in learning to adopt the ways of the white people. He asked me if I remembered the great chief that came to see us last summer. He told me he saw him in the big white camp, and was invited by him, the great chief, to accompany him on a ride out. On the appointed day, taking their seats in a luxurious carriage, they started for their ride, and during the course of their travels, they approached a beautiful mansion surrounded by clustering pines and magnificent fields of corn. They entered the avenue and drove towards the house, for the purpose of inquiring as to the ownership of such a splendid demesne. They alighted and knocked for admittance, when, lo, behold, an old grey-haired man, venerable and majestic in appearance, opened wide the portals of the mansion to admit them. On asking him if he was the owner of the splendid house and surrounding fields of dropping corn, he answered yes, and on further inquiry the old man told them it was his sons who had assisted him in beautifying his property. The great chief then told the old man that he must give him one of his sons to teach the Blackfoot and help them in growing such splendid fields of corn as he possessed. The old man answered that he had already given one son to the Blackfoot and could ill spare another, but on being pressed, he finally consented to sacrifice himself and give them another.

THE WENDIGO LAY DOWN

The Wendigo or Windigo is the spirit of cannibalism and the personification of greed among the Algonkian-speaking Indians who comprise about two-thirds of Canada's Indian population. Is it permissible to slay a person possessed of the Wendigo? "Killed a Wendigo: Two Cat Lake Indians to Be Tried in Winnipeg for Murdering Their Chief" appeared in the *Medicine Hat Weekly News* (Medicine Hat, Alberta), 2 November 1899. The Dominion Police was founded as a security force and intelligence unit in 1868; in 1920 it was incorporated into the Royal Canadian Mounted Police. Rat Portage is the old name of Kenora, Ontario.

Rat Portage, October 29 — R.G. Chamberlain, of the Dominion police, Ottawa, and A.B.J. Bannatyre, Indian agent at Lac Seul, are in town with three Indians in their custody. Two of the Indians are charged with shooting their chief last winter at Cat Lake, about 350 miles northeast of Dinorwie. The story told by the two prisoners is essentially as follows: The chief of the Cat Lake Indians called Abw ah-sa keh-mig, became a wendigo, or insane, and ordered the prisoners to shoot him. A council of the tribe was called and they discussed the matter for two days, when they arrived at the conclusion that the chief's orders would have to be obeyed. The wendigo lay down in his wigwam and indicated with his hand where they were to shoot him. After he was dead, wood was heaped upon his body and the fire kept going for two days, thereby, according to the belief of the Indians, thoroughly destroying the evil spirit of their chief.

The matter was reported to Mr. Bannatyre, but as the Cat Lake tribe are non-treaty Indians, special legislation was passed last July to cover the case. Constable Chamberlain went to Lac Seul, where Mr. Bannatyre and two guides joined him, and they made the 700 mile journey in twenty days. The arrest of the two Indians was effected without trouble and when seen by a correspondent yesterday smoking their pipes at the Russel house they appeared to rather enjoy their captivity. The third Indian was brought along as a witness. Two of them had never seen a railroad or train before and only one of them had ever seen horses or cows. They are magnificent specimens of the red man and are above the average of their race in intelligence.

They are being held here for an order to take them to Winnipeg for trial, as the assizes are over here. The greatest wonder of the prisoners since their arrival here has been how the white man gets his living. They say everyone seems to be walking about doing nothing. By doing something their idea is hunting or fishing. Messrs. Bannatyre and Chamberlain say they are under great obligations to J.W. Anderson and Robt. Arnett of the Hudson Bay posts at Lac Seul and Cat Lake respectively, for assistance on the trip.

2

GHOSTLY STORIES

A pedlar takes refuge in a derelict cabin in the woods, where his life is threatened by a menacing, ghostly hand!

On a dark and stormy night, a traveller who is returning home approaches a fork in the road and is surprised to see old Angus cautioning him to take the longer rather than the shorter route. He accepts the advice and returns home safely … to discover that old Angus has been dead for six weeks!

These are a couple of the stories to be found in the first section of this book. The stories are written in the first person singular. They are narratives, not descriptions of narratives written by other people.

Could anything be more exciting than hearing or reading the details of an encounter with a ghost, an encounter recalled in the very words of the witness? The words themselves are enough to send shivers up and down the spine!

A good ghost story is a story about people as much as it is a tale about ghosts. Some people believe in the existence of ghosts; others do not. (Query: Do ghosts believe in the existence of people?) So these stories are about human beings, about men and women, about people who are struggling to find reasonable, rational explanations for what are essentially unreasonable, irrational experiences.

Terror and surprise lie at the heart of a good ghost story. There is terror in these stories; there is also the element of surprise. So the reader should beware! Some of the stories in this section are not all that predictable. They might not end the way the reader expects them to end.

As previously noted, a good ghost story requires the elements of terror and surprise. But it should also offer a suggestion of the supernatural.

COLONEL REAGAN'S GHOST

Prospectors live by hope and often by superstition. "Colonel Reagan's Ghost" appeared in the *Free Press* (Ottawa), 28 February 1900. The story is apparently reprinted from the *Dawson Weekly News*.

Colonel Reagan's Ghost — Incident in the Life of an Old Cassiar Miner — in the Winter of '72

The *Dawson Weekly News* of January 26 has the following:

J. Reagan is a typical old-time prospector. He has followed the fortunes of many mining camps since the early '50s in California and now that he has reached the ripe old age of 75 winters with hardly a friend to lend him a helping-hand his lot in life seems gloomy and despair has helped to break his once robust frame and subdue his once indomitable spirit. He came to Dawson in the rush of 1898 from the Cassiar mining district, but in the hurly-burly rush for desirable ground he was pushed aside and lost in the scramble. The old-time method of prospecting and then recording was not the way of the Klondike to make a success and so his funds have run short, and he now depends upon a few old-time friends to give him shelter and provisions. He has been living in a little cabin on the hillside but his wood becoming exhausted and his provisions about gone he has found a temporary shelter at the Flannery hotel.

In the early '70s, when the Cassiar mining district was in its heyday of prosperity, Colonel Reagan was well-to-do, having a rich paying claim on Tibbett Creek. In those days of frontier hospitality no man came to Reagan's cabin without receiving food or shelter. He was known all over the diggings as an eccentric character, devout in the observance of his religious duties and lavish in his gifts when called upon to help a fellow miner. He was held in considerable reverence by the Indians as a great medicine man, having cured several of the tribe of their prevailing sicknesses.

He was a good talker, and the story he tells of meeting a ghost during the last years of his life in the Cassiar mining district is interesting. He never tires of telling it, for he says that that experience has taught him that this manifestation of the unknown in the spirit world proves to him the existence of a hereafter and the truth of the immortality of the soul. He is a very little man — about 5 feet 4 inches in height, attenuated in form, with a large head covered with gray straggling locks and bright eyes that mark him as a man of an iron resolution ready to battle with the vicissitudes of life as long as he had a breath in his body. As he narrated, at the Flannery hotel last night, the story of meeting with the stranger in the lone cabin, the fire of zealous belief kindled in his eyes and seemed to bring back the scene of 28 years ago. He said:

"It was a cold and bitter night in the winter of 1872 when I crossed over the ridge and came to Dick Willoughby's cabin at Buck's Bar, on the Cassiar River. It was full of miners and they directed me to an empty cabin across the stream which was said to be haunted. I pulled my sled over to the shelter and entered, finding two rooms, one of them containing a fireplace which had not been used for some time. I started a fire and fried a little bacon and made some tea. As I was eating I looked up and found a stranger by my side. I did not hear him come through the doorway and was naturally surprised. He was an Englishman, smartly dressed and wore no coat. He had his arms folded across his breast and gazed upon me. His eyes seemed to look through me and I felt very uncomfortable.

"Finally I addressed him and asked him if he owned the cabin. He shook his head and said no. I asked him where he came from and he pointed to a number of graves standing white on the hillside. I had now become thoroughly alarmed and asked him if he was going to stay for the night.

"He pointed to the graves and beckoned me to follow him. As he was dressed in a strangely fashioned suit foreign to our miner's clothes I was puzzled and began to believe that he was a supernatural being, a genuine ghost. I finally pulled myself together and offered him some of my bacon, bread and tea, but he silently left the room without a sound of footsteps. When he had disappeared the fire blazed up into a flame and roared up the chimney, my frying pan rattled and banged on the floor and finally balanced in the flames while the bacon turned to a deep blood red hue. I almost swooned with fright. When all of a sudden the fire subsided and I was alone with my thoughts. I looked at the bacon and it had still the blood-red hue and to this day I could never solve the mystery."

MY GHOSTLY GUIDE

"The woods are full of creepy things." So runs a line from a child's song. At least one of these "creepy things" is a sentinel or guardian angel of sorts. "My Ghostly Guide" is reprinted from the *Free Press* (Ottawa), 15 January 1891.

My Ghostly Guide — A Lumber Merchant's Story

In January 1853 I was engaged as assistant clerk in a large lumbering camp in the woods about a hundred miles north of the Ottawa River. Our main shanty, was by the side of an outlet of the Red Pine Lake about two miles from the south side of the lake itself, a sheet of water of oblong shape, about a mile and a half wide and five miles long. There was a fairly good road from the edge of the lake to the shanty, and from the north or opposite side of the lake, a road had been made for some miles through the forest, to a point where a smaller camp had been established, and where a number of our men were engaged in making timber. From the main shanty to the smaller one was probably twenty miles. One day my chief, Mr. Simpson, sent me off with some instructions to the foreman in charge of what we called the Crooked Creek camp. I started with my snowshoes on my back and moccasins on my feet, at a brisk pace. It was a bright clear day. The road to the lake had been well worn by teams, and as there had been a thaw covered with frost, the ice on the lake was hard and smooth. The road from the lake to the Crooked Creek camp was rather rough and narrow, and a stranger might have difficulty in following it. However, I knew the route well, and arrived at my destination in good time, just as the men were returning from their work, with axes on their shoulders. I spent the night in the camp, being asked innumerable questions, and hearing all the petty gossip the men had to relate. It must be remembered that these shanty men go into the woods in October or November and excepting in rare instances hear nothing whatever from the outside world until they come out in the spring. Next morning I executed my commission and about ten o'clock started back for the main camp. I had not travelled more than half the distance when a snowstorm set in. In the woods the flakes fell down steadily, and I had no difficulty in keeping the road. It was about sun down when I reached the edge of the lake. The snow had reached the track across the ice and there was nothing to guide me to the entrance to the road to our main camp on the opposite shore. Out on the lake the storm was blinding, but I did not doubt my ability to reach the other side and find the road. So I started across the lake. When less than half a mile from the edge of the woods the snow was so thick that I could see neither shore. Moreover it was getting dark and exceedingly cold. If I should lose my way on the lake and have to spend the night there I would certainly perish. What was to be done? I turned in my tracks and managed to reach the North Shore again, stopping in the shelter of some bushes to recover my breath. Should I stay there all night? To tramp back to Crooked Lake camp was my first decision, but on reflection I remembered that any person travelling that road at night was liable to be attacked and eaten by wolves. Moreover I was hungry and fatigued. While I was thus communing with myself, jumping up and down and slapping my hands to keep myself warm, I saw a man dressed in a grey suit with a tuke on his head and a scarf around his waist, about 200 yards out on the lake, beckoning to me to follow him. I at once jumped to the conclusion that Mr. Simpson had sent one of the axe-men to meet me and guide me across the lake. So I ran with all my might towards him, calling to him at the same time. When I came close to the spot where he had stood, I looked around. He was not there, but a lull in the drift showed him some distance further on, still beckoning me to follow. No reply came to my calls to the man to wait for me, but every few moments he would appear some distance ahead beckoning me towards him. I could not tell what to make of the man's eccentric behaviour, but thought possible he was angry over being sent to look me up, and was taking this method of evincing his displeasure. At last I saw him on the shore, pointing towards the woods, and reaching the spot where he had been standing I found myself at the point where the road to our camp left the lake. The road was easy to follow, and I hurried forward, still somewhat puzzled over the refusal of my guide to wait for me; and wondering also why he had not brought a horse, and sled. I reached the camp just as the men had finished their supper, and everybody was surprised at my return. Mr. Simpson said he supposed that even if I had started from Crooked Creek camp in the morning I would have turned back when the snow storm came on. Somewhat bewildered I asked which of the men it was that guided me across the lake and pointed out the road to the camp. "Why did he not wait for me?" I asked in a rather injured tone. The men looked at one another in amazement. Not a man had been out of the camp that evening. Every man had returned from work at the usual time and remained in camp until my arrival. We were nearly seventy miles from the nearest settlement and there was no camp nearer than the one at Crooked Creek. Every person in the camp became restless and nervous. That man who guided me across the Red Pine Lake was not a being of flesh and blood, was the general conclusion of the shanty men and my description of his disappearances and reappearances tended to strengthen their theory. The experience was such an inexplicable one that very few of the inmates of our camp slept that night. I was grateful for my rescue, and it was evidently that whoever my guide was it was not my destiny to be eaten by wolves or frozen to death in attempting to cross Red Pine Lake in a snow storm.

THE SCHOOL TEACHER'S STORY

Most ghost stories are not stories so much as sketchy accounts of sensations, impressions, suppositions, conjectures, and speculations. The present account is an exception. Few accounts of wraith-like visitors are as detailed as this one. It was contributed by a teacher named P.A. O'Neill. "A Genuine Ghost Story" appeared in the columns of *The Irish Canadian*, 29 November 1883.

A Genuine Ghost Story — How the Spirit was "Laid"

An article in the *Fortnightly Review*, entitled "Phantasms of the Living," has induced me to relate here the circumstance of an apparition which I myself saw, and to the fact of seeing which I am prepared to make affidavit. I will premise by saying that I by no means belong to the superstitious class. On the contrary, I am strongly inclined to skepticism, and was at that time.

In 1877 I was engaged to teach in the third district of Ennismore, Peterboro' County, Ont. As was customary at that time, and is yet, the school teacher boarded round. But in this particular case a widow, possessor of a small farm, undertook the business of boarding the schoolmaster. After remaining with her for some time, she told me that she had concluded to rent or sell (I forget which) her small farm; consequently I should have to look out for another place to board. I was naturally a little perplexed, for upon the condition of boarding permanently with her during my engagement, I had accepted the situation.

However there was nothing for it but to acquiesce. So, next Sunday, I set out for mass to the one parish church of Ennismore. I knew there was a farmer living four miles distant, with a comparatively small family, who had a very large farm house. Originally it had been intended for a country tavern, with a row of horse stalls, large dance hall, etc., after the manner of the time. But through some cause, generally attributed to the dullness of the times, the house had fallen back to the rank of an ordinary farm house — a giant among its neighbors.

After mass it is a custom — especially an Irish custom — to assemble for some time and gossip in front of the church before driving home; and you may be sure that Ennismore marks no exception to the general rule. After the usual courtesies had been exchanged I broached the subject of board for the school teacher to my friend, Mr. — (the only name which shall be held sacred in this relation). He said that, particularly for the sake of his two boys, nothing would suit him better than to board me; but he had no sleeping room for me. I naturally wondered at this, and frankly told him that a man living in the largest farm house in the township, with a comparatively small family, could not be hard pressed for sleeping room.

"Well," said he, "I don't own the farm; I merely lease it from the owner. But one-half of the house is entirely useless to me, except the lower half, which I use as a granary; for in the upper half is a very large room with a very fine bed in which no one will sleep."

Said I: "Did you ever try to sleep there yourself?"

"God forbid!" was the reply.

I was somewhat surprised at this remark, and begged to know the cause of the trouble, but all the information he would volunteer was that the room was haunted. It was the only available room he had in the house for a stranger, and he could scarcely offer hospitality to anyone in it, when nobody could sleep in it. The end of it was that I laughed down my worthy friend's superstition; occupied the next day the haunted room; congratulated myself upon having so large, cool and fine a room in hot July weather; ate generously of a most bounteously furnished table — nothing better in the world than in Ennismore; and, altogether rejoiced in my good luck in the change from the scrimpy widow's board to the generous farmer's cuisine; and enjoyed many a quiet laugh at the ghost's expense.

My first experience of her ghostship was while sitting on a rail fence in a warm August day at twilight, talking to a friend at a considerable elevation above the house. My friend, who seemed to know the room I occupied, suddenly, with an exclamation of surprise, turned to me and said:

"Look, Daly, there's some one in your room, and it's a woman, too."

I looked in the direction indicated, and sure enough there was a light in the room and a shadow upon the window curtains showed a woman moving to and fro. Of course I was somewhat nonplused, but I accounted for the circumstance by thinking that some of the girls of the house were engaged in the room in the performance of the ordinary domestic duties. Still I thought this a little strange, knowing the abhorrence entertained by every member of the family of entering the so-called haunted room.

On returning that evening I congratulated the farmer's wife on her courage in once more throwing open the room. She stared at me with blank astonishment. She wouldn't, for all the world, having anything to do with the room. Why, did I suppose she had? I told her what I had seen. There had been nobody there, as far as she knew. I went up stairs; the door was locked, the lamp unlit, the wick as I had left it, no evidence in the world that anybody had been there since morning. I considered the whole thing an optical illusion, and went to sleep. My dreams were not disturbed.

Three or four nights after, however, operations began. I awoke about the witching hour of night — so my watch admonished me — feeling chilly. The covering was all off the bed. I jumped up and found that the bedclothes had been removed and placed on the floor in a heap below the foot-board. I replaced them deeming I had kicked them off, and thought no more about it. But the same thing occurred several successive nights, so that it became a worry to me; and at last I got worked up to such a nervous pitch that I could not sleep at all. Toward the middle of the night I distinctly felt the bed clothes begin to move downward. I clutched at them grimly, and quite an exciting struggle for their possession began. But my invisible antagonist proving the stronger I saw everything disappear slowly but surely through the open space between the foot-rail and the floor-board.

Meanwhile, I had turned on the light, and leaping from the bed exclaimed: "Now I've got you!" in no enviable frame of mind, either. I seized a stout cudgel and explored the foot of the bed, and everywhere in the room; found the door securely locked and bolted. Not a single vestige of my nocturnal visitant except the heap of bed clothing on the floor. To say the least, I was awed as well as puzzled; and not knowing what other deviltry might be forthcoming, I took care to keep the light burning the rest of the night.

I need not say I slept no more but lay awake thinking. What could it be? Nevertheless, a bright thought struck me. I was not going to be driven out of my comfortable quarters by any ghost who played such a shabby track as this, for by this time I began to think it was a ghost, after all. Still, if stealing bedclothes was all it could do it wasn't much of a terror; and I'd fix that. The next morning I procured a wide slat and nailed it securely across the open space at the foot of the bed. Several nights passed; no more annoyance from that source.

I had then, and still have, a habit of placing my boots at the side of the bed before retiring for the night. One night, at the usual hour, I was awakened by a sound as loud as a pistol shot succeeded by dead silence. I immediately jumped up, and, upon investigation found one of my boots missing. Looking around I espied it under the bed close to the wall, against which it had been thrown with such violence that it chipped off some of the plaster. Certainly my nocturnal visitant exhibited a strange inclination for working close to the ground.

By this time I was in a towering passion, and seizing the remaining boot I sent it flying with an oath accompanying it in the direction the other had apparently come from. I listened for a reply, but none coming, I got up on the bed. Scarcely had I lifted my legs from the floor when the boot was thrown back with such force that I felt the wind strike my leg as the missile passed it. Had it struck me it would surely have broken the limb. My investigations ceased for that night. I lay still and let the boots alone. Yet, after that, not wishing to undergo the same experience, I took the boots to bed with me, and nothing more of that kind occurring, I began to flatter myself on having laid the spirit. Besides, I was strengthened in my opinion by the congratulations of my neighbors, who looked upon me as a man of extraordinary moral courage, and, as my landlord had laughingly remarked, "undoubtedly ghost-proof." Of course I mentioned my experience to no one. I feared ridicule, in fact, and really believed that I would solve the mystery, and prove the ghost theory to be all nonsense.

Nothing occurred for several weeks afterward. I enjoyed the old farmer's hospitality meanwhile, taught my school and made my mind easy. One night, however, I was rudely disturbed from this happy frame of mind. I awoke with a feeling of terror. My usual resource I at once turned on the light. Then I beheld a sight which filled me with mingled fear and amazement. There stood, evidently, my ghostly visitant, staring at me; — a woman, pale and wan, yet with traces of beauty on her face. She was dressed in an ordinary black dress, with a black ribbon around her throat. But the thing which riveted my attention most was the expression of dire sorrow and awful despair upon her countenance. I never saw anything like it, not even in the faces of those condemned to an ignominious death. Once or twice the lips parted as if to speak; then, I suppose, as the expression of horror upon my countenance increased, there was a slight frown. With a strange fascination I continued to gaze for what appeared to be a minute. Then I made a movement towards the woman, when she appeared to go through the doorway. I examined the door, however, but found it locked as usual, and bolted. I listened, but heard no footsteps or other sounds on the stairs.

Then, returning to my couch, I concluded, as I am now thoroughly convinced, that I had seen a spirit. I received, however, a severe nervous shock, which was plainly visible to my kind host at breakfast next morning. He questioned me, and I related to him the circumstances herein set forth. From him I ascertained the name of the owners of the farm, and when vacation occurred I hied me to Peterboro', where Mr. Sullivan lived, to get an explanation of the mystery. Of course I slept no more in the haunted room.

Mr. Sullivan was quite friendly in his manner. "Yes," he said; "that woman was my wife's sister. She died in that bed in that room of consumption. We did all we could for her in her last sickness. She had the priest with her, received the last sacraments, but, though suffering terribly from disease, seemed terribly unwilling to die. Yet, why she should not rest with the multitude who sleep in Christ, and rest in peace, we do not know. We did all we could to make her comfortable, and in return she has driven us from our farm. She appeared to my wife one night, shortly after death, and so terrified the woman that she came near joining her ghostly visitant in the other world. Nothing would ever induce my wife to sleep in the house again, so I had to move here, engage in another occupation and rent my farm. She has never troubled us here, but seems to confine her visits to the room where she died. To me the whole thing is unaccountable."

I assured him it was equally so to me, and took my departure.

Now, why was this spirit so spiteful against anybody sleeping in the bed she died on? Why did she visit the scene of her demise at all? Rev. Mr. Searless, in the Catholic World, says if the spirit of the friend appears to us and gives "reasonable proofs of his identity we may of course put faith in what he may tell us of his experience since his departure." But no such faith is needed in this essay, as the apparition will never be called upon for proofs of identity, or spoken to at all. The poor spirit may abandon hope. The scene is the heart of an exclusively Irish settlement, and there is not a man, woman or child who would dare to speak to it. It is graven upon the Irish mind, the superstition — coming, it is said, from druidical days — that he who speaks to a spirit shall surely die within a year.

The old house may sink and rot and pass away, and the day of judgement come, but in Ennismore it never will be known why this uneasy spirit revisits the "glimpses of the moon."

Perhaps, however, some adventurous stranger, bolder than I am, or rather with more presence of mind, may wish to undergo my experience and solve the mystery. The house is there yet; is easily accessible; the door of the room locked, and the room itself abandoned to its ghostly tenant.

THE PEDLAR'S GHOST STORY

Toronto Telegram, October 20, 1870

Several years ago, I was engaged in the business of peddling among the frontier towns of Canada. The route over which I was accustomed to travel usually occupied me about six weeks; and so scattered were the settlements which I visited, that not infrequently I was obliged to encamp for the night in the woods. I carried my goods in a pack upon my back, and was accompanied in my journey back and forth by a huge hound mastiff — one of the most intelligent brutes I ever saw, and devotedly attached to me. Of course I was armed. In addition to a pair of good revolvers and a knife, I carried a cane, which I used as a staff in walking, but which I could, upon occasion, instantly convert into a most deadly weapon. It was charged with a heavy load of buckshot, and was quite as effective as a blunderbuss.

Much of my journey lay through a rough country just beginning to be broken up by the pioneers; and often for miles I had to travel through forests which none but the trapper, or men engaged in some business like my own had ever visited.

One afternoon I was seated on the bank of a little stream, resting from my walk; and being warm and tired, I proceeded to bathe my face. While thus engaged, I noticed a little path, which led from the water's edge up into the forest. I knew at a glance that it was made for deer and other animals coming down to drink; and, impelled by curiosity, I determined to follow it up for a short distance. I had passed less than a quarter of a mile, when I suddenly came upon an opening in the woods, of several acres, in the centre of which stood a good substantial log cabin. Going to the door, I pushed it open, and took a survey of the premises. There were but two rooms in the building — one on the ground, and a loft overhead, which was reached by a short ladder. At one end of the lower room was a huge fireplace, strewed with ashes and a few pieces of charred wood; while at the other, in one corner, a pile of fir boughs were flying, showing that some traveller had made it a shopping-place for the night; but it must have been long before, for the branches he had gathered for a couch were dried and dead.

Glancing at my watch, I saw that it was half-past five, and the sun was nearly down. Thinking myself fortunate in securing so good a camping-place, I proceeded to gather some dry sticks and kindle a fire. Dry wood there was in abundance, for directly in front of the cabin stood a pine tree, which the lightning had shivered, scattering splinters and boughs for rods in every direction, and I soon had a cheerful fire blazing and snapping on the hearth. Then, gathering a few armfuls of fir boughs for a bed, and extemporizing a rough seat, my dog and I betook ourselves to supper. He seemed to be as well pleased with the situation as myself, and after eating the food I gave him, went and stretched in the doorway — for it was a pleasant spring evening — and composed himself for a nap, while I, filling my pipe, indulged in a smoke and a reverie.

For a long time after my pipe had gone out, I sat watching the fire creeping up the dried wood, now burning steadily, and now leaping with burning flame, as it caught at some part more combustible than the rest. At length, tired with my day's journey, I nodded and fell asleep, but was soon awakened by the growling of my dog. Rising and rubbing my eyes, I went cautiously to the door, and looked about me. Everything was quite, and the full moon just peering over the tops of the forest trees, streaked the clearing here and there with patches of mellow light.

"What is it, Brave, old fellow, eh?" said I, speaking to the dog.

He wagged his tail, whined, and snuffed the air uneasily. Satisfied that something was wrong, I cocked a pistol and went out into the moonlight, closely followed by the dog. I went round the cabin; there was nothing to be seen. I peered into the shadows of the woods about me — all was still, save that the branches now and then swayed to and fro with the evening wind.

Satisfied that there was nothing within the opening, yet feeling a little uneasy, I entered the cabin, replenished the fire, and was about to close the door, when, as if in answer to a threatening growl from the dog, there came a quick, sharp blow against the side of the building, similar to that which could be produced by striking with a piece of board. With a short, savage bark, Brave sprang out of the open door, while I, with a pistol in readiness for instant use, followed. There was nothing to be seen, although I made a most careful search, and everything was as quiet as before; but there was something very strange about it, for the dog came to me with a half whine, half growl, his hair bristling, and he sniffling the air and looking uneasily overhead. A thought struck me. Had not some persons been in the cabin, and, seeing me coming, concealed themselves in the chimney, and were they not now, with some object in view, trying to frighten me? Impossible! for the smoke from the resinous pine I had burned would soon have driven them out, or suffocated them in their hiding-place.

"Brave," said I, "we are a couple of fools; there is no one here, and everything is all right; if it isn't we'll make it right in the morning."

As I spoke these words I reached the door, and was in the act of entering, when, without the least noise, with a motion silent as death itself, a huge bird, black as midnight, came swooping past so close that it almost brushed my face with its wings. On that instant the dog sprang, and though his motion was as swift as lightning itself, and I could swear that he grasped it in his jaws, yet I heard them clash together with a snap like a steel trap, while the bird, swooping upward, settled itself on a branch of the withered pine.

"Born in the woods, and scared by an owl," I repeated to myself; but looking at the dog, I saw that he had slunk into the cabin, and was shivering with fright.

Almost angry at his actions, I commanded him sharply to come to me, and he obeyed, though reluctantly.

"Now, Brave," said I, you are too wise and old a dog to be scared by a paltry owl, though he is a big one. He'll be giving us some of his precious music presently; and as I don't care about that kind of a serenade I'll drive him back into the woods."

So saying, I picked up a handful of stones and began trying to frighten away my unwelcome visitor. But the more I wanted him to leave, the more he wouldn't go; and though on several occasions I was sure I struck him, still he never altered his position or budged an inch. Now, when I begin to do a thing I like to carry it through; and so, without thinking what the consequences might be, I drew one of my pistols and fired at the strange bird. The report rang sharply out upon the night air, and went echoing through the forest and over the hills for miles and miles away. Half frightened at what I had done, and provoked that he did not stir, I fired again and again. How strange it was that I could not hit that bird! Did I miss my aim? I am a good shot — it was almost light as day, and he was not over twenty feet distant.

Going into the cabin, I reloaded my pistol, and being now fully aroused and provoked at my want of success, I determined that this time at least he should not escape me. I got my cane, adjusted it, took deliberate aim, and fired. The piece was heavily loaded, and the discharge almost deafened me; but when the smoke had cleared away and I looked upwards, the bird had gone.

"I thought I'd settle you that time," I muttered.

Gone! Yes it was gone — but where? I looked into the air above me, on the ground around me; I peered into the tree to see if perchance it had lodged in any of the branches; I listened, that I might hear it flutter, if but wounded; but there was no sound save the wind moaning through the dead branches of the tree above me, that stood withered, scalped, and ghastly, like a thing accursed.

Partially satisfied in that the bird had disappeared, and musing on the strange occurrence, I took my way into the cabin, reloaded my piece, securely fastened the door, and calling my dog close to me, lay down on the branches to sleep, resolving that I would suffer no more mysterious sounds or strange birds to annoy me. With my faithful dog at hand, and my arms in readiness for use, a feeling of security came over me, and I fell into a sound slumber.

I must have slept for several hours, for when I woke the fire was burning but feebly, and its flickering, dying flames cast weird and grotesque shadows on the wall. But what was the strange presence in the room that made my flesh creep and the perspiration to stand in cold drops upon my brow? There was nothing that I could hear; yet a strange sense of impending and appalling danger almost paralyzed me. It came at length, as I knew it would — a wailing sound, at first faintly heard, but swelling louder and louder until it deepened in its hideous intensity to the pitch of an unearthly yell; then again all was still.

I sprung to my feet; there was nothing in the room but my dog, who stood with burning eyes and bristling hairs glaring at the opening in the loft overhead.

"By all the beings of earth and air!" I shouted, "I'll see this thing out, if it cost my life!" And kindling the fire to a roaring flame, I seized a blazing brand in one hand and a pistol in the other, and climbed to the loft above.

I searched in every nook and corner where even a mouse might hide. I went round it again and again; I descended to the open air and peered into places which I had examined a dozen times before. Nothing was changed. The old pine still stretched its long, gaunt arms in the moonlight, and the wind sighed and moaned like the wail of a wandering spirit through its shivered boughs.

I entered my cabin, took up my pack, and resolved to pass the remainder of the night beneath the open sky; but a feeling of pride prevented me; and closing the door once more, I flung myself upon my bed.

Suddenly, as I lay pondering on the mysterious manifestations, a livid gleam, like lightning, shot from the loft overhead; and that yell came once more — not as at first, slowly and indistinctly, but sharply and fearfully sudden; then it died away like a death groan. The fire, which was burning brightly, with a sudden hiss went out, and the room was left in utter darkness. Then a little vapory ball of light appeared at the opening in the lift; it grew brighter and brighter, till the room was as light as day; and from the centre of that vapory ball, a hand appeared — a hand! With moving fingers that seemed searching the air for something they found not. It moved towards me; at first the hand alone, but soon a wrist, and then an arm appeared, lengthening, lengthening, and slowly stretching out to grasp me. Great heaven! Was there no end to that arm? My dog was crouched beside me, but not in fear now; his eyes were fixed with a steady glow upon the moving hand, and every nerve was braced for a deadly spring; and when at least it had reached so frightfully near that I might have reached it with my hand, and I might have touched it, and I shouted, "Take him, Brave!" the noble creature leaped, with panther spring, from the ground beside me. There was a growl, a crash, and a smothered fall, and then I was caught in a vice-like grasp. I struggled to free myself, but in vain; and when at last a pair of clammy arms were passed close to mine, I gave a shriek of terror and despair, and felt my senses leave me.

I knew no more till I woke up to find my faithful dog locking my face and whining piteously, and I lay on the bank of the stream where I had stopped to rest.

'Twas only a dream after all, but so frightfully real did it appear, that it was hours before I recovered my strength or composure of mind.

It was the last trip I ever made upon the route, for I never could shake off the impression left upon me by the dream. I believe it to have been a warning of danger ahead, and I shudder now, and ever shall, as I think of that afternoon nap in the woods of Canada.

A THRILLING ADVENTURE

A Pedlar's Startling Experience at a Backwoods Tavern in the Early Days of Ontario

Canadian Statesman, December 24, 1889

In all my travels, over thousands of miles of country, I was never really terrified but once; and then I confess I had a fright which

I did not recover from for weeks, and which I still never recall without a secret shudder. My life might be said to have hung on a bare thread; and nothing but heaven's kind providence, interposed in a most miraculous manner, saved me from the awful doom.

In the regular pursuit of my vocation, I was travelling through Western Canada, when, towards evening of one hot, sultry, summer day, I found myself passing through a long stretch of swampy woodland, along what might much better have been denominated a horse-path than a road. I had taken a rather obscure by-way, in the hopes, if I found few customers, to find those who would pay well; but I had made a serious mistake, in that I had discovered none at all. In a walk of eight tedious miles, I had seen only three dwellings, and these miserable shanties, one of which was unoccupied, and the other two with ragged families who had no money for trade. At the last house, I inquired the distance to the next, and I was informed that four miles further on I would come to a main road, where there was an inn for travellers; and towards this I was now making my way, with the intention of putting up there for the night.

I came in sight of the road and the inn just as the sun was setting behind a drift of clouds, that seemed to betoken the gathering of a storm. Tired and hungry as I was, with night setting in upon me in such a lonely country, I was very glad to come in sight of a place of rest, and went forward in comparatively good spirits.

The inn was a brown stone building, two stories in height, and quite respectable looking for that region of country. As I came up to it, however, I fancied it had a certain air of gloom, which had a rather depressing effect upon my spirits; but then this, I thought, might be caused by the absence of sparkling lights and bustle, and seeing it at the hour of twilight. No one met me at the door; nor did I perceive a human being in or about it till I had entered the unlighted bar room, where a man, who was sitting in a corner, rose and came forward, with a slight nod of salutation.

"Are you the landlord?" I inquired.

"I am," was the answer.

"I suppose I can put up with you for the night?" I said.

"Certainly," he answered, glancing at my trunks. "Shall I take care of them for you?"

"I will merely set them behind your bar till I retire for the night, and then I will take them to my room. I suppose you can give me a single apartment to myself."

"Oh, yes, easy enough — my house is large, and will not be crowded to-night."

"Have you any other guests?" I inquired, feeling, from some cause for which I could not account, strangely ill at ease.

"There is no one here yet," he replied; "and it is getting rather late for the drovers, who often stop with me."

It was a relief to think that drovers were in the habit of putting up at the house, for that implied a certain honesty in the landlord, and a consequent security for lonely travellers; and I really needed this reflection to counterbalance a strange sense of something wrong, if not absolutely wicked and dangerous.

I informed the host that I was very tired and hungry, and wished a good supper and a good bed, and he assured me that I should be provided with the best he had. He went out of the room, as he said, to give the necessary directions and get a light. He was gone some ten minutes, and returned with a candle in his hand, which he placed on the bar. I had taken a seat during his absence, and, being a little back in the shade, I now had a chance to scrutinize his features closely without being perceived in the act.

I did not like the appearance of his countenance. His face was long and angular, with black eyes and bushy brows, and the whole expression was cold, forbidding, and sinister.

He remarked that the night was very warm and sultry, and that it was likely to be showery, and then inquired if I had come far that day, and which direction? I informed him of my tedious walk over the by-road, and unguardedly added that I did not think my day's experience would incline me to travel through that region again in a hurry. He asked me where I was from, if I had seen many persons that day, if I was an entire stranger in that part of the country, and so forth, and so on — to all of which I gave correct answers.

Thus we conversed till a little bell announced supper, when he ushered me into a good-sized dining room, and did the honours of the table, trying to make himself very agreeable. That there was somebody else in the house I had good reason to believe — for I heard steps and the rattling of dishes in an adjoining room — but the landlord himself was the only person I saw during the evening, if I except a glance at a disappearing female dress as he was in the act of lighting me to my room.

My bedroom was small, but looked clean and neat, and contained an inviting bed, curtains of chintz at the single window, a chest of drawers, a looking-glass, a wash stand, a couple of chairs, and was really quite as well furnished as many an apartment in hotels of far greater pretension. With all this I was pleased, of course; and judging by the appearance that there was nothing wrong about an inn so properly conducted, I bolted my door, raised the window for a little fresh air, looked out and discovered the night was intensely dark, undressed, blew out my light, jumped into bed, and almost immediately fell asleep.

I was awakened by a crash of thunder, that was rolling over and shaking the house to its foundation at the moment my senses returned to me; and being rather timid about lightning, and remembering to have heard that the electric fluid would follow a current of air, and also recollecting that I had left my window open, I sprang up hastily to close it. As I did so, my head barely touched some soft substance, just above me; but the fact produced no impression upon my excited mind at the moment. I reached the window, and for an instant stood and looked out to get a view of the approaching storm; but, as before, I could not see anything at all — all was as black as the darkness of a pit — and as before, too, the air was perfectly still — so much so, that I fancied I felt a stifling sensation. I was the more surprised at this that I thought I heard the roar of the wind, and the falling of rain; and certainly there was another clap of thunder, whose preceding flash of lighting I had not perceived.

Awed by the mystery, I hastily let down the sash, and returned to the bed in a state of some trepidation; but, as I put out my hand to feel my way in, it came into contact with a mattress nearly as high as my neck from the floor. Now really terrified by a sense of some unknown danger, and half believing that the room was haunted, I clutched the mattress convulsively, and felt over and under it, and found it was separate from the bed on which I had been sleeping, and was slowly descending!

Gracious heaven! how shall I attempt to describe that moment of horror, when I first got a comprehension of the whole diabolical plot! a plot to murder me in my sleep! I was walled up in a room prepared with machinery for the express purpose of murdering the unsuspecting traveller, and had been saved from the awful fate by the report of heaven's thunder. The window of course was only a blind to deceive, placed inside of a blank wall, which accounted for my seeing nothing from it and getting no current of air when the sash was raised; and the mattress I had hold of was arranged to be lowered by pulleys, and held down by weights upon the sleeping traveller till life should be smothered out of him. All this I comprehended as by a sudden flash of thought and as I stood trembling and almost paralyzed, there came a quick rattling of cords and pulleys, and the upper bed dropped down with a force that denoted the heavy weights placed upon it.

But though left out from under it — alive as it were, by a miracle — what was I now to do to preserve my life? As yet, all was dark, and no one appeared; but I now heard voices speaking in low, hushed tones and knew that soon the truth would be discovered, and in all probability my life attempted in some other way. What was I to do? How defend myself from the midnight murderers? I had no weapon but an ordinary clash-knife, and what would this avail against two or more? Still, I was determined not to yield my life tamely; and as in all probability every avenue of escape was barred against me, I resolved to crawl under the bed and take my chance there. Mechanically, while considering, I had felt for my clothes and drawn on my pantaloons; and now cautiously trying the door, and finding it, as I had expected, fastened on the outside, I stealthily glided under the bed, and placed myself far back, close against the wall. I had barely gained this position, when a light shone into the room from above; and looking up between the bed and the wall, I saw an opening in the ceiling, about five feet by eight, through which I suppose the upper mattress had descended; and, standing on the edge of this opening, looking down, was the landlord of the inn, and beside him a tall, thin, sinister virago, who looked wicked enough to be his wife, as undoubtedly she was.

"All right, Meg," he said, at length: "he is quiet enough now;

and if not, I can soon finish him;" — and with this he took the candle from her hand, and leapt down upon the bed, and then sprang off upon the floor. "Now hoist away," he continued, "and let us go through with this job as quick as possible."

Again I heard the noise of ropes and pulleys, and knew the upper bed was being raised, which in another moment would disclose to the human monster the fact that my dead body was not under it. What then? Merciful heaven! It must be a struggle of life and death between him and me! — and I was already nerving myself for the dreadful encounter, when I experienced a kind of transitory sensation of a crash and a shock.

The next thing I remember, was finding myself exposed to the fury of the tempest — the wind howling past me, the rain beating upon me, the lightning flashing, and the thunder roaring. I was still in my room, but it was all open on one side of me, and it took my bewildered sense some time to comprehend the awful fate of heaven's peculiar providence.

The lightning had struck the portion of building I was in, and had thus given me life and freedom!

As soon as I fairly comprehended this, I leapt to the ground outside, escaping injury, and ran for my life. I took the main road, and ran on through the storm, as if pursued by a thousand fiends, as I sometimes fancied I was. I ran thus till daylight, when I met a stage-coach full of passengers, hailed the driver, and told him my wonderful story. He thought me mad, but persuaded me to mount his box and go back with him. On arriving at the inn, he found a confirmation of my fearful tale.

The house had not only been struck, but, strange to relate, both the landlord and his wife had been killed by the bolt of heaven, and were found dead among the ruins!

I subsequently had to appear before a magistrate, acting as coroner, and depose to the facts and the jury returned a verdict in accordance therewith.

I got away from that fearful region as soon as I could; but to this day I have never fully recovered from the effects of that night of horror at the inn!

WARNED OF DANGER BY A GHOST

The Meeting on the Road and the Specter's Words of Guidance — The Shade Was "Not Wrapped Up for Driving" — and Refused the Invitation to Ride, as "Walking Was Warmer"
Regina Leader Post, March 11, 1890

Such a glorious night! The snow sparkled like diamond dust, and the sleigh runners squeaked as they passed over it, with frosty sound so dear to the heart of the true Canadian.

The moon had risen, and it was as bright as day. The horse's breath seemed to fill the air with clouds, and his coat already began to sparkle with frost. Oh, it was good to be home again! "Canada for the Canadians." Is it any wonder we love our beautiful country with such passionate devotion?

From these high and patriotic thoughts I was aroused by coming to a turn in the road, a fork. Now there were two roads to the village from this point, one leading down a long, steep hill, at the bottom of which an aboideau, or primitive bridge, built of fire trees and brush, with alternate layers of earth and stones — a sort of earthwork, in fact — spanned a deep treacherous little creek, in which the ice piled in huge blocks in winter, and, as it was an estuary of the river, it was a dangerous spot when the tide was high. Taking this road would cut off more than half a mile of my journey, so I decided to try it, despite a curious reluctance on the part of my horse. The road certainly did not look as if it was traveled much, but just at the turn the snow had drifted off, leaving it nearly bare. So I forced the unwilling nag into the roadway and jogged on cautiously.

The spot bore an unpleasant name, and a still more unpleasant reputation. It was called "Ghost's Hollow."

Fifty years ago, in the old days when the province was thinly settled and a weekly stage coach was the only means of communication between the different towns, the horses of a heavily laden coach had taken fright at the top of the hill, and dashing down at mad speed gone over the aboideau. The tide was full in at the time and the creek filled with great floating blocks of ice. There were none to help in that lonely spot, so every one had been drowned, and the superstitious country people insisted that on wild winter nights any one standing at the top of the hill and listening intently could hear the muffled sound of sleigh bells, the shouts and the splashing and struggling of the horses. Certain it was that, when the tide was very low and the wind high, the water rushing through the sluices under the aboideau made an eerie, gurgling sound that was not by any means cheerful. I could hear it now with painful distinctiveness, though there was no wind. And my thoughts traveled back to my boyhood and to old Angus McDonald, a queer old Scotch farmer, with whom I had been a favourite, who had taught me how to make fox traps and to shoot rabbits, to believe in omens and to be frightened in dreams.

He was a superstitious old fellow, who declared that he had the gift of second sight, and who had always insisted that to hear the sound of the groans and struggles in "Ghost's Hollow," was a sure forerunner of coming misfortune to the one hearing them.

I smiled to myself as I remembered it, and made a mental note that I would tell Angus the first time I saw him, and ask him what he made of the omen now.

The horse stopped so suddenly that I nearly fell over the dashboard! And directly in front of the sleigh I saw a man plodding slowly along through the snow. I could have sworn that he was not there half a minute before, and yet he could not have come out of the woods without my seeing him. "Holloa!" I called. He turned slowly, and I saw that it was old Angus himself.

"Why, Angus, old fellow," I said, "what in the world are you doing in this lonely spot? Jump in and I'll drive you home. I was just thinking about you."

"Many thanks, Walter, for yer offer and yer thoughts, too; but it's a cold night, and I'm not that wrapped up for driving; walking's warmer," he answered.

"But what brings you out here on such a night, Angus?" I persisted. "Your rheumatism must be better than it was, or you would not run such risks."

"Ay, the rheumatism's a not that bad, I was seein' to the fox traps, an' then I heard the bells an' knew some one was going down the hill, so I came out to warn them. The 'bito's' all down, Walter, an' you'd get an ugly fall amongst those ice cakes if ye went over; turn back, boy, an' go the long way."

"But, Angus," I cried, "I don't like to have you here."

"I'll do well enough, lad; I'm going home now, good night."

"Good night," I answered reluctantly, "I'll see you to-morrow."

He made no answer and I turned the trembling horse, who pranced and snorted and tried to bolt until he realized that he was going the other way. When I looked back Angus was gone.

Once on the main road again we went like the wind, and soon the lights of home shone out, and in a few minutes more I was in the hall being shaken hands with, and kissed and questioned, passed around from one to the other like a sort of cordial, exclaimed over and commiserated because I had not any tea, and reading a welcome in Maggie's sweet eyes that was more "truly sustaining," as the old ladies say, than all the tears in the world.

"Walter, dear," said Maggie, "you have not been taking care of yourself. You look terribly worn and pale."

"Never mind, Maggie," I answered, "I am going to rest and get strong again now."

The boys were both home for the day.

Jack was in the civil service and Will was in a bank, both younger than I, and already winning their own way in the world I thought with a sigh.

Then mother came in to tell me my supper was ready, and every one came into the dining room to see that I was taken care of. Maggie poured out hastily made coffee, and if I could only have shaken off a curious feeling of languor that would creep over me, I should have felt as if I were in Paradise, after my long months of solitude.

"By the way, Walter," said Jack suddenly. "How did you happen to come the marsh road, as of course you did, or you would not be here — you know you always take the old coaching road because it was a little shorter. Was it by chance, or did they tell you at the hotel that the aboideau was down?"

"I believe they did tell me," I answered. "At least the hostler called after me, but I did not hear him. So I took the coach road, and if it had not been for poor old Angus McDonald I should be floundering among the ice cakes now instead of sitting here. I met him before I had more than started down the hill, and he told me about the 'bito,' as he called it."

For a full minute after I spoke there was a dead silence. Then Jack opened his mouth to speak, but was checked instantly by a look from father. Maggie grew very pale, and then flushed uneasily, and mother said something hurriedly about my having missed the train, and how disappointed the girls had been.

Something had evidently happened, for every one seemed constrained, but made nervous efforts to talk, so I was glad when the meal, which had begun so merrily, came to a close.

I went back to the parlor with the girls and tried to feel as I did when I first came in, but it was of no use, and, hearing Jack's footstep crossing the hall, I slipped out and stopped him.

"Look here, Jack," I began, "did I say anything out of the way at supper?"

"No! Oh, no," said Jack, uneasily; he had evidently received private instructions to hold his tongue, and he found the task a hard one.

"Very well," I answered shortly; "if you don't choose to tell me, I'll go out in the kitchen and ask the servants. They will tell me fast enough. Now what was there in my saying I had seen old Angus to startle any one so?"

"Well, if you will have it, there was a good deal. Angus died six weeks ago. I can't imagine how we forgot to write you about it — Walter!!!"

I can't tell much about what happened after that, for the reason that I don't know. Jack says I just staggered and fell, as if I had received a blow. And when I was able to take any interest in what was passing around me it was nearly the last of January, and I had lost count of time for many weeks.

A BOY'S GRIM ADVENTURES

He Didn't Believe in Ghosts, but Had Several Scares — The Phantom Dog that Excited the People of Charlottetown, and How It Was Brought to Bay

Daily Examiner, Charlottetown, P.E.I., November 24, 1894

There are people here and there who believe in ghosts, but even among children the belief is disappearing. One of the readers of the Recorder, Jr., asked me lately:

"Have you ever seen a ghost?"

"No. Have you?"

"Never," was his reply, "but I'd like to see one if there are such things."

"You'd get a jolly good fright if you did," I said, and he wanted to know what made me think so. He didn't believe in ghosts.

"Neither do I, but it isn't pleasant to see what some people might take for a ghost."

This remark whetted my young friend's curiosity, and he wanted to know if such an experience had ever been mine. Before he got through with me he had drawn out all my knowledge of ghosts. My disbelief in them dated from my earliest boyhood and yet one of the most decided frights that ever befell me was experienced after the years of manhood had been reached. Late one night, while walking along a lonely road, giving no thought to even such solid and dangerous beings as highwaymen and footpads, much less to ghosts, I was startled by a misty appearing figure that seemed to spring out of the ground close to my side. It seemed as tall as a man, and was so pale and ghostly that quick as thought I leaped back from it and scarcely knew what to think or do. As suddenly as it appeared it disappeared, and after a little hesitation my walk was resumed, my glance turning rather anxiously in the direction where the strange figure had been. Two or three steps brought me abreast of a hitching post painted white. In the faint light shed by the stars it looked pale and misty. Was that what had scared me? Why, it was scarcely four feet high, and the figure appeared to be nearly two feet taller. And then the figure had disappeared as suddenly as it appeared! That was something which puzzled me until I leaped back just as before, and the hitching post disappeared also. My leap had brought a bush between me and the post, and the mystery was explained.

"But what made the hitching post appear so tall?" my young friend asked, after he had heard the story.

"Partly the fact that white objects always appear to be larger than the same objects would appear to be if darker; partly because a white body looming up in the darkness always appears to be larger than it really is; but mostly because in my fright my vision was distorted. Probably the last fact would explain many of the ghost stories we hear. You have seen on marshes that pale light known as the will-o'-the-wisp, or jack-'o-lantern, and known by learned people as *ignis fatuus*. In some places it is regarded as a ghost, and ignorant people fear it very much. It was a common sight in the vicinity of a certain graveyard that I knew of, and yet there were people who declared that these lights were ghosts, for they had seen them grow into tall figures and assume human shape. But of course that was all nonsense. The will-o'-the-wisp you know is the flame of phosphorus rising out of the stagnant water or moist soil of marshy ground and igniting in the air. It is a very pretty sight and certainly not to be feared, except as a warning that the demon of malaria is near. Another pretty effect of phosphorescence light is seen at sea, and I have spent many hours gazing over the side of ships at the breaking of the ghostly flame on the waters as we rushed along. Once I sat on deck nearly the whole night on the Bay of Fundy watching the great splashes of such light made by the huge schools of fish that were swimming near the surface.

Among the stories drawn out by the lad who had led me into the subject was of a phantom dog which at one time was a source of terror to many of the people of Charlottetown, Prince Edward Island. All kinds of strange things were told about it and mothers awed their wayward sons by telling how the typical bad boy of the town was out on the river skating one night when his mother thought he was in bed, and was frightened almost to death by this phantom dog. Its eyes were like balls of fire and it ran round and round the bad boy, snapping with its sharp white teeth and growling with a terrible deep growl. How that bad boy ever got home he could never tell, but he skated no more at night, while the rest of us were particularly careful not to go near the river at night unless there were older people with us.

Now there was plenty of ground for the stories told of the phantom dog. He had been seen many times and had been traced to his hiding place, which was under a big barn on a bluff overlooking the river. He had been fired at many times, and as some good marksmen had tried their skill on him, it was believed that he had been hit more than once. Yet he did not cease his nocturnal rambles, nor was there ever found a trace of his blood. Even sensible people began to suspect that he was an evil spirit. Crowds used to gather on the bluff at night to watch for him and fire at him, but he always escaped unharmed. Although regarded by many as a ghost he had a very earthly appetite, as one butcher in the town could testify, for one night he bounded into the butcher's shop, seized a large joint of meat and was off again before the butcher and his two sons had recovered from their fright. At last some practical fellow suggested that the only way to get at the dog was to take up the floor of the barn, and one evening several hundred men and boys gathered there to assist in the work. They were armed with guns, pistols, axes, pitchforks, clubs and all manner of other death-dealing instruments. The barn was surrounded so that the dog might not escape, and the floor was soon taken up. More than half the crowd expected something horrible to happen, but all that happened was the dog was found, and after a vain attempt to fight his pursuers, was pinned to the ground with a pitchfork and killed. He was a big Newfoundland dog, a tramp, and his coat was so thick and so matted with tar that it was no wonder if it turned the bullets fired at him. The town breathed easier on learning that he was not a demon in the form of a dog. It was supposed that he had strayed from some ship which left him to a vagabond's fate.

That same town was a great place for ghosts, and it held several haunted houses. Part of my boyhood was passed in one of these houses, and my room was the one in which the ghost was said to appear. A woman who had lived in the house had fled to this room one day when her clothing had taken fire, and, falling against the door, burst it open. When help reached her she was lying dead on the threshold. The story went that at rare intervals after that her ghost was heard rushing toward the door, which flew open, accompanied by the noise of a falling body. My parents were too sensible to put any faith in that yarn, and for months I studied and slept in the room undisturbed, either by any strange sounds or by any fear of them. I had what my parents called a bad habit of sitting up half the night to read, and was indulging in this habit one night, sitting with my back to the door, when suddenly the door flew open with a crash. Some story tellers tell of people's hair standing on end with fright. Mine didn't, and I felt of it; but there was a creepy feeling all over me, and the crown of my head felt as if it were full of quills. Did I expect to see a ghost? No, indeed. My eyes turned quickly toward that door, expecting to see a burglar. There was nothing to be seen, so seizing my lamp I fastened it to the door, calling to my father that somebody had broken into the house. A search from attic to cellar revealed no intruder, and on inquiry an outside door and window [were] found locked. My father gave me a lecture on letting imagination run away with me, and would not believe a word about the door flying open.

"You left it open," he said.

But this was denied so persistently that he finally went to my room with me, and, closing the door, we sat there some time, when there came a rustling sound and the door flew open. He hastened out into the entry, only to find nothing, and returned to the room, puzzled. No sooner was the door closed that it flew open again, and thus the mystery was explained, for my father was standing near it, and felt the door jar under his feet. Up to this time neither of us had noticed that a very high wind was blowing. It was such a storm as was not frequent there, and the wind striking the house from a certain direction caused such a vibration of the beam under the door that the door was thrown open. Repairs were made to the house a little later, and nothing more was ever heard of that ghost. — W.

THESE UNQUIET FORMS

The following story is well told and comes from the Christmas issue of the *Victoria Daily Colonist*, 25 December 1897. I am sure that the reporter's story was read by families gathered round the fireplace and appreciated by many a young listener!

A Real Ghost Story — Two Strange Visitants Who at Night — Appeared to a Citizen of Victoria — White Figures Who Flitted into an Undertaker's — And Asked to Be Buried

Though in these days of prosaic commonplace, many of the old-time Christmas ways are falling into disuse, still there is a lingering charm even to the minds of the "grown ups," not to mention the little people, of a thrilling ghost story. Who of those who have come from the colder parts of the world does not remember some night before the lights were lit, and when the forks of flame cast strange shadows on the wall, the little circle gathered round the grate while the story-teller was relating some blood-curdling tale in which ghosts bore a leading part? One who has not known this pleasure has lost — well, it is only those who have experienced it who can remember the delicious thrill of creepiness crawling up the back when a snap of the burning log, or the sudden falling of a coal on the fender, came just at the climax of the tale. Such great writers as Dickens and Thackeray well understood this feeling and ghost stories figure prominently in their Christmas tales. But though one often hears of ghosts, and though some fellow knew another fellow who saw one, it is very, very infrequently the case that it is granted to any favored individual to see a real live ghost.

Just imagine what one would feel to see two ghostly figures flit into one's house and ask to be buried — two restless souls who begged to be laid at rest. Yet this is just what happened in this city of Victoria in these days of the commonplace.

On Thursday night, when the black clouds shrouded the moon and the far-off electric light on Douglas Street shone so as to hide the pitfalls in the sidewalk, a closed carriage suddenly pulled up in front of Hanna's undertaking rooms. The door of the vehicle was opened and from the coach there glided to the sidewalk two white figures, shrouded from head to foot in long flowing robes. At such a time of night no mortal man surely could have traversed six feet of sidewalk without becoming entangled in a nail or stubbing a toe on a projecting plank, but these ghostly figures flitted smoothly the boards and entered the undertaker's shop.

Evidently these unquiet forms were weary of this world, for they had no sooner entered the store than they asked to be buried. There hung around these visitants a strange aroma, and by its scent the young man in the establishment knew that he was in the presence of spirits (apparently rye). He declined to bury the spirits; but one of them, stretching himself at full length in a coffin, begged to be buried. At this juncture Mr. Hanna returned and naturally, as the spirituous visitants had neglected their burial certificates, he as a good citizen had to refuse their pleadings. They might be dead, but without a certificate the poor spirits must float around and curse the red tape that forbade them to be interred without dying in the regular way.

Mr. Hanna not only refused to bury the strangers, but turned them out and telephoned to the police. Ghost stories were all very well to read about, but he had no use for any spirits at his place as he is a temperance man.

The police sallied forth to hung the ghosts and later on captured one without his shroud, refreshing himself at a bar — and so it turned out that they were not ghosts after all, but a couple of young men who thought they were having a good time. The one captured was charged with being drunk, as he evidently was, and as he failed to show up in the police court yesterday morning his bail of $10 was forfeited. And so it turns out a very commonplace story after all; not nearly as interesting as if Mr. Hanna had taken the ghosts at their word and buried them.

A NOVA SCOTIA SENSATION

Dead Woman Appears to Her Friends

A Daily Evening News, Saint John, N.B., December 16, 1873

For some days past rumors have been in their circulation of spiritual manifestations witnessed by persons living in the vicinity of Tuft's Cove, which is some three miles outside of Dartmouth, N.S. The reports at last assumed such an importance that one of our reporters, whose faith in spirits of any kind is not very strong, decided to interview the people, and see what the story amounted to. The persons whom he interviewed appeared to be intelligent, and not over inclined to believe in ghosts. Their narrative is in substance as follows: About four months ago, "Agnes," wife of Briton McCabe, and daughter of a Mrs. Barnstead, died, and was, of course, buried.

She and her husband lived some 12 miles from Dartmouth, on the Windsor Road, and before she died she was, at her own request, removed to her mother's house, at Tuft's Cove. There she died; was laid out by a Mrs. Gay, and was buried in the rural churchyard nearby. On Friday, the 12th inst., Mrs. Gay was sent for by Mrs. Barnstead, mother of the deceased woman; and upon going over she was somewhat startled at being informed that "Agnes had come back"— a statement which Mrs. B. proceeded to explain by stating that for some days previous herself and the other inmates of the house had heard mysterious rappings in different parts of the premises; that they attributed the noises to a mischievous young girl who lived with them; but that they had that morning been satisfied that such was not the cause, for she and the rest had distinctly heard the voice of her dead daughter Agnes. They were, the old lady said, all gathered in the room, when the mysterious rapping was heard, and afterwards the voice of Agnes was heard exclaiming in low tones, "Mother, Mother, Mother." Though all were startled, the mother answered the voice, asking what was wanted. The voice replied, "I am a spirit; I have been sent to warn you all. I was buried alive, and was awoke by hunger. I lived for two days after I awoke, and forced the end out of my coffin. I am come to invite you all to glory." Then the voice sang three verses from three different hymns, familiar to the family; and in reply to some questions again addressed them. They asked would they dig her up; the reply was "I am dead now, and my soul is full of glory." They asked what caused her death, and the voice made a reply which at present it would not be judicious, perhaps, to make public. (It may be stated that the doctors attributed the woman's death to a wasting of the system.) Some one then sent for a brother of the deceased woman, and he on coming heard the familiar voice. Upon the circumstances being stated to him, he said, "Agnes, do you want to see me?" and then he saw what appeared to him to be his sister's eyes, float past him, and felt a hand softly touch his shoulder. At this juncture Mrs. Gay was sent for, and she heard the voice address some of the members of the family by name, and heard a rapping on the floor beneath her feet. Then the voice said, "I am going now, and I will not come again until the last day; and that will be soon." After that the noises ceased; and since then there has been nothing seen nor heard. As before stated, the people from whom these particulars were obtained are intelligent, and do not appear to be at all superstitious. The suspected and mischievous girl was made to stand quietly by during the seance, with her hands folded, and was watched. So they have no doubt that she at least had no hand in the manifestation. The family do not appear at all alarmed; and not afraid of ghosts in ordinary; but have an abiding faith that the spirit of their departed friend and relative has been with them. They tell their story straightly, and express their willingness to testify under oath to all they have said. It is talked of to exhume the remains, but the husband of the deceased has not yet been communicated with; and until that is done it is not probable that any action will be taken in the matter. — *Halifax Express.*

A HALLOWEEN STORY

How an Appointment Was Kept — A Vacant Chair and a White Figure

Daily Evening News, Saint John, N.B., November 21, 1883

Our contemporary, the *Montreal Gazette*, not given to much intentional joking, publishes the following this morning. It may be taken, as our contemporary says, for what it is worth, and is regarded by many more from a humorous point of view than a matter of even shallow fact: —

An incident of a rather peculiar nature occurred in this city on last Halloween, which has given rise to considerable conjecture and surmise. The facts, as obtained from one of the participants by a representative of the *Gazette*, briefly stated, are to the effect that seven young ladies, all of Montreal, at a Halloween gathering ten years ago, agreed to meet again on the same evening ten years after: the stipulation was "dead or alive," the young lady who made use of that expression remaining the other six of the agreement a short time after by sending them each an invitation for Oct. 31st, 1883. This lady was evidently the originator of the little reunion, and laughingly promised to be present, even if dead, and it were at all possible for her to do so. About four years ago the young lady died very suddenly. She is described as having been of a quiet, religious disposition, and very tall.

The remainder of the ten years rolled by, and the time for the reunion came. Accordingly, on All Hallow Eve the six met at the house of two of their number, who were sisters, for tea; but, according to the original arrangement, a chair was left vacant for the missing one. This chair was draped in black, while in front of it on the table were some withered flowers, gathered from the grave of the deceased. Nothing remarkable occurred during the repast, save that the young lady next to the empty chair spoke of a strange nervous sensation, but this was not thought of at the time. After tea they started to move to the parlor, immediately adjoining, the young lady last mentioned leading the way and carrying in her hand the bunch of withered flowers. The parlor was quite dark, saving the light which streamed in from the dining-room as she opened the door. At that moment she cried, "Look! look!" and pointed into the parlor, where three or four of them saw distinctly a tall white figure standing at the door leading from the parlor to the hall. She who had first seen it retreated quickly, and was just leaving the dining-room by the door from that room to the hall, when she again saw the figure, and her cry brought three of the others to the door, and all saw it glide quickly along the hall from the parlor door to the door leading to the street, which seemed to open of itself and close after the figure had passed through.

Only one of the six failed to see the figure at all, she having in both cases been too late, consequently she was very dubious, and believed the apparition to be merely some kind of a practical joke, and at once went and inspected the door of exit, but this was always kept locked and latched from within, and was found to be still secure, so the trick theory was apparently out of the question as a solution of the mystery.

Our informant saw the figure twice and describes it as being "just the right height," that is to say, very tall, and wholly draped in white; no hands or feet were to be seen and the face was concealed; it seemed to glide rather than walk and moved very quickly; it did not touch the door at all, and did not appear to pass through it, but the door seemed to open of itself and close behind the figure.

The sensation produced by the figure was as if it were chuckling to itself for having kept the promise to be present, laughing at the scare produced — at least, our young lady informant states such to have been her sensations in so far as she had any apart from the dominant sense of fear.

Such is the story and we give it for what it is worth without attempting to offer either explanation or comment.

HAUNTED CELLS

Ghost of McConnell, Murderer, — Said to Walk in the Corridors of Hamilton Gaol

Kingston Weekly, January 14, 1884

Eight years ago Michael McConnell, a Hamilton butcher, murdered Mr. Nelson Mills, a gentleman living in the West End of the ambitious city. McConnell was hanged for the crime on March 14th, 1876, and the Hamilton Spectator states the gaol is now believed to be haunted by the spectre of the murderer. Says the Spectator: With McConnell's death it might reasonably be supposed that the affair would end, but it seems that his perturbed spirit will not rest quietly beneath the cold, cold ground and stubbornly persists in haunting the east yard, and what is known as the east basement corridor. On the western side of the corridor the "black holes" or punishment cells are situated. These are small apartments provided with nothing. Prisoners are put there for six, twelve or twenty-four hours, according to the nature of the offence. Now a man might naturally be presumed to have a horror of staying in a dark and comfortless cell, but prisoners dread to go, not only for that reason, but because they declare they are haunted by the ghost of the man who was hanged on that wild March morning so many years ago. At night they say the ghost flits from room to room and tramps up and down the long corridor with a ceaseless stride. On the night of March 14th they claim that the awful scene on the scaffold is all gone over again, and a ghostly figure, with a black cap on top, falls through a trap door and dances for a minute in mid air. Then all is still. The figure straightens out, and death claims its own. The turnkey of the jail said to a Spectator reporter that the bravest and best prisoner in the place would cry like a child and consent to undergo any punishment sooner than be put into one of the black holes with McConnell's ghost to keep him company. But men who had never been accused of cowardice will shrink and shiver and pray not to be consigned there. Governor Henry was spoken to. He laughed at the idea and said he had never heard of it before. But, all the same, any man who had spent any part of a night in one of the black holes will tell you that McConnell's ghost keeps him company, and they all stand in mortal fear of being sent in with it.

3

HAUNTED HOUSES

People love stories about haunted houses. Indeed, the alliteration … "haunted houses"… trips off the tongue so easily!

There is a notion that no dwelling place is whole if it lacks its resident spirit, whether that spirit be guardian or ghoul. That dwelling may be a shack, log cabin, cottage, house, farmhouse, home, flat, apartment, suite, residence, mansion, castle, or palace; it makes no difference. Every region has its *genius loci*, its spirit of place.

Here are some stories of haunted houses that once stood in villages, towns, and cities throughout the land. The reader today would have to travel in time as well as in space to visit these domiciles, for it is unlikely that today even one of them is still standing.

(Query: When a haunted house goes up in flames, where does its ghost go?)

AN AUTHENTIC GHOST STORY

Correspondence of the Advertiser
Tilbury East, December 2, 1869
London Advertiser, December 6, 1869

In a small settlement in the backwoods, some twenty-five miles west of the town of Chatham, there is a vacant lot, where once resided a worthy farmer, who put up a house, cleared about fifteen or twenty acres of land, and then exchanged it for a farm in a more eligible situation. He left it in the spring of 1867, since which time (with the exception of twelve months) it has remained unoccupied. This fall, however, a young man rented it of the proprietor for four years; and he, with his wife and child, moved into it, and thought himself settled for some time to come. But alas for human hopes! he had not been there long when he found to his dismay that the house was occupied with some inhabitants from another region. This was made known to him in various ways. A potato came rolling from the upper room down the ladder, and he (the tenant) had not taken a potato upstairs. A corn cob fell on the furniture, then to the floor, and did not roll; but the tenant being a brave man, was not to be driven away by such trifles; and it was not long before a piece of glass fell — a piece that a neighbor was almost sure was seen on his mantle piece the day previous. Pieces of firewood fell through the upper floor where there was no way for them to come. Nor was this all. Lumps of clay fell, striking one man on the head, and the wife on the eyes, blackening them. The pieces of clay, when handled, were decidedly hot. The tenant's father and one or two more were eye-witnesses of some of these unearthly scenes. This may seem a joke to some — not so to the poor man — who on Saturday, the 25th of November, 1869, procured an ox-team and sleigh, loaded on his goods, and solemnly departed to the house of a neighbor, to muse on the transient nature of all sublunary things. The evening he left — the cause of his leaving being well known in the neighborhood — about a dozen men and one or two boys, some of whom were routed from their slumbers by the alarmed parties, assembled at the house, and remained there till eleven p.m., whether armed or not I do not know. But nothing unusual was to be seen, and they retired to their homes to think over the events of the day.

Could not some plan be adopted to hinder their works? Picture to yourself this scene if you can. A young man in the prime and vigor of early manhood, with his beloved wife and child, driven from a home they had just entered by some unearthly beings without consciences, for no other apparent purpose but that they might reign there supreme. Should these beings, stimulated by their success, be inclined to make further trouble in this neighborhood or elsewhere, some steps will have to be taken to oppose them. — "B."

A HALIFAX MYSTERY

Very little was said in the Halifax papers about some strange occurrences said to have taken place in a certain house in that city recently. The *Amherst Gazette* gives the following in relation to the matter — the result of an "interview with a resident of Halifax":

Daily Examiner, Charlottetown, P.E.I., December 19, 1878

The house of Mr. M. occupied during the manifestations, and from which he was obliged to remove on account of their effect upon members of his family, is a very respectable looking two-story building, with shop in lower flat — the whole having been occupied by him. He now occupies another building not far from it, having been obliged to remove through "circumstances over which he had no control," though he assured us that he had resolutely determined not to leave the house until "the power" pitched him from it by force, and only changed his mind on account of the severe illness produced upon his daughter — the one principally wrought upon — and his wife who became prostrated from attending her.

About the first of September last the house referred to was occupied by himself and family as tenants, and had been for 2 years and 7 months. The family consisted of himself and wife, three daughters, aged 18, 22 and 25, a son of 27, who worked in the shop, two young men as boarders, one of them being the husband of the eldest daughter, and an apprentice. The following is his statement corroborated by his son, in reply to our questions: —

The first intimation I had of anything unusual was one night about the first of September, soon after all the house had retired. I had fallen asleep, and was aroused by my wife saying some one was rapping at the door; then both heard it. On going to the door I found no one, but the rapping continued. I aroused the household, and all heard the noise — 3 raps in quick succession, then a pause — which seemed to be in the outer wall, and continued for some time. For a week this occurred at nights, after which it took place in the daytime also, following, apparently, the two girls to all parts of the house, from cellar to attic. I often had people on the roof and stationed outside to watch, but there was no visible cause.

One evening it was found that the knocking kept time with a tune which one of the young men whistled, and this afterwards occurred in the case of several tunes of different measures, and it became so accommodating as to beat the time of any tune asked. We frequently asked questions, and replies were given by raps, always correctly, so far as we could decide, except that it erroneously gave us to understand that the place would be destroyed in 20 days, at which time we had left, though the furniture had not all been removed. About the 10th day the young men's trunks in their rooms, as well as tables, would pile themselves on the bed; the parlor table turned upside down; clothing was thrown from hooks; a bed stead on which two girls were lying one Sunday afternoon moved from the wall to the centre of their room, at other times beds in three rooms moved; in fact, something moved in every room in the house.

For a time the disturbance was greatest in the room of one of the young men, where heavy chests were moved. One evening a large homemade hearth-rug followed one of the girls down the staircase. At length the disturbances took place whether the girls were in or out.

While we were moving I stood, one day, just at the top of the staircase, with my hand on the balustrade, when I saw a heavy roll of oilcloth, which had been taken from the floor of the second story, coming towards me. It made no grating on the floor, and came eight or ten feet, stopping within a foot of where I stood. Many pots of flowers, occupying a whole stand, moved from the stand to the floor, on one occasion, without the breaking of a pot or the spilling of water in the saucers. Sometimes all the chairs in the room would simultaneously revolve, and turn bottom upwards.

One evening one of the young men said he was playing the piano, when the time was beaten by distinct thumps. We heard the jarring in the shop below and went up in order to see what was taking place, and found the young man considerably terrified.

A lady — a relative of the landlord — came in one evening and conversed with the invisible by means of raps. The landlord afterwards told me he could not expect me to stay and be thus annoyed, and I finally resolved, in the interests of my family, to leave, though I now regret that I did not remain myself, to see whether I would be ejected bodily. The woman who cleaned the house as we removed — a resolute person — found the broom following her down stairs, and left, nor could she be induced to return.

I kept working in the shop a short time after removing from the dwelling apartments. One day one of my daughters was fitting a pair of boot tops at the sewing machine, when something appeared to strike her on the back and she was thrown down. The rapping continued in the shop after removal from the other apartments, but nothing of the kind was heard after the whole had been vacated.

Several people who came in charged us with being, voluntarily, the cause, and I almost resolved to allow no more persons to enter except sensible people who might see that we would not willingly subject ourselves to all these annoyances, to illness, the payment of heavy doctor's bills, and finally the loss in removing from premises with which we were well suited. Even my pastor annoyed me by remarks he made and which he must retract before I can again feel as I should under his pastorate. Still, I blame no one for disbelieving, as without experiencing it I could not have believed such things would take place. All that bothers me is — I wish the cause could be ascertained.

This is but a brief account of the manifestations as reported to us. From other sources we learn that the origin seems to have been similar to that of the Amherst transactions, namely, a fright experienced by one of the young ladies. At the time of our visit their new quarters had been occupied but a short time, and the trouble had not followed them. It will be seen that there are some striking similarities in the two cases.

A GHOST STORY

Canadian Statesman, Bowmanville, Ont., February 23, 1887

This story was told by a Toronto doctor about an epoch in his very early career, when he was collecting bills for a subscription book publication firm, somewhere in the interior of the Province, and stopped to lodge in a house, where the only sleeping place that could be provided for him was in the room with a corpse. He had been indiscreet enough in engaging his lodging to show his roll of bills. He heard suspicious movements about the house in the night; the entrance of someone by a back door and a whispered consultation somewhere. His candle had been taken out after he had got to bed. Presently there was a hoarse whisper from someone in the centre of the room where the corpse was laid out —"Come here!" His blood froze in his veins. "Come here!" the whisper repeated. Obeying an irresistible impulse, he crept, trembling, to the side of the dead. The corpse was sitting bolt upright upon the table where it had been laid. "Look out!" said the corpse; "they are after your money, and may murder you — they're capable of it." The young man took up a post by the window, which couldn't be opened, however. But he stayed there, and by-and-by, when someone crept stealthily into the room, and he heard the ghastly lunging of a knife into the bed clothes where he had lain, he leaped through the window, and took the sash with him as he went out. As the doctor began to tell his story, the wood fire on the hearth, which had been blazing brightly, flickered and burned low, as if cold, damp blasts had been blown over it. When he described the rasping accent with which the dead man uttered his call, "Come here!" the fire suddenly went out, leaving only the glimmering fringe of light around the edges of the lighted sticks. A current of cold rain came from some unknown quarter just at this moment. The "conditions were favourable" for the narrative. When it was over there were any number of questions. Was the dead man really alive? Did he revive for the moment only and sink back into unequivocal death when he had delivered his warning? Of course the doctor, who had not remained to discover the secret of the thing, could not answer these questions.

HAUNTED BY FIRE

Alleged Case of Spontaneous Combustion in New Brunswick
Montreal Star, August 20, 1887

A correspondent in Woodstock, N.B., of the Boston Herald writes: "The people of Woodstock are mystified by the strange scenes which for the past forty-eight hours have been enacted in a little two-story frame house in Victoria street occupied by Reginald C. Hoyt, a picture-frame dealer. His family, consisting of his wife, five children and two nieces, are in a state of dread and anxiety. Since 1 o'clock a.m. yesterday no less than forty fires have broken out in the house. Bedding, furniture, window shades, clothes and various household articles have been partially destroyed. Only untiring vigilance has prevented the house and its contents from being burned to the ground, and this would also have caused the destruction of the other wooden buildings in the neighborhood. The fires can be traced to no human agency, and even the scientists are staggered. Without premonition, with no lamp lighted or stoves in use, various articles would burst out into flames. Now, it would be a curtain high up out of reach, then a bed-quilt, another bedroom would begin to smoke and smolder and as if to puzzle the theorists, a carpet-covered lounge was found to be all afire underneath among the jute stretched above the springs. A basket of clothes in the shed burst into flames and the basket itself was partially consumed. A child's dress hanging on a hook, a feather bed, a straw mattress and two articles in the same room were ignited, and would have been consumed but for water copiously poured on them. The news spread that Hoyt's house was haunted and great crowds flocked there. It was the talk of the town last night.

UNCANNY DOINGS

At the House of Joseph McDowell, Kent Co., Ontario — Mysterious Rappings, and Stones — Fired by Unseen Hands — The Bushes Full of Grinning Skeleton Faces — A Terrible beast Appears to a Little Girl — (Special Cor. Toronto Globe)

Daily Sun, Saint John, N.B., October 4, 1894

Chatham, September 26. — Having heard rumors of mysterious and uncanny happenings at the home of Mr. Joseph McDowell, on the 15th concession of Raleigh, a reporter drove out yesterday morning to ascertain whether or not the reports had any foundation in fact, and, if so, to get all possible particulars, and, if possible, to solve the mystery which surrounds the place.

Arriving at Mr. McDowell's, the scene of operations, we found Mrs. McDowell alone in the house, with little 13-year-old Lettie, an adopted daughter, who has been with her upwards of six years. Mr. McDowell, who was ploughing, was sent for, and, while awaiting his arrival, his wife told the following:

"I was standing outside, near the door, Saturday morning, after we had milked and had breakfast, working my butter. Lettie was just behind me washing the dish-pans. The rain-barrel was at the corner of the house, about ten or twelve feet away, and in plain sight of both of us, when a stone the size of a small goose-egg fell upon a board which was over the top of the barrel; but, though I looked up, I paid no further attention to it and thought nothing more of it until afterwards. I continued to work my butter, when showers of gravel came from under the house, where there was an opening barely large enough to let a cat through, and, flying to a considerable height in the air, fell on our heads, quite a bit of it getting into the butter I was working. I then kept watch, to see where the gravel came from, when the same thing occurred a second and third time, in rapid succession, and, though we could plainly see it go, we could not see anything throwing it. I took my butter and went into the cook-house, and, even after I was in there, a lot more gravel flew in the open door at me, and more stones went into my butter. I could see Lettie as she was standing at the door of the cook-house, and I know that she had no hand in it, and, besides, Lettie would not do such a thing. I told her to open the screen-door, so that I could take my butter in the kitchen. She tried to do so, but the door was swollen so that she could not. I set my butter down in the cook-house, and found the screen-door very hard to open. I then went back to get my butter, and just as I reached it a lot more stones came into it. I told Lettie to run down to the field and tell her father about it and tell him to come up to the house at once; which he did. In the kitchen I picked the stones out of the butter and put it in a crock, and started mixing bread. After I had been at that a little while large stones began to come through the window, breaking four panes of glass, and after them came nearly a bushel of gravel. When Lettie returned without Mr. McDowell, the stones were still coming in, and I myself went to fetch him, as the former run had made the girl feel sick. Cautioning Lettie to remain in the house, I left, and, during my absence, some animal, about three feet long, with a head like a cat and the same kind of whiskers as that animal, came to the screen-door and tore it with its claws. Lettie told it to go away, whereupon it growled at her, terrifying the poor child so that she dropped a stick of wood which she had picked up to defend herself, and ran, screaming, into the adjoining room. When I returned she was so upset with what she had seen that I could scarcely pacify her."

Mr. McDowell, who had left his ploughing to give what information he could, arrived at this juncture and took up the narrative:

"When Mrs. McDowell came running for me in the field and told me what had happened, I came up as soon as possible, and seeing the pile of gravel and stones which had come in the window, told her not to touch it until I came back. I then went out and brought in one of my neighbors, Ed. Murdock, and we took out of the house over a bushel of the dirt, and sand and gravel were piled up on the window-casing, on the outside, to the height of the bottom of the glass. This I scraped off with my hand."

When asked as to previous occurrences, Mr. McDowell said: "Some months ago tobacco worms seemed to be gathering around the house from all quarters and made their way everywhere. One day my wife was washing in the cook-house when many of the disgusting things fell from the roof on her back and all over her. These worms, which came by hundreds, never touched anyone but my wife, and, after a visit of nearly a month, left as they had arrived, going in a body down the road.

"Soon afterwards myriads of red ants came up the concession, and, arriving at the house, came in and made an extended stay. These also would bite my wife most unmercifully, and not touch either myself or Lettie. I took her away for a while, and during the time she was away she was not bitten, but the moment she came home the ants met her at the gate. I then took her to a doctor, but he could make nothing of her case and could do nothing for her. After the ants had gone away up the concession in a body, crickets came in most unusual numbers, and they, like the others, appeared to have special liking for my wife. A couple of weeks ago there were mysterious rappings all about the house, but we paid no attention to them; but on Friday night last the main trouble commenced and since then I have not slept a wink. I started to go to the station and had got to the railway, which passes about 40 rods in front of the house, when I heard something pounding. It sounded as though it was here, and I wondered what my wife was doing, but thought no more of it until on my return I learned that she and Lettie were sitting in the room when a great pounding and moaning were heard under the house, followed almost immediately by the same noise on the roof. Then came a rap like a man's knock on the front door, beside which Mrs. McDowell was seated. My wife says the knock was undoubtedly upon one of the panels of the door, and, as the wire fly-screen was shut and hooked, this startled her so that she would not open the door, but peeked out of the window, where, though it was a bright moonlight night, nothing was to be seen. Just after this an animal, similar to the one seen by Lettie on Saturday, was heard and seen by the latter sitting upon its haunches on the window sill, with its forepaws against the top of the second pane from the bottom, looking in. And every day since then, with the exception of yesterday and today, stones and gravel were thrown in and peculiar noises heard. On Sunday, my wife, with her sister, Mrs. Michael Broadbent, were in the cook-house, when stones were thrown in on them. Mrs. Broadbent went to the barn for her husband, who was there with quite a number of men, including myself. He went to the house with her, and he also saw the stones coming in.

"Nothing of this kind has occurred when I was present, and never yet when there is a crowd of folks around."

Upon being questioned as to what she saw, Lettie said: "The animal which came to the screen and tore it was the most terrible looking thing I ever saw. It was over two feet and a half long, with rough, shaggy, brown fur, a face somewhat like that of a man, but entirely covered with hair; it had long whiskers and ears like those of a cat. A short, bushy tail completed the picture. When mother went to get father I was reading aloud, when I heard the beast at the door, and when I looked up it had its head through a hole it had ripped in the screen.

"It growled at me, and I threw a stick of wood at it and ran into the other room. While there I thought I heard it in the room, but cannot be sure, as I kept the door shut until mother came back. Monday night, while Mr. McDowell was at the station, I saw the same animal sitting at the window, with its feet upon the pane. I also saw the stones coming into the house. The most of them came right up the side of the house from under the back doorstep, and when on a level with the window turned right off sharply and went in. After I had shut myself in the room on Saturday I looked out of the front window and saw the beast jump the fences and go away towards the bush. It did not run, but jumped, all the time taking over half the width of the road in a leap."

Daniel Broadbent, upon being questioned, said: "Night before last (Monday), between dusk and darkness, I went with my brother, Albert Broadbent, to Joseph McDowell's farm, to see for myself what there was, and whether or not there was any truth in the many incredible reports which were being circulated concerning the mystery surrounding the place. I took my double-barrelled shotgun with me. Upon arriving at the farm, I sat on a log a few feet away from the cook-house. Mr. McDowell asked me to come in and have tea with him; but, having had supper just before going,

I thanked him, and said I would stay where I was. I had not been there fifteen minutes when a considerable quantity of gravel, amongst which were several stones about the size of a hen's egg, fell in a perfect shower on the top of the cook-house and upon us. It appeared to be coming straight down, and landed with great force. A few minutes later it fell again, whereupon I got up, went to the door and told Joe I had seen enough to satisfy me. I stayed until nearly 9 o'clock, but neither heard nor saw anything more. Before taking up my position on the log on which I was sitting, Albert and I thoroughly searched every nook and cranny which could possibly afford a place of concealment for any practical joker, and I know the missiles were not thrown by human hands, though where they came from is, and must remain, a mystery."

An old resident, who stands high in the estimation of all — his name will be withheld for the present — in reply to the reporter's question as to the cause of the supernatural visitations, said: "It is nearly half a century since I came to these parts, having come here when I was but a young man, and at that time there stood in the bush just about where Joe McDowell's little house now stands, a small deserted and tumble-down log hut, which, even at that early date, no one would pass after night. A little bit after I came here — I was in my prime then and proud of my unusual strength — I heard tell of the 'haunted hut,' as folks called it, and openly made fun of those who refused to pass. I never thought of trying it myself until one day one of the young men remarked that they noticed, with all my brave talk, I myself never travelled that path. It was immediately arranged that I was to make the trip that same evening at dusk, leaving half the party at one end of the path and meeting the rest of them about half a mile past the hut. I started in the best of spirits and took with me a good pistol with which I was a first-rate shot. When I arrived near the hut the very atmosphere seemed stifling and peculiarly oppressive, and yet I was not afraid, but pushed on until I arrived just about where the present haunted house now stands. What happened then I never knew further than that I met a man dressed in plain, badly worn clothes going the opposite direction. When I was nearly up to him I said: 'I thought I was the only one around here not afraid to pass the — ghost, but I see I am not," and I put out my hand to shake hands with him and congratulate him on his pluck. He took my hand in his, when to my horror I discovered I held the hand of a skeleton, and then I saw that the head of the one whose hand I held was only a fleshless skull, the stare of whose empty sockets seemed to fairly freeze the very marrow in my bones. At the very moment I took its hand the bush on every side seemed full of grinning skeleton-faces, which glared at me from behind every tree, and filled the air with hideous, discordant laughter. Then fine gravel began to rain down upon me, after which came stones of increasing size, which bent me to the ground insensible. When I recovered consciousness I was lying on a lounge in my own house. They told me they had found me lying on the cow-path through the bush. I never told the story to anyone till today. Nor did I ever go near that spot again after nightfall."

A GHOST STORY

It Comes from Stanstead Plain

Daily News, Sherbrooke, Que., April 16, 1900

Stanstead, April 16. — Stanstead has a "haunted" house. It is right on Main Street, and the tenants bear absolute testimony to the presence of the spirits. Tea tables, which have been cleared away, are found set for breakfast in the morning; pictures hanging in their accustomed place in the evening are found on the floor in the morning, trunks securely locked at night, are found opened at daybreak and contents strewn about. Such things are repeated night after night. Children suddenly awake during the night, and cry out that someone is near them. Footsteps are distinctly heard passing from room to room in the dead of night. The ghost was most persistent in removing a certain picture from the wall. The room was finally locked and the key placed out of reach. The result was the same. Next morning, the picture was again on the floor, face downward. This was repeated several times until the picture was placed in another place where it was allowed to remain. The mystery is deep. Those who believe in ghosts credit the weird tales of their doings in this house — there are others who do not.

4

HAUNTED PEOPLE

Is it places that are haunted, or people?

There are numerous descriptions of haunted houses. There are, as well, a number of accounts of haunted people, people who could be described as cursed. (They could hardly be described as blessed!) Their strange powers are not ours. For instance, there is Caroline Clare, the "human battery." She is the subject of the first account, which seems to have originated in the *Hamilton Spectator*. Research has failed to establish that she even existed. She may be a ghost! In addition, the name of "Dr. Tye, of Thamesville" appears in no Ontario medical records for the 1870s. The Wandering Jew turns up as a "mysterious personage" in one of these tales. One name by which this spectral figure of immense age is known is Ahasuerus. It is said that Ahasuerus was a resident of Jerusalem who refused to help Jesus carry the Cross. In an uncharacteristic display of pique, Jesus turned to Ahasuerus and said, "Tarry till I return." So he wanders the face of the earth until the Second Coming. A haunted person for certain and for eternity!

A HUMAN ELECTRIC BATTERY

(Hamilton, Ont. Spectator)
Daily Sun, Saint John, N.B., June 23, 1879

About two years since a daughter of Mr. Richard Clare, Caroline by name, and then seventeen years of age, living on Lot 25, on the 2nd con. of Rodney, was taken ill. Her disease could not be correctly diagnosed, and had many peculiar features. Her appetite fell off, and she lost flesh till from a strapping girl of 130 pounds weight, she barely weighed 87 pounds. There did not seem to be any organic complaint. The bodily functions were not impaired, the falling off in this respect was not such as in itself would alarm her friends. After a lapse of a few months she took to her bed. Then it was that a change occurred in her mental condition. Formerly she was noted rather for lack of conversational powers, but now fits or spasms would come over her, on the passing away of which, her eyes would become set and glazed, her body almost rigid, and while in that state she would discourse eloquently and give vivid descriptions of far-off scenes, far exceeding in their beauty anything which she had ever seen or presumably ever read of. On the passing away of this state she exhibited a great degree of lassitude and indisposition to move, and was taciturn and surly in reply to any questions. This continued till about a month since, when an extraordinary change occurred. The girl, although still not gaining flesh, appeared to rally. She became light-hearted and gay, and her friends anticipated an early release for her from the room to which she had been confined so long. Their expectations were not vain, for she is now about the house apparently as well bodily as ever. But a most remarkable development has taken place: She is constantly giving off electrical discharges, and seems to be a perfect battery. A person, unless possessed of the very strongest nerves, cannot shake hands with her, nor can anyone place his hand in a pail of water with hers. By joining hands she can send a sharp shock through fifteen or twenty people in a room, and she possesses all the attraction of a magnet. If she attempts to pick up a knife the blade will jump into her hand, and a paper of needles will hang suspended from one of her fingers. So strongly developed is this electrical power that she cannot release from her touch any article of steel which she may have taken up. The only method yet found is for a second party to take hold of the article and pull while the girl strokes her own arm vigorously, from the wrist upward. On her entering a room a perceptible influence seizes hold of all others, and while some are affected with sleepiness, others are ill and fidgety till they leave, and even for a considerable time afterwards. A sleeping babe will wake up with a start at her approach, but with a stroke of her hand she can at once coax it to slumber again. Animals also are subject to her influence, and a pet dog of the household will be for hours at her feet motionless as in death. A curious part of the phenomena is the fact that the electricity can be imparted by her to any article with which she habitually comes in contact. The other day a younger sister, while doing the house work, took up a pair of corsets belonging to Caroline, and on her hand touching the steel she was compelled to drop them with a loud cry and an exclamation to the effect that she had run a needle into her finger. Wooden spoons have had to be made for her, as she cannot touch metal. Altogether the case is a most remarkable one, and attracts scores of visitors to the house of Mr. Clare. Medical men are especially interesting themselves, and it has been stated that Dr. Tye, of Thamesville, will read a paper on the subject of the meeting of the Provincial Medical Association which is to be held in London in the course of this summer. Mr. Clare is the father of a family of seven children, none of whom, except Caroline, show any abnormal qualities.

A MYSTERIOUS PERSONAGE

Is He the Wandering Jew?

Daily Colonist, Victoria, B.C., December 9. 1880

Several persons who have had occasion to be out-of-doors at night recently report that they encountered a man of striking and mysterious mien — his figure tall, his head bowed upon his breast, silently stalking along the dark and silent streets of the suburbs. During the severest weather, when the thermometer scored 22 degrees of frost and the snow covered the land in heaps and drifts, this man was met long after midnight labouring through the drifts. When the change came and the rain poured down for two days and nights, when even dumb brutes sought shelter, still the stranger was met plodding his weary way through the mud and slush, his garments soaked with the moisture, his head still bent on his breast, pressing on in search of — Heaven only knows what. Newspaper carriers have met him on their routes — silent, grim and mysterious, stalking steadily on. Members of the Club wending their way home have been startled to observe him like an apparition rising, as it were, from the ground and hurrying away in the gloom. Two guests from the Pioneer dinner on last Saturday night met the stranger on Fort Street, and tried to open a conversation with him. But he replied not to their salutation, nor raised his head nor quickened nor slackened his pace, but with the same measured, purposeless stride and dejected air turned off at Blanchard street and plunged into the darkness. Throughout the "silent watches of the night" the mysterious footfalls are heard on the sidewalks, but with daylight the man disappears and is seen no more until the sable mantle is again let down. Some imagine that the highwayman who asked Mr. Price to "stand and deliver" the other morning and this strange man are identical. Others associate him with the recent burglarious visitations; and others have ventured to think that he may be the Wandering Jew, who as a punishment for his brutality on a certain memorable occasion was condemned to "go on till the end of Time." Our own opinion is that the man's mind is distraught and that, following out an idiosyncracy, he wanders in a purposeless manner through the city after dark and seeks his bed at daylight.

THOUGHT READING

Mr. Stuart Cumberland's Marvellous Experiments in Victoria Hall
Winnipeg *Free Press*, August 10, 1886

Mr. Stuart Cumberland yesterday evening gave a marvellous exhibition of his power of mind reading in Victoria Hall to a somewhat small but very attentive and enthusiastic audience. A committee of the best-known people in the room was selected to sit on the platform and keep things along. This committee included the Rev. Mr. Gordon, Hon. Dr. Wilson, Mr. Bedson, Mr. F.W. Buchanan, Mr. Pearce, and others.

Mr. Cumberland began his seance by a difficult experience. He wanted a gentleman to pick out in the audience some lady, and think of her constantly; he on his part undertook to find the lady while blindfolded himself. To make the experiment somewhat parallel to the classical story of Paris and Stonore, he produced an apple, which he said would be given to the lady so selected as a souvenir of the occasion.

There was this difference between the two circumstances, he said, that while Paris had only to select the fairest of three ladies, the critic in this case would have to choose from a galaxy of beauty. After some difficulty in getting a man to make a selection Mr. Cumberland pounced on Mr. F.W. Buchanan. The latter, having chosen the lady, retired to the anteroom with the Rev. Mr. Gordon and to the latter confided the name of the person picked upon. Then the experiment began.

Mr. Buchanan was told to concentrate his thoughts on the lady. Mr. Cumberland, then blindfolded, placed Mr. Buchanan's wrist on his temple for a moment during which time he stood wavering. Suddenly he made a dash for one of the aisles, down which he rushed, dragging Mr. Buchanan after him; then hesitating for a moment he branched down a line of seats and made his way directly to where Miss Mingaye sat. Mr. Gordon then announced that Mr. Buchanan had selected Miss Mingaye prior to the experiment. The mind-reader was rewarded with the most enthusiastic applause.

After the experiment he was quite blown and exhausted as though he had received a severe nervous shock. He several times took occasion to state that there was nothing supernatural in anything he did: Natural laws controlled his experiments, and their success was in exact ratio to the intensity with which the person operated on concentrating his thoughts on the subject of the experiment.

All his experiments were marvellous, but some were more wonderful than others. For instance, he wanted someone in the audience who had a pain somewhere in his body to come forward and let him blindfolded find it. No one appeared, because, as Mr. Gordon remarked, this was a very healthy climate, so Mr. Cumberland said that a pain would have to be manufactured, and deputed Mr. Gordon to take Mr. Bedson out of the room and prick him with a pin. This was done, and Mr. Cumberland, having blindfolded himself, seized Mr. Bedson's right hand, held it to his temple, and then began searching for the pain. He went up the arm and touched the face, but was not satisfied. He was heard to say "most peculiar"; then dropping Mr. Bedson's right hand he took his left. This time he went directly to the right hand, and lingered for a moment at the back, but he was still unsatisfied. He then asked Mr. Gordon who had made the picture to give Mr. Bedson his left hand and him his right. This time he went directly to Mr. Bedson's right hand and almost instantly located the spot on the side of the hand at the base of the little finger —"the exact spot" to use Mr. Gordon's phrase.

Mr. Cumberland then explained the cause of his hesitation. When he first tried to find the pain with the right hand it was impossible to do so because the pain being in the hand moved along with it. At the spot on the back of the hand where he had first stopped, there was an old sore which had been paining Mr. Bedson for some days.

Another experiment was the drawing on a blackboard of an object thought of by a person whose hand he held. The person was Mr. Secretan, and Mr. Cumberland, blindfolded, slowly drew the outlines of a dissipated looking bottle, with a bit cork and a label "Gin" on the side.

The final experiment was the most difficult, as it certainly was the most interesting and amusing of the lot. It was the enactment of a mock murder scene. First a man was to be selected as the murderer; Mr. Cumberland was then to retire, and the murderer was to stalk down from the stage, seize a victim, drag him on the stage, and there despatch him with one of six knives. Two robbers were then to go through him and hide the swag in various parts of the room. He, blindfolded, was to pick out the victim among the audience, take him up to the stage, despatch him over again with the same knife and in the same spot. He was then to take the robbers and find the hidden articles.

Having outlined the programme, it then became necessary to select the murderer and the robbers. Mr. James Fisher was proposed as the murderer and Mr. Leacock as the victim, but finally Mr.

Pearce was selected as the horror and Dr. Wilson and Mr. Buchanan as the professional robbers. Mr. Pearce in selecting a victim hit on an unwilling one, who refused to be dragged from his seat. Quite a wrestling match occurred, greatly to the delight of the audience. A more willing person was found and the entertainment was in every way a success.

Tonight Mr. Cumberland will give another seance when he will write out on a blackboard the number of a bank note thought of by any person.

FIRE SPOOK AT MILLVILLE

Forty-seven Fires in Forty-eight Hours — Mysterious Fires Break Up a Quiet Country Home — (Fredericton Gleaner)
Daily Sun, Saint John, N.B., June 7, 1888

The fire spook is again at large. This time it is carrying on its work of devastation in a hitherto quiet home at Howland Ridge near Millville.

On Friday and Saturday of last week it was currently reported about town that mysterious fires, similar to the Woodstock fire mystery, had broken out in the house of Duncan Good near Millville, and was destroying his property and peace and happiness. The report, however, was not credited at the time, but has since been confirmed by eye witnesses of the mystery. The report is true enough — too true for Mr. Good's liking. It is the talk of the whole country round about and hundreds have gone to visit the scene of desolation. Mr. Estey, merchant at Millville, was among those who visited Good's place at the time the fire spook was doing its work.

He states that while he was there and examining the different places where the fire had broken out, an almanac hanging from a peg on the side of the wall suddenly caught fire, and in an instant the almanac was enveloped in flames. He stood aghast. He was informed that that was the 47th fire that had thus mysteriously occurred during the 48 hours previous to his visit. Curtains, bed clothing, cushions, carpets, books, articles of clothing, had alike been visited by the fire spook. The fires, however, occurred only in the daytime, and when they were least expected. Not only were the mysterious fires confined to the house, but the barns and outbuildings were also haunted by the strange visitant, one of the barns being totally consumed by the fire spook.

Mr. Pinder, of Nackawick, was also an eye witness of one of the unaccountable fires and has many remarkable stories to tell about its work. During Wednesday of last week the fire fiend proved the most destructive, fire breaking out in nearly every hour of the day; first in the house, then in the barns or some of the outbuildings.

Our Millville correspondent writes under date of June 1st:

At last we have a thorough sensation, all our own, which looks as if it might have the effect of giving us a world-wide celebrity. On Howland or Beckwith Ridge, some two miles east of this village, live a family named Good, who have for years been working and living along the same as the rest of us poor mortals, with nothing pointing to the great celebrity they are now enjoying. This sylvan quietness was broken suddenly last Monday by the appearance of fire in their dwelling, which was easily extinguished, but this forerunner was followed on the following day by the breaking out of fires, very mysteriously, in different parts of their dwelling, consuming clothing, bedding, papers, etc., in fact of whatever appeared to be of an inflammatory nature. This continued all through Tuesday and Wednesday, until the family were compelled to remove from the dwelling. One of the odd phases of the affair is that the fire does not catch at night, or while anyone is looking for it.

On Thursday, about one o'clock, their barn caught and was consumed, with some farming implements and about six tons of hay.

Mr. Good, in describing the fire in the barn to your correspondent, said it appeared to flame up instantly, and in an inconceivably short time the flames burst from every quarter. The fire resembles very much the burning which caused so much excitement in Woodstock about a year ago.

The inhabitants, for miles around, have visited the scene, and it is rather amusing to listen to the different causes assigned for this. It may well be styled mysterious fire, witchcraft, visitants from the world of spirits, judgements for sins, &c. It appears to have brought to the surface all the latent superstition natural to the natural man. The most sensible reason, according to my mind, and I have minutely examined the premises, is put forth by Mr. Earle, railway agent here, who claims it is caused by the escape of natural gases only inflammable when coming in contact with certain gases contained in the atmosphere we breathe. Let the cause be what it may, it is certainly to us mysterious.

Your correspondent would very much like to see the matter thoroughly investigated by scientists, and a preventive found.

Mr. Good's loss will be quite a serious one to him, and take years of patient toil and frugality to replace.

KILLED BY A METEOR

Regina *Leader-Post*, June 18, 1889

Intelligent persons have ceased to believe in dreams and visions. In fact, one might say that this moribund century has been the golden age for the doubting Thomases who have successfully attacked everything that was dear to our grandmothers and calculated to make the hair of the timid stand on end. Witches have been relegated to dismal obscurity; ghosts have been compelled to seek pastures green in the Antipodes or in the delta of the Niger; and the scions of the worthy publishers of Egyptian dream books are subsisting on the interest of the dollars paid to their fathers in years gone by, by credulous old women and sillier old men. Yes, it is safe to say that even Ichabod Crane, were that worthy alive today, would not run away from the headless specter of the Mohawk Valley. Reason, we hear on every side, has triumphed over superstition, and cold materialism had taken possession of everything and everybody.

And yet, if we look around us, with eyes and ears wide open, we can see and hear things every day which reason prompts us to doubt, but which reason cannot explain. Such an occurrence the writer is about to relate for the benefit of those who believe that the Bard of Avon spoke the truth when he said to his friend,

"There are more things in Heaven and earth,
Horatio,
Than are dreamt of in your philosophy."

Erasmus Johnson, the hero of the strange story about to be related, was one of the brightest and most promising students of a western college whose professors and tutors were noted for their orthodoxy and opposition to spiritualism and materialistic doctrines. Erasmus was, moreover, a son of a Presbyterian elder and had received a home training which, while narrow and unprogressive, kept his mind in healthy condition. He entered college with a clear head and a determination to acquire as much knowledge as possible. His intellectual pursuits did, however, not interfere with physical recreation, and no student displayed more energy and abandon in a game of football or a rowing match than he. Combining with his mental and physical superiority a truly altruistic disposition, he soon became a favorite with everybody.

No party in the pretty little college town was considered a success unless Erasmus Johnson contributed his presence to the occasion, and every church society was anxious to have him take a part in the various entertainments given under its auspices. He sang for the Methodists, handled the Indian clubs for the Presbyterians, recited poems for the Congregationalists and read essays for the Unitarians whenever requested to do so. He took long walks with his pedantic instructor in botany; talked philosophy with the cranky individual who taught that science in the college, and discussed German and French poetry and prose with the long-haired Teuton who presided over the destinies of modern languages and literature. He pulled an oar with his associates, acted as pitcher for the college ball nine, and was the recognized hero of the gymnasium.

That such a man should have had any faith in supernatural visions is out of the question. And yet, two weeks before the day set for the commencement exercises, Erasmus Johnson, whose face had always been a mirror of smiles and joy, appeared before his class in an almost indescribable condition. His face looked haggard and worn, black rings had formed under his eyes, his form seemed to have lost all elasticity, his hand trembled incessantly. The excitement caused by this sight was intense. In a moment he was surrounded by seven or eight of his "chums," who labored under the impression that he suffered from a sudden attack of illness.

"What is the matter?" asked his friends in chorus.

"A dream!" responded Erasmus with a sad smile.

"A dream!" repeated the students, incredulous and inclined to take the matter as a joke.

"Yes, a dream," reiterated Johnson; "a terrible dream which I can not drive out of my head, although it is as silly as it can be."

"What is it?" came from many lips.

"I dreamed that I would be killed on my wedding day in a strange and peculiar manner," explained Johnson in a hesitating way, which clearly indicated that he felt ashamed of himself for having made the confession.

The reply called forth unbounded merriment, which lasted until the professors entered the lecture hall.

Poor Johnson was made the butt of everybody's ridicule and even the young lady to whom he was engaged to be married ventured to poke fun at her lover's dream.

Meanwhile the commencement exercises had taken place and Johnson had been awarded the class honors as well as a gold medal for a powerful and beautiful Latin poem. He was lionized by his class, the faculty and townspeople; but never did a young man receive applause with more reserve. Ambition and hope seemed to have a dwelling place in his heart no longer. They had been superseded by melancholy, by a hideous specter born of a dream.

A few hours before his departure from the scenes of his intellectual triumphs, he called on his most intimate college friend, who did everything in his power to revive the energy of his unfortunate visitor; going even so far as to suggest to Johnson the advisability of breaking his engagement. To this the young man would not consent, because, despite his fears and misgivings, he could not persuade himself that he had good grounds for such an action which might, moreover, break the heart of the woman he loved.

"Whatever else I have lost," he said to his friend, "my honor remains unsullied, and I would not wreck Julia's happiness on account of an uncertain something at which the world and even you laugh. No, Jack, we will be married on the 5th of August, whatever may be the consequences."

The following morning Johnson was with his parents. It is superfluous to say that they did everything in their power to overcome their son's melancholy mood. He listened to them patiently and smiled sadly when he saw his good old mother in tears. He even went so far as to simulate a cheerfulness he did not feel. He listlessly supervised the preparations for his approaching nuptials, and, accompanied by a number of relatives and friends, left for the home of his affianced on the evening of the 4th of August. The party arrived at its destination the next morning.

Johnson had passed a restless night in the sleeper, and when he arrived at the house of his future parents-in-law, looked even more careworn and haggard than usual. His friend, Jack, who also stopped at the house, was shocked, and upon inquiring for the cause of his friend's ghastly appearance, learned that the hideous dream which had wrecked his happiness had again haunted him. By dint of will power he managed to suppress his anguish, however, and succeeded in appearing before the woman he was about to marry in a seemingly happy frame of mind. The couple chatted for awhile, discussed their prospects, and dwelled at some length upon the joys that seemed to be before them.

The wedding ceremony was to be performed at 7 o'clock in the evening at the Presbyterian Church of the little city. Shortly before the hour the bridal party arrived; a half hour later the newly wedded couple received the congratulations of their friends. The groom, sad and dejected until he had entered the church, seemed like another man. His old smile once more illuminated his face, his eyes flashed happiness, and his form was erect as in the days of old. One after the other of the assembly pressed his hand and was dismissed with a pleasant word. His friend Jack was once of the last to offer his good wishes. As he approached Johnson the latter whispered:

"Thank God, Jack, the danger is over. I am married and still alive."

A few minutes before 8 o'clock the bride and groom left the church. Johnson was gay and attentive, and replied wittily to the bon-mots hurled at him by the crowd. The couple reached the sidewalk. The bride was handed into the carriage, and the groom was about to follow her. At that moment he heard a whistling noise above him, and looking up to explain the strange phenomenon, was struck on the forehead by a missile of extraordinary power. He fell heavily on the carpet-covered walk, and when his friends ran to his rescue they found — a corpse. Erasmus Johnson had certainly met his end in a strange and peculiar way. A meteorite fully two inches in diameter had crushed his skill. His dream was fulfilled. Was the vision then a coincidence or a warning? Let every reader answer the question for him or herself.

5

DREAMS AND VISIONS

We talk of seeing ghosts, but more often than not, we sense the presence of ghosts. Indeed, they are sensed rather than seen.

When they are sensed, the heart begins to beat rapidly; the hands tremble; beads of sweat appear on the brow; the hairs on the head stand up on end; the stomach feels like it is tied in knots; goose pimples run up and down the spine; a dread feeling floods the nervous system ....

Ghosts are more often sensed in this way than seen with the eyes. Yet there is another way that ghosts are sensed, and that is in dreams and visions. Do states of sleep or reverie permit the dreamer or the visionary access to worlds invisible to the eyes? Do these worlds correspond to a new level of reality, one that is inaccessible to non-dreamers and non-visionaries? Since the year 1900, when Sigmund Freud published his treatise *The Interpretation of Dreams*, the answer to that question has been a resounding No! Freud is associated with the theory that dreams and visions are expressions of subconscious desires and dreads. Before Freud, the answer to that question was an equally resounding Yes!

A century ago the theory was that dreams and visions offered a form of knowledge which, while not veridical, yielded information about the world beyond the world of our senses, the one we know so well. The pre-Freudian idea is not to be lightly discounted. Consider this: Let us call dreams and visions by another name. Let us call them, let us say, "altered states of consciousness." Then it seems that during sleep or reverie, during contemplation or meditation, during lucid dreaming or guided imagery, we are put in contact with aspects of ourselves and possibly with worlds outside ourselves that are otherwise inaccessible to the conscious mind.

The newspaper stories that appear in this section of the book suggest that the information inaccessible to us in normal states of consciousness is available to us in dreams and visions. That information is a form of knowledge about the past, about the future, and about action at a distance.

The terminology of psychical research and parapsychological investigation may be applied to the past, the future, and remote action. Psychic archaeology is the study of the knowledge of the past through mediumisic means. Prophecy, prediction, revelation, foreknowledge, and prolepsis are concerned with present-day knowledge of the future. Action at a distance often turns on clairvoyance and clairaudience as well as psychokinesis.

It is worth remembering that one of the fascinations of good ghost stories is that they seem tantalize us with revelations about our past, our present, and our future.

EXTRAORDINARY, IF TRUE

Nova Scotian, Halifax, N.S., November 26, 1860

A correspondent of the Miramichi *Colonial Times* writing from Youghal, New Brunswick, October 28, relates the following extraordinary circumstance. He says that one night last spring he had a peculiar dream, repeated several times during the night, of digging up a large quantity of money at a certain locality called Tinker Point. On visiting the spot in the morning, he was so impressed with the accuracy with which the locality had been described in his dream, that he resolved to test the truth of the nocturnal revelation still further, and, furnishing himself with pick and spade, commenced digging. He says:

"After working for a time, and almost going to give it up for a bad job, my spade struck upon some wooden substance which proved to be a coffin, in which was the remains of a human body, of extraordinary length and size, measuring 8 feet 6 inches, which apparently has been buried some years ago. There was no appearance of flesh or clothing, and when the coffin was opened there was no difficulty in discerning the outlines of a huge well-developed body, but immediately after the air coming in contact with it, the body seemed to dissolve leaving nothing but the immense skeleton and a quantity of dust. In the coffin was found some old rusted implements of warfare. In a small earthenware vessel singularly sealed, I found an old manuscript written on parchment in some foreign language, but not being able to decipher or translate the contents of the same, I some time ago deposited it with Mr. End of this place, but having not since had any conversation with that gentleman on the subject.

"The skeleton I have had conveyed to Dr. Nicholson's office, where the curious have an opportunity of feasting their eyes on this giant!"

A STRANGE APPARITION

Evening Journal, St. Catharines, Ont., August 17, 1866

St. Catharines, August 16.
To the Editor of the Journal:

SIR, I would beg leave to call your attention to a very strange incident in connection with the fire the other night, which at the time made a strong impression on my mind; but believing that it was perhaps a mere hallucination of my own brain, induced by the sudden awakening at or near the hour of midnight, when the mind is most susceptible of supernatural influences, I did not give expression to my thoughts or the matter until I learned to-day that others beside myself witnessed the same startling phenomenon.

When awakened that night by the most startling of all cries — the cry of fire at midnight — I jumped out of bed, and dressing myself as hastily as possible, I ran down Queen Street on the south side, and when I had reached that part of it situated between St. Paul and King streets, where the shade of the trees are deepest, I distinctly saw a figure moving on the other side to that on which I was going.

Now, Sir, I think I am not superstitious, in fact I have always prided myself on my total want of faith in spiritual visitations, but there before my vision, and evidently with the consent of all my other senses, was a figure the first view of which brought me to a sudden halt and recalled lines long since impressed on my memory —

> "For he reared at the sight of the lady in white,
> And he paused in his mad career.
> She spoke and her words, when I heard them aright,
> They curdled my blood with fear."

The light from the burning building was just casting its lurid glare upon the dark and mazy atmosphere which prevailed at the time, and was bringing into view, in exaggerated proportions, every object within its influence. Whether it was this strange effect or my excited imagination I dare not say, but there, directly between me and the light of the conflagration, rose up a figure which I should judge was at least 10 or 12 feet in height and was from the knees upwards completely clad in white. Below the knees I thought I could discover a pair of legs and feet, which, considering the strides they were making, ought to have been enveloped in the seven league boots, which I remembered to have read of in my young days, but which were not, if my eyes were at all faithful to their trust, for they appeared to be as naked and bare, as if they were prepared for footing turf or searching for flag in a bog hole in the Emerald Isle. The head was surmounted with a cap, the climax of which, owing I suppose to the velocity with which the feet moved, stuck out behind to a great distance and left a trail which enabled me to follow its course for some time.

You may judge, Mr. Editor, what the effect of such an apparition was upon me at the moment, but as I watched it moving it suddenly disappeared before it reached the corner of King Street and I saw no more of it. I am not, as I said before, superstitious, but I am certain there was something in it, and I would like to know what it was. I could not tell whether it was male or female, for I am not sure whether such distinctions exist in the spiritual world, but I am inclined to think it belonged to the latter gender.

However this is not of material importance — but I would like to know from you whether you have had an intimation before this of such an apparition, or whether I am really the victim of my own imagination. I have thought that perhaps if followed up it might be made to account in some way for the origin of the fire; but this is a mere speculative hint, not worth much in itself. Do, Mr. Editor, try and unravel the mystery and you will confer a great favour on the community generally and myself particularly. — QUIS.

A STRANGE STORY

A Lost Man Found by Means of a Dream — A Speedy Answer to Prayer — From the Mail
Toronto News, October 12, 1882

Kingston, October 11. — A most marvellous occurrence transpired at Inverary a few days ago, the most interesting facts of which arrived here today. Lawrence Carey, an old man 70 years of age, got lost in the woods on Thursday morning, and a vigilant search of three days failed to find him. On Sunday morning about 100 men took part in the search, but they all met at Carey's house with the same story — no trace of him. An open-air prayer-meeting was held, and the Rev. B. Young engaged in prayer for the safe deliverance of the lost one to his friends. While he was enumerating Carey's many virtues as a friend and a neighbour, there was scarce a dry eye in the whole assemblage; Mrs. Hogan, a relation of Carey's, overcome by her emotion, was carried off the ground in a fainting fit. Before the meeting had broken up, as if in answer to Rev. Mr. Young's affecting appeal, joyous shouts were heard, and Mr. Magee, of Inverary, came up in hot haste with the glad tidings that the lost was found.

Magee, it appears, had been engaged in the search all day Saturday, having always taken a very warm interest in Carey. On Saturday night he had a startling dream, in which he avers the Holy Virgin appeared to him, and described to him the exact spot where Carey was to be found. In the morning he related his dream to a number of neighbours, and told them that he thought he knew such a place as the one described in his dream about two miles north of Hart's dwelling. They hooted at the absurdity of the thing. As night approached, however, and no trace of Carey had been found, his strange dream made such a deep impression on his mind that he started to go in quest of the place resembling the one described to him. He found it without much difficulty, a large opening in the earth between two hills, some six or eight feet in depth, apparently formed by some convulsion of nature. The walls are rocky and precipitous, and there at the bottom, strange to say, lay Carey, the object of all their search, buried in a deep sleep. Mr. Magee lost no time in arousing the unconscious sleeper, who, through exposure and want of proper sustenance, was unable to stand upon his feet. He could give no satisfactory account of how he had got there, nor how long he had remained in what would have assuredly been his living tomb had it not been for Magee's discovery. It appears that he left home on Thursday evening to look for the cattle, but lost his way, and wandered about in the darkness until he fell into the pit in which he was found, and was through physical infirmities unable to get out.

SEEN IN THE SPIRIT

A Charlottetown Servant Girl's Vision of the Fate of a Missing Man

Winnipeg Free Press, January 25, 1888

A Charlottetown, P.E.I., Despatch says:

Eighteen months ago Charles H. Yeo returned from Winnipeg to visit his relatives in Prince Edward Island. On New Year's Day, a year ago, he was in Charlottetown on his return to Winnipeg. While here he visited the house of a relative, and after leaving it disappeared as mysteriously and completely as if the earth had swallowed him. He had several hundred dollars on his person, and, no trace being obtainable, his parents offered $500 for information of his whereabouts, dead or alive.

That was last summer. Nothing more was heard of it till this week when the grand jury met, and Miss Tuck, a domestic, appeared and told a most extraordinary story. Upon hearing of the reward offered for Yeo's whereabouts, she prayed that she might discover the secret. In answer to her prayer she had a vision.

In the spirit she saw a man walking up and down in front of a certain house. Her description of the man tallies completely with that of Yeo. A man, whom she minutely describes, came out of that house and asked Yeo to go to the rear stable to see a horse. The two were joined by two others while there. The first-mentioned stranger drew a knife and stabbed Yeo to the heart. The murdered man's pockets were searched and a large amount of money obtained and divided among the three men. The body was stowed in an oat bin, and subsequently the bin and the body were taken some distance away in a sleigh, a hole cut in the ice by the same three men and the body thrown in, when the men returned to the city.

This story of her vision has produced a profound sensation. The investigation is still proceeding.

REMARKABLE DREAMS

I have a great deal of respect for David Boyle and for that reason I am reprinting two dreams that he collected as they appeared in one of the columns that he wrote for the series "Canadian Folk-Lore" published in *The Globe* (Toronto). The series of columns appeared on Saturdays between November 1897 and May 1898, and they were widely read and occasioned much interesting correspondence from readers. The excerpt reproduced here is taken from the column on the subject of "spirits" which appeared on 5 May 1898.

I should backtrack and explain that David Boyle (1842-1911) was a self-taught man with a passion for the past. Trained to be a blacksmith, he became Canada's premier archaeologist. All his life he was enthusiastic about the discovery, the examination, the preservation, and the protection of the antiquities of Ontario, be they physical objects (like bones or arrowheads) or intellectual property — Algonkian legends and myths, farmers' customs and beliefs, etc.

The Globe of Boyle's day evolved into today's *Globe and Mail*. It is a shame the newspaper these days does so little to commission columns as serious, as stylish, and as enlightening as Boyle's. There is nothing in the contemporary *Globe* to match this century-old series. Boyle notes that the previous week's column caught the eye of "a Toronto gentleman." The gentleman remains unnamed, but Boyle describes two of his dreams. The first dream is an anticipation of the assassination of Thomas D'Arcy McGee on Sparks Street in Ottawa on 7 April 1868. The second dream is also prophetic, for it offers specific details as to the death of a dear friend otherwise unknown to history. D'Arcy McGee was a Member of Parliament, a Father of Confederation, and an eloquent orator whose fiery speeches against the Fenian cause made him as many enemies as they did friends.

I try to avoid reprinting accounts of weird experiences that have been prepared by unidentified informants; the accounts invariably leave out significant details (such as where and when the event or its anticipation occurred), details that could, possibly, corroborate the story that is being told. Anonymous accounts generally read like folklore; possibly they are. If so, David Boyle was right in reproducing them. Yet I have to ask myself: Are these two "remarkable dreams" veridical? In other words, are they truthful? There is no way of proving that they are truthful or that they are concoctions after the fact. The matter will never be proved one way or the other. In the meantime, they make delightful reading today.

Remarkable Dreams

> A Toronto gentleman, who encloses his card, gives us two very remarkable instances of dream verification, for which he vouches.
>
> "I notice," he says, "in Saturday's *Globe*, several accounts of strange dreams, etc., and with your permission will relate one that I think has never been related before, because the person who told it to me would not allow it to be made public, for fear that his friends would laugh at him. He is now dead, and while I reserve the right to keep his name out of print, I think the dream sufficiently interesting to chronicle.
>
> > "D'Arcy McGee was advertised to lecture some thirty odd years ago in the Music Hall, Toronto, and my relative, being a prominent man in connection with the Mechanics' Library, as it was then, and a prominent citizen, was taking a great deal of interest in the work, being at the hall almost every

evening for a week. The night McGee was shot my friend wakened up about midnight, and sitting up in bed, wakened his wife, who asked if he were ill. 'No,' he responded, 'but I have had a very nasty dream. I thought I saw D'Arcy McGee shot.' His wife replied: 'You have been thinking so much of him lately it has naturally made you anxious and restless.' After some minutes they both went to sleep again. In the morning they were at breakfast when *The Globe* arrive, and almost the first thing they read was that D'Arcy McGee had been shot dead at Ottawa. Mr. — was so upset by this news and his dream that he was unwell for days. He made his wife promise never to tell the dream to anyone, but it was told to me years afterwards, as a great secret.

"Can any person explain this to me? The person who dreamed this dream was one of the best known men in Canada, and no one would doubt his word or that of his wife.

"Some six years ago a very dear friend and neighbour of mine was taken suddenly ill. He immediately sent for me. I found him in bed, with what was only a very severe cold. That night I dreamed he would die Thursday morning at three minutes to 3. So impressed with this dream was I that I told it to my wife in the morning. Tuesday night I sat up with him. Wednesday two other friends sat up, but I was there, too.

"About 11 p.m. the other two wanted me to go home and rest, telling me I could take their places on Thursday. I then told them of my dream, and said I would remain until 3 o'clock, and if my friend was alive then I would go home. He was resting all day and did not seem seriously ill. About 1 o'clock he took a turn for the worse, and died exactly at three minutes to 3, as I had dreamed."

6

HAUNTED SHIPS AND TRAINS

During the Victorian period in Canada and in other countries, ghosts were known to flit about the fireplace in the parlour or the hearth in the pantry. But ghosts are not bound by the walls of the homestead. There are ghosts that board ships that sail the Seven Seas! In this chapter you will encounter an fleet of phantom frigates, spectre brigs, fire-ships, phantom vessels, and voodoo ships. For good measure there is a nod towards spirited railway travel! Seafarers were known to avoid jinxed vessels. The last of the marine stories in this section of the book is a departure from the norm, for it is written in verse rather than in prose. It is signed "S." (It is possible that "S." is the pen name of the once-popular Canadian versifier otherwise known as "Serenus," Susie Frances Harrison; but this is just speculation on my part; though it is in her style, there is no proof that she composed "The Phantom Ship.") In the meantime haunted ships sail continue to plough the haunted waters of the Seven Seas! Haunted trains are not unknown!

THE SPECTRE BRIG

The Examiner, Charlottetown, P.E.I., 26 January 1863

The fall of 1853 saw me on board the bark Swordfish, bound from New York to Yarmouth, Nova Scotia, thence to Liverpool and a market. I cannot imagine what odd freak decided the owners of the bark to give her a name so inappropriate, for the swordfish is known to be of uncommon symmetry, and moves with the quickness of light, while its ungainly namesake was tub-built, blunt-bowed, short-sparred, requiring four men at the wheel in a gale of wind to keep her within six points of the compass, and then she would make more lee-way than a Dutch galliot.

However, she proved to be a tolerable sailor, despite her unpromising appearance, and the fifth day out, we made the Seal Islands, in the Bay of Fundy, and a few hours later were moored alongside the wharf at Yarmouth.

Here we were informed that our cargo would not be in readiness for several days, and as but little remained to be attended to aboard the vessel, I concluded to take a cruise over the city and surrounding country.

The city has a gloomy and antique appearance, looking as though the blight of ages had fallen upon her buildings in a night. The houses are of a style and architecture in vogue half a century ago, being built still earlier by Tory refugees, who fled from the Colonies during the Revolutionary war.

Many of these were offshoots of noble families in England, and clinging to their sovereign with fanatical blindness, they fled to this and adjacent provinces, where their descendants have managed to keep up a dingy show of gentility in their old tumble-down tenements.

Their hatred of republicanism, a hatred gathered and intensified through many generations, until it has become almost a passion, is only equalled by their love and veneration for their sovereign. The poorer class, mostly Irish and Scotch, are ardent admirers of republican institutions, and are outspoken in their sentiments.

Between them and their more aristocratic neighbours exists a bitter feeling partizan hostility which increases in intensity with each succeeding year, and must, ere long, break forth in a rougher shape than a mere war of words.

The Home Government is fully alive to this and accordingly grants every indulgent consistent with its dignity. But still the people are dissatisfied. They feel that there is a lack, a moral blight that deadens their enemies and clouds their prospects.

They know their country to be rich in mineral wealth, yet it remains undeveloped. Rich in its fisheries, yet they are unprofitable.

One day, while taking a stroll on the high ground bordering the bay, and watching the tide as it came in from the sea, rolling in the solid wall thirty feet in height that reared and rumbled like distant thunder, I chanced to hear some remarks made by a group of persons near me, that drew my attention. Not wishing to play the part of listener, I was turning from the spot when the foremost speaker of the party exclaimed:

"I tell you, gentlemen, it is no illusion! There is not a person for miles around who has not heard or seen the 'Spectre Brig.' Furthermore, if you will remain a few days longer, you can satisfy yourselves of the truth of my statement, as it is nearly time for her annual visitation."

Being interested by these strange remarks, I turned and joined them. During the conversation that followed, I referred to the above and requested to be enlightened as to its meaning, addressing myself to the person who had attracted my attention. He looked at me as though surprised at the request, but seeing I was a stranger, he replied:

"Certainly, sir; with pleasure if it will be of any interest to you."

Seating ourselves, he then proceeded to relate the story, as nearly as I can recollect as follows:

"Fifty years ago, the brig Yarmouth, commanded by Capt. Bruce, and manned by a crew from this neighborhood, sailed from this port to the West Indies. Days and weeks went by, and the time for her return came and passed. Apprehensions began to be felt for her safety as the days went by, and daily an anxious crowd of women and children might have been seen gathered on the headlands that overlooked the bay, straining their eyes seaward in the faint hope of catching a glimpse of the missing vessel that had borne away a husband, a brother, a father, or son. Each night only witnessed a deeper disappointment, and at last apprehension had become almost certainty, and people began to speak of her as a thing of the past.

"A year had just passed away, when one night as the watchman was going his rounds among the wharves, he chanced to look seaward, and was surprised to see a vessel covered with canvass from truck to kelson, standing boldly into the harbour, although it was blowing a living gale sufficient to swamp the strongest craft with half the amount of sail. On she came, plowing before the blast like a thing of life until she had reached within a cable's length of the shore; when suddenly her main topsail was backed, her anchor dropped into the water with a splash, followed by the rattling of the chains as it ran out through the hawse-hole. At the same instant her tacks and sheets were let go, her sails clowed up and furled, and in less time than it takes me to narrate it she had swung round with the current and was riding quietly at a single anchor.

"As she swung broadside to the wharf the astonished watchman recognized her, and started up town with a tearing rate. 'The Yarmouth has come.' The glad cry ran from house to house and street to street, and in a few minutes a crowd of people had gathered upon the wharf making the air ring with their cheers, while wives, mothers and sisters were kneeling and with streaming eyes returned thanks for the wanderer's return.

"As yet not a sound had been heard or an object seen aboard the brig to denote that a soul was near her. Every one recognized her as she lay silent and dark, rising and settling with every wave.

"Finding their efforts to arouse the crew to be of no avail, they procured boats, and in spite of the violence of the wind, put out to board her. Bending stoutly to the oars with a hearty good will they soon found themselves within a few yards of her, when they were surprised to hear a hoarse voice exclaim, 'Keep off! Keep off!' Hardly believing their senses, they returned to the shore, which they had scarcely reached before a thick black fog, peculiar in that land of fogs, swept in from the sea and enveloped everything in an impenetrable veil. Surprised and terrified at what they had seen, the people returned to await the morning, hoping, yet scarcely daring to believe that with daylight everything would be explained. The gale still continued, and as morning broke, the vapor raised for a few moments, but not a vestige of the vessel of the preceding night was to be seen.

"Another year went by and the phantom vessel again appeared under nearly the same circumstances, and all attempts to board her resulted as before.

"'Thus,' continued my narrator, 'nearly fifty years have gone by, and still she makes her annual visit at just such a period of each succeeding year. Of late no attention is paid to her whatever, her arrival being hardly noticed, as she comes in invariably at midnight, and disappears within an hour.'"

Here the story concluded, and thanking my informant for his kindness, I arose, bid the party good-bye, and returned to my vessel and retired to my berth, as it was getting late.

I felt feverish and restless, and lay tossing about for several hours. Not being able to rest, I got up, dressed myself and went on deck, where the night air soon cooled my heated blood, and I was about to go to my stat-room again, when my attention was arrested by hearing a loud splash in the water, followed by the rattle of a chain as it was rapidly paid out. Looking out into the harbor, I saw to my astonishment, a large, old-fashioned full-rigged brig laying quietly at anchor, with sails snugly furled and everything in ship-shape style. I was at first considerably startled, as I knew it would be impossible for any sailing vessel to come in and anchor when not a breath of wind was stirring. Not believing in anything of a supernatural character, whether it be ghost or ghoul, hobgoblin or witch, I resolved to pay the strange craft a visit, feeling confident it was the "spectre brig," whose history I had heard a few hours before.

Going to the forecastle, I turned out two of the men, and ordered them to lower away the boat, throw out a pair of oars, and jump in, which they promptly did. I followed them over the side, and taking the tiller, sat down to wait the result.

In a few minutes we were within a dozen yards of the stranger, and rising in the boat I hailed:

"Brig, ahoy!"

No answer.

"Brig, ahoy!" I again shouted, with all the force of my lungs, but still no answer.

The third hail resulted as before.

There she lay, grim and dark, her sides covered with barnacles and clothed with seaweed. Not a sound could be heard, not even the creaking of a block, or the rattling of a rope.

Determined to board her at all hazards, I directed the men to pull with all their strength, and lay the boat alongside, while I grappled the rigging.

Bending themselves to the oars they sent the light boat seething through the water like a dart; but when, apparently with an oar's length of her side, the stranger craft began to grow indistinct, like a vapor. A moment her outline could be plainly seen, stamped against the sky, and the next she had vanished wholly, without a sound, without a sigh.

A thick fog soon set in from the bay, and we were compelled to grope our way to the shore as best we could, feeling awed and perplexed at what we had seen.

In vain I have tried to explain this phenomenon, but without success, and at last I am forced to the conclusion that it must remain one of those secrets that must continue until the Last Great Day, when the "heavens shall roll away like a scroll, and the mysteries of the universe stand revealed!"

A MIRAGE OF SOME SORT

The Maritimes are fabled for their "fire-ships" and "phantom ships." The former vessels appear on the horizon and appear to be ships that are aflame. They strike terror in the hearts of Maritimers. The latter vessels are ghostly galleons manned by spectre crews. They too strike terror, though there are fewer sightings of phantom ships than there are of fire ships. Over the centuries fisherfolk and seafarers on the Bay of Chaleur have reported spotting the alarming sights of fire-ships scudding across the horizon. They regard such sightings as forebearers or harbingers of bad luck. In the account offered here, there is a reference to the Intercolonial Railway which linked Halifax and Montreal. "Bay Chaleur's Phantom Ship" appeared in the *Halifax Morning Herald*, 17 July 1885.

Bay Chaleur's Phantom Ship
(Special correspondence Halifax Herald)

Chatham, December 16. — The reports in regard to the phantom ships seen in the Bay Chaleur have been revived. Operators at Jaquet River and Charles stations on the northern division of the Intercolonial, report that the phantom, which is said to be an exact likeness of a full-rigged ship on fire, was plainly seen for miles along the Bay shore on Monday night. Various legends more or less ancient are current concerning the apparition or whatever it may be. The story is that long ago a mutiny occurred on a ship in the Bay Chaleur, and that so fierce was the conflict that the only person to escape barely survived to reach the shore and tell the terrible story of the conflict. Another story, still more improbable, is to the effect that during the continuance of the apparition a good many years ago, a boat put off from the shore with several men to see the strange thing, neither boat nor men being heard from afterwards. The phantom ship does not appear at very regular intervals, and had not been seen before Monday night for about two years. It appears to come quite close to the shore at times, and is probably a mirage of some object in the surrounding country similar to a ship.

THE HAUNTED SHIP

Daily Patriot, Charlottetown, P.E.I., January 3, 1887

A St. John *Globe* reporter had a talk with a gentleman who came from Bathurst on Friday. He says the ship *Squando* still lies on the bar about a mile and a half from the beach and about six miles from the town of Bathurst. He has been on board the vessel on two or three occasions. He says that the two watchmen declare that there is something supernatural on board. They have not seen anything, but have heard strange noises. One night both men laid down to sleep in the cabin, one in the forward cabin and the other in the after cabin. The men who was sleeping aft was aroused during the night by hearing a terrible commotion going on in the forward cabin. He called out to his mate and asked him the cause of the noise. Receiving no reply he went to the forward cabin. Stretched on the floor was the body of his companion. Finding that he could not arouse him from his faint by shaking him he dashed a pitcher of water in his face. This brought him to his senses. When asked how he got out of his bunk he said he did not know — he was thrown out by some invisible hands. On another night the two men walked the deck all night to ascertain if the noises were caused by some practical joker from the shore. No one came on board, but the noises were still to be distinctly heard in the cabin, as if a struggle were going on. The men say they do not believe in ghosts, but they are at a loss to account for the strange, weird things they have heard. The captain of the vessel also persists in saying she is haunted. He has had the clothes torn off him when sleeping at night, by invisible hands. One night he pulled the clothes over his head, and no sooner had he done so than they were stripped off him to his very feet. He, too, declares that he has not seen any supernatural beings on board. These tales have awakened considerable interest in the vessel along the North Shore. When the bay becomes sealed with ice it is probable that a determined effort will be made to lay the ghost or ascertain from whence the supernatural sounds proceed.

THE PHANTOM SHIP

A legend of Cape Despair, and the fleet sent out by Queen Anne in 1711, which was lost in a storm in the Gulf. The Gaspé fisher-folk say that the ship is thus seen on moonlight nights in April.

"'Poet's Corner," *Daily News*, St. John's, Nfld., September 1, 1902

Off the Gaspé coast, when the sea lies calm,
And ne'er a breeze doth sigh,
And the Moon of Bright Nights shineth fair,
Within a cloudless sky;
With a sudden surge the waters rise,
And the Phantom Ship doth bear
Down the towering waves, through the flying foam,
On the rocks of Cape Despair.

And o'er her bulwarks in silence grim,
A spectral host doth lean,
In the garb of old-timer soldier-men,
When Anne was England's Queen:
While one stands forth on the plunging brow,
To front the soundless storm,
With one arm clasping to his breast
A woman's white-clad form:

Like the panther crouched to spring is he,
As his wild eye sweeps the shore,
While the woman's snowy garments stream
On a ghostly wind of yore;
And the watchers through the midnight hear
A woman's anguished cry,
As with lightning flight through waters white,
The Phantom Ship goes by!

The stars wane wan in the skies above,
And the moonlit sea grows dark,
As the seething surge of the hurricane
Sweeps o'er the fated bark
And the stars shine forth in the skies again,
O'er the rugged Gaspé coast;
But the Phantom Ship hath met her doom,
With all her gallant host.

"S."

GHOSTS OF THE ROUND-HOUSE

The history of the nineteenth century, as well as its literature, is rich in haunted castles, haunted houses, haunted shacks, haunted sailing ships, haunted stage coaches and carriages. Indeed, there were even haunted railway trains, coaches, and round-houses. At first it seems odd that a railway train should be haunted. After all, the epitome of technology in the latter half of the nineteenth century was an engine pulling a tender, a mail coach, a passenger coach or two, followed by a caboose. But upon consideration, it is not odd at all. Transcontinental passenger trains are rich in human drama; not for nothing is Agatha Christie's best-known crime novel set aboard a train: *Murder on the Orient Express.* Canada has no train to match the luxury and drama of the Orient Express, but in its day the Canadian Pacific Railway ran transcontinental trains of considerable glamour. Once they steamed out of Montreal's Windsor Station for points West, their lounge cars and cabin cars would be ideal settings for mayhem, not to mention ghostly mischief! Here is a ghost on the rails, courtesy of an unidentified newspaperman with the *Toronto News*, 9 March 1897.

Ghosts in the Cabe — A Wild Weird Tale of Phantoms from Kingston — Special to The News

Kingston, March 9. — Ghosts at midnight stalk about in the Kingston & Pembroke Railway round-house. Last Thursday night Charles Davidson and Walter Latto, night watchmen, heard a noise and found the form of a negro named Commodore, killed on the road, seated on the cab of an engine. He seemed to be choking and trying to speak. The watchmen were terror stricken. Next night the forms of three men killed on the road passed before the watchmen. The trio were readily recognized. They all seated themselves on the engine which, it is said, caused their death. There is considerable excitement over the affair. The railway management speak in terms of praise of the reliability and soberness of the watchmen. A committee will likely investigate. The second night the watchmen fired shots, but the spectres seemed unharmed.

A HAUNTED LOCOMOTIVE

Earlier I referred to the haunted round-house. Here is the story of a haunted locomotive engine. This news story appeared in the St. John's *Daily News*, St. John's, Newfoundland, 9 December 1904.

A Haunted Locomotive on the Intercolonial — Engine 239, — The Man Killer — Said to Be Infested with a Ghostly Visitor — Several Engineers Have Been Killed on Her — Has Unenviable Record

Has the I.C.R. a haunted engine?

This question is agitating the minds of the public generally, and particularly the knights of the throttle and their assistants in the cab who are employed on the government railway.

Is 239 haunted?

Is this ill-fated engine hooded?

The general opinion of I.C.R. men is that she is, and this particular locomotive is now looked upon with fear and trembling.

Superstition has its devotees in every calling of life. At the cradle the anxious mother will be heard saying, "The goblins will catch you if you don't watch out." Time goes on and as one enters the state of manhood he has his misgiving, his forebodings, governed by his superstitious make-up; the sailors at sea, the soldier in the battlefield, the ordinary individual in every day life — each has his problems in this respect.

Probably no calling has more cause for superstition than that of the man in front, or in other words, the man who handles the throttle and lever, and to whose exactness, wisdom and foresight is intrusted the lives of the travelling public.

Coming back to the direct basis of these few preliminary remarks, no doubt the past history of engine No. 392 will be read with interest.

It is said, and on good authority, that since the construction of this locomotive for the I.C.R. several fatalities are recorded. Trainmen, and the public generally remember the disaster at Belmont when Sam Trider, who for thirty-odd years ran an engine between Moncton and Truro, met his death. The train on this occasion was running by Belmont station. Suddenly there was a smash and a general mix-up. No. 239 had left the rails. From what cause is as yet a mystery. She swayed to and fro and suddenly lunged to the right, toppling over. Fireman Harry Campbell was thrown through the cab window and landed in a pile of snow dazed but uninjured, while Sam Trider, the engineer, met death at his post.

Again, 239 was in the wreck at Windsor Jct. In this, Driver Wall, an old and trusted I.C.R. man, lost his life. It was late in the evening and a C.P.R. train driven by Wall, and the freight from Halifax with Driver Mel. Copeland, were to cross at the junction. Copeland passed the semaphore and danger signals, and the crash came. Four persons including Driver Wall were killed and several more or less injured. Upwards of 70 cars were derailed, many being dashed over the embankment and smashed into kindling wood.

On another occasion, No. 239 jumped the rail at Humphrey's mills and the driver and firemen miraculously escaped death or at least serious injury. Again, north of Moncton, she met with a serious mishap.

After each accident she was sent to the Moncton shops and repaired, and the query was frequently voiced by I.C.R. men, "Who will be her next victim?"

At all events, even the I.C.R. round house cleaners at Moncton have a great aversion to working on 239. A story of a somewhat ghostly character is told.

It is reported that not long ago a cleaner while doing some work around a locomotive, casually glanced into the cab, says that he saw a man standing at the throttle. Not having seen any one enter the cab he hailed the supposed driver, and receiving no reply, again looked in, but the man had vanished. He made immediate enquiries, but nearby workmen had not seen anyone entering or leaving the cab.

The cleaner in question is positive that he saw a man there, and no argument can alter his opinion.

At all events the general opinion among the men is that 239 should now be consigned to the scrap heap.

Repairs and renovations to this locomotive during her career on the I.C.R. have gone to prove her a veritable white elephant.

The engine has been in the service of the I.C.R. for some two years and her record is an unenviable one. — *St. John Times.*

7

FAMOUS HAUNTINGS

At times it seems that there is a ghost for every community in Canada. Possibly I am exaggerating; my files bulge with ghost stories, but I do not have a story for every village, town, or city in the country. Yet when a community has an independent local newspaper, there is likely to be a ghost story — if not a ghost — lurking about! (During the Victorian period the newspapers were livelier than they are today and they were not yet links in various newspaper chains.) In these stories his "ghostship" (to use one of the wry terms of the time) customarily took up residence in the oldest structure in town, whether it be a log cabin, a pioneer farmstead, a court house, or the crypt of a church!

Little of this lore has survived the years. Hardly any of it has been handed down to us today except as it is preserved in the columns of daily and weekly newspapers. There are many reasons for the sparseness of traditions of ghosts and hauntings in English Canada during the 18th and 19th centuries. One reason is that the educated people in the community, who were the doctors and the lawyers, the businessmen and the bankers, scoffed at intangibles like spirits. Intangibles could not be bought or sold so they had no "net worth." You might think that the clergymen of the day would be sensitive to "spirit beings" but that did not prove to be the case. From the pulpit the priest or the minister regularly denounced what he saw as superstitious beliefs and practices. It was suggested that such things were "the work of the Devil" and hence to be avoided at all costs by right-thinking people.

Another reason that the knowledge of traditional hauntings died out is that most hauntings are local affairs and not national ones. They are often sporadic occurrences rather than recurrent hauntings. Farmer Brown sees the spectre of his dead son near the bed in the upstairs bedroom of his farmhouse, the room on the right of the stairs. Or groups of neighbours are drawn to Farmer MacDonald's farmhouse because of reports of poltergeist-like activity: mysterious fires, descending nails, flying dishes, strange sounds, eerie messages inscribed on walls, etc. Then, abruptly, everything returns to normal. So the haunting may be a one-day affair or a seven-day wonder. No matter its duration, it is rooted in the region, on a quarter-section perhaps, and the distances to the next crossroads are measured in miles. Such is the local fame of the ghost or poltergeist in nineteenth-century Canada.

Despite the scepticism of the local populace, regardless of the remoteness of many of the communities, there were some hauntings in the country before the turn of the twentieth century that were notable at the time and are notable even in today's terms. They are unforgettable even in the period that produced the excesses of *The Amityville Horror* and the inanities of *The X-Files*. These early hauntings attained a level of fame (or infamity), a degree of note (or notoriety), that few if any hauntings could since claim. These are stories of ghosts and hauntings that are known outside their hamlets. Some of them are recognized nationally and even internationally.

Six of the most haunting stories that are appreciated by connoisseurs of true ghost stories throughout the English-speaking world are featured in this section of the book. These stories happen to have occurred in Canada during the eighteenth and nineteenth centuries. These stories are among the most thrilling in the book. They are classic tales and accepted as true ghost stories by ghost-hunters, psychical researchers, and parapsychologists. These stories are known as the Wynyard Apparition, the Baldoon Mystery, the Great Amherst Mystery, the Binstead Haunting, the Dagg Poltergeist, and the Mackenzie River Ghost. Four of them are reprinted here from the columns of nineteenth-century newspapers, with the exception of the Baldoon Mystery (which was originally described in a newspaper of the period but is reproduced from a booklet printed by that newspaper) and the Mackenzie River Ghost (which seems not to have been recounted in a newspaper article during the Victorian period but so that it may be represented in this book is reproduced from its first appearance in a nineteenth-century publication.)

There is much literature about the Wynyard Apparition, Canada's most famous crisis apparition. (A crisis apparition occurs when the spirit or apparition of a dying person appears to a relative or friend in another part of the world at the point of dying or great stress.) The account carried in these pages suggests it is little more than a folklore (what today we might called an urban myth). Indeed, it seems to be a well-travelled tale; yet in its classic form it concerns Lieutenant (later General) Wynyard and Captain John C. Sherbrooke (later Lieutenant-Governor of Nova

Scotia and still later Governor General of Canada) and it took place on October 15, 1785, at approximately four o'clock in the afternoon, in the quarters of the British garrison in Sydney, N.S. Here it is treated as a traditional ghost story, one that grows in the telling and moves around a lot. But it also appears in the standard biography of Governor General Sherbrooke written by A. Patchett Martin.

The Baldoon Mystery concerns the poltergeist-like activities that took place on the McDonald farm near Baldoon, the Scottish farming community located northwest of Chatham, Ont. All manner of disturbances were reported by farmer John McDonald, members of his family, members of the farming community, and travellers and mediums during the three-year period from 1829 to 1831. The disturbances included a hail of bullets, stones, lead pellets, water, and sporadic fires. It is said that at one point the small wooden farmhouse heaved from its foundations. One night it was consumed in flames and burnt to the ground. These disturbances were never satisfactorily explained, though many fanciful tales were told about them, including the curse of a witch and the summoning of a witch-doctor.

The fame and fascination of the Great Amherst Mystery spread far and wide because of the professional interest in the matter of a New York actor named Walter Hubbell who was attracted by newspaper accounts of the poltergeist-like activities that in 1878-79 were taking place at the Cox family cottage in Amherst, N.S. Hubbell coined the phrase "the great Amherst mystery," and he did his best to publicize and popularize the disturbances, first through a road-show starring himself and the poor young woman Esther Cox, and second through the printing of his book titled, inevitably, *The Great Amherst Mystery*. Hubbell had no way of knowning that the effects he described as taking place in the Cox cottage would, fifty years later, through a stroke of fate — call it the result of serendipity — be replayed in the haunting of Borley Rectory, Sussex, England. Borley Rectory was known as "the most haunted house in England," and if that was so, the Cox family cottage has a claim to being considered, in its day, "the most haunted house in Canada."

The case of the Binstead Haunting was discussed in the late nineteenth century but was forgotten in the twentieth century. The account of the haunting appeared in the prestigious *Journal of the Society for Psychical Research* as part of the section titled "On Recognised Apparitions Occurring More than a Year after Death" (*SPR Journal*, July 8, 1889). The SPR was founded by British scientists to conduct psychical research, study mediumship, document hallucinations, and investigate what was quaintly called "spirit-survival."

The author of the account is identified, quaintly, as "Mrs. Pennée, of St. Anne de Beaupré, Quebec, daughter of the late Mr. William Ward (a Conservative M.P. for London), and sister of the late Rev. A.B. Ward, of Cambridge." The calm of the estate, located outside East River, P.E.I., was compromised by events that took place in its past and that led to the appearance of "a woman with a baby" in one arm who stirred ashes in the fireplace with the other.

The text of the account printed here (with some additional comments by the SPR's editor) is based on the version that appeared in the journal rather than the one that was published in the newspaper. The newspaper's account was headed "A Real Ghost!" and began with the following words: "The English Society for Psychical Research is still vigorously pursuing its investigations and is about to publish part XV of its proceedings, containing articles on apparitions, duplex personality, seances with the celebrated medium, D.D. Home, &c." Minor variations in punctuation and spelling were noted, but the principle difference between the versions is that the newspaper story is shorter than the journal story. The newspaper story ends before the introduction of the second and third letters. The longer version appears here.

The Dagg Poltergeist is the case of a "an invisible inhabitant of the woodshed" on the Dagg family farm in Shawville in 1889. There are at least two interesting features to this story. The feature to be noted first is that the effects of the poltergeist-like spirit were observed taking place by many members of the community in the Ottawa Valley who swore on oath that the manifestations occurred precisely as described. The story's second feature is the presence of Percy Woodcock, the reporter who offered readers of the *Brockville Recorder and Times* exclusive, eyewitness accounts of events and experiences on the farm before giving them exposure across the North American continent. The National Film Board of Canada has produced a documentary about the Dagg Poltergeist called *The Ghost that Talked* with psychical researcher R.S. Lambert as narrator.

The Mackenzie River Ghost, the most famous true ghost story of the Northwest, received its broadest readership through its appearance in *Lord Halifax's Ghost Book* (1936), prepared by Charles Lindley, Viscount, an influential and widely read compilation of English ghost stories. The events themselves took place in the Great Northwest in 1853-54; a fur trader, accompanying a corpse by dogsled from Fort McPherson in the Mackenzie River District to Fort Simpson, heard the corpse utter the command, "Marché!" at times that turned out to be critical to the survival of the group. It is told here in the words of Roderick MacFarlane (1835–1920), Fellow of the Royal Geographical Society, a fur trader in the Northwest Territories for over forty years. It was MacFarlane who established Fort Smith in 1874, and it was at his instigation that the first steamship for travel on the Mackenzie River was constructed in 1886. MacFarlane was the principal witness of the eerie events and experiences recorded in this account. He recalled his experience at the request of a scholar at Oxford University in 1883. The full account appeared as "Ghost Story" in *The Beaver*, December 1986–January 1987. (That account, the original one, is reproduced here.) It was given semi-factual, semi-fictional treatment by the British officer and explorer Sir W.F. Butler in *Good Words* (1877). It was retold by Ernest Thompson Seton in *Trail and Campfire Stories* (1940). Noted ghost-hunter R.S. Lambert, in *Exploring the Supernatural: The Weird in Canadian Folklore* (1955), recalling the story, called it "the most convincing of all Canadian apparitions."

Anyway, here are six of Canada's classic spooks!

THE WYNYARD APPARITION

Supernatural Appearance
Montreal Herald, November 6, 1822

Sir John Sherbrooke and George Wynyard were as young men, officers in the same regiment, which was employed on foreign service. — They were connected by similarity of taste and studies, and spent together in literary occupation, much of that vacant time which was squandered by their brother officers in those excesses of the table, which some forty years ago, were considered among the necessary accomplishments of the military character. They were one afternoon sitting in Wynyard's apartment. It was perfect light, the hour was about four o'clock; they had dined but neither of them had drank wine, and they had retired from the mess to continue together the occupations of the day — I, ought to have said, that the apartment in which they were, had two doors in it, the one opening into a passage, and the other opening into Wynyard's bedroom. There were no other means of entering the sitting room but from the passage, and no other egress from the bed-room but through the sitting room; so that any person passing into the bed-room must have remained there, unless he returned by the way he entered. This point is of consequence to the story. As these two young officers were pursuing their studies, Sherbrooke, whose eye happened accidentally to glance from the volume before him towards the door that opened in the passageway observed a tall youth, of about 20 years of age, whose appearance was that of extreme emaciation, standing behind him. Struck with the presence of a perfect stranger, he immediately turned to his friend, who was sitting near him, and directed his attention to the guest who had thus strangely broken in upon their studies. As soon as Wynyard's eyes were turned towards the mysterious visitor, his countenance became suddenly agitated. "I have heard," says Sir John Sherbrooke, "of a man's being as white as death, but I never saw a living face assume the appearance of a corpse, except Wynyard's at the moment. As they looked silently at the form before them — for Wynyard, who seemed to apprehend the import of the appearance, was deprived of the faculty of speech, and Sherbrooke, perceiving the agitation of his friend, felt no inclination to address it — as they looked silently upon the figure, it proceeded slowly into the adjoining apartment, and in the act of passing them, cast its eyes with an expression of somewhat melancholy affection on Wynyard. The oppression of this extraordinary presence was no sooner removed, than Wynyard, seizing his friend by the arm, and drawing a deep breath, as if recovering from the suffocation of intense astonishment and emotion, muttered in a low and almost inaudible tone of voice: "Good God! my brother!"

"Your brother," repeated Sherbrooke, "what can you mean, Wynyard? there must be some deception — follow me," and immediately taking his friend by the arm, he preceded him into the bed-room, which, as I before stated, was connected with the sitting room, and into which the strange visitor had evidently entered. I have already said that from this chamber there was no possibility of withdrawing but by the way of the apartment through which the figure had certainly passed, and as certainly never had returned. Wynyard's mind had received an impression at the first moment of his observing him, that the figure whom he had seen was the spirit of his brother. Sherbrooke sill persevered in strenuously believing that some imposition had been practised. They took note of the day and hour in which the event had happened; but they resolved not to mention the occurrence in the regiment, and gradually they persuaded each other they had been imposed upon by some of their fellow officers, though they could neither account for the reason, or suspect the author, or conceive the means of its execution. They were content to imagine any thing possible rather than admit the possibility of a supernatural appearance. But though they had attempted these stratagems of self-delusion, Wynyard could not help expressing his solicitude with respect to the safety of the brother whose apparition he had either seen or imagined himself to have seen, and the anxiety which he exhibited for letters from England, and his frequent mention of his fears for his brother's health, at length awakened the curiosity of his comrades, and eventually betrayed him into a declaration of the circumstances which he had in vain determined to conceal. The story of the silent and unbidden visitor was no sooner bruited abroad, than the destiny of Wynyard's brother became an object of universal and painful interest to the officers of the regiment; there were few who did not inquire for Wynyard's letters before they made any demand after their own, and the packets that arrived from England were welcomed with more than usual eagerness, for they brought, not only remembrances from their friends at home, but promised to afford a clue to the mystery which had happened among themselves. By the first ship no intelligence relating to the story could have been received, for they had all departed from England previously to the appearance of the spirit. At length the long wished for vessels arrived; all the officers had letters except Wynyard. Still the secret was unexplained. They examined the several newspapers; they contained no mention of any death, or of any other circumstance connected with his family, that could account for the preternatural event. There was a solitary letter for Sherbrooke still unopened. The officers had received their letters in the mess room at the hour of supper. After Sherbrooke had broken the seal of his last packet, and cast a glance on its contents, he beckoned his friend a way from the company, and departed from the room. All were silent. The suspense of the interest was now at its climax; the impatience for the return of Sherbrooke was inexpressible. They doubted not but that letter had contained the long expected intelligence. At the interval of one hour Sherbrooke joined them. No one dared be guilty of such rudeness as to enquire the nature of his correspondence; but they waited in mute attention, expecting that he would himself touch upon the subject. His mind was manifestly full of thoughts that pained, bewildered and oppressed him. He drew near the fire place, and leaning his head on the mantle piece, after a pause of some moments, said, in a low voice, to the person who was nearest to him, "Wynyard's brother is no more." The first line of Sherbrooke's letter was, "Dear John, break to your friend Wynyard the death of his favourite brother." He had died on the way and at the very hour on which the friend had seen his spirit pass so mysteriously through the apartment.

It might have been imagined, that these events would have been sufficient to have impressed the mind of Sherbrooke with the conviction of their truth; but so strong was his prepossession against the existence, or even the possibility, of any preternatural intercourse with the souls of the dead, that he still entertained a doubt of the report of his senses, supported as their testimony was by the coincidence of vision and event. Some years after, on his return from England, he was walking with two gentlemen in Piccadilly, when, on the opposite side of the way, he saw a person bearing the most striking resemblance to the figure which had been disclosed to Wynyard and himself. His companions were acquainted with the story; and he instantly directed their attention to the gentleman opposite, as the individual who had contrived to enter and depart from Wynyard's apartments without their being conscious of the means. Full of the impression, he immediately went over, and at once addressed the gentleman; he now fully expected to elucidate the mystery. He apologized for the interruption, but excused it by relating the occurrence, which had induced to this solecism in manners. He had never been out of the country; but he was the twin brother of the youth whose spirit had been seen.

This story is related with several variations. It is sometimes told as having happened in Gibraltar, at others in England, at others in America. There are also differences with respect to the conclusion. Some say that gentleman who Sir John Sherbrooke afterwards met in London, and addressed, as the person whom he had previously seen in so mysterious a manner, was not another brother of General Wynyard, but a gentleman, who bore a strong resemblance to the family. But however the leading facts in every account are the same. Sir John Sherbrooke and General Wynyard, two gentlemen of veracity, were together present at the spiritual appearance of the brother of General Wynyard; the appearance took place at the moment of dissolution; and the countenance and form of the ghost's figure were so distinctly impressed upon the memory of Sir John Sherbrooke, to whom the living man had been unknown that on accidentally meeting with his likeness, he perceived and acknowledged the resemblance.

If this story be true, it silences the common objections, that ghosts always appear at night, and are never visible to two persons at the same time.

THE BALDOON MYSTERY

Wallaceburg News, Wallaceburg, Ontario
Reprinted from the booklet *The Baldoon Mystery* (1871)

It was rumoured that there was a great mystery going on at McDonald's, and I, like a great many others, went to see for myself. I saw stones and brick bats coming through the doors and windows, making the hole whatever size the article was that came in. Parties would take these same things and throw them into the river, and in a few minutes they would come back again. I saw a child lying in a little cradle, when the cradle began to rock fearfully and no one was near it. They thought it would throw the child out, so two men undertook to stop it, but could not, still a third took hold, but stop it they could not. Some of the party said, "Let's test this," so they put a Bible in the cradle and it stopped instantly. They said that was a fair test.

The gun balls would come in through the windows and we would take them and throw them into the river, which is about thirty-six feet deep, and in a few minutes they would come back through the windows, so we were satisfied that the evil one was at the helm. I saw the house take fire upstairs in ten different places at once. There were plenty to watch the fires, as people came from all parts of the United States and Canada to see for themselves. No less than from twenty to fifty men were there all the time. The bedsteads would move from one side of the room to the other, and the chairs would move when someone was sitting on them and they could not get off. They thought the devil was going to take them, chair and all. I saw the pot, full of boiling water, come off the fireplace and sail about the room over our heads and never spill a drop, and then return to its starting place. I saw a large black dog sitting on the milk house while it was burning, and thinking it would burn we threw sticks at it, but it would not stir, but, all at once, he disappeared. I saw the mush pot chase the dog that happened to come with one of the neighbours, through a crowd, and the people thought the devil was in the pot. It chased the dog all over the house and out of doors, and mush stick would strike it first on one side and then on the other. The dog showed fight, and turning round caught hold of the ring in the stick, which swinging, would strike him first on one side of the face and then on the other. It finally let go of the dog's teeth and went back to the pot. I was acquainted with Mr. McDonald and knew him to be an upright man and in good standing in the Baptist Church.

This is my true statement of what I saw.

William S. Fleury

THE GREAT AMHERST MYSTERY

A Nova Scotian Mystery — (From the Amherst, N.S., Borderer)
Daily Colonist, Victoria, B.C., December 4, 1878

Running in a southerly direction from Church street, Amherst, and parallel with Main street, is a thoroughfare which leads in the direction of the railway station. A short distance below Church street corner is the house occupied by Mr. Daniel Teed, a respected resident of the town, who holds a position in the Amherst Shoe Factory. The house is an ordinary two-story dwelling. In the rear is a barn, to which we shall refer. The occupants of the house are Mr. Teed, his wife and infant, Miss Esther Cox, and Miss Jane Cox. The last named are sisters of Mrs. Teed, and are young women past twenty years of age. Miss Esther is the central figure in the story. Her health has been good, and she has lived until recently undisturbed by mysterious influences, and in ignorance of the theories of practices of spiritualistic mediums. The first indication of anything unusual was a mesmeric trance, by which she was overcome during her early illness, eight weeks ago. One night she retired to bed with her sister Jane, and scarcely had she done so when a noise was heard in a pasteboard box, containing scraps of cloths, which was under the bed. Little attention was paid to this, as it was supposed to be the work of a mouse, nor were the girls much disturbed when they heard it in the straw of the ticking. They went to sleep and their slumbers were not interrupted. On the following night they again retired, and again the mysterious noise was heard. This time it was of a more positive character, for the box was violently overturned. Much alarmed, the sisters called their brother, who responded to their call, righted the box, placed the cover on it, and set it in the middle of the floor. The effect was most surprising, for not only was the box again overturned, but the cover flew through the air and landed on top of the table. As often as the test was made, so often did the same result follow, and as was natural enough, much alarm was felt at these extraordinary manifestations. The unknown (we hardly know the term to apply to it) now entered upon its work in earnest, and for four nights it continued its freaks, varying its method of each occasion. When the girls went to bed, it would seize the quilts and drag them to one corner of the bed, pillows would be pulled from under Esther's head by the invisible influence, and with such force was this done that she was unable to hold on and prevent the articles moving. Strange rappings were next heard in various places where Esther was, and during the day as well as night. Mr. John White went to the house one morning and as Esther went out to the barn a terrific pounding which is described as resembling a hundred and fifty-six pound weight falling in succession on the roof, commencing at once, and continued until Esther ran back to the house. This pounding has always been loud when she has gone to the barn, but it has been fully as loud around the house. When Esther goes into the cellar it sounds as if a colossal fist were pounding on the beams with the fury of a demon. In order to test Esther's good faith, her hands have been tied behind her back, but the pounding was instantaneous and as loud as before. Other persons have accompanied her and have satisfied themselves that the noise was made by no human agency visible to mortal eye. Sometimes the pounding is in one room and sometimes in another. It is as heavy as the blows of an axe would be, but has more of a dead sound as if it were a flesh-covered fist. Rapping commenced in the early history of the case. It resembles a drumming on a board with the fingers and nails of a person's hand. It was the first heard on the slats under the bed, on the wall and around the bedpost. To an unpracticed ear it is suggestive of telegraphy, but it is not that, and is more like the tippy-ti-tap of an impatient boy. Dr. Carritte, as the medical attendant, has endeavoured to trace the noise to some agency, but has failed to do so. Esther has been placed sitting on the top of the bedclothes, where the slightest motion of her body could be observed, but though she has remained motionless the noise has continued. She has been seated on a chair placed on thick rugs in the middle of the floor, and the rapping was as if some one were tapping on the wall with the knuckles. Sometimes it taps on the legs of a table, a chair, a shelf — anything so long as Esther is present. More than this it is musical. It beats the measure of "Yankee Doodle" and "Somebody tapping at the Garden Gate" while it regularly keeps time with any one [who] whistles or sings. During Esther's sickness it frequently slapped her in the face, causing much pain and leaving a conspicuous red mark. Esther is not a facile writer, but when she takes a pencil in her hand and places it against the wall, it is guided by an influence which she cannot resist, and writes sentences of which she has not the remote thought. We are sorry to say that some of these sentences are very wicked ones and are most horribly profane. The writing is not at all like Esther's, but it is said to be exactly like that of a certain young man. Not only is the language far from choice, and such as Esther is not capable of using, but the spelling is most atrocious. "I ded rit to her Cister," is intended to signify "I did write to her sister." The sentences are incoherent, but they have declared that they are from the man in question, and his latest proclamation is that there will be great sport in three weeks' time. On one occasion, the unknown is said to have scratched a word on the plaster when no one was present. A Mr. Campbell was in the house, and the name "Cammal" was scratched on the wall as if with a pin. The word is there, however it got there. The scratching noise, like nails scratching over a smooth board is heard frequently, and is enough to send the chill down the backs of nervous persons. The bed on which Esther has slept is marked in various places, as if a hot iron was rapidly passed over it in an irregular manner. On one occasion, when twelve persons were in the room, Esther lay in bed, with her hands outside the cover-lid. The bed clothes were violently agitated; but the pillow acted as if literally "possessed of a devil." It would leap towards Esther's head, strike her and bound back, and this it continued to do several times. Two persons then took hold of the corners of it and stood several feet away from the bed. The pillow straightened itself out horizontally in the direction of Esther, and those who held it declare that a weight of twenty-five or thirty pounds seemed pulling against them. When it could not get away it elongated itself to its utmost capacity just as a piece of elastic rubber would do, and wriggled and squirmed like a leech in a jar of water. A hat placed on the bed stood on the edge of its rim and pirouetted and danced around as if suspended by a string. This was witnessed by at least a dozen persons, several of them being ladies of high respectability.

On Saturday last, we are told, Esther felt the influence at work on her shoe string, and in another moment, though the string had been tied in a hard knot, the boot was unlaced. Later manifestations are in the nature of chair and table tippings. A few days ago the cradle in which the baby was lying was rocked for some time by invisible hands. An ordinary wooden chair on which Esther was sitting, with her feet on the rug, began to tip backwards and forwards, and she was rocked as if in a rocking-chair. Chairs follow her. She went to the street door, and a chair followed her the entire distance. She went into the pantry, closing the door after her, and when she came out every chair in the kitchen had piled itself against its neighbor at the door, as if seeking admittance. On Tuesday, when she was walking through the cellar, a basket of beets took a notion to follow her, and travelled actively over the floor, accommodating itself with great ease to any irregularities in the planking. Another curious thing, at times, is the action of the water in its pail when Esther is present. The water will be violently agitated into a whirlpool, and will foam like the waves of the tide.

Among the clergymen who have visited the house are Rev. Messrs. Temple, Jarvis, and Sutcliffe, of Amherst, and Rev. Edwin Clay, M.D., of Pugwash. The latter well-known gentleman is a biologist and is thoroughly versed in what is known as psychology and animal magnetism. He came under the impression that he could put an end to the disturbance, but after devoting the best part of two days to the effort he went away baffled, and wholly unable to account for the manifestations, of the existence of which he had such positive face to face proof.

The Yarmouth Herald, referring to the mystery, says: — "A similar case in Yarmouth about seventy years ago attracted much local attention, and has been familiarly known as the 'Rub-a-dub.' There are persons still living who remember the excitement it created at the time."

THE BINSTEAD HAUNTING

I will conclude my quoted cases with a somewhat painful and complex narrative, which ought, I think, to be considered when we are trying to form a conception as to the true significance of "haunting" sounds and sights.

Daily Examiner, Charlottetown, P.E.I., November 28, 1889

XIV — The following case, which we owe to the kindness of Mr. Wilfrid Ward (and of Lord Tennyson, for whom it was first committed to writing some years ago), is sent by Mrs. Pennée, of St. Anne de Beaupré, Quebec, daughter of the late Mr. William Ward (a Conservative M.P. for London), and sister of the late Rev. A.B. Ward, of Cambridge.

Weston Manor, Freshwater, Isle of Wight.
1884.
It was in the year 1856 that my husband took me to live at a house called Binstead, about five miles from Charlottetown, P.E. Island. It was a good-sized house, and at the back had been considerably extended to allow of extra offices, since there were about 200 acres of farm land around it, necessitating several resident farming men. Although forming part of the house, these premises could only be entered through the inner kitchen, as no wall had ever been broken down to form a door or passage from upstairs. Thus the farming men's sleeping rooms were

adjacent to those occupied by the family and visitors, although there was no communication through the upstairs corridor.

It was always in or near the sleeping apartment, immediately adjacent to the men's, that the apparition was seen, and as that was one of our spare bedrooms, it may have frequently been unperceived.

About 10 days after we had established ourselves at Binstead, we commenced hearing strange noises. For many weeks they were of very frequent occurrence, and were heard simultaneously in every part of the house, and always appeared to be in close proximity to each person. The noise was more like a rumbling which made the house vibrate, than like that produced by dragging a heavy body, of which one so often hears in ghost stories.

As spring came on we began to hear shrieks, which would grow fainter or louder, as if someone was being chased around the house, but always culminating in a volley of shrieks, sobs, moans, and half-uttered words, proceeding from beneath a tree that stood at a little distance from the dining-room window, and whose branches nearly touched the window of the bedroom I have mentioned.

It was in February (I think), 1857, that the first apparition came under my notice. Two ladies were sleeping in the bedroom. Of course, for that season of the year a fire had been lighted in the grate, and the fireplace really contained a grate and not an American substitute for one.

About 2 o'clock, Mrs. M. was awakened by a bright light which pervaded the room. She saw a woman standing by the fireplace. On her left arm was a young baby, and with her right hand she was stirring the ashes, over which she was slightly stooping.

Mrs. M. pushed Miss C. to awaken her, and just then the figure turned her face towards them, disclosing the features of quite a young woman with a singularly anxious pleading look upon her face. They took notice of a little check shawl which was crossed over her bosom. Miss C. had previously heard some tales concerning the house being haunted (which neither Mrs. M. nor I had ever heard), so jumping to the conclusion that she beheld a ghost, she screamed and pulled the bedclothes tightly over the heads of herself and her companion, so that the sequel of the ghost's proceedings is unknown.

The following spring I went home to England, and just before starting I had my own experience of seeing a ghost. I had temporarily established myself in the room, and one evening, finding my little daughter (now Mrs. Amyot) far from well, had her bed wheeled in beside mine that I might attend to her. About 12 o'clock I got up to give her some medicine, and was feeling for the matches when she called my attention to a brilliant light shining under the door. I exclaimed that it was her papa and threw open the door to admit him. I found myself face to face with a woman. She had a baby on her left arm, a check shawl crossed over her bosom, and all around her shone a bright pleasant light, whence emanating I could not say. Her look at me was one of entreaty — almost agonizing entreaty. She did not enter the room but moved across the staircase, vanishing into the opposite wall, exactly where the inner man-servant's room was situated.

Neither my daughter nor myself felt the slightest alarm; at the moment it appeared to be a matter of common occurrence. When Mr. Pennée came upstairs and I told him what we had seen, he examined the wall, the staircase, the passage, but found no traces of anything extraordinary. Nor did my dogs bark.

On my return from England in 1858 I was informed that "the creature had been carrying on," but it was the screams that had been the worst. However, Harry (a farm-servant) had had several visits but would tell no particulars. I never could get Harry to tell me much. He acknowledged that the woman had several times stood at the foot of his bed, but he would not tell me more. One night Harry had certainly been much disturbed in mind, and the other man heard voices and sobs. Nothing would ever induce Harry to let anyone share his room, and he was most careful to fasten his door before retiring. At the time, I attached no importance to "his ways," as we called them.

In the autumn of the following year, 1859, my connection with Binstead ceased, for we gave up the house and returned to Charlottetown.

I left Prince Edward Island in 1861, and went to Quebec. In 1877 I happened to return to the Island, and spent several months there. One day I was at the Bishop's residence, when the parish priest came in with a letter in his hand. He asked me about my residence at Binstead, and whether I could throw any light on the contents of his letter. It was from the wife of the then owner of Binstead, asking him to come out and try to deliver them from the ghost of a young woman with a baby in her arms, who had appeared several times.

After I went to live in Charlottetown, I became acquainted with the following facts, which seem to throw light on my ghost story.

The ground on which Binstead stood had been cleared, in about 1840, by a rich Englishman, who had built a very nice house. Getting tired of colonial life, he sold the property to a man whose name I forget, but whom I will call Pigott (that was like the name). He was a man of low tastes and immoral habits; but a capital farmer. It was he who added all the back wing of the house and made the necessary divisions, &c., for farming the land. He had two sisters in his service, the daughters of a labourer who lived in a regular hovel, about three miles nearer town. After a time each sister gave birth to a boy.

Very little can be learnt of the domestic arrangements, since Pigott bore so bad a name that the house was avoided by respectable people; but it is certain that one sister and one baby disappeared altogether, though when and how is a complete mystery.

When the other baby was between one and two years old, Pigott sold Binstead to an English gentleman named Fellowes, from whom we hired it, with the intention of eventually buying it. The other sister returned to her father's house, and leaving the baby with Mrs. Newbury, her mother, went to the States, and has never returned. Before leaving she would reveal nothing, except that the boy was her sister's, her own being dead. It was this very Harry Newbury that we had unwittingly engaged as a farm-servant. He came to bid me farewell a few months after I left Binstead, saying he would never return there. In 1877, I inquired about him, and found that he had never been seen since in Prince Edward Island.

In another letter dated September 24th, 1887, Mrs. Pennée adds:

Another fact has come to my notice. A young lady, then a child of from 5 to 10, remembers being afraid of sleeping alone when on a visit at Binstead on account of the screams she heard outside, and also the "woman with a baby," whom she saw passing through her room. Her experience goes back some 10 to 15 years before mine.

In a further letter, dated St. Anne de Beaupré, Quebec, January 23rd, 1889, Mrs. Pennée gives additional facts, as follows:

(1) Mrs. Pennée interviewed Father Boudreault, the priest sent for by the C. family to exorcise the house. Father B., however, was on his death-bed; and although he remembered the fact that he had been sent for to Binstead for this purpose, he could not recollect what had been told him as to apparitions, &c.
(2) Mrs. M., who first saw the figure, has gone to England, and cannot now be traced. Mrs. Pennée adds: — "The lady in question told several people that she saw a woman with a baby in her arms when she slept at Binstead; and, like myself, she noticed a frilled cap on the woman. The woman whose ghost we imagine this to be was an Irish woman, and perhaps you have noticed their love of wide frills in their head-gear."
(3) Mrs. Pennée revisited Binstead in 1888, and says, "The tree whence the screams started is cut down; the room where all saw the ghost is totally uninhabited; and Mrs. C. would not let us stay in it, and entreated us to talk no further on the subject. From the man we got out a little, but she followed us up very closely. He says that since the priest blessed the house a woman has been seen (or said to have been seen, he corrected himself) round the front entrance, and once at an upper window."

The list of cases cited in this and the previous paper, while insufficient (as I have already said) to compel conviction, is striking enough to plead for serious attention to a subject which will never be properly threshed out unless the interest taken in it assumes a scientific rather than an emotional form.

THE DAGG POLTERGEIST

A Disincarnated Being — The Clarendon Spirit Tells Who He Is to a Psychist — Voices from the Other World — A Sworn Report Concerning the Strange Doings at Dagg's House
Ottawa Free Press, November 25, 1889

The enterprise shown by the Free Press in despatching a reporter to personally enquire into the strange proceedings at the house of

George Dagg, a farmer residing at Clarendon Front, Pontiac County, has attracted general attention to that spirit-haunted locality, and the result has been a general rush of curiosity seekers to investigate these phenomena. Those who went could make nothing out of the matter and for the most part laughed at the whole affair and attributed the alleged supernatural occurrences to human agency. A correspondent apparently a past master in black art did explain the cause of the persecution of the Dagg family but in too vague a manner to satisfy the general public. It has remained therefore for Mr. Percy Woodcock, an adept in psychological matters, to act as the medium between the spirits, who, he claims, are the cause of all the trouble and an unbelieving public. That gentleman's adventures are little else than marvellous and the sworn testimony he exhibits seems to prove satisfactorily that there actually exist airy spirits beyond the ken of mortal eye. Mr. Woodcock, who is well known as an artist in Ottawa, Montreal, New York and Paris, spent three days with the Dagg family and certainly did not waste his time. The spirits "cottoned" to him at once, for he had hardly arrived at the house before an invisible inhabitant of the family woodshed addressed the artist as follows:— "I am the devil; and I'll have you in my clutches." Mr. Woodcock declined to be scared, and therefore the spirit called him opprobrious names.

A conversation then ensued between Mr. Woodcock, the voice and Mr. George Dagg who afterwards jointed them, lasting for five hours without a break. Mr. Woodcock took the position that he had to deal with an invisible personality, as real as though there in the flesh, and on this basis endeavored to shame him into better behavior and stop persecuting the Daggs who had admittedly done him (the voice) no harm. On the other hand the voice resisted for a long time, but finally seemed to yield to the expostulations of Mr. Woodcock and Mr. Dagg and agreed to cease the use of obscene language and finally admitted that it had been actuated solely by the spirit of mischief, of having fun, as it termed it, and had no ill will against anybody except Woodcock and the little girl Dinah, to whom he seemed to have a decided antipathy. Mr. Woodcock's later experiences are of the same remarkable nature. In order to convince the outside world that there was no humbug in the matter, he drew upon a "report" which seventeen responsible citizens of the neighborhood signed. This document sets forth that the curious proceedings treated of being on the 15th of September and were still in progress on the 17th November. The events chronicled are, briefly, that fires broke out spontaneously in different parts of the house,that stones were thrown by invisible hands through the window; that various household articles were thrown about by invisible agency; that a mouth organ was heard to be played and seen to move across the floor; that a rocking chair began rocking, that when the child Dinah is present (?), a deep gruff voice like that of an aged man had been heard at various times, both in the house and out doors, and when asked questions answered so as to be distinctly heard, showing that he is cognizant of all that has taken place, not only in Mr. Dagg's family but also in the families in the surrounding neighborhood; that he claims to be a disincarnated being who died twenty years ago, aged eighty years; that he gave his name to Mr. George Dagg and Mr. Willie Dagg, forbidding them to tell him; that this intelligence is able to make himself visible to Dinah, little Mary and Johnnie, who have seen him under different forms at different times, at one time as a tall, thin man with a cow's head, horns, tail, and cloven foot, at another time a big, black dog, and finally as a man with a beautiful face and long white hair, dressed in white, wearing a crown with stars on it.

The above document is signed by the following:— John Dagg, Portage du Fort, Que.; George Dagg, Portage du Fort, Que.; William Eddes, Radsford, Que.; William H. Dagg, Arthur Smart, Charles A. Dagg, Bruno Morrow, Portage du Fort; Benjamin Smart, William J. Dagg, Shawville, Que.; Robert J. Peever, Cobden, Ont.; R.H. Lockhart, John Fulford, Portage du Fort; George G. Hodgins, Richard E. Dagg, Shawville; George Blackwell, Haley's, Ont.; William Smart, John J. Dagg, Portage du Fort.

After Mr. Woodcock left on Sunday night the following extraordinary manifestation is said to have been given. The voice requested that some persons whom it named should be sent for. As these gentlemen were far away Rev. Mr. Bell, a Baptist clergyman, was persuaded to come. Mr. Bell read a chapter from the Bible, the voice accompanying him through it and occasionally going in advance of the clergyman. When they knelt to pray the voice responded. Mr. Bell prayed for the family whom he said had brought the trouble upon themselves by trampling the Bible underfoot, or words to that effect, and finally exorcised the spirit, commanding him in the name of the Saviour to depart, whereupon the spirit laughed and said it was all words, that Mr. Bell had better stick to photography. Mr. Bell left without directly speaking to the voice at any time.

Afterwards the voice sang a hymn in so beautiful a manner as to cause the women present to shed tears. On Monday morning Mr. Woodcock went over to the house again and whilst there the three children came rushing out of the house wild-eyed and fearfully excited, saying that they had seen a beautiful man dressed in white with gold things on his head and stars in it, and that the man spoke to them. The child Dinah said she heard the man say that Woodcock had said that he was not an angel, but that he would show that he was. Thereupon the apparition went up in the air in a blaze of fire and disappeared. This final transformation scene is supposed by Mr. Woodcock to be the last of the mysterious events at the Dagg mansion. It seems a pity that Mr. Woodcock's visit and the ghastly pranks should cease at the same time.

THE MACKENZIE RIVER GHOST

Roderick MacFarlane

On the fifteenth day of March 1853, Augustus Richard Peers, a fur trader and post manager in the service of the Hudson's Bay Company, departed his life at Fort McPherson, Peel's River, in the Mackenzie River District, Arctic America. Although he had occasionally complained of ill health, his death after a few days' sickness at the comparatively early age of thirty-three years was entirely unexpected. He was of Anglo-Irish origin, an able officer, much esteemed by his friends and popular among the Indians. During a residence of, I think, eleven years in that remote district, he had been stationed for two or three Outfit seasons at "Head-quarters," Fort Simpson, and afterwards at Forts Norman and McPherson. In 1849, Mr. Peers was married to the eldest daughter of the late Chief Trader John Bell of the Hudson's Bay Company. They had two children. In 1855 the widow remarried the late Alexander McKenzie, who succeeded Mr. Peers at Fort McPherson.

While a resident of both Norman and McPherson, the deceased had been heard to express a strong dislike, in the event of his death, that his bones should rest at either spot. Mr. Peers was thought to have made a holograph will some time previous to his demise; but if so, he must have mislaid or destroyed it, as no such document ever turned up.

Having entered the service of the Company in 1852, I was appointed to the Mackenzie River District the following year, and reached Fort Simpson five months after Mr. Peers's death, where I met his widow and infant children. In the autumn of 1859, at the urgent request of Mrs. McKenzie and her husband, it was decided that the long contemplated transfer of the remains of Mr. Peers from their place of interment at Peel's River to Fort Simpson on the Mackenzie, should be carried out that winter. Mr. Charles P. (now Chief Trader) Gaudet, then in charge of Fort McPherson, agreed to convey the body by dog train to my trade post at Fort Good Hope, a distance of three hundred miles, while I undertook to render it at its final destination, some five hundred miles further south.

Fort McPherson is situated about one degree north of the Arctic Circle. The soil in its neighbourhood is marshy, and frost is ever present at a shallow depth beneath the surface. On being exhumed by Mr. Gaudet, the body was found in much the same condition it had assumed shortly after its burial. It was then removed from the original coffin, and placed in a new and unnecessarily large coffin which, secured by a moose skin wrapper and lines on a Hudson's Bay dog sled or train, made it an extremely awkward and difficult load for men and dogs to haul and conduct over the rugged masses of tossed-up ice which annually occur at intervals along the mighty Mackenzie River, especially in the higher and more rapid portion of its course towards the northern ocean.

On the first day of March, 1860, Mr. Gaudet arrived at Good Hope and delivered up the body to my care, and I set out for Fort Simpson. The coffin was fixed on one team or train of three dogs conducted by an Iroquois Indian from Caughnawaga, near Montreal, named Michel Thomas (since deceased), while the second train carried our bedding, voyaging utensils and provisions. I myself led the march on snowshoes, and after seven days of very hard and trying labour, owing to the unusual depth of the snow and much rugged ice, the first two hundred miles of our journey to the nearest point (Fort Norman) from Good Hope, was successfully accomplished. At this place Mr. Nicol Taylor (now deceased) strongly pointed out that unless the coffin was removed, and the body properly secured on the train, it would be almost impossible to travel over the vast masses of tossed-up ice which were sure to be encountered at certain points between here and Fort Simpson. As I had previously gone twice over the ground in winter, and had already had some experience of bourdions, I acted on his advice, and we had subsequently good reason for congratulation on having done so.

After one day's rest at Norman, we started on the last and longest portion of the journey. There was no intervening station at that time, and we met few Indians. The Iroquois Thomas remained with the body train. The baggage train and man from Good Hope were exchanged at Norman for fresh animals and a new driver named Michel Iroquois. Mr. Taylor also assisted me in beating the track for the party, he having volunteered to accompany the remains of his former master and friend, Mr. Peers.

A full description of winter travelling in this country may be learned from the pages of Franklin, Back, Richardson and Butler. Here it may be briefly stated that we got under way by four o'clock in the morning; dined at some convenient spot about noon, and after an hour's rest, resumed our march until sunset, when we laid up for the night, generally in a pine bluff on the top or close to the immediate bank of the river. Clearing away the snow to the ground for a space of about ten feet square, cutting and carrying pine brush for carpeting the camp and collecting firewood for cooking and warming purposes, usually occupied us for about an hour. Another hour would see supper over and the dogs fed, and by the end of the next sixty or more minutes, most of the party would be sound asleep. Except on two occasions to be presently mentioned, the train carrying the body of the deceased was invariably hauled up and placed for the night in the immediate rear of our encampment, and except also on the first of the said occasions, our dogs never exhibited any desire to get at same, nor did they seem in the slightest degree affected by its presence in our midst.

About sunset on the fifteenth day of March, 1860, the seventh anniversary of poor Peers's death, we were obliged to encamp at a short distance from Roche qui trempe a l'eau, the rock by the riverside of Sir Alexander Mackenzie, as there was no better place within reach. The banks here were high, rocky and steep, and we had to leave both trains on the ice; we experienced much difficulty in scrambling up the bank with our axes, snowshoes, bedding and provisions for supper and breakfast. The dogs were unharnessed and remained below, while the weather was calm and comparatively fine and mild. The bank rose about thirty feet to the summit where, on a shelving flat some thirty feet beyond, we selected a position for the night. All hands then set about making the camp, cutting and carrying the requisite supply of pine brush and firewood.

After being thus busily employed for ten or twelve minutes, the dogs began to bark and we at once concluded that Indians were approaching us, as this was a part of the river where a few were frequently met with. We, however, continued our work, the dogs still barking, though not so loudly or fiercely as they usually do under similar circumstances. Neither the dogs nor sleds were visible from the camp, but only from the summit of the river bank. While talking with Mr. Taylor about the expected Indians, we all distinctly heard the word "March!" (I may remark that French terms are almost universally applied to hauling dogs and their work in the Northwest Territories of Canada.) It seemed to have been uttered by someone at the foot of the bank who wished to drive away the dogs in his path, and we all left off work in order to see who the stranger was; but as no one appeared in sight, Michel Thomas and myself proceeded to the aforesaid summit, where, to our astonishment, no man was visible, while the dogs were seen surrounding the body train at a distance of several feet, and still apparently excited at something. We had to call them repeatedly before they gave up barking, but after a few minutes they desisted and then somehow managed to ascend the bank to our encampment, where they remained perfectly quiet for the night, and thereafter continued as indifferent as before in respect to the deceased's body.

It struck me at the time I heard it that the word marche was enunciated in a clearer manner than I had ever before known an Indian to do so, as they seldom get beyond a mashe or masse pronunciation of the term.

On the eighteenth day of March we were compelled to travel two hours after dark in order to find a suitable encampment, and although we discovered a tolerably good place near the head of a large island on the Mackenzie, yet it was not an easy matter to ascend a perpendicular bank of some twelve feet in height. The baggage train being now rather light, by tying a line to the foremost dog, we managed to drag it and them to the top. The same plan answered with the dogs of the body train; but we considered it beyond our power to get it up, and we were therefore reluctantly obliged to leave it below. After cutting a trail through thick willows for about thirty or forty yards, we reached the edge of a dense forest of small spruce, where we camped. The customary operations were at once attended to, and when most of the work was over I turned up with some firewood from a distance where I had been collecting a lot for the night.

Mr. Taylor then asked me if I had heard a very loud call or yell twice repeated from the direction of the river.

I said, "No," as my cap ear protectors were closely tied down owing to the cold wind, and the thicket very dense.

The two Iroquois corroborated Mr. Taylor's statement, but to settle the matter and find out if any Indian had followed our tracks, we all proceeded to the bank, where nothing could be seen or heard, and we at once decided on having the body train hauled up by sheer force, and it proved a tough job to do so.

We remembered our experience of the fifteenth of March, and when we set out early next morning we had reason to congratulate ourselves on taking this trouble, as on reaching the spot from which we had removed the body train, we discovered that a carcajou or wolverine had been there during the night. To those who know the power of this destructive animal, I need not say that he would have played havoc with the aforesaid remains.

Fort Simpson was at length reached without a recurrence of anything of an unusual nature, in the forenoon of the twenty-first of March, and the body was duly buried in the adjacent graveyard on the twenty-third of that month. Shortly after my arrival, Mr. Taylor and I recounted everything to Chief Trader Bernard R. Ross (since deceased), the district manager, who had been an intimate friend and countryman of Mr. Peers. Mr. Ross was a good mimic and had an excellent memory. He was asked to utter the word *marché* in the voice of the deceased, and while I at once recognized the tone as similar to that heard by us at our encampment of the fifteenth of March, Mr. Taylor had no doubt whatever on the subject.

During my stay at Fort Simpson, I occupied a shakedown bed in the same room with Mr. Ross, and at a distance from his of some eight or ten feet. On the first or second night after retiring and extinguishing the candle light, while conversing on the subject of the rather remarkable occurrences narrated herein (including the supposed disappearance of his will) relating to the deceased, I became over poweringly conscious of what struck me then and since to have been the spiritual or supernatural presence of the late Mr. Peers. The feeling, however, came on so very suddenly and scaringly that I instantly covered my face with the blanket and remained speechless. After an interval of perhaps only a few seconds Mr. Ross (whose voice had also ceased) in a somewhat excited tone asked me if I had experienced a very peculiar sensation. I answered that I had and described the feeling, which he assured me agreed exactly with what he himself had just undergone. I know from experience what nightmare is; but while it is most unlikely that two individuals who were carrying on a conversation in which they felt a deep interest should be thus attacked simultaneously, it may be stated that neither of us had partaken of any wines, spirits or anything else which could have brought on a nightmare.

I leave it to others, if they can, to give a reasonable account or explanation of the facts I have here stated; but if it be assumed as an axiom that the spirits of some of the dead are occasionally permitted to revisit former scenes and to take more or less interest in their discarded bodies, then from what we have incidentally learned of the late Mr. Peers's sentiments in respect to the final disposition of his remains, what other or more natural course would the spirit of such a man be expected to take with the view of preventing any unnecessary desecration of them than that apparently adopted on the nights of the fifteenth and eighteenth of March, 1860?

From the position of our camp of the fifteenth of March, it may be taken for granted that it was almost impossible to have hauled the body train up such a steep and rugged rocky bank. Dogs are invariably hungry at the end of a long day's travel and, as the weather was fine that day, they may have scented the still fresh and perfect remains, and probably desired to get at them, while their barking at and position around the sled would, on any other hypothesis, be at least equally strange and unaccountable. Of course, there was danger from wolves and wolverines, but it is presumed that spirits know more than mortals. On the night of March eighteen, however, although the bank was very difficult of ascent (to get up one had first to raise and push a man till he laid hold of the root of a stout willow by which he hoisted himself to the top, and then threw us a line which aided the rest) it was not insurmountable; and as a most vicious and destructive animal actually visited the spot where we intended leaving the body train for the night, but for the calls and yells referred to, I again ask what other course than that mentioned would any man or spirit possessed of future knowledge be likely to take? And as to the extraordinary feeling experienced by Mr. Ross and myself at the moment when we were talking about the deceased and his supposed will, if it be possible for spirits to communicate with mortals, might this not have arisen (as I actually felt at the time) from a desire on his part to convey some information to us who evinced so deep an interest in the matter but which, from losing our presence of mind, we missed the opportunity of ascertaining?

The foregoing facts made so indelible an impression on my mind that I firmly believe that my present account of them does not in any material point differ from what I communicated to Mr. Ross at the time, and repeatedly since to others. I also distinctly remember the occasion on which I gave similar details to General Sir William F. (then Captain) Butler, K.C.B. It was at Green Lake post, North-West Territory, in the month of February 1873. Captain Butler soon after proceeded to Ashanti, where he experienced a very severe attack of illness, and he, moreover, wrote me that he had taken poetical licence with my narrative, and this will naturally account for the discrepancies between the statements I have given in this paper and his story of same in *Good Words* for 1877.

8

SUMMONING THE SPIRITS

Ghosts and spirits flit across the pages of history, mysteriously appearing and disappearing before the eyes of the perplexed public. They come and go during times of crisis; they seem to cluster around historic sites.

Spirits certainly prefer some sites to others. Edinburgh Castle has been a favoured haunt over the centuries, and so for more than a century was Borley Rectory before it burned to the ground in 1939. In Canada, the spirits favour no special sites. Having made that statement, I should perhaps qualify it. There are no regularly haunted sites in Canada, where you can go with the expectation that you will behold a ghost or a spirit, but there are some places of visions. Throughout the nineteenth century, Roman Catholics made pilgrimages to the shrine of Sainte-Anne-de-Beaupré outside Quebec City, where there are reports of Marian visions, apparitions of the Blessed Virgin Mary, as well as attestations to "miracle cures." So even in Canada the spirits come and go as they see fit.

Is it possible to summon a spirit? In the past, witches and warlocks were reputed to possess a special power or ability to invoke the denizens of the spirit world and command them to do their bidding. The possession of this power over the spirits was based on family history (being the seventh son of a seventh son, etc.), initiation (in a coven), study and discipline, or divine intervention. Self-styled necromancers, self-proclaimed wiccans, and so-called black magicians all maintain they have such powers, commonly known as the Black Arts.

Is it possible to exorcise a spirit? The power to banish spirits has been claimed by witches and warlocks, and also by priests and ministers of the Christian denominations employing the power of the Holy Writ. The Rite of Exorcism may be found in the pages at the end of the *Anglican Book of Common Prayer*. When such powers are used, they are to be used sparingly, with the special dispensation of the bishop of the diocese. The rite of exorcism is performed from time to time but seldom if at all in public.

Before the middle of the nineteenth century, communication with the spirit world was non-recurrent, sporadic, indirect, one-way, with the ghost or spirit putting in an appearance and standing, floating, gliding, passing through closed doors or walls, but saying nothing. When confronted by human beings, most ghosts are notably mute. It is as if they having nothing at all to say, their mere presence saying what has to be said. They have nothing to say to us; their visage is their message.

The modern Spiritualist Movement was born in the 1850s and flourished in Canada and elsewhere for over a century. During their seances, spiritualists claimed the power to contact specific spirits of the dead: fathers, mothers, sons, daughter, grandfathers, grandmothers, aunts, uncles, nieces, nephews, "discarnate entities" all. Contact was sometimes hampered by the presence of "lying spirits," discombobulated entities, mindless energies, which interfered with the transmission. They simply got in the way like that static that is heard interfering with long-distance radio reception.

Spiritualism as a movement may well be a thing of the past, but it is wise to remember that in the country's major cities there are spiritualist churches with active congregations. The practice of communication with spirits, undergoing a name change in the 1960s, was reborn as *channelling*. The old-fashioned *spirit medium* is now the new-fashioned *channeller*. The word *seance* is no longer used; instead the word *session* is employed to describe a sitting during which, once summoned, the spirit of a 200,000-year-old entity may answers the petitioner's questions with bewildering accounts of what life was like so long ago. This used to be called *direct-voice mediumship*. Now it is known as *channelling*.

Next to a New Age channeller like Shirley MacLaine, the local fortune-teller (Madame Delia perhaps) is an unassuming and unglamorous creature, a Gypsy woman maybe, who reads palms, crystal balls, Tarot cards, auras, whatever. Most fortune-tellers are women, for no known reason, and she may work out of her house or out of a store-front parlour. Her rates are posted. Satisfaction is guaranteed. All questions about Love, Life, Health, and Money are answered with 100 percent accuracy, guaranteed.

By the end of the nineteenth century, in Canada as in the rest of the Western world, the world of the spirits had become a democratic one. These days the spirits of the dead and the intelligencies of entities that were never born may now and then be summoned and questioned at will — to the satisfaction of all.

SPIRIT RAPPINGS

From the Halifax Christian Messenger — By The Rev. S.T. Rand
The Islander, Charlottetown, P.E.I., September 23, 1853

I have lately had an opportunity of witnessing those mysterious operations, which have made so much noise in the world, called "Spirit Rappings." I did not "go to see" them. I paid nothing for the sight, and as I ascertained several facts respecting the matter which may be of service to the public, in guarding them against imposition, I have considered it my duty to make them known.

I lately read what I considered a very good article upon the subject in the *Christian Visitor*. I became satisfied that to consult a "medium" as an oracle is decidedly wrong, and felt strongly inclined to attribute the whole thing to Satanic agency. On the former point my views are fully confirmed. I have not ascertained beyond a question, that not the slightest dependence can be placed upon those responses, beyond what is known by some of the parties in contact with the operators. It can tell you all that you know, and it can tell you nothing more. By innumerable experiments, made by an intelligent friend of mine, himself a powerful medium, he has ascertained that the responses are entirely controlled by those spirits in the room that still inhabit houses of clay. Many experiments illustrative of this important fact, I not only saw but participated in. Without being a medium, and being declared by the "spirit" incapable of that dignity, I have myself called him forth to do my biddings, and in spite of the mediums made him give just such answers as I chose. But I had better pursue something like method in my statement.

1. It is not deception, nor sleight of hand on the part of the operators. On this head I am perfectly satisfied. I was well acquainted with the operators on the occasion referred to. My own brother and my own nieces composed the party. I know they would not attempt to impose upon me. Nor could they have succeeded had they been so disposed. I put questions to the table myself, and spoke in a language which no one

in the room understood but myself. They knew nothing of the questions put, and consequently could not have known what answers to give. Yet were the answers at such times all appropriate and correct.

2. It is something very mysterious. Several persons sit around a table with their hands upon it. In a few minutes one asks, "Are there any spirits present? If there are, rap." A rap is distinctly heard. "Rap again," says another. The rap is repeated. "Rap three times." "Rap, rap, rap," is distinctly heard. There is a peculiarity about the sound. It appeared more like the pattering of rain than anything else I could think of.

"Now then," says one of the party, "will you answer a few questions. If you will, tip the table towards me." The obsequious table tips in the direction indicated. "Is the spirit of King William the third present? If he is, let the table rise up and stand upon two legs." The table rises — the laws of gravity being to all appearance completely set at defiance — and stands on two feet. "Now then will your majesty show us how your majesty's horse leaped upon the banks of the Boyne?" Instantly the table rises on its "hind legs" and leaps "upward and onward," giving no bad representation of the picture of the event, so commonly seen, and of which every individual at the table and in the room are thinking at the moment.

This dignified question and answer will give some idea of the mode of conversing with the supposed spirits of the departed. You may obtain names and numbers, and the answers, "Yes" and "no," in several ways. "Tell me," said I, "my age." At the bidding of one of the mediums, the table rocked from side to side, striking the floor with its feet forty-three times. "Now spell the name of my wife." "Now," says the medium, "when I mention the first letter of aunt's name, tip towards me." She then began the right one, *J*, when the table tipped as ordered. The process was repeated, and the letters were indicated which correctly spelled the name *Jane*.

The table would cut up all sorts of pranks and shines at the bidding of the "mediums." I saw it stamp and dash about as if in anger. I saw it "shake its head," for a decided "no!" I saw it rise up and balance momentarily on one leg, and all this simply at the bidding of the operators, whose hands were laid gently upon the top of it. I call this mysterious. I cannot explain it.

3. But if I am perfectly satisfied that there is no magic, nor "satanic agency" in the matter, I am just as confident that the "spirits of the departed" have nothing to do with it whatever. And I *know* that it cannot be depended on as an oracle, to inform us what will happen hereafter, or what has happened already. What we know to be true it can tell us with wonderful precision. Beyond that boundary line it cannot conduct us. All is uncertainty, contradictory, bungling, guess-work. It may hit right, just as we may hit right in our surmises, and in the judgements which we may form on different subjects. But this is all. Its answers will turn out wrong in so many instances, that no dependence can be placed upon it.

I must advance proof of this point. If it be true then, the folly and wickedness of appealing to the "spirit rappings" for a knowledge of the other world, or the truth of Religious doctrines is manifest. In advancing this proof I shall mention facts which go at the same time to confirm the position that the whole thing is conducted and controlled by the minds and wills of the operators, and those other embodied spirits who are present at the time.

1. Argument first. I myself repeatedly received answers which I knew to be untrue. The following questions were put, my hands not on the table: "Have I any money about me?" The answer was correct, affirmatively. "Now then what is it? I have but one kind, is it silver, paper or gold?" I was first told that it was silver. But this was not true. So it had to be "guess again." Accordingly I was assured that it was paper. Wrong again. Try once more, for I had stated that it was not copper. So it very correctly informed me the third time that it was gold. But what fool could not have done that? Surely a "spirit," be he bad or be he good, ought to have been able to get at my pocket and peep into my purse somehow, and find out that there were two sovereigns in it. Manifestly if he had to guess three times between silver, paper and gold, in so plain a case as that, he could not be trusted in the matter of more intricacy. But it was evident that the operators

were "guessing," and that the answer each time was just what they were thinking of.

2. I was informed — proof second — that questions of the following import are often proposed. "How many children have I?" Answer correct. "How many of them are sons?" Answer correct again. "Now then, what will the next one be?" to this "important" question the "spirit" has only to guess between "two," and so occasionally hits right, but it just as often hits wrong.

I ask again of what manner of service can the "Spirit rappings" be, as an "oracle," if I cannot be informed with absolute certainty respecting an event of that kind, which is upon the eve of accomplishment? But I was assured by the mediums themselves, that answers to such enquiries were as likely to prove false as true.

Here then are the facts of the case. The enquirer knows how many children he has. He knows too how many are boys and how many are girls. His mind is upon this, and his own mind controls the answer. Here is a mystery — he feels it to be so — and he is convinced that there is no deception on the part of the operators; and he naturally enough concludes that if the spirit can tell him so correctly what he knows, it can tell him what he does not know. But here he is mistaken, and my brother assured me that he invariably found the answers were in accordance with what was uppermost in the mind of the enquirer, or of the individual whose mind happened to control the table. Sometimes a majority seems to carry the point. For instance, if a majority of the minds present decide in favor of the Roman Catholics, or Universalists, the spirit is sure to say they are right. If they be Baptists, then the Baptists are said to be right. I heard this question put in a variety of forms, but the answer was invariably that the Baptists are in the right. Nor would the spirit admit that they were in an error, not even in the smallest matters. We happened to be, the most of us, Baptists in sentiment. But one of the mediums was a Methodist, and she assured us that when "they" had a majority present, the "spirits" would stand up as stoutly as the Methodists.

Now grant me, either that our religious controversies are

continued as strenuously as ever in the other world, or that it is the work of "embodied" spirits, and not that of the "departed."

But, finally, I could control the "thing"— whatever it be — myself, and make it give just such answers as I choose, whether true or false. I did this repeatedly. On one occasion I set them to spell the name of a friend. While, with my own hands upon the table, I would fix my thoughts upon the proper letter, the table would rise very correctly as soon as the "medium" had, in going over the alphabet, reached that letter. In this way the first name was correctly obtained. "That will do," said I. But the curiosity of my young friends was now excited, and they wished to know the other name. And they said, "We will find out in spite of you." "Very well," said I, "go on." But I fixed my mind upon the wrong letter, and "rap" would go the table, as soon as this letter was reached. The result was, that they could not find out the name, any way they could fix it. So I was informed that it invariably occurred, when an individual enquired the number of his own age, or that of another, if we were laboring under a mistake at the time, the same mistake would be made by the "spirit" with whom he was conversing.

Now, I ask, is it not absurd to suppose that because I have made a mistake of ten years in the age of my grandmother at the time of her death, she herself too must have forgotten, and that she cannot rectify the mistake, until, by dint of reckoning and pencilling, I have myself ascertained the correct number? Verily if we have got to cipher out their ages for the "rapping spirits," before they can tell us how old they are, they must be miserably qualified to instruct us. My brother assured me that just such an event as this he had known to occur.

So when stolen property is enquired after. "Did so-and-so steal my wheat?" asks a Frenchman. "Yes." "Well I thought so." "Count off the number of pecks he took." "Thump, thump, thump," goes the table. "Ah! just three pecks! well I thought it was about that."

Some lady had lost her silver spoons, or some article of wearing apparel, and she very strongly suspected that one of the female servants had taken the article. The spirits were appealed to for information. The "medium" of course knew nothing of the affair. He therefore left the whole "control" to the lady. She enquired, "Have I lost anything?" The answer was in the affirmative. "What is it? When the article is mentioned let the table tip." Various articles were run over, and as soon as the "spoons" are mentioned, the table tips. "Have they been stolen?" The answer in the affirmative. "By one of the servants?" "Yes." "Now when the name of the servant is mentioned, let the table tip." Several names are mentioned, and as soon as the suspected person's name is uttered, the table moves as directed. Now it might so happen that the poor girl suspected of taking the spoons, &c., might have taken them; but if it be the fact that the answer comes, not according to what is true, in the case, but according to what the enquirer, or some other person present, supposes to be true, then it is certain that its answers are not to be confided in, and every one must see how wicked and cruel it would be to fix a crime upon any one upon such testimony. And yet how easily might an unprincipled "medium" use this power for evil purposes! This is not all. The mediums themselves may be deceived, and so be innocent "mediums of mischief." My brother assures me that it was not until after repeated experiments, and cool, careful investigation, that he became satisfied that the answers come out invariably in accordance with the knowledge or belief of some person or persons in connection with the table.

In conclusion I would just observe, that I cannot offer any explanations respecting the really mysterious part of the affair. I cannot tell — I believe no one pretends to tell — how mind controls matter in any case. I know not why, nor how, my hand or foot rises at the bidding of my will, any more than I do know the table rises by being commanded. I have many a time explained to my friends the working of the "Electric Telegraph," so far as to convince them that it is not the work of the devil. But I believe no one yet pretends to know why electricity magnetizes iron, nor what either electricity or magnetism is. The time, however, has gone by when intelligent men were wont to ascribe every new phenomenon to supernatural agency. Investigation, cool continued, and extending to the collection of as many facts as possible, is now the course pursued. No doubt mischief has been done by the "Rappings." But what has not been made an instrument of evil? one might ask. Eclipses, comets, earthquakes, and lightning, have frightened people out of their wits. They are natural phenomenon notwithstanding. At all events, the epithet "religious," so far as I can see, may as properly be associated with the "Telegraph" as with the "raps."

SPIRIT-RAPPINGS

The Islander, Charlottetown, P.E.I., October 14, 1853

We intended to have reviewed the Rev. Mr. Rand's letter on this subject, about the time it was copied into the *Islander*, but had to postpone it for more pressing matter. The facts which came under Mr. Rand's personal observation we, of course, receive implicitly; and in deducing opposite conclusions therefrom, our enquiry shall be conducted with the courtesy due to a gentleman, and especially a clergyman, himself engaged in the investigation of truth.

What has been called "spirit-rapping" originated in the States a few years ago, and bore, from the first, very strong traces of imposture. Questions put regarding the souls of the departed were answered by two or three raps on a table, and hence the designation of the delusion. Our space will not permit us to follow Mr. Rand through all his long communication, and we shall, therefore, briefly remark that he does not attribute the rappings to spiritual agency, but to some occult principle which produces answers in accordance with the knowledge, or belief, at the time existing in the mind of the querist. The table, moreover, has got from rapping or "tipping" sideways in answer, and even elevating itself on two or three feet at the word of command. How those tabular motions were effected we do not pretend to say, but we have read that a respectable mechanic in New York revealed that he had been applied to, to construct tables with the requisite machinery to produce similar results, and that he had manufactured them accordingly.

We do not think Mr. Rand's example, that he could control the answer of "the thing," from the belief, or imagination, existing in the mind, at the time, very satisfactory, or happy. He requested the name of a friend to be spelled, and the table correctly gave a rap, when the "medium," or showman, as he may be called, in repeating the alphabet, came to the right letter. In this way the first name was correctly spelled; and it must be admitted the guess was a good one. But in spelling the second name, says Mr. Rand, "I fixed my mind on the wrong letter," and the rappings were wrong too. But here Mr. Rand commits an inadvertence himself. Knowing the name of his friend, and how it should be spelled, it was not possible for him to think, or imagine, that it was spelled with other letters, unless memory had deserted her seat, and hence the example adduced proving too much, proves nothing. When that blunder was perpetrated by the "medium," Mr. R's hands were on the table, but the blundering was as bad, or worse, as it happened, when they were off. In the latter position he requested to be informed what sort of money he had in his pocket, whether gold, silver, or paper, and it was only at the third trial, when further error was impossible, that the answer was correct. What childish trifling is this! But if the intelligence of one mind can flow into another by mere volition, where shall we stop? When we find an ignorant "medium" thus unfolding some of the most obtruse and recondite problems in mathematics, we may then consider the subject worthy of serious attention, but not until then. Again, when an innocent man is likely to be condemned on circumstantial evidence, for a capital offence, does not his whole soul yearn, with a yearning unknown to the trifles under review, to impress his knowledge on the minds of the jury, but ineffectually; and ineffectually we maintain it will be, though they all be "in communication" around a table.

Mr. Rand remarks: — "I cannot tell — I believe no one pretends to tell — how mind controls matter in any case. I know not why, nor how my hand or foot rises at the bidding of my will, any more than I do know the table rises by being commanded." It is true we know no more how the will operates to give motion to the muscles which move the limbs, when in a healthy state, than we do know an idea is formed on the brain, or any other of the first principles of the Great Architect of nature; but the cases are not analogous. It is true that Mr. Rand believes there is no sleight-of-hand or jugglery in the motion of the table, but it is both possible and probable that he is mistaken. Like the transfer of knowledge discussed above, the believers in table turning, or tipping, prove, or allege, too much. If a chain of communication be formed round a table by the junction of hands laid thereupon, and if no muscular force be exerted, the influence will be equal throughout, and the table motionless. But if muscular pressure be greater at one part than another some tables of ordinary enough construction will "tip" to that side. But a parallel difficulty to the imparting of knowledge meets us in those tabular motions. If the human will alone can overcome the force of gravitation over inert matter, even to the weight of a single grain, where shall, where can we stop in the ascending scale? But a very slight illustration will satisfy every reasonable man that the power of the human will to produce motion in the human body is very limited, and absolutely impotent beyond its organization. The mechanism of the body is precisely adapted to produce motion, but if that mechanism be out of order, motion will be suspended, let the individual will it ever so heartily. The human fore-arm, as every body knows, is of considerable breadth, and formed of two bones which afford ample space for the development of the muscles, or cords, which move the hand and fingers. But if those bones be broken, the most earnest will of the patient cannot move a hand or finger though the muscles and nerves which connect them with the system be in their place. And are we to be seriously told that the will, which cannot move its own little finger, can move a mass of inert matter exterior to the body, be it a table or a house, for the mystery, or the miracle, is not one whit greater in the one case than in the other.

Mr. Rand concludes by likening "the thing" to the mystery of electricity or magnetism, but the case is not in point. A great variety of facts in natural philosophy, apart from first principles, are not yet understood; but every investigation of table-tipping from the mere operation of the will, precludes it from the possibility of being a fact at all. Electricity and magnetism are probably only light in the peculiar state of chemical combination, and if they be, the laws of that combination, we may rest assured, will yet be detected; but the motion of the table cannot be referred to electricity.

The Acadian Recorder endorses the view taken by Mr. Rand, and positively affirms that "the ideas and thoughts passing through the mind of a thinking being are actually communicated to a foreign body, THE WOODEN TABLE!" In that event, the table must have a soul, too. The Recorder beats the Hindoo mythology hollow. It only inculcates the transmigration of souls from one animal to another, but the Recorder extends it to wood, metal or rope. It asks triumphantly if mesmerism, clairvoyance or ventriloquism be understood. Clairvoyance, or the alleged faculty of seeing things at a distance, has been completely falsified in the case of the most celebrated operators in England, in their visions and predictions of Sir John Franklin. Mesmerism is simply the effect of the imagination, and as it will blanch the hair, unsettle the brain, and arrest the current of life, we shall not attempt to prescribe limits to its effects over the body which enshrines the mind; but where we see results produced which we know cannot proceed from imagination, we may fairly suspect a confederacy to practice deception. Dr. Franklin fortunately happened to be in Paris when the sensation caused by Dr. Mesmer was at its height. The mania seemed of sufficient importance for the Government to appoint commissioners to investigate the delusion: and Franklin was requested to accompany them. A man was introduced who had been previously mesmerized; he was carefully blindfolded, and Mesmer turned out of the apartment. The Commissioners and Franklin retired to a distant part of the room to watch the conduct of the "medium." He, thinking that Mesmer was operating upon him, shortly went through all the phenomena of mesmerism from the effects of the imagination alone. On the Report of the Commissioners, those exhibitions were prohibited, as Franklin thought improperly, because, as he said, if imagination originated some diseases it might cure others.

Ventriloquism, which is classed with the other assumed mysteries, can be more definitely settled. The word is of Latin derivation and signifies speaking from, or by means of, the belly. But the word is a complete misnomer, and serves no other purpose but to mystify the art. Ventriloquism is spoken by the mouth, but the peculiar articulation can only be acquired after severe study and practice, and even then few persons possess organs of speech well adapted to its perfect utterance; but ventriloquists keep their own secret. The ear is an indifferent judge of the direction of souls, and when it can seeks assistance from the eye; for the eye seeing the lips firmly closed, in ventriloquism, is itself deceived, and instead of assisting, powerfully deceives the ear. Now, as the voice of a ventriloquist may seem to proceed from any part of a room, can we be sure that those spirit-rappings are not produced by ventriloquism! Mr. Rand says the sound is peculiar, and so it should on that hypothesis.

Mr. Rand is satisfied that "it is not deception, nor sleight of hand on the part of the operators." This is merely matter of opinion, and some sleight of hand tricks are so dexterously executed as to throw the miserable and clumsy exhibition of table-tipping completely into the shade. In confirmation of that assertion we might quote examples innumerable, but must confine ourselves to one illustration in which both ear and eye were incomparably better deceived, but being exhibited as a juggle, was received as such, without a pseudo-philosophy endeavouring to elevate the deception into something almost miraculous. The case occurred in India a few years ago; and the narrative, which some of our readers may recollect, was published by an eye-witness, and was so incomprehensible that we would have considered it a romance, had Mr. McKenzie, lately of New London, not had then a brother, an officer in the army, serving in India, who was present, and wrote his brother a detail of the juggle quite confirmatory of the published account.

A Juggler, accompanied by a little girl, about eight or ten years of age, made his appearance in the barrack-yard, and proposed exhibiting his art for the amusement of the officers and men. Leave being granted, he prudently, as matters turned out, requested a guard for his protection. This being furnished, and an area cleared on the ground trampled hard by the daily parade of the troops, the juggler was left to the practice of his art. It is obvious that the nature of the ground prohibited even the idea of any subterranean communication. He was provided with a long wicker basket, or hamper, open at one end, which he dropped over the child, to shield her completely from the view of the spectators. He and the little girl entered into conversation, which gradually seemed to excite angry feelings in the mind of the conjuror. They at last became so ungovernable that he threatened her life, for which the child implored unavailingly. He twice passed a sword through the hamper, and twice drew it forth covered with blood. The screams of the child subsided into dying moans, until all was hushed in the silence of death. At this the Regiment, which was an Irish one, manifested so strong an intention of inflicting summary justice on the supposed murderer, that in great alarm for his safety, he hastily raised the hamper, and to the astonishment and consternation of the spectators, there was under it neither blood nor child. No sooner was it raised than she pressed through the ring, into the area, where stood the juggler, and threw herself affectionately into his arms.

Talk of your "Table-tipping!" Faugh!

TABLE MOVING IN TORONTO

Newfoundland Express, St. John's, Nfld., November 12, 1853

The phenomenon of table moving was witnessed by the writer, in this city, the other night. A description of the operation may interest the curious who may not have had an opportunity of witnessing a like performance themselves. The table selected was a common dressing table, of black walnut, about three feet and a half in length and eighteen inches wide. Its weight would be about 30 lbs. The four feet were placed in glass tumblers. Eight persons seated themselves round the table; taking no care either to insulate themselves or the table. They placed the palms of their hands on the surface of the table; but their fingers did not form an actual connection, the nearest hands being often as far as an inch apart, and sometimes more. A good deal of scepticism was expressed by at least one-half the operators; but one or two who had witnessed the success of previous experiments, expressed a confident conviction that the operation would be successful. One of the operators took his hands off the table several times; and by this means caused some delay in the motion. About three-quarters of an hour had elapsed and there was no visible motion of the table. "I don't believe it will move a bit," one would say; "it's a humbug," another would respond, till at least half the operators had given vent to their scepticism in one form or another. About this time one of the eight, who had witnessed the success of a similar operation before, got down on his knees, and to the great amusement of the company, began to say,— addressing the table,— "rise up on the south-east corner;" repeating his instructions very frequently. In a short time the table began to follow his directions; and the corner rose up so far as to allow the tumbler [to be] taken away. Subsequently the table followed the instructions to rise on the south or the north side, as desired; it also rose on one leg and twirled round the room, the operators going with it and keeping their fingers on the surface. Several questions were asked, and the table instructed to reply by rising up on one side and descending with its two feet rapidly on the ground. Some of the questions and answers were:

"How many apples are there in the basket — on the table? — a rap for every apple."

The table rose on one side and struck its feet against the ground eleven times. The apples were counted and found to be eleven.

"How many pictures and daguerreotypes are there in the room? — a rap for every one."

The number was rapped out correctly; the raps being given at about the rate of one every second.

"How many buttons has Mr.— on his vest? — a rap for every one."

Four raps; pocket examined, and found to contain only one copper.

"How many chairs are there in the room?"

The answer gave one below the actual number.

"How old is Mrs.— ?"

Raps 27; the right answer.

"How old is Mr.— ?"

Raps 32; the right number. They were also right in two or three other cases of ages.

"How old," asked one of the party, "was my mother's father when he died? — five years for every rap."

Fifteen raps were made, at about the rate of one every second; but the number was deficient by 20.

A great many questions were asked; and the table invariably

lifted two legs from the ground to answer them; and it happened that more than half the answers were correct. The first idea that struck the writer was that the principal operator guessed at the answers; and as many of them were such as he would have some knowledge of, he might by some means be enabled to control the motions of the table; for be it understood the table never moved but when directed. How this is to be accounted for is the question. Is it that the minds of all the persons whose hands are on the table are directed to the same object, when one of their number directs a particular motion of the table; and that the united volition of all the parties exerts some unseen power? The table did not move at the direction of every person whose hand was placed upon it, but only of particular individuals. This appeared a singular if not suspicious circumstance. But when the chief director of the movement and three of the others left the table; the writer who had hitherto been merely a spectator of the proceedings, put his hands on the table, and with three others moved it at least a hundred times; it having always obeyed his directions; why or wherefore was as unknown to himself as to any one else present. It may be, as Professor Faraday asserts, that the motion of the table is produced by involuntary muscular action; but the parties themselves are not conscious of exerting any force upon the table; and it will move when touched only by the tips of the fingers. — *Toronto Leader.*

AN EVENING IN SPIRIT LAND

Winnipeg Free Press, August 12, 1879

Every available seat in the city hall was filled last evening — the occasion being Prof. Cecil's widely advertised "Evening in Spirit Land,"— a novel entertainment in this city.

The Professor, after making some explanations as to the nature of the exhibition, invited the audience to name a committee of three from amongst themselves to watch the proceedings on the platform, and Messrs. S.J. Van Rensselaer, A.M. Brown and W.F. Luxton were selected for that purpose.

On stage was a mysterious-looking "cabinet," in which were tambourines, bells, horns and other instruments and two chairs. These, with the ropes to be used, were examined by the committee, and pronounced to be what they apparently were. The Professor and his assistant then entered the cabinet, and being seated on two chairs were tied hand and foot by the committee as securely as could possibly be done. Van was asked to close the cabinet doors, but before he could fasten one, he received a slap on the ear, and for a few minutes enjoyed a Fourth of July pyrotechnical display. Van sat down. Mr. Luxton's turn was next — same result. Mr. Brown, ditto.

However, the doors were finally closed, and immediately the bells began ringing, the horns tooting, the tambourine and triangle joining in the chorus, while hands appeared through apertures in the cabinet doors, and above the cabinet. The doors were opened, and the mediums were found tightly tied.

The Professor had previously announced that perhaps the spirits would work and perhaps they wouldn't — but there didn't seem to be any "perhaps" about it.

The next thing on the programme was the Hindoo box trick — an apparently ordinary heavy chest was locked, tied with ropes and the knots sealed with wax, after having been carefully examined by the committee. This box was placed in the cabinet, and so was the Professor's assistant. The doors were closed, and on being opened one minute afterwards the box was still found there, but the man had disappeared. The box was opened and the man was found snugly ensconced inside. The spirits were evidently working well and the spirits of the audience were also high, as was evidenced by the loud applause which followed this trick-manifestation.

Then the Professor's hands were tied with a handkerchief, and a rope slipped through his tied hands, Mr. Brown holding the two ends of the rope, but the Professor slipped it off without untying the handkerchief or breaking the rope.

Prof. Cecil then entered the cabinet alone with some ropes, and in a very few minutes was found tied apparently more securely than when the committee had undertaken the job — and he only took three-quarters of a minute to do it. The knots were sealed, the cabinet closed, and in a few seconds the Professor was discovered with his coat off. Mr. Luxton's coat was then placed in the cabinet — the Professor being assured that, being a temperance man, there were no "spirits" in the garment — but it didn't make any difference. In a few seconds the coat was on the Professor. Then they sewed it on him, and almost instantaneously it was thrown out of the cabinet, still sewed.

Mr. Brown went into the cabinet with the Professor, and shortly appeared crowned with a tambourine, although he had hold of the medium all the time. Then Van went in — apparently to stay — and firmly grasped hold of the hands of the Professor, who was still tied. Van's coat was thrown out first, then his vest — and on opening the cabinet it was seen that he had still a firm hold on the Professor. The cabinet was closed again, and the spirits commenced taking off Van's unmentionables — but stopped in time to save an awful scene. Van's watch was found in the Professor's pocket. The Professor's mouth was then filled with water, yet he played on a mouth organ and then he released himself from the ropes.

An officer was asked to come forward with handcuffs. Policeman Grady accepted the offer, and appeared with a set of bracelets belonging to the city. These he placed on the Professor, who retired to the cabinet, and shortly appeared entirely free — the handcuffs being found fastened to the handle of a pitcher and the rung of a chair, which were in the cabinet. The Professor was placed in a pillory, which was locked and sealed, but he easily and quickly escaped from his uncomfortable position. He was then tied and a gag placed in his mouth, but he pronounced distinctly any word required of him by the committee.

His young assistant was then mesmerized, and tied in the cabinet, and spirit hands wrote on a slate, a message to Mr. Brown from Katie King reading, "You are a bad man." Spirit faces appeared about and around the cabinet — one being that of Captain Kidd, the pirate, and another of Van's grandmother. The hall being darkened, a ghost came out from the cabinet and sang a song — but his, her, or its voice wasn't much like a ghost's, at least any ghost we ever read about or talked to, the sepulchral tones being wanting entirely.

Then the tricks of the spiritualists were exposed and an explanation given of how he slipped out of the rope in the handkerchief trick, which was very simple — after one knew how — and the entertainment concluded, the Professor promised to expose other tricks this evening.

During the evening, the audience were kept alternately completely mystified and roaring with laughter — as the incomprehensible or the ludicrous was presented. Mr. Ormande presided at the piano, and played some selections with great skill, contributing materially to the enjoyment of the evening. The Professor's entertainment gave unbounded satisfaction to the great majority of the audience, although there were some who expressed themselves that more expositions should have been given. Doubtless these will get all they want tonight.

UNITED SPIRITUALISTS' ASSOCIATION

This account of a public demonstration of spirit-communication conducted by the United Spiritualists' Association is particularly lively. Many such accounts are earnestly dull, but this one is decidedly irreverent! It was contributed by an unidentified reporter who attended the seance and it captures to perfection the often irrelevant exchanges that occur during trances. "Red-Haired Man Upsets Spirits" appeared in the *Toronto Daily News*, 4 January 1909.

Red-Haired Man Upsets Spirits —"Say, Old Chap, What have I got in My Noodle" — "Nothing," said Medium — "Stung, Old Sorel Top, Stung,"— Chuckled a Visitor at Spiritualistic Seances in Labor Temple

It was the presence of the "impudent young man" in the hall of the Labor Temple early Sunday evening that was responsible for the spirit messages showing an objection to come.

His rude words "blurred" the "influences" as they approached. Sometimes the material conditions did overpower the "spirituality of the pure, thinking Spiritualists."

They formed an obstacle, and this interfered with the messages.

This was why there were only two demonstrations at the inaugural meeting of the United Spiritualists' Association last evening in the Labor Temple. People were disappointed, of course, but Dr. Angus told them to look for better things next Sunday; perhaps during the week. A close watch will be kept upon that impudent young man.

He had red hair, that young man, and did not take the seance in the proper spirit. He wanted to play upon the word, and also upon the demonstrator.

Things had not got started properly when he interrupted in a rude voice: "Say, old chap, what have I got in my noodle?"

"Old chap" and "noodle" were unspiritualistic terms.

Dr. Angus yielded in the temptation to answer him in kind, and retorted "nothing whatever."

Now the youngest gamine on the streets could carry on this conversation one more step; thee is only one word in the English language that is the proper comment, and it came:

"Stung, old sorel top, stung again." It was a middle-aged man who found breath in the midst of muscle-straining laughter to utter these words.

Still another picked up the thread of conversation, remarking: "Didn't I tell you the guy who was to run this meetin' was a wise duck out of the west? Ha, ha!"

And the "sorel top" came back with his: "My hair is red, but I'm glad the spirits have fermented right after the reduction fight, too. Ha, ha!"

Dr. Angus glared upon the disturber and threatened him with a material condition in the shape and substance of a policeman. Also asked him to "slip out" if there lingered any token of respect within his heart for the family. Also, if there wasn't, and he didn't slip out, every one else would.

He started to slip out, but "material conditions" were still present. He had paid a silver collection at the door, and Dr. Angus ordered his money to be refunded. The treasurer offered him ten cents. No, it was a quarter he had paid. Well, give it to him, then. Four others followed — sympathizers, Silver collection for them, too, at the door.

Five minutes passed in stillness. Dr. Angus passed his hand over his forehead to blot out that impudent young man from his thoughts. After announcing a couple of "trumpet seances" during the week, he was about to let them depart, but they asked for a few "demonstrations."

He wasn't sure about the law.

But you can give spirit messages.

Very well, then.

More silence — more closed eyes, and bent heads.

"One, two, three, four"— the impudent young man was now out of ken —"the influences to hand say that a sister of a wife who is sitting in the front row and has only been in the faith a short time is advising her of the conditions surrounding her. I think the sister's words are: 'Peace be with you in the hour of trouble.' It seems to me that her name is Elizabeth."

At once an elderly woman shouted out in a half-hysterical voice: "That's right; that's right."

The medium went on: "There is a young lad on a long bench about the centre. His name is Trillie, or Willie, or something like that, and his last name Frox or Fox. He is also a new beginning in Spiritualism and is eager to grasp its principles."

But the expected reply did not come. Where was Willie Fox, or Trillie Frox, Willie Frox or Trillie Fox? The impudent young man may have still been working on him, too, for he did not answer, and Dr. Angus feeling his malign influence still in the air, said it was all over for this time.

9

GHOSTLY AND GHASTLY JESTS

The stories in the book's section have a mood and a spirit that is all their own.

Here are stories that are odd or offbeat. Some of the stories are ghostly; some of them are ghastly. Most of them are jabs, jokes, or jests.

The reporters who conducted interviews and wrote these news stories for their newspapers must have had fun researching and drafting them, striking poses, expressing irreverent opinions, casting doubts on the events and experiences of others, ridiculing the witnesses, belittling the proceedings, etc.

In other words, their news stories were written with some humour. They, too, are part of our "haunted heritage."

A GHOST

Victoria Daily Colonist, October 20, 1883

The other night at an hour when churchyards are supposed to yawn, (though what for, goodness only knows), an honest burgher of Victoria was awakened simultaneously with his wife by hearing the piano played. Now, considering there were no other residents in the house, it is small wonder the couple were startled.

After listening to the sounds, which still continued, the wife said: "Oh, Joshua, those are no earthly notes, but played by the inhabitants of another sphere, O-o-oh!" and vividly realizing such an awful possibility the frightened woman, as a means of protection, buried her head beneath the bed-clothes. "That's played out," said her more prosaic spouse, "get up and we'll go see what it is." "Oh no, there are spirits in the house," said Mrs.— , to which Joshua replied, "Yes, there's half a case of gin, and I'm going down to see that it's all right. Come on!" And together they descended the stairs and walked towards the room in which the piano was kept, the husband with considerable presence of mind making his wife with the candle go first (doubtless to protect her from an attack in the rear). Pushing the door slowly open they looked around the room when a fearful "mia-ow" caused Joshua to fly back up the stairs, six at a time, and jump with a yell of terror into the bed, (he afterwards said it was to divert from his wife any possible pursuit by the assailant whom he thought to be in hiding). Putting the best face he could on the matter, he called out, "It's all right, old woman, you can come up now!" In the words of Pinafore, "It was the cat."

HUGGED BY THE MAN IN WHITE

Lively Apparition Causes Consternation at Brampton — Search for the Sprite — Although He Makes His Appearance Nightly — All Efforts to Capture Him Have Proved Unsuccessful
Toronto News, October 20, 1897

The good people of Brampton are greatly agitated over the nightly appearance in their midst of a real up-to-date ghost of the male persuasion whose specialty seems to be hugging the fair and young section of the population and frightening the old. The ghost was first seen on the road near the town hall by two young ladies who were returning home from a friend's at a rather late hour. The vision appeared to have risen out of the roadway and seemed to be eight feet high and attired from head to foot in a flowing white raiment. As he approached the terror-stricken woman he seemed to glide instead of walk, but his arms proved to be solid enough as he embraced them. One of the ladies fainted, but the screams of the other attracted attention and the Spook suddenly disappeared, seeming to melt into the air.

Next night the ghostly visitor was met in a different part of the town by an elderly lady, who courageously advanced until she was within a dozen feet of the object, when it once more suddenly disappeared. For several nights nothing more occurred to startle the people, but every night last week the Spook was met on different streets, until at present there is hardly a young woman in Brampton who will venture out alone after dark.

A few nights ago Rev. William Walsh, the Anglican clergyman, was proceeding home from church when he saw a tall white object in the roadway. He quietly approached until he got within a dozen yards of the supposed Spook, when it started off at a lively gait, uttering frantic shrieks as it ran. Mr. Walsh, who is quite a sprinter, for a time kept up with the fugitive, but was finally obliged to give up the chase. Next night William Howell, a clerk employed in Peaker & Co.'s hardware store, was escorting two young ladies home from choir practice when the Spook once more appeared. The ladies fled in wild terror, but Howell started after the ghost and an excited chase ensued. Howell got almost within striking distance when the ghost emitted a shriek and disappeared.

Greatly mystified, Mr. Howell related his experience to his friends and they arranged a party to effectually lay his ghostship. Several young ladies who had seen the "horrible object" and one who was actually embraced by the amorous ghost, are now very ill, suffering from nervous prostration, and the alarm has become so general that Sheriff Brodie has been appealed to for protection. A determined effort will be made this week to develop the mystery with shot guns as the medium.

THE DEVIL IN CHURCH

Hornerite Congregation Gets a Scare at Madoc — Boys Say It Is a Joke

Ottawa Free Press, December 6, 1897

A very strange thing occurred recently at a Hornerite meeting held at the meeting house of that sect, situated seven miles north of Madoc, known as "McCoy's," says the Tweed News. The people came as usual to their place of meeting, an old wooden building, through the cracks and crevices of which the wind blew with many a ghostly and weird sound. As the meeting progressed, and as the preacher arrived at that part of his discourse in which he had occasion to speak of the devil, there arose immediately in their midst, through and from beneath the floor, a spectre so awful in appearance that the audience and preacher alike were wholly paralyzed with fear. The latter had hardly ceased speaking when there rang out a voice terrible to hear:

"I am the devil; I'll have you. Ha, ha, ha."

Fire issued from his mouth and nostrils. He needed not this to proclaim himself, as from his appearance his identification was an easy matter. He is described as having two horns, one protruding from either side of the head, a cloven foot and a clanking chain, two flaming eyes like balls of fire and a large appendage at the rear. His ears were perpendicular and pointed at the top, and a fiery blaze encircled his whole body and head. His figure was tall and slim and his position erect, and when he spoke the building shook as if by an earthquake.

He had not yet ceased his sardonic "Ha, ha," when the terrified people and preacher alike rushed pell-mell for the door over seats and one another in their frantic endeavors to rid themselves of so awful a presence. Following them closely, this fiery fiend's sardonic voice was again heard and seemed more terrible than before. "I am the devil; I'll have you. Ha, ha, ha."

No further warning was needed. The terrified people fled in all directions, leaving "His Satanic Majesty" in full possession of their meeting house.

A few days after the occurrence some of the sports of the neighborhood whispered about that it was a practical joke, conceived by them, but the Hornerites refuse to believe them.

SPIRITED AWAY

The Albertan, Calgary, Alberta, May 11, 1908

"Who's there?" shouted the occupant of a hotel bedroom, as he heard a noise in the corner of his room. There was no answer, and the noise stopped.

"Anybody there?"

No answer.

"It must have been a spirit," he said to himself. "I must be a medium; I will try." (Aloud): "If there is a spirit in the room it will please rap three times."

Three distinct raps were given.

"Is it the spirit of my sister?" No answer.

"Is it the spirit of my mother-in-law?" Three very distinct raps.

"Are you happy?" Nine raps.

"Do you want anything?" A succession of very loud raps.

"Will you give me a communication if I get up?" No answer.

"Shall I hear from you tomorrow?" Raps very loud in the direction of the door.

"Shall I ever see you?" he waited long for an answer, but none came, and he fell asleep.

Next morning he found the "spirit of his mother-in-law" had carried off his watch and purse, his trousers and overcoat.

10

APPARITIONS AND FIRESTARTERS

In this section will be found some of the odds and ends of the spirit world, including apparitions, inexplicable spooks, and widely-feared "firestarters."

"A Ghastly Apparition" is reprinted from the *Toronto Mail*, 20 November 1880. The last paragraph adds an unusual note. The reader is left wondering what loot would "be serviceable" to a ghost.

"Chasing a Ghost." Some ghosts, like this one, are tangible. And a lot of fun! "Chasing a Ghost" appeared in the *London Advertiser*, 11 March 1881.

"Spooks, or What" appeared in the *Toronto World*, 7 November 1891. This is the first of two entries about the enigmatic Jennie Bramwell. See also the next entry for a further consideration of this interesting — indeed classic — case of the fire-setting poltergeist.

"That Ghostly Firebrand" appeared in the *Toronto World*, 12 November 1891. In this account Jennie's last name is given as Bromwell rather than the more customary Bramwell.

A GHASTLY APPARITION

A Strange Spectre Haunting Niagara's Lone Places — Evidences of Nocturnal Appearances of an Extraordinary Nature

Niagara, November 19. — The town is in a state of excitement over a ghastly apparition which has haunted the place of late. Tales of a blood-curdling nature are told by belated travellers. The appearance is differently described by those passed by the spectre, possibly owing to the unnerving nature of the occurrence, and these contradictions have given ground for contemptuous scoffing at the whole story by the incredulous. The experiences are nevertheless growing more numerous, and even men are chary of going abroad after dark. A farmer leaving town the other night about eleven o'clock, the moon being bright, avers that he saw the thing rise from among the tombs in the churchyard, and trail toward him. It had the semblance of a woman with long white garments and fair hair, apparently floating, or else with far more than the average length of limb. The farmer closed his eyes, and turning his horse drove back into town at a furious gallop, his animal seeming to share the fright. He never looked around until safely in the heart of the town. Another account states that at one of the lonely crossings in the outskirts of the place the woman was seen crouching beside a low fence. The spectators, two in number this time, did not at first recall the stories of the apparition, and went toward the thing under the impression that some vagrant was crouching there for shelter. As they went near, a peculiar sensation affected them both, and without speaking to each other or exactly knowing why, they stopped involuntarily and turned away. As they did so a shuddering thrill went through them, as they say, and they broke into a wild run for the nearest lights.

Other tales have contradictory points, but all agree that the apparition has the form of a woman, and possesses a strange floating motion. There is much speculation in the place over the matter.

Later. — Five successful burglaries have been accomplished, and three unsuccessful ones attempted, lately in the town, and the evil deeds are still going on. It is possible that the burglaries have been committed by the ghost, although there is nothing to show this positively. The people of the town argue that the spectre has not been guilty of the crimes, as nothing has been taken which would be serviceable to a ghost.

CHASING A GHOST

A Stratford Girl Tests Her Lover's Bravery

Stratford, March 10. — A young gentleman, son of one of our enterprising merchants, who, by the way, has a sweetheart, has upon different times, when coming home rather late, seen what he has always supposed to be a spirit at the long bridge, near Mr. Wm. Hanson's lumber yard. He says he has seen it three or four times, and on one occasion chased it, but could never find out what it was. He did not think it was in reality a ghost, but fancied it to be the work of some boys, bent on having some fun at his expense. He resolved next night, let come what would, he would find out what it was. In company with his sweetheart they went to Col. Burgess' "Sleigh Party." It was rather late when they reached home, and the young man stayed, as usual, very late. On returning home he encountered the ghost again, and set out post haste after it. He ran as fast as he could, but the ghost ran faster. All at once the ghost stopped. He ran on, and caught it just as it was making off for the second time. It was real flesh and bone he had hold of, and it did not take him long to wheel her ghostship (for she proved to be a female ghost) right about face, when, horrors upon horrors! What do you suppose it was? None other than the young lady he was with not ten minutes before. When asked why she had played the part of the ghost, she replied: "Well, Sammy, my dear, I wanted to see if you really were the coward Emily — said you were. But I am satisfied to take you for 'better, for worse, for rich or for poor.'" She had kept her secret well. Their wedding-day is not far off.

SPOOKS, OR WHAT?

Mysterious Doings in a Torah Farmer's House — An Incorporeal Firebug — Cats Take Fire, Towels Burn up and Wood Disappears — Queer Pranks in Broad Daylight — A Young Girl's Name Connected with the Mystery — Over Fifty Years in the House in One Day — The Ghost's Queer Pranks Astonishing All the Neighbors, Who Are Visiting the Scene by Hundreds — What the Inmates Say — These Strange Phenomena Have Now Been Going on for Over a Week

Beaverton, Ontario, November 6. — The residents of the sleepy township of Thorah have been for the past week considerably excited by the reports of curious antics rumored to be performed by supernatural means, in a house owned and occupied by Robert Dawson, a reputable farmer on the first concession of Thorah, about three miles from this village. The story, told by neighbors arriving here, was that an adopted daughter of Mr. and Mrs. Dawson had been seriously ill with brain fever; that about a week ago she went into a trance and on awakening suddenly jumped up, exclaiming, "Look at that!" and pointing with her finger towards the ceiling of the house. The rest of the members on looking towards the point indicated by the girl were surprised to see the ceiling on fire. They immediately extinguished the fire and nothing more was thought of the matter until the following day, when the girl again startled the family with the same exclamation and the interior of the house broke out in flames. This performance, according to the rumor, was continued every day thereafter.

From an investigation by The World's Ghost Exterminator, it is evident that the ghost sleeps just at present, but for a time it was fully as persistent as the one detailed for Banquo's special benefit.

The house is situated about one hundred yards from the road on lot 17, con. 1, Thorah — about seven miles from Cannington and three from Beaverton. It is a small and rather an ancient structure and is built of logs. There is a window in the front of the house, but no door; entrance to it being by a door in the rear through an old summer kitchen.

On arriving at the house Mrs. Dawson, the wife of the farmer, introduced the girl, whose name had been mentioned in connection with these mysteries. She was engaged in washing dishes. The girl was adopted by Mr. and Mrs. Dawson from an immigrant home in Belleville some time ago. She was originally from England, where she was known as Jennie B. Bramwell, but since coming to her present home she has adopted the name of Jennie B. Dawson. Miss Bramwell, or Miss Dawson, is a bright intelligent girl of about 14 years of age. She is well educated and an excellent conversationalist.

After being shown over the premises, both up stairs and down, Mrs. Dawson tells this story of the girl's illness and the mysterious fires:

On Monday afternoon, Oct. 25, she and her husband went to a neighbor's to spend a few hours, and on returning home in the evening Jennie informed them that the house had been on fire and pointed out the place — near the chimney. Mr. Dawson, thinking that there might still be some fire around the chimney, remained up all night to watch it, but nothing occurred during the night. After breakfast on Tuesday morning Mr. Dawson went out to the barn to load some grain to take to market, and Mrs. Dawson also went out into the yard. They had scarcely left the house when the girl, Jennie, came out shouting the house was again on fire. On entering the house they found that the west gable end was on fire. With the aid of water the fire upstairs was extinguished, but no sooner had that been accomplished than the fire broke out in several places on the wall in the room in the lower flat, and while extinguishing it there it again broke out on the wall in another room in the east end — there being no visible connection between any of the fires. They finally succeeded, with the assistance of some neighbors, in getting the fire extinguished. The next day the fire again broke out, and as on the former day, when it was extinguished in one place it would suddenly break out in some other place, several feet away.

On one occasion, while the fire was burning at the extreme west end of the house, a picture hanging on the wall at the opposite end of the house suddenly took fire and was consumed before their eyes. On examination it was found there was no fire near it. The family had now become thoroughly aroused, and after succeeding in extinguishing the fire, they removed the stove from the house as they had an idea that the fire was caused by it. But the removal of the stove had no effect, as on the following day — Thursday — the fire again broke out. While sitting looking at the wall fire would suddenly break out on it; a stick of wood lying in the old summer kitchen suddenly took fire and was partly consumed; a piece of paper pulled from the wall and thrown on the floor would immediately take fire and burn up. A towel which Mrs. Dawson had been using to wipe a table with on being thrown onto another table suddenly took fire and would have been consumed had not water been thrown over it, and a basket hanging in the woodshed also took fire.

The dress of the girl Jennie took fire and she narrowly escaped being burned to death. Mrs. Dawson also had her right hand burned while helping to extinguish the fire. Wherever the fire appeared it would char into the wood over half an inch in a second, and the other side of the board or log would instantly become so hot that a person could not place their hand on it. A peculiar thing connected with these fires was that as soon as any of the burning lumber, paper, cloth or wood (no matter how furiously they were burning in the house) was thrown outside the fire would immediately die out. After all the fires had been extinguished Mrs. Dawson pulled a piece of paper from the wall and rolled it up in a piece of old muslin dress and roped it on the centre of the floor and, accompanied by Mr. Dawson and the rest of the family, stepped outside to see the result. No sooner had they stepped out of the door than the muslin and the paper became ignited and burned furiously. Friday was no exception — in fact the fire was ten times as bad, there being nearly 50 fires in different parts of the house that day. But the climax was reached on Saturday when a kitten, which was lying in the centre of the floor of one of the rooms, became enwrapped in flames and rushed out into the orchard, where the flames, like that on the wood, paper, etc., immediately died out. On the kitten being examined it was found that the hair on its back was badly singed. The fires in the house also broke out twice that day.

Mrs. Dawson, to prove what she said, showed the towel, basket, kitten, etc., which had so mysteriously taken fire, and everything was as she had stated. The kitten, which was examined closely, was badly singed. Mr. John Shier, brother of Mrs. Dawson, was also present and corroborated what his sister had told, as did also the girl Jennie. Mr. Shier also added, "That when he was first told of the fires he just laughed, and so lightly did he treat it that he did not visit the place until Wednesday and saw the mysterious fires himself." He was there when the cat took fire and when the linen and towel were burned, but neither he nor Mrs. Dawson or any other of the members of the family could in any way account for the origin of these fires. Neither can any of the neighbors who were at the fires.

On asking if it was true that the girl Jennie was ill or subject to fits, Mrs. Dawson said: "The girl was taken ill some weeks ago with whooping cough, but when she was recovering from that she was taken down with brain fever, but was now all right again." During the girl's illness the doctor in attendance injected into her arm morphine, and immediately after the girl went into convulsions and for some time after was subject to them. However, she could in no wise connect the girl's illness with the fires.

The house is still standing, but all the partitions have been removed from the top story, and the furniture has been taken to a neighbor's. A peculiar feature was that no fires occurred at night — all being in daylight, and they appeared to be more numerous during the two days when the stove was outside.

Chemist Smith Thompson and Editor Robinson of *The Cannington Gleaner* have visited the scene and are unable to explain the phenomena. Everything has been suggested that reasoning minds could imagine as a natural cause for the phenomena, but they have in turn been rejected. Human agency and electricity have been mentioned, but at every fresh suggestion of cause the apparently angry author of the mysterious fires repelled the insinuation by blazing out in a new place and destroying all topographical calculations. If it be human agency the one who constructed the machinery must be an expert and a model of ingenuity. If it be electricity the house must be charged more powerfully than any building yet tested.

There is a great stir in the neighborhood and the house is daily visited by scores. All are politely received and given every facility for inspecting the rooms, charred articles, etc. Both the girl and Mrs. Dawson tell their story in a plain, unvarnished manner, devoid of exaggeration and seemingly with a firm faith in the supernatural character of the manifestations. Mr. and Mrs. Dawson have lived on the place for a number of years and are well-to-do, kind and highly respected people. The neighbors speak in the highest terms of them and also of the girl Jennie. The neighbors are all deeply impressed with both what they saw and what they were told.

THAT GHOSTLY FIREBRAND

An Investigator Who Failed to Investigate — The Case Still a Mystery

Brockville, November 11.—The young girl Lillie Bromwell, whose name was mentioned in connection with the mysterious fires in the house of Farmer Dawson near Beaverton, has been returned to Fairknowe Home here. Mr. Burges told a *Recorder* reporter very emphatically that the statement made by *The Globe* that the girl has a knowledge of chemistry is all nonsense, that she possesses no such knowledge, and with this emphatic statement *The Globe* reporter's theory falls to the ground and he will have to begin over again. Mr. Burges states that the Dawsons had got the girl from the orphans' home when she was about five years of age, some nine years ago, and so far as he is concerned he is not inclined to believe that the girl had anything to do with the manifestations.

The Globe reporter after fully questioning the girl's adopted parents admits that the fire could not have been started with matches, and then proceeds to show that the girl had a knowledge of the rudiments of chemistry, and that she procured phosphorus and thus the mysterious fires are accounted for. No one is forthcoming who sold the girl phosphorus, so the reporter concludes that she must have stolen it from a neighboring drug store, and then admits that "it is difficult to see how she applied it." We should think it is. If the reporter knows anything about phosphorus he must know that no mere novice in chemistry could have produced the effects, or could have handled it without danger of burning themselves, so that theory is untenable.

11

GHOSTS AND POLTERGEISTS

Here are some well-known names — James Boswell and Dr. Samuel Johnson — and some once-known names, especially that of Sir Gilbert Parker, parliamentarian and historical novelist. Along the way the reader is introduced to the so-called Great Amherst Mystery, one of the enduring mysteries of the Maritimes in the nineteenth century. The events that took place at the Cox homestead in Amherst, N.S., we widely reported throughout the Eastern Seaboard and, because of a quirk of fate, were replayed a half-century later at Borley Rectory, Sussex, England. The link between the two was a young woman and an older Anglican minister, their romance and marriage, and their "living" at Borley, which attracted the attention of Britain's leading ghost-hunter, Harry Price, who boomed it and turned Borley into "the most haunted house in England" and hence in all of Europe and America — the Amityville Horror of its day. The story is told in some detail in my book *Mysterious Canada.*

THIS INEXPLICABLE CALLING

The great Scottish biographer James Boswell delighted in what he termed "the mysterious." Whenever an opportunity would arise, he would ask the great Cham, Dr. Samuel Johnson, to give his opinion about the existence of ghosts or the significance of apparitions. One of Boswell's worries was that the reading public would confuse his own enthusiasm for "the mysterious" with Dr. Johnson's measured and reasoned response to it. So the biographer took the trouble in his *Life of Johnson* to explain, as he did in the entry for 15 April 1781, his repeated references to the subject: "But the truth is, that the author himself delighted in talking concerning ghosts, and what he has frequently denominated the mysterious; and therefore took every opportunity of leading Johnson to converse on such subjects." Indeed, Boswell quoted the following sage observation of Dr. Johnson on 3 April 1778: "It is wonderful that five thousand years have not elapsed since the creation of the world, and still it is undecided whether or not there has ever been an instance of the spirit of any person appearing after death. All argument is against it; but all belief is for it." With his characteristic clarity and customary energy, Boswell recorded another opinion of Dr. Johnson which was expressed during a conversation on a variety of matters that took place in London on Sunday, 15 April 1781. Present on the occasion were Dr. Johnson, Alexander Macbean, and Boswell himself who at one point referred to the subject of a superstition, "being called," which was once widely observed in Great Britain. Dr. Johnson was then in his early seventies. Macbean was a fellow lexicographer, the author of *Dictionary of Ancient Geography* (1773) which bears Dr. Johnson's preface. According to a footnote added to Boswell's text, the "acquaintance" who is mentioned as Boswell's legal clerk was a gentleman named Brown. James Boswell's celebrated *Life of Johnson* first appeared in 1791. The source for the passage below is the Oxford University Press's new edition of 1953, prefaced by R.W. Chapman, based on Boswell's third edition. Boswell began by referring to an observation of Dr. Johnson's.

> Of apparitions, he observed, "A total disbelief of them is adverse to the opinion of the existence of the soul between death and the last day; the question simply is, whether departed spirits ever have the power of making themselves perceptible to us; a man who thinks he has seen an apparition, can only be convinced himself; his authority will not convince another, and his conviction, if rational, must be founded on being told something which cannot be known but by supernatural means."
>
> He mentioned a thing as not unfrequent, of which I had never heard before — being called, that is, hearing one's name pronounced by the voice of a known person at a great distance, far beyond the possibility of being reached by any sound uttered by human organs. "An acquaintance, on whose veracity I can depend, told me, that walking home one evening to Kilmarnock, he heard himself called from a wood, by the voice of a brother who had gone to America; and the next packet brought accounts of that brother's death." Macbean asserted that this inexplicable calling was a thing very well known. Dr.

> Johnson said that one day at Oxford, as he was turning the key of his chamber, he heard his mother distinctly call Sam. She was then at Lichfield; but nothing ensued. This phenomenon is, I think, as wonderful as any other mysterious fact, which many people are very slow to believe, or rather, indeed, reject with an obstinate contempt.

THE AMHERST "MYSTERY" AT MONCTON

"The Amherst 'Mystery' at Moncton — Esther Cox Interviewed — The Spirit Disturbs a Church" is reprinted from the *Daily Sun* (Saint John, N.B.), 23 June 1879, where it originally appeared as one part of a *pot-pourri* of items under the general title "Canadian Curiosities." The *Daily Sun* credited the *Despatch* (Moncton, N.B.), 18 June 1879, with first printing the article. The Great Amherst Mystery was an interesting case of poltergeistery that centred around the discontented young woman Esther Cox. It was reported throughout North America at the time and subsequently influenced manifestations at Borley Rectory, "the most haunted house in England" which burnt down in 1939.

> Miss Esther Cox, the spirit medium, commonly known as the "Amherst mystery," arrived here in care of friends on Friday afternoon last, and a detailed account of the manifestations and workings of "the mystery" were given in Ruddock's Hall on Friday evening and Saturday. Sunday evening, Miss Cox essayed to attend service at the Baptist Church, but during the first singing "the spirit," which had been quiet for some days, again manifested itself by rapping, apparently on the floor of the pew in front. When told to stop by Miss Cox it would cease the noise for a moment, but then break out worse than ever. Throughout the prayer it continued, and when the organ began for the second singing the noise became so distinct and disturbing that Miss Cox and party were forced to leave the church. Upon reaching the house on Wesley Street, where they were stopping, "the spirit" seemed to enter into Miss Cox, and she was sick and insensible until morning. Lying upon the bed she seemed for a time as though in great pain, her chest heaving as though in a rapid succession of hiccoughs — and the body and limbs being very much swollen. A medical gentleman of this town, who saw

her at this time, states that the symptoms were as those of a functional heart disease, probably caused by nervous excitement. The heart was beating at an exceedingly rapid rate and the lungs seemed gorged with blood, so that a portion was forced into the stomach, causing the patient to vomit blood afterwards. A sound could be distinctly heard in the region of the heart, resembling the shaking of water in a muffled bottle, supposed to be caused by blood in a cavity being shaken by the violent jerking, hiccoughy motion of the body. As to the cause of the affection, that is the mystery.

Towards morning Miss Cox relapsed into a state of somnolence, and later in the day woke seemingly entirely recovered. She states, however, that on Monday afternoon, while sitting near the window of a room on the ground floor, a fan dropped out of the window, she went outside to recover it, and on returning, a chair from the opposite side of the room was found upside down near the door, as though it had attempted to follow her out of the room. No one else witnessed this occurrence. Again, while writing a letter, "the spirit" took possession of the pen and wrote in a different hand altogether, other and entirely different words from what were intended. In fact it wrote of itself, the young lady being able to look in another direction and not show the least interest in what the pen was writing. A gentleman who was present at the time asked "the spirit" its name, when it wrote in reply "Maggie Fisher," and stated that she had gone to "the red school-house on the hill in Upper Stewiacke" before Miss Cox did, but left when she went. Miss Cox did not know this Maggie Fisher, but it seems that one time she did attend the school indicated, and that a girl of that name, now dead, had attended previously.

Monday night Miss Cox was again attacked, and held under the power of "the spirit" much the same as the night previous.

A representative of the "Despatch" called on "the mystery" yesterday afternoon, but she not being "under the power" of course no "manifestations" could be seen. The young lady appeared quite pleasant and affable, and looked well. She considers her trouble to be a spirit, and is more perplexed with it than any one else. She says that she cannot tell by any premonitory symptoms when the manifestations are going to commence, is becoming rather frightened concerning "it," and is very easily annoyed and excited by any noise except that which she herself may cause.

If the spirit is willing and the flesh not too weak, Miss Cox will leave for Chatham by train today.

SATAN IN A CHURCH

Satan in a Church — Most Mysterious Happenings — In a Catholic Church Near Quebec — Fire Bursts from the Altar, Floor, — Surplices and Other Unexpected Places

This article is reprinted from the *Free Press* (Winnipeg, Man.), 28 October 1889.

Quebec, October 26. — Parishioners of the adjacent parish of St. Catharines, Port Neuf, are greatly excited over mysterious happenings in connection with the recent fire at the presbytery and church there. It seems flames would suddenly, and without any apparent cause, burst out in most unexpected places among the surplices, in bags, clothing, brooms, front of the altar in carpets on the floor, and it is even asserted that the tablecloth was consumed on the table at which the Curé was sitting. At the request of the church authorities, the Cardinal has sent up Monsignor Hamel and a couple of his other household clergy to investigate the matter. A couple of Provincial Police have also been despatched to the scene of these mysterious happenings.

A HAUNTED HOTEL IN CANADA

A Haunted Hotel in Canada — Queer Antics in a House — on the Shores of the Lake of Two Mountains

This news story appeared in the *Daily Sun* (Saint John, N.B.), 8 October 1880. What is being described is the action of a poltergeist, not a ghost.

Montreal, October 4. — The spirits are at work in Hudson, a pretty village on the shores of the Lake of Two Mountains, Ottawa River, forty miles from here, and the authorities, both spiritual and temporal, are appealed to by the affrighted people, who are mainly French. The Hudson Hotel, John Park proprietor, for two weeks past has been haunted. The manifestations occur in broad daylight. Closed doors are thrown violently open by unseen agency, and furniture, beds, linen, cooking and farming implements, and food engage in a general waltz and are badly mixed up. On Friday afternoon last the evil genius held high holiday in one of the bedrooms, notwithstanding the presence of several of the neighbours, who saw with great alarm the work of the unseen agent. An hour later two successive fires were started in the stables, but were extinguished with slight damage. On Friday night the revels increased to such an extent that, early on Saturday, the priest was summoned and exorcised the demon. Peace reigned supreme until the departure of the clergyman at about 11:00 a.m. Then the bottles of liquor in the bar showed great vitality and a fire broke out in the hay lot of the stables which were burned to the ground. The surrounding outhouses were saved with difficulty. On Sunday the priest, assisted by the clergy from the Indian village of Oka, just across the lake, again exorcised the demon, who remained passive until after nightfall, when he confined his antics to the upper flats. A strict watch is set to discover if possible the actual cause of the disturbances and to prevent fire, as should the hotel be fired the whole village would be endangered.

A LONDON MYSTERY

Here is a news item from the *Free Press* (Winnipeg, Man.), 29 January 1895. See also the next item (where the family name is given as Ascott).

A London Mystery — "Spirit" Rapping Exciting Residents of the Forest City

London, January 28. — A sensation has been caused in the city by the strange doings at the residence of John Arscott, 1,755 Ann Street. Saturday and Sunday the house was thronged with people including ministers and professional men, and all were to say the best, puzzled by the extraordinary manifestations, which consist of loud scratchings on the wall at the command of the eleven-year-old daughter. The latter says she first noticed the noise on Friday, and that it followed her from room to room. Her father examined the walls and cellar but found nothing unusual. The girl spoke to invisible spirits and asked that her question be answered, one rap to signify "yes" and two raps "no." A large number of queries were put and invariable correct replies were returned. None of the other members of the family can produce the manifestations, which are not heard if strangers are in the same room as the girl. A *Free Press* correspondent visited the house yesterday and was astonished at the results. He asked that his age be told. The girl entered the next room, though in full sight of the visitors all the while, and after putting the question loud strikes were heard corresponding in number of the scribe's age. The number of coins he held in his closed hand was also correctly told. Scores of questions were put by others, and in no case was the reply incorrect. The noise is heard in any room which the girl may enter. The house has been so besieged by callers that the Arscott family, who are highly respected church-going people, have decided to send the child away and deny admission to strangers. They profess to be much annoyed at the publicity given them and are at a loss to account for the noises.

GENTLY RAPPING

"Gently Rapping" appeared in the *Herald* (Calgary, Alta.), 1 February 1895. See the previous item (where the family name is given as Arscott).

London, Ontario, January 30 — The public are more than ever mystified over the strange doings at the Ascott residence. The little girl, Ada, who controls the rappings on the wall, was taken to the house of a neighbour named Bayes last night by her family, who feared she would collapse under the nervous strain. She no sooner entered the place than loud scratchings on the wall were heard by a company of invited guests, including newspaper reporters, who were curious to know if the girl could produce the manifestations away from home. Questions were put and answered correctly as before. Several city ministers alluded to the matter as a "fake" from their pulpits on Sunday and the Ascott family have asked them to investigate it.

A DOUBLE OF THE LIVING

Today it is hard to fathom why Sir Gilbert Parker (1862–1932) was in his heyday the most widely read of Canada's historical novelists. The uniform collected edition of his literary works numbers twenty-three volumes. Among his romances only *The Seats of the Mighty* (1896) retains residual interest because its action sheds light on the attitudes of the English and the French at the time of the Conquest of Quebec. Although born in Ontario, Parker spent most of his life in London, where he served as a Member of Parliament in 1900–18. He was knighted in 1902, created a baronet in 1915, and appointed a Member of the Privy Council in 1916. Robertson Davies was wont to muse that someday his own novels would share the fate of Parker's and their "uniform edition" would catch dust in large public libraries.

It seems that Parker, along with two other Members of Parliament, experienced the apparition of an absent Member. The incident occurred shortly before the Easter break 1905 in the House of Commons, Westminster. "A Double of the Living" is the title given to his incident. It was so titled by Walter Franklin Prince, the psychologist and psychical researcher, in *Noted Witnesses for Psychic Occurrences* (Boston: Boston Society for Psychic Research, 1928; reprinted by University Books, 1963). Prince based his account of the incident on his translation of the episode as it was described in the second volume of *La Mort et Son Mystère: Autour de la Mort* (Paris, 1921) by the French astronomer and writer Camille Flammarion.

Parker wrote that he saw the "double" of his friend Frederick Carne Rasch (1847–1905), M.P. Two other Members of the House who admitted that they also saw the "double" of Rasch were Sir Henry Campbell-Bannerman and Sir Arthur Divett Hayter. It had to be his "double" because at the time of the vision Rasch was not in the House but at his residence and on his sickbed. With these words Prince introduced Parker's brief account:

> Some time before the Easter parliamentary recess, Major Sir Carne Rasch had an attack of influenza, which brought about a disordered state of his nervous system. His condition became so grave as to prevent attendance in the House of Commons, despite his desire to support the Government at the evening sitting immediately preceding the vacation, and which might be of serious consequence. It was then that his friend Sir Gilbert Parker was astonished and grieved to see him near his accustomed seat. This is how Sir Gilbert expresses it:
>
> "I wished to participate in the debate. My eyes fall on Sir Carne Rasch, seated near close to his habitual place. As I knew that he had been ill, I made him a friendly gesture and said, 'I hope you are better.' But he gave me no sign of response, which surprised me much. His countenance was very pale. He was seated, quietly supported by one hand; his face was impassible and severe. I pondered a moment what I had better do; when I looked in his direction again he had disappeared. I was sorry and immediately began to search for him, hoping to find him in the lobby. But Rasch was not there, and no one had seen him."

12

PREMONITIONS

A *premonition* might be defined as a vision of the future that lies half way between a *prediction* and a *prophecy.* It is a *forewarning* or a *forerunner.* A *prediction* is a judgment based on intuition or imagination. A *prophecy* is a general anticipation of "things to come" based on "the way things are." A *forecast* is an educated estimate based on past performance and present possibility. A *prognostication* is something that seems unexpected but which should have been expected — what sociologist Robert K. Merton called as "a self-fulfilling prophecy." Because the premonitions in this section involve true knowledge of the future or accurate information about events taking place in remote regions, they are associated with the powers of ghosts and spirits. They influence present-day attitudes and behaviours and hence future outcomes. They are associated with dreams and with a sense of certainty. Naturally only dreams or visions that "come true" are recorded, so the "hit rate" is one hundred percent.

QUEBEC EARTHQUAKE PREDICTED

Marie de l'Incarnation could well be the most remarkable woman ever to have lived in this country. Marie Guyart (1599–1672) was born in Tours, France, and from her earliest years she seemed concerned with matters both material and mystical. As a child she had a dream in which she saw the Lord and heard him ask her, "Do you want to be mine?" She immediately replied, "Yes." She did not immediately enter a convent but entered into the state of marriage and bore a son. Then her husband died. Not long after she was widowed, she experienced what she called her "conversation." This occurred on 24 March 1620 in her twentieth year. She felt herself immersed in the blood of the Son of God. The experience left her with "a clearness more certain than any certitude." In later years she described it as "an inner paradise." For more details of this sort, see Marie-Emmanuel Chabot's entry on her life in Volume I of *The Dictionary of Canadian Biography*. Marie Guyart entered the Ursuline order at Tours, taking her vows in 1633 and the name in religion of Marie de l'Incarnation. She dreamt of a vast country full of mountains, valleys, and heavy fogs. In another dream or vision she beheld the Lord speaking to her and saying, "It was Canada that I showed you; you must go there to build a house for Jesus and Mary." In 1639, she set sail for Quebec. There is no need to go into detail concerning her life in New France, but it is important to realize that she regarded her actions as guided by God, so certain was she of her apostolic vocation. It gave her strength to establish the Ursuline order in New France, to establish a convent school to educate young French and Indian girls, to master the Algonkian language and compile word lists, to write an immense number of letters. From the time of her death in Quebec in 1672, she was venerated as a saint. Bishop Laval wrote that "she was dead to herself … and Jesus Christ possessed her so completely." She has subsequently been sanctified by the Vatican. A couple hundred letters of the estimated 13,000 that Marie de l'Incarnation wrote in New France have been preserved. They are rich in descriptions of the spiritual and secular life. Joyce Marshall translated and edited *Word from New France: The Selected Letters of Marie de l'Incarnation* (Toronto: Oxford University Press, 1967). Marie de l'Incarnation had a strange experience and she wrote the following letter in confidence to her son on 20 August 1663. "My very dear son," she wrote, continuing….

> I have waited to give you an account separately of the earthquake this year in our New France, which was so prodigious, so violent, and so terrifying that I have no words strong enough to describe it and even fear lest what I shall say be deemed incredible and fabulous.
>
> On the 3rd day of February of this year 1663 a woman Savage, but a very good and very excellent Christian, wakened in her cabin while all the others slept, heard a distinct and articulated voice that said to her, "In two days, very astonishing and marvellous things will come to pass." And the next day, while she was in the forest with her sister, cutting her daily provision of wood, she distinctly

heard the same voice, which said, "Tomorrow, between five and six o'clock in the evening, the earth will be shaken and will tremble in an astonishing way."

She reported what she had heard to the others in her cabin, who received it with indifference as being a dream or the work of her imagination. The weather was meanwhile quite calm that day, and even more so the day following.

On the fifth day, the feast of St. Agatha, Virgin and Martyr, at about half past five in the evening, a person of proven virtue (Mother Marie-Catherine de Saint-Augustin), who has frequent communication with God, saw that he was extremely provoked against the sins committed in this country and felt at the same time disposed to ask him to deal with these sinners as they deserved. While she was offering her prayers for this to divine Majesty, and also for souls in mortal sin, that his justice be not without mercy, also beseeching the martyrs of Japan, whose feast was being held that day, to consent to make application for this as would be most suitable to God's glory, she had a presentiment — or rather an infallible conviction — that God was ready to punish the country for the sins committed here, especially the contempt for the ordinances of the Church.

She heard the voices of these demons saying, "Now many people are frightened. There will be many conversions, we know, but that will last but a little time. We will find ways to get the world back for ourselves. Meanwhile let us continue to shake it and do our best to turn everything over."

The weather was very calm and serene and the vision still had not passed when a sound of terrifying rumbling was heard in the distance, as if a great many carriages were speeding wildly over the cobble-stones. This noise had scarcely caught the attention than there was heard under the earth on the earth and from all sides what seemed a horrifying confusion of waves and billows. There was a sound like hail on the roofs, in the granaries, and in the rooms. It seemed as if the marble of which the foundation of this country is almost entirely composed and our houses are built were about to open and break into pieces to gulf us down.

Thick dust flew from all sides. Doors opened of themselves. Others, which were open, closed. The bells of all our churches and the chimes of our clocks pealed quite alone, and steeples and houses shook like trees in the wind — all this in a horrible confusion of overturning furniture, falling stones, parting floors, and splitting walls. Amidst all this the domestic animals were heard howling. Some ran out of their houses; others ran in. In a word, we were all so frightened we believed it was the eve of Judgement, since all the portents were to be seen.

I close this account of the 20th of the same month, not knowing where all this commotion will end, for the earthquakes still continue. But the wondrous thing is that amidst so great and universal a wreckage, no-one has perished or even been injured. This is a quite visible sign of God's protection of his people, which gives us just cause to believe that he is angry with us only to save us. And we hope he will take his glory from our fears, by conversion of so many souls that had slept in their sins and could not waken from their sleep by the movements of interior grace alone.

THE STELLARTON FORTUNE-TELLER

Apparently a Mrs. Coo, a well-known fortune-teller in New Glasgow, Nova Scotia, predicted the explosion in the Foord mine. She was subsequently interviewed by a reporter from Halifax who published his story in the *Halifax Chronicle*. "The Stellarton Fortune-Teller" is reprinted in *The Mail* (Toronto), 20 November 1880. Yet to be located are original reports of the Foord mine disaster and Mrs. Coo's prophecy. Many a prophet or fortune-teller is "wise after the event." Maybe Mrs. Coo is one such person.

The Stellarton Fortune-Teller — Interview with the Woman Who Predicted the Colliery Disaster

The Stellarton correspondent of the *Halifax Chronicle* has the following: — Enquiry among the miners showed that it was quite true that this and the other disaster had been foretold by this Mrs. Coo before spoken of. Most of the miners regarded it as a good joke, and even still are sensible enough to say the woman only made a lucky guess. But some of the more superstitious did put faith in it, and the day before the explosion it was the subject of conversation in many of the shanties. One woman, it is said, was so impressed with a belief in the prediction that she hid her husband's boots the next day and delayed him so long in hunting for them that the explosion occurred before he went down the shaft. It seems, however, that her warnings of danger in the mine were not always the same. To some men who consulted her she said working in the pit would be safe up to a certain day after the second breaking in of water, but to others this day was different, thus showing, she said, that some would be in danger before others; but in the majority of cases the 12th was regarded as the day. This evening I went over to consult this oracle in the outskirts of New Glasgow. I was shown her house, a little one-story building. We knocked at the door, which was opened by a rather pretty young woman, and, in response to our enquiry for Mrs. Coo, were at once shown into the parlour, a comfortably furnished room in which a cheerful fire was burning. The black cat was not there, nor were there any noticeable sulphurous fumes, which was reassuring. On the table was a church hymn-book, a couple of fashionable novels from Mudie's Library, London, and one or two school books. We now waited anxiously for the appearance of the soothsayer — expecting, of course, to see an old hag with a crutch and sinister eye, such being the general idea of the soothsayer, but she turned out to be a by no means ill-looking woman of great size, with a brawny arm bared to the elbow which might have levelled a man with one blow. She is about forty years of age, and the wife of a foundry workman, now absent in the States. Not being in very good circumstances, and having other mouths to feed as well as her own, she read destiny in a tea-cup at a dollar a read. I inquired if she had really predicted the disasters to the Foord pit. She replied in the affirmative, and, moreover, said she had predicted the destructions of the Drummond colliery weeks before it occurred, naming several persons who had consulted her in reference thereto. Could she tell anything further about the Foord pit? She could, "but business was business." This meant coin, and the difficulty having been smoothed over she raised the book of fate in the shape of a white tea-cup with powdered tea grounds in the bottom. She began to read out whole sentences, the most of which were nothing but the talk peculiar to all similar humbugs, made up of words the meaning of which the reader herself evidently did not know. Here and there she would look up and explain the meaning of what she saw. There will be another breaking in of the water, but not loss of life, which may mean the pouring in of water now going on. There would be two more men killed very shortly by something falling on them, or in some sudden and violent manner. One of these was a large and handsome man, and had a loud voice; the other was shorter. She could see that no fire was yet near the shafts, and none would go into the North side of the cage pit or the old Bye pit. She could see six bodies near together and not far from the main shaft bottom. She described them. The Foord Pit was not lost, and much money would be made from it by one who now had great anxiety. One number from now, whether month or year she could not tell, the men might take their picks and enter the mines once more with safety. Nearly all the bodies would be recovered. These and many more prophecies did the woman get out.

Much more did she tell, and all with an evidence of deepest earnestness, which would certainly lead one to suppose that the woman really believed what she was getting off. When asked if she thought she was doing right in thus pretending to read the future, she denied the pretense, said it was a gift she had, and that she would be no man if, when she saw danger in the path of mankind, she did not warn them, for a price of course. It seems the woman has been pursuing this business for many years, and I am told in many instances her prophecies turned out correct, and these were heralded forth, but nothing is said of the hundreds of other instances where her guessing was as wide of the mark as it is to be hoped the present prediction of further loss of life about the Foord pit soon may prove to be.

THE MIDWIFE'S PROPHECY

This extraordinary prophecy was recorded in the family Bible that belonged to Antoinette and Carl Hartley of Montreal. The prophecy was made and recorded on 20 February 1896 by a midwife Madelaine Donat. According to Robert Tralins in *ESP Forewarnings* (Toronto: Popular Library, 1969), the prophecy came to pass in all particulars. As well, Tralins noted, the prophecy only came to light following the deaths of their children, Carl and Edith. The Montreal-born twins felt themselves to be in telepathic communication; apparently they died at the same time on schedule — 5:00 a.m., 5 May 1965, Carl in Pasadena, California, Edith in Wilkes-Barre, Pennsylvania. Tralins concluded his account of "The Midwife's Prophecy" with these words: "A search is currently underway for other such 'prophecies' which quite possibly might have been inscribed upon the birth records written in other family bibles of children delivered by this little-known Canadian midwife, Madelaine Donat. Information concerning this will be appreciated by this writer."

> I attest and bear my sign and seal herewith and duly record that on this 20th day in February, in the year of our Lord, 1896, that I have delivered of Mrs. Antoinette Hartley and her husband, Mr. Carl Geo. Clayton Hartley, one fine baby boy and one fine baby girl. The son and the daughter are healthy and sound and do not bear any marks or deformity. The son is to be called Carl Gerald. The daughter is to be called Edith Anne. I predict that they shall live extraordinary lives for three score and eight years and that they shall be blessed with the higher powers of God until the hour of five upon the fifth day of the fifth month at which time one will call upon the other to withdraw from this earth. So be it that this birth record and document shall forever attest to what I, the undersigned hath writ here:
>
> Her Hand And Seal at Montreal, Quebec
> [Signature]
> Madelaine Donat, Midwife.

A PROBLEMATIC DREAM

Cromwell F. Varley was a British-born engineer who was employed in Newfoundland. In 1860, he experienced what he called "a problematic dream" at Harbour Grace, Newfoundland. It is taken from the interesting collection *Noted Witnesses for Psychic Occurrences* by Walter Franklin Prince. Prince was a noted psychologist and psychical researcher, and his book is an annotated anthology of more than 170 experiences of a "spontaneous" nature, as distinct from accounts of planned experiments. His book was published by the Boston Society for Psychical Research in 1928. Gardner Murphy contributed a new introduction to the 1963 reprint edition published by University Books Inc., New Hyde Park, New York.

"This incident was told by Mr. Varley, a prominent English electrician, to the London Dialectical Society," wrote Prince, who cited as his source *Report on Spiritualism of the Committee of the London Dialectical Society* (London, 1873). Prince went on to discuss the curious characteristics of this dream, which he considered to be "problematic."

> This is one of the most interesting dreams for study with which I am acquainted. On the one hand it is easy to form a theory of normal explanation. While dreaming he heard the sound, correctly guessed that it was caused by a falling plank, inferred that therefore there was probably a yard near the house containing timber, also inferred from the sound that the plank must be too heavy to be lifted by one man, and correctly guessed that there were two. All this, although a happy combination of accurate inferences and guesses, might be possible. But Mr. Varley testifies that he dreamed he saw the stack of timber and two men approach, ascend the stack and lift the plank, and that he dreamed a device to make himself wake, before he had the sensation of noise in the dream. An ordinary person might during the time which had elapsed since the dream, nine years, have misplaced the order of its details, but it is less likely that a man of science strongly impressed and bound to study his recollections on waking, should have done so. But there is some evidence tending to show that dreams affected by real sensory impressions do sometimes rearrange the time order so as to present on waking the illusion that the cause of the sensory impression was imaged before the impression itself was received. But it is at least exceedingly rare that a dream should present imagery corresponding to the real facts, as though by inferences, and yet not connect that imagery at all with the sensory impression as its cause, but attribute the cause to something entirely different. Mr. Varley's dream correctly pictured the real external facts, yard, stack of timber, two men, plank and fall of the plank, but ascribed the sound to a bomb! If "clairvoyance," whatever process that term really covers, is deemed established by a mass of other evidence, it is perhaps simpler to ascribe this particular case to it.

Prince was not the only researcher intrigued with Varley's vision. A number of Varley's experiences were reproduced in shortened form by Leslie Shepard in the first volume of his monumental work *Encyclopedia of Occultism and Parapsychology* (1979). Shepard noted that Varley seemed able to bring about "the liberation of the double in the state of sleep…."

> I have had another case in 1860; I went to find the first Atlantic Cable; when I arrived at Halifax my name was telegraphed to New York. Mr. Cyrus Field telegraphed the fact to St. John's and then to Harbour Grace; so that when I arrived I was very cordially received at each place, and at Harbour Grace found there was a supper prepared. Some speeches followed and we sat up late. I had to catch the steamer that went early the next morning and was fearful of not waking in time, but I employed a plan which had often proved successful before, viz., that of willing strongly that I should wake at the proper time. Morning came and I saw myself in bed fast asleep; I tried to wake myself, but could not. After a while I found myself hunting about for some means of more power, when I saw a yard in which was a large stack of timber and two men approaching; they ascended the stack of timber and lifted a heavy plank. It occurred to me to make my body dream that there was a bombshell thrown in front of me which was fizzing at the touch-hole, and when the men threw the plank down I made my body dream that the bomb had burst and cut open my face. It woke me, but with a clear recollection of the two actions — one, the intelligent mind acting upon the brain in the body, which could be made to believe any ridiculous impression that the former produced by will power. I did not allow a second to elapse before I leapt out of bed, opened the window, and there were the yard, the timber, and the two men, just as my spirit had seen them. I had no previous knowledge at all of the locality; it was dark the previous evening when I entered the town, and I did not even know there was a yard there at all. It was evident I had seen these things while my body lay asleep. I could not see the timber until the window had been opened.

EXPECT THE END OF THE WORLD

Millennial sects are always with us. The world "as we know it" is always about to come to an end. Are we living through the so-called End Time? Here is an answer from someone who lived in the year 1891. For another answer, ask a human being who will be living in A.D. 2999! "Expect the End of the World" is reprinted from the *Toronto World*, 12 November 1891.

Expect the End of the World
A Curious Religious Sect Flourishing at Sarnia — Their Peculiar Creed

Sarnia, Ontario, November 11.—There is a religious sect flourishing here who call themselves Israelites. They have recently become possessed of the idea that the world is about to come to an end, and as England, according to their belief, is the great rallying place for them to gather before that event takes place, they have all given up their situations to-day, and are selling their property preparatory to taking their departure. They appear to have suddenly come to this determination at the instigation of an Israelite of distinction from Detroit called Michael, who arrived here on Saturday with eight followers. When Michael was asked by the purser for his fare on the boat from Detroit, he demanded that he and his brother Israelites should be carried free of charge. He said that the Gentiles must provide for the Israelites. The purser good-naturedly obeyed the command and brought the party to Sarnia. The chief peculiarities of the Israelites outside of their religion are their long flowing locks and beards. They neither shave nor permit their locks to be shorn.

13

SPIRITS AND SPIRITUALISTS

When a scholar finally writes a global history of the Modern Spiritualism Movement, a number of Canadians will be featured in the study. Many notable mediums were born in this country, including the Fox Sisters (Maggie, Katie, Leah), who remain controversial mediums to this day, and Mina Crandon ("Margerie the Medium"). The work of Iris and George Owen in the study of seances will be noted as well. In the nineteenth century, before the terminology of the Spiritualist movement was adopted by psychical researchers and the public, mediums (today's channellers) were often called "witches."

THE SEEDS OF SPIRITUALISM

There is nothing inherently "mysterious" about the events and experiences described in the following account. Nonetheless it is interesting for the light it sheds on the partisan and denominational nature of Protestantism in the Maritimes in 1856 and also on the role of visiting speakers in promoting causes, both popular and unpopular, like Spiritualism.

The account was written by Emma Hardinge, the British spiritualist, who is also known as Mrs. Emma Hardinge-Britten, and it recounts one of her strange experiences on Prince Edward Island. It is reprinted from her volume of memoirs of travel titled *Modern American Spiritualism: A Twenty Years' Record of the Communion between Earth and the World of Spirits* (1869).

> From Montreal to Prince Edward's Island [*sic*], Mrs. Hardinge extended her visits until the largest cities and villages of that section of the province became alive to the truths of Spiritualism, and earnest in evoking the abundant medium-power with which the Canadians seem to be endowed.
>
> At Bloomfield, a small village near Picton, Prince Edward's Island, the Universalists, triumphing over a powerful combination of other sectarian denominations, who brought their united forces to bear against them, at last succeeded in raising funds to build a church for themselves, which, for a time they could not open in the face of the bitter antagonism with which their opinions were assailed.
>
> Taking advantage of the author's brief visit to the neighbouring towns of Picton, the Universalists, uniting with a number of progressive Quakers who resided there, invited her to open their church with a spiritual lecture. This announcement caused the remark, from the anti-progressives of the place, that "the Universalists had been obliged, at their repeated remonstrances, to sweep and garnish their house, even to the expulsion of the devil of Universalism, but lo! now they were about to take unto themselves seven devils worse than the former one, in the shape of Spiritualism."
>
> The lecture, however, whatever its origin might have been in satanic imaginations, was a brilliant success. The building was crowded from floor to ceiling, and even the eminence on which it stood was packed with dense masses of human beings, who crowded round the open windows eager to catch the faintest vibration of the speaker's voice from within. Poor hungry multitudes! They had fed so long on the stale crumbs of moldy traditions, listening to the dim echoes from the corridors of a buried past, that the very shadow of the bright life angel that flitted across their path in the shape of Spiritualism, seemed to them like manna fallen from the skies. At the close of the lecture, according to her custom, the speaker invited questions; and after many had been answered and she was about to dismiss the multitudes who still lingered unwilling to

part with her, a fine old octogenarian Quaker, whom the excessive heat of the throned building had induced to strip off alike his coat and stubborn hat, sprang on a bench, crying, "One more question, blessed spirits; only one more. Tell us, I pray thee, will she, thy medium, ever be permitted to come amongst us again."

With the sad words of answer, "Never more in the mortal form," the vast assembly separated; but the seeds of Spiritualism were sown on far more imperishable foundations than the mound which supported the church where it was first proclaimed in Bloomfield.

THE QUESTION OF SPIRIT CONTROL

The full title of this article is "Some Physical Phenomena Bearing upon the Question of Spirit Control," and it initially appeared in the *Proceedings of the Society for Psychical Research*, Volume XI, 8 July 1889. It was contributed by Charles Hill-Tout, who is identified as the Principal of Buckland College, Vancouver, B.C. (In the original account the contributor's name appears as "Charles Hill Tout," but the customary hyphen has been added here.) In some detail in these pages, Hill-Tout recalls a series of "strange impersonations" that occurred to him, and he takes pains to analyze and explain them in terms of what he calls "the dramatizing faculty." In doing so, he finds no need to invoke theories of spirit manifestation or spirit possession. As well, he dismisses notions of clairvoyance or mind-reading, concluding that what he observed happening to him "will be adequately explained without resorting to any such occult agency." Hill-Tout's argument is inherently interesting and in line with present-day psychological thinking with respect to theories of alters, multiple personalities, disorders of dissociation, possession, etc. The article is also interesting because of its influence. Psychical researcher Frank Podmore thought it important enough to quote from it and consider its analysis of mediumship in Volume II of his study *Modern Spiritualism* (London, 1902). Podmore's account caught the eye of the writer P.D. Ouspensky, who referred to Hill-Tout's researches in the chapter titled "On the Study of Dreams and on Hypnotism" in his major work *A New Model of the Universe* (London, 2nd edition, 1931). Ouspensky identified in Hill-Tout's article instances of "the phenomena of impersonation," and the Russian philosopher found that precedents existed for it not only in the psychical literature but also in his own life. The final point of interest is the author himself. Charles Hill-Tout (1858–1944) was an English-born anthropologist who settled in Canada in 1891 and became the headmaster at a boys' school in Vancouver. He went on to found and similarly head Buckland College in that city. He conducted field work among the Salish population of the Fraser Valley where he owned land. "Hill-Tout became perhaps Canada's most important amateur anthropologist," George Woodcock noted in his entry on the man in *The Canadian Encyclopedia*. Elected to the Royal Society of Canada in 1913, Hill-Tout served as president of its anthropological section. He was also a fellow of the Royal Anthropological Institute of Great Britain.

Some Psychical Phenomena Bearing upon the Question of Spirit Control

A wave of interest in psychical matters passing over our locality about three years ago, due in part to the transit across our horizon of a psychic star of some magnitude from the neighbouring Western States, enabled me to bring about the formation of a small body of inquirers for the purpose of first-hand investigation into spiritistic phenomena. A half-dozen of us arranged to meet twice a week. It would be tedious to give in detail the results of our "sittings"; it will be sufficient to say that our experience was of a very mild type. Sitting in the dark as a rule, subjective lights in the form of luminous vapour were occasionally seen by myself and one other member. I was at first inclined to attribute these to our imagination, but as they seem to be a matter of common experience in spirtistic circles, I suppose they may be regarded as having some sort of reality of their own, and may perhaps be taken as evidencing incipient powers of clairvoyance in the seers.

The lady members of our circle, particularly a mother and her daughter, were taken almost from the first sitting with spasmodic twitchings and movements in the fingers and arms. Sometimes these movements were very violent, causing them to slap and thump the table with such force as to seriously bruise their fingers and hands. Often we were obliged to withdraw their hands by main force from the table, — the ladies being unable of themselves to do so, — or to place something between their hands and the table to soften the effects of the blows.

With the exception of these two ladies, none of the other sitters were much affected on these occasions, though at times an almost irresistible impulse came upon myself to imitate their actions; but though I occasionally allowed the impulse, at the suggestion of the other sitters, to have full play, it never with me took the bit between its teeth and got beyond my control. I could always stop at once any movements in my limbs, or change the attitude of my mind, by an effort of will. Almost from the first an overpowering drowsiness would come upon some of us, especially upon myself and Miss G., the young lady who beat the table so violently. My head would become as heavy as lead, and I sometimes had the greatest difficulty in sitting in my chair. At times this stupor would get the better of me, and my head would drop to the table, seemingly drawn down to it by some force in the table itself. After an interval of a moment or two, I could sit up again. My spiritistic friends assured me on these occasions that if I would give myself up to the influence upon me I should pass into the trance state, and I think it possible that I might have done so if I could have sufficiently subdued my very wakeful critical faculty. But this I at this period found a great difficulty in doing, and it was not till much later that I was able to watch the effect of this influence upon myself and learn something of its mode of action.

And now, in referring to my own experiences, if my remarks appear to be egotistic and centre rather much in myself, this, I beg to say, is due rather to the nature of my topic than to any desire on my part that it should be so. Being ever wishful to test the theory of spirit intervention and control, I dropped in one evening upon some friends, professed "spiritualists" of many years' standing, and after a little conversation we sat, myself, my friend and his wife, for manifestations. After about half an hour I felt a strange sensation stealing over me. I seemed to be undergoing a change of personality. I seemed to have, as it were, stepped aside, and some other intelligence was not controlling my organism. I was merely a passive spectator interested in what was being done. My second self seemed to be a mother overflowing with feelings of maternal love and solicitude for some one. The very features of my face seemed to be changing, and I was distinctly conscious of assuming the look of a fond and devoted mother looking down upon her child. I even inwardly smiled as I thought how ridiculous I must be looking, but I made no effort to resist the impulse. I now felt I wanted to caress and console somebody, and the impulse was strong upon me to take my friend in my arms and soothe and cheer him. I resisted the impulse for some time, but finally yielded to it. In doing so, I had a distinct feeling of relationship to my friend. After a little while I became myself again. My friend was confident that I had been influenced by the spirit of his dead mother, as he had a distinct impression of her presence at the time, which very probably accounts for the feeling of relationship I experienced, as well as for my impersonation of the maternal character. I shall show presently how very susceptible I became, under like conditions, to all kinds of suggestion; and if this fact be taken into consideration here, I think it will adequately account for what took place without resorting to my friend's hypothesis.

However, I am bound to state as against this view that I afterwards learnt that he was in trouble and worry over his business, and was in need of cheering and encouragement; and that, moreover, a few months later, a terrible calamity overtook him in the loss of two of his children by drowning. The effect of this experience upon myself was very curious too. For the rest of that evening and most of the next day I experienced a most delightful sense of rest and contentment, and a feeling of relief from the strain and worry of life, as if somebody else had taken the burden off my shoulders on to his own.

The night following this, I accepted an invitation to be present at a sitting held at the home of another believer in spiritism. This gentleman's wife is mediumistic to a mild degree. She sat apart by herself, and the husband and I sat at a small table. Presently, after a little singing which closed with the hymn "Nearer, my God, to Thee," she asked me if any relative of mine had died from lung trouble, as she was suddenly experiencing a great difficulty and pain in breathing. She was sure, she said, that this unusual impression was due to my presence among them. At first I could remember no one belonging to me who had died or suffered from lung trouble; though, as a matter of fact, my father had actually died from bronchitis and pleurisy some twenty years before. My memory had gone back rather to my mother who had died since, but from quite another cause. I mentioned the cause of my mother's death and asked her if she thought it referred to that. But no, it was not that; "it was somebody who had passed away with lung trouble." I now suddenly remembered my father's death and its cause, and acknowledged to her that my father had died from lung trouble. At this she, or rather (as she expressed it), the influence which she called my father, manifested satisfaction; from which she inferred that he was pleased to be recognised. I remember too, now, and noted as a curious coincidence, which may or may not mean anything, that the hymn we had been singing when the impression came upon her, viz., "Nearer my God, to Thee," had been a great favourite with him. I mention this fact because at every subsequent meeting, the singing of this hymn always produced in her when we were both present together the same sensations; and because of the suggestive influence it had later upon myself.

My friends, of course, claimed that this occurrence was irrefragable evidence of spirit manifestation; but though there was some appearance of ground for their claim, I was still unable to regard what had occurred as in any sense a satisfactory proof of spirit communion, or of the persistence of my father's personality, and still less can I do so today. I may add that I learnt through the medium that I was an object of special care to my father, who was always actively overlooking my welfare and interests, and I received answers more or less satisfactory to a number of questions I put with regard to future movements on my part. But as the medium could only answer in the form of "yes" and "no," somewhat after the fashion of the table, I could not regard this as very important or conclusive.

A little time after this, at meetings where I met a greater number of sitters, I began to manifest a phase of mediumship myself, or so the sitters regarded it. I should also say that every medium I had so far met had always informed me that I possessed mediumistic powers. On one occasion a public medium of the Mrs. Piper type singled me out from a mixed audience as a person of peculiarly mediumistic temperament, stating that she saw me surrounded by a luminous haze, which she interpreted as marking in me a particular phase of mediumship. What this phase was I have now forgotten. I merely mention the fact for what it is worth, and as possibly explaining, in part, the events which happened later.

At one of these larger sittings, after the table had rapped out answers to a serious of questions put to it, confirming in part, and contradicting in other instances, what we had been told on previous occasions, the movement in the table began to subside, and the influence began to centre in me. I may say here that this has been my unvarying experience throughout the whole course of my observations, that while the table is rapping out answers no one sitting at it is affected or influenced; although those of impressionable temperament are liable at any moment, when the interest in the questions and answers flags, I find the power centering in themselves. On this particular occasion I was affected to an unusual degree, experiencing violent twitchings in my limbs, and sensations of painful chilliness that made my teeth chatter again. I sat, as I always did now, passively waiting for what might transpire. All sorts of impulses seemed to be moving me, and I noticed how susceptible I was becoming to the slightest, even half-realised suggestion offered by the course of my own thoughts, or by the chance remarks made by the other sitters. I presently felt myself being drawn, as it seemed to me, towards the floor on the left side of my chair. I yielded to the influence and fell prostrate out of my chair on to the floor with considerable force; and though the others thought I must have hurt myself, I certainly felt no inconvenience from the fall. I lay groaning for a little while and then got up and sat in my chair again.

Some one now suggested that we should sing, and this being done, I immediately became affected by the music, which moved me in a very extraordinary manner. I fancied myself realising the whole scene clearly; — in a great cathedral I seemed to be the presiding priest at the close of a great function pronouncing the benediction. I appeared to be looking down from a great height upon the congregation and, lifting my hands, I went through the form of blessing them. It will be observed in all these phases or states that I seemed to be two individuals, — one my ordinary, critical, observant self, closely watching what took place in and around me, the other the character that seemed to be personating itself through me. Presently, with a change in the music, the scene changed and I now became an operatic singer. I sing tenor a little, but am not, strictly speaking, a musical person. But now I seemed to have a perfect control and mastery over my voice, and I sang with impassioned tones sever notes above my normal compass pleading and gesticulating to some invisible but felt female presence in the air above me. I have no recollection of the words I uttered, I was carried away and intoxicated with the passion I felt. I stretched my arms aloft, invoking the presence I felt, but could not realise, above me. There were moments during this phase when I lost consciousness of myself and surroundings.

The singing of the others ceasing, the scene again abruptly changed. I say abruptly, for this exactly expresses the suddenness of the change. In going over the events of this evening the next day I was struck with this, and being familiar with the abrupt changes sometime produced in the hypnotic by the varying suggestions of his operator, accounted for my own sudden change of character in the same way. And I do not doubt that, of the dozen or more personalities I characterised that night, every one was due to a suggestion of my own mind, or to something in my immediate environment.

But to proceed. After what I have described took place, some one suggested more music, as the influence seemed to work upon me better under music, and the hymn "Nearer, my God, to Thee" was started. Before the first verse was finished, I began to experience strange sensations. I stood up and began to sway to and fro, and soon lost all sense of my surroundings. I seemed to be far away in space. The feelings of distance and remoteness from all other beings were very marked, and a sense of coldness and loneliness; oppressed me terribly. I seemed to be moving, or rather to be drawn downward, and presently felt that I had reached this earth again; but all was strange and fearful and lonely, and I seemed to be disappointed that I could not attain the object of this long and lonely journey. I felt I was looking for some one, but did not seem to have a clear notion of whom it was, and as the hopelessness of my search and the fruitlessness of my long journey forced itself upon me, I cried out in my wretchedness and misery. I felt I could neither find what I wanted nor get back from whence I had come. My grief was very terrible, and I should have fallen to the ground but that the other sitters had gathered round me, and some of them held my hands.

Just at this moment, the lady who had experienced the oppression on her lungs at the first singing of this hymn, made the remark, which I remember to have overheard, "It's his father controlling him," and I then seemed to realise who I was and whom I was seeking. I began to be distressed in my lungs and should again have fallen, if they had not held me by the hands and let me back gently upon the floor. As my head sunk back upon the carpet, I experienced dreadful distress in my lungs and could not breathe. I made signs to them to put something under my head. They immediately put the sofa cushions under me, but this was not sufficient — I was not raised high enough yet to breath easily, and they then added a pillow. I have the most distinct recollection of the sigh of relief I now gave as I sank back like a sick, weak person upon the cool pillow.

I was in a measure still conscious of my actions, though not of my surroundings, and I have a clear memory of seeing myself in the character of my dying father lying in the bed and the room in which he died. It was a most curious sensation. I saw his shrunken hands and face, and lived again through his dying moments; only now I was both myself — in some indistinct sort of way,— and my father, with his feelings and appearance.

Presently the sense of loneliness came over me again. I seemed to be all alone, and wanted and cried out for my son, that is for myself. I continued in great distress, though the others assured me that my son was there present. I suppose the suggestion took effect, as I presently seemed to be holding and fondling myself as the son I came to speak with. I seemed to be at the same time both my father and myself, his son. We communed together and comforted each other, and all the little misunderstandings of the old days were made clear; and I made him understand that as a man and a father myself, I was now better able to appreciate his attitude towards me in the past. As a boy, I had always regarded him as very harsh and had no warm feelings for him, and it seemed as if the knowledge of his part of this fact had made him restless and unhappy ever since his death, and had, through the singing of this favourite hymn of his, brought him back to this sphere again. After this I presently came to myself and got up again, and in a little while readily assumed or impersonated several other characters before the meeting broke up.

With regard to this strange impersonation of my father in his dying moments, I think the suggestion made through the remark

I overhead, that it was my father controlling me — coupled with the prior suggestion conveyed through the singing of the hymn which had now become associated in my mind with my father's personality — sufficiently and convincingly accounts for all that took place, without calling in the actual presence of my father's spirit self. The peculiar manner in which the details of the scene worked themselves out I can fully account for in my own mind. The peculiar feelings of loneliness, the chilly vastness, the tracklessness of the surrounding space, and the fact that I could not find the object of my search, together with the sense of the hopelessness, the uselessness of my efforts — all sprang from a story I had heard read aloud many years ago, and which took a great hold upon my imagination. It was a ghost story from the ghost's point of view, and told of the return of a restless spirit to the earth and to the scenes of its former existence; the strangeness and intense disappointment it felt at night being able to make itself known to the loved ones of its past life, &c., &c.

The other details relating to the imaginary conversation are also what would be likely to take place if such a thing as my father's return in spirit were possible, and therefore what would most likely take place if I could be made to believe he were present with me. For often of late years, when I have felt that my children misunderstood the motives which prompted certain conduct on my part towards them, my thoughts have involuntarily gone back to my own youth and training, and I have frequently longed that my father might be alive, that I might make him feel that I understood and appreciated him better now and would gladly seek his advice and counsel in the training of my own children. And in the same way I might, if it were needful, adequately account for all the salient features of the other impersonations.

While seeking in no way — in thus accounting for these experiences of mine by the natural workings of my own subconscious self — to deny that we may under certain conditions and circumstances be influenced by intelligences outside ourselves, I cannot admit that my own experience, at any rate, is to be accounted for in this manner. I know myself — and my susceptibility, even under normal conditions, to suggestion in all sorts of forms, not necessarily verbal — so well that no alternative remains to me but to believe that what I did was due simply to every-day suggestion in one form and another. Building and peopling chateaux en Espagne was a favourite occupation of mine in my earlier days, and this long-practised faculty is doubtless a potent factor in all my characterisations, and probably also in those of many another full-fledged "medium." At any rate I hope I have made it clear that before we can admit that phenomena such as I have described are due to the influence or presence of disembodied spirits, that is, discarnate men — as is commonly done,— the personal equation that here manifests itself so strongly under the dramatising faculty which we all possess in a much greater degrees than is commonly supposed, and which is very active in strongly imaginative temperaments such as mine, must be eliminated. And when this is intelligently and rigorously done, I venture to think that a very large proportion of cases now attributed to spirit control will be adequately explained without resorting to nay such occult agency.

In conclusion, let me say that I have not written this hurried and fragmentary account of my experiences to establish any theory of my own, or to run a tilt against over credulous spirits. My purpose has been simply to point out how liable we are in these as in other matters to be the victims of self-deception; and how guardedly and critically we should receive all evidence of this kind. So strongly do I feel in this matter myself that I would personally refuse to accept phenomena of a vastly more startling nature than any that have come under my observation or that I have experienced as, in any sense, evidence of spirit control, unless the whole character and antecedents of the medium were thoroughly known and were such as to render an explanation of the kind I have given wholly inadmissible and out of place. And as it is of the very essence of mediumship *ex hypothesi* that it be impressionable and therefore readily open to suggestion, I do not see that we can ever hope to obtain evidence not open to these objections and, therefore, evidence that we can accept and rely upon.

A WHITE-ROBED FIGURE

"A White-Robed Figure" appeared in the *Brandon Mail*, 10 April 1884. The account was apparently reprinted from the *Toronto Mail* (Toronto, Ont.). It has been slightly edited for presentation here.

> Perhaps the most wonderful case of somnambulism that has been known in Toronto for years occurred recently at an early hour. Shortly after two o'clock a gentleman was proceeding homewards along King Street near Simcoe when he suddenly observed by the gas light a spectral-looking figure about one hundred yards in front of him on the opposite side of the street. The air was perfectly still so that ordinary footsteps on the sidewalk could be heard for some distance, but not a sound of any kind proceeded from the figure which moved towards him. When he first caught sight of it the figure was moving along in front of the Government House grounds, and, as it drew near the corner of Simcoe Street he perceived that it was clothed in white. The sight at first almost froze his blood with terror. He was on the point of resigning himself to belief in a supernatural agency when it occurred to him that he might as well face it out, and see where the apparition would go to. It kept its course silently and as if there was not a human being within a 1,000 miles of it, until it reached York Street, the gentleman followed stealthily on the other side of the street. At York Street there stood P.C. McFarlane. Both were at a loss to think what sort of a "ghost" it was making towards them. P.C. Davis approached it to stop, when a sudden ejaculation of surprise and horror came in a man's voice. In a few moments the constable learned that the "mysterious apparition" was an unfortunate young man who was in a somnambulistic fit. When he had sufficiently regained his senses to realize where he was, he gave his name and address. As he was nearly dead with cold, the officers proceeded with him at once to his home. It appeared that he had leaped in his night-dress from his bedroom window, which is situated on the second floor of a house on Windsor Street. Strange enough, he was not awakened by the fall, but went to work and scaled a seven-foot fence and reached Wellington Street by means of a lane. He then walked along Wellington to John, up which he proceeded to King,

and along King to York, where luckily he was noticed by the policemen. As he is a young man of very respectable connections, his name is suppressed.

A SPIRITUALIST IN MONTREAL

Popularity as distinct from genuine fame is so fleeting that the description of anyone as "well-known" is doomed to be self-defeating. For instance, who has ever heard of Dr. Orton, the author of this contribution? "The following was communicated by Dr. Orton, a well-known New York physician, to the Spiritual Telegraph of March, 1858." These are the words of Emma Hardinge, British spiritualist, also known as Mrs. Emma Hardinge-Britten. In her day she was widely respected as one of the editors of the London publication *Spiritual Telegraph* and is recalled today as the author of a number of books including *Modern American Spiritualism: A Twenty Years' Record of the Communion between Earth and the World of Spirits* (1869). Mrs. Emma Hardinge-Britten travelled throughout the English-speaking world and promoted the spiritualist cause. According to the contemporary newspaper reports of her public appearances in Montreal, she completely confounded the critics in that city, a city noted for its hostility to spiritualism. (A half century later, Sir Arthur Conan Doyle, a famous rather than "well-known" advocate of the spiritualists' cause, would declare that the city was hostile to the message of "spirit-return" because of its population which was predominantly Roman Catholic. Both Doyle and Hardinge-Britten were well aware of the Church's traditional stand on mediums and psychics.) The account in Hardinge-Britten's book concludes with these words: "The 'important results' prophesied by Dr. Orton, in additional remarks omitted in this place, have indeed been accomplished. From Montreal to Prince Edward's Island [*sic*], Mrs. Hardinge extended her visits until the largest cities and villages of that section of the province became alive to the truths of Spiritualism, and earnest in evoking the abundant medium-power with which the Canadians seem to be endowed."

Dr. Orton's Tour — Mrs. Hardinge at Montreal — Waterford, February 18, 1858

I have just had the satisfaction of meeting Mrs. Hardinge here, at the house of General Bullard, on her return from Montreal, and of learning, from the Canada papers she has brought along, the results of her Northern mission, which have been, and promise still to be, of a most interesting character. It seems that before leaving the States, at Rutland, Vermont, she was informed that her presence at Montreal as a public speaker, but on account of her sex and the doctrine she advocated, was likely to produce some disturbance; and that certain persons were threatening to procure her arrest, should she undertake to lecture, as a disturber of the public peace; hence, she was advised not to proceed.

On her arrival at Montreal all this proved true. Nevertheless, she proceeded to the fulfillment of her engagement. On entering the hall where she was to speak, on the first evening, she was met by sneers and audibly discourteous remarks, on the part of some of the audience. This, however, ceased when she had spoken a few words, and all remained quiet and attentive to the close of the lecture.

The audience on this first occasion was not large; but amongst it was a strong array of learning,— of priests, lawyers, doctors of various orders, and reporters. The time having arrived for questioning the speaker, a Jewish rabbi, of great scholarship and intelligence, was placed in the van as chief spokesman. A period of profound and exciting interest succeeded. The questions, at least some of them, according to the journals of that city, were put with the obvious purpose of confounding the speaker; but, according to the same authority, each successive attempt was promptly frustrated, and the tables turned upon the querists. It was declared that the speaker must have devoted her life to study, in order to be able to exhibit the learning she displayed. The rabbi announced that it was plain that she was acquainted with the Hebrew language, and interrogated her on that point. She replied that she had never studied the Hebrew. But very shortly after, she tripped him on a point relating to that language, and reasoned him down until he acknowledged his error. At the close of the session, the victory remained triumphantly with the speaker.

On the second evening the hall was crowded, but with the lecture, the exercises terminated. No one, according to the journals referred to, seemed willing to enter the list and oppose himself to the ready with an acknowledgement of the speaker.

Two more evenings of crowded audiences, at an admission fee of twenty-five cents, succeeded with like results. The questions were again resumed, but with no better success on the part of the querists. On all points raised, the lady speaker remained confessedly master of the field; and with a fifth and free lecture on the Sabbath, on which occasion, she was tendered, and occupied the Unitarian Church, Mrs. Hardinge closed her labours at Montreal, where Spiritualism seems, previously, only to have been known in name.

THE GREATER SPREAD OF THE TRUTH

A.W. Sparling, with his handlebar moustache, looks alert and inquisitive in his portrait which appears in *What Converted Me to Spiritualism: One Hundred Testimonies* (1901), the collection made by B.F. Austin. Sparling is identified as a resident of Toronto. The important role played by physical and trance mediums in Spiritualists' circles in the late-nineteenth century is highlighted in his testimony. One of the most impressive mediums was Mrs. Etta Wreidt. She was popular enough to catch the eye of W.L. Mackenzie King, the Prime Minister of Canada, who on a number of private occasions consulted her. Readers knowledgeable about parlour magic will be aware that "the envelope and slates," mentioned below, is well known to be a conjuror's trick, the stock-in-trade of magicians as well as a piece of paraphernalia that is for sale in magic shops the world over.

My first experience in the spiritual phenomena carries me back to the year 1863, again to 1873 and 1875. Of course at that time I knew nothing of Spiritualism, and hence looked upon the strange happenings as supernatural occurrences. It was not till the winter of the year 1897 that I, through curiosity, and with much prejudice, was induced by a friend to attend some of the addresses and manifestations that were being given in this city. My first attendance was at a trumpet seance at 25 Walton St., this city, my wife and another friend accompanying me. We were complete strangers to everyone present and had never seen, met, or heard about the medium, Mrs. Etta Wreidt, of Detroit, until she took her place in the circle. After the services were opened with singing of such hymns as "Shall We Gather at the River?" "Sweet Hour of Prayer," "There Are Angels Hovering Round," "Nearer My God to Thee," &c., I came to the conclusion that these Spiritualists were not as godless and as closely leagued with the devil as they were represented to be. The medium suggested that we sing her guide's (Dr. Sharp) favorite piece, "God Save the Queen," so it appeared that in spirit life they still retained their loyalty to country and to Queen. This was sung, and during the singing of it another voice joined in, which seemed to be at different times in various parts of the room and above our heads, and on its conclusion a strong male voice bid the medium, "Good evening," and spoke to each one with great courtesy, stating that each one's friends were there and desirous of talking with them, also requesting that we act as ladies and gentlemen and exercise the same reverence as we would if we were in any church. The medium being seated next to me, I, as soon as the circle was formed and the light turned off, took hold of her address and placed my foot in front of her, so that if she should attempt to leave her seat I would be aware of it, and also if she should be a ventriloquist I could detect it. I may say that as far as the medium was concerned during the whole of the seance I had her under test conditions satisfactory to me, and the result proved that she was perfectly honest and took no part in the manifestations that occurred. Our children and friends came and gave their names and identified themselves so completely, telling of circumstances and things that were only known to ourselves, and bringing messages of love, comfort, cheer, hope and encouragement, proving their continuity of life and interest in us, and the fact of spirit return. This seance led to further investigation of the phenomena, and a private sitting was had with the same medium and others, and the evidence obtained through independent writing, in which blank paper was placed in a sealed envelope between two common school slates, securely fastened, and never leaving our sight or possession and held above the table in the air, was satisfactory. The envelope and slates being opened by ourselves and all precautions against fraudulent methods being taken, I am satisfied as to the genuineness of spirit communication in that way.

Again I have had the great pleasure of seeing my dear arisen mother twice this summer and talked face to face with her, and also have in my possession now a spirit portrait of her and two of my children; also that of my wife's mother, who have all entered the higher life. These portraits were obtained through the mediumship of the Bangs Sisters during their late visit in Toronto and were produced in from 20 to 25 minutes and witnessed by several, amongst whom was a thorough sceptic as to the phenomena and who was also a materialist, and who examined the canvasses that were brought there by my own son Wesley, and opened by him and placed in position in the front of the window in the light and saw the production of the portraits. The testimony under oath of the witnesses to the production of these pictures can be had by anyone doubting the facts, the witnesses being fifteen in number, the canvasses used being the common Steinback used by all artists and obtained at the Art Metropole on Yonge St., a reliable firm. We will be pleased to have any of the readers of the Sermon or of this volume call and inspect them and each say it is beyond their power to produce such work, and place their value as works of art at from $75 to $100 each.

In conclusion let me say that the phenomena and fact of spirit return are demonstrated beyond the peradventure of a doubt and proven by the testimony of thousands. We as Spiritualists do not ask the investigator to "Believe — believe or be damned," but simply say "Come and see," as the Samaritan woman did of old. Thus they will be led into fuller and diviner truth and enjoy a joyous liberty and find in our glorious phenomena and philosophy the key that unlocks that mysterious and so-called sacred book, the Bible. I trust that this simple story may add to the greater spread of the truth, especially among my old circle of friends in this and other places and lead them to investigate and find the truth.

PHOTOGRAPHING THE SPIRITS (SORT OF)

Spirit photography was in vogue from the 1880s to the end of the Great War. It was a continuation of the tradition of fairy paintings identified with the Pre-Raphaelite movement in Britain. Spirit photography and photographic trickery went hand-in-hand, as noted by W.V. (Ben) Uttley, a local historian, in *A History of Kitchener, Ontario* (1937, 1975). He made this point when he discussed a certain photographic studio in Berlin (today's Kitchener) in the 1910s. Nothing immediately is known of Dr. Minchin and photographer Huber. The Market Hotel was built in 1886.

> Photographers of the early days included Mr. Schneuker, George Seiler, A.S. Green, S.J. Yost, A.A. Perrin, and H.A. Huber. Since their day, colour photography and motion picture cameras have come in. Among the prominent houses of today are the Binning Studio, the Denton Studio, and the Suffolk Studio.
>
> Once a clairvoyant and her husband stationed themselves in Casper Heller's Market Hotel. She claimed that when she went into a trance a number of celestial spirits surrounded her. Dr. Minchin suggested that they photograph the spirits. The man was willing. Dr. Minchin consulted with Mr. H.A. Huber. On the evening before the day set for the photographing, a large chair in which the clairvoyant was to sit was placed in a central part of the room and around it four men with flour on their faces and in long white sheets, who were photographed. The next evening the woman was placed in the chair and the negative exposed. Result: a lady and four spirits around her. Both husband and wife were delighted with the picture. He sent it to an American spiritualistic paper, which published it. New York papers copied the story. There was much excitement over it. Scientists, however, laughed at the claim. Reporters were sent here to interview the Doctor and from him learned that it was a practical joke.

THE "SPIRIT PHOTOGRAPHY" OF DR. T. GLEN HAMILTON

It may be argued that the appearance of ghosts and spirits was nowhere more in evidence, anywhere in the world, than in Winnipeg between the end of the Great War and the beginning of the Second World War. The sole rival claimant may well be Borley Rectory, which psychical researcher Harry Price described as "the most haunted house in England." At the time Price owned the rectory, so as a "ghost-hunter" and journalist he had a vested interest in "booming" the strange events reported there. It is true that Borley had a long tradition of haunting, but there are no unambiguous photographs of ghosts or spirits to back his claim, whereas there are more than seven hundred photographs of spirit-manifestations that occurred in the parlour of the residence of Dr. T. Glen Hamilton on Henderson Highway in Winnipeg's fashionable Westgate district. Herein lies the story …

Dr. T. Glendinning Hamilton (1873–1935) was an upstanding and productive member of high society in Winnipeg in his day; he was also a psychical researcher by avocation. He served as a physician, as president of the Manitoba Medical Association, as a university professor, as an elected member of the Manitoba Legislature, and as an Elder in the Presbyterian Church. At the same time, he was drawn to mediums and for almost three decades he conducted seances in the parlour of his home. In those days, mediumship was an acceptable form of social recreation, in the same way that trance-channelling gained acceptance in New-Age circles throughout North America in the 1980s and 1990s. Dr. Hamilton was also an enthusiastic photographer, so he set up banks of cameras to document the physical manifestations of his mediums. His cameras could not record the thought processes of his mediums, who were largely unlettered local women of East European background, but he could record the accompanied movement of furniture and the production in his parlour of a mysterious substance called ectoplasm (or "teleplasm" as he preferred to call it).

Dr. Hamilton presided over hundreds of seances and experiments in telepathy (or thought transference) conducted in 1918–21 and telekinesis (or movement at a distance) in 1921–28. The materialization of "teleplasm" was attained in 1928–33. Throughout it all, his "spirit-photography" remains the visible, physical record of the phenomena that he and other members of his spiritualistic circle witnessed. These black-and-white photographs taken of the mediums and their effects remain his most characteristic contribution to the field of physical research, and also the most difficult to explain, short of the charge that the mediums who "sat" for him were engaged in fraudulent activities themselves. None of the participants was ever accused of fraud or deception.

Dr. Hamilton was unapologetic about his avocation but necessarily circumspect in the conduct of his seances. However, sympathetic souls visiting Winnipeg were invited to join the sessions. Sir Arthur Conan Doyle, touring America to promote the spiritualist cause, joined Mrs. Elizabeth Poole. She "charged" the table by placing her hands on it for a moment. The table was then put inside a cabinet shaped like a phone booth and the lights were turned off. Two of the group held Mrs. Poole's hands. Doyle stood in front of the cabinet. The table moved violently up and down and lunged at Doyle, who was so impressed that he described the evening at length in his travel book, *Our Second American Adventure* (1923). He returned to visit the Hamilton Circle two more times — following his death, according to the transcripts of the voices of the mediums.

Another sympathetic visitor was William Lyon Mackenzie King who joined the Hamilton Circle for an afternoon session on 29 August 1933. Here is what he subsequently confided in his diary, according to C.P. Stacey in *A Very Double Life: The Private World of Mackenzie King* (1976): "The afternoon was quite the most remarkable one.... I believe absolutely in all that Hamilton & his wife & daughter told me." As the leader of the Opposition and as the future Prime Minister of Canada, he was perhaps in dire need of some encouragement. The circle contacted the spirit of the late Robert Louis Stevenson and he supplied some word of reassurance. The author of *Treasure Island* was popular with spiritualists and his spirit certainly approved of these seances, for R.L.S. is recorded as saying, "It is good work you are doing for your fellow-man. Commence again. R.L.S."

The most astonishing of the seven hundred photographs are the ones that display the production of teleplasm. The first photograph of a "teleplastic mass," which emanated from the mouth of the medium known as Mrs. Y., was snapped on 20 March 1927 by Dr. Hamilton's assistant, William Creighton, M.D. Thereafter there was no deficiency of teleplasm or photographs of the gauze-like matter — gobs of it, strings of it — issuing from the facial orifices of the mediums. These photographs are gruesome images.

Today the plates and prints of the "spirit-photography" are lodged as part of the Hamilton Family Fonds (PC 12), University of Manitoba Archives and Special Collections, which has granted permission for their reproduction. Also part of the fonds are voluminous manuscripts including early drafts of Dr. Hamilton's book about his beliefs and experiments which was subsequently published as *Intention and Survival: Psychical Research Studies and the Bearing of Intentional Actions of Trance Personalities on the Problem of Human Survival* (1942) edited by his son, J.D. Hamilton. The book argues for what at the time was called "human survival," the notion that the soul, psyche, spirit, phantasm, or "astral double" survives the physical death of the body and spends an interlude in the "summerland" or "bardol state" that exists in "the afterlife" or between successive incarnations.

Dr. Hamilton's daughter, Mrs. Margaret Hamilton Bach, herself a spiritualist, deeded the material to the University of Manitoba in 1979. The closing words of that book are Dr. Hamilton's testament to the worth of the work that he undertook and its enduring merit: "That our small share in this unfoldment may lead to still greater discoveries is my greatest hope. How far off these great days are I cannot venture to surmise, but that they will come, I am certain."

Top: Dr. T. Glendenning Hamilton appears here in an autographed photographic portrait, 1930.

Bottom: This bank of cameras and other photographic equipment was used to capture the effects and manifestations during the seances, circa 1930.

Visible through the cloth that drapes this "spirit-cabinet" is an outline of a side-table, 1926.

The side-table seems to levitate and invert of its own accord, within the "spirit-cabinet," as if by telekinesis, 1926.

The side-table appears to bounce around, spooking the mediums and other observers, 1926.

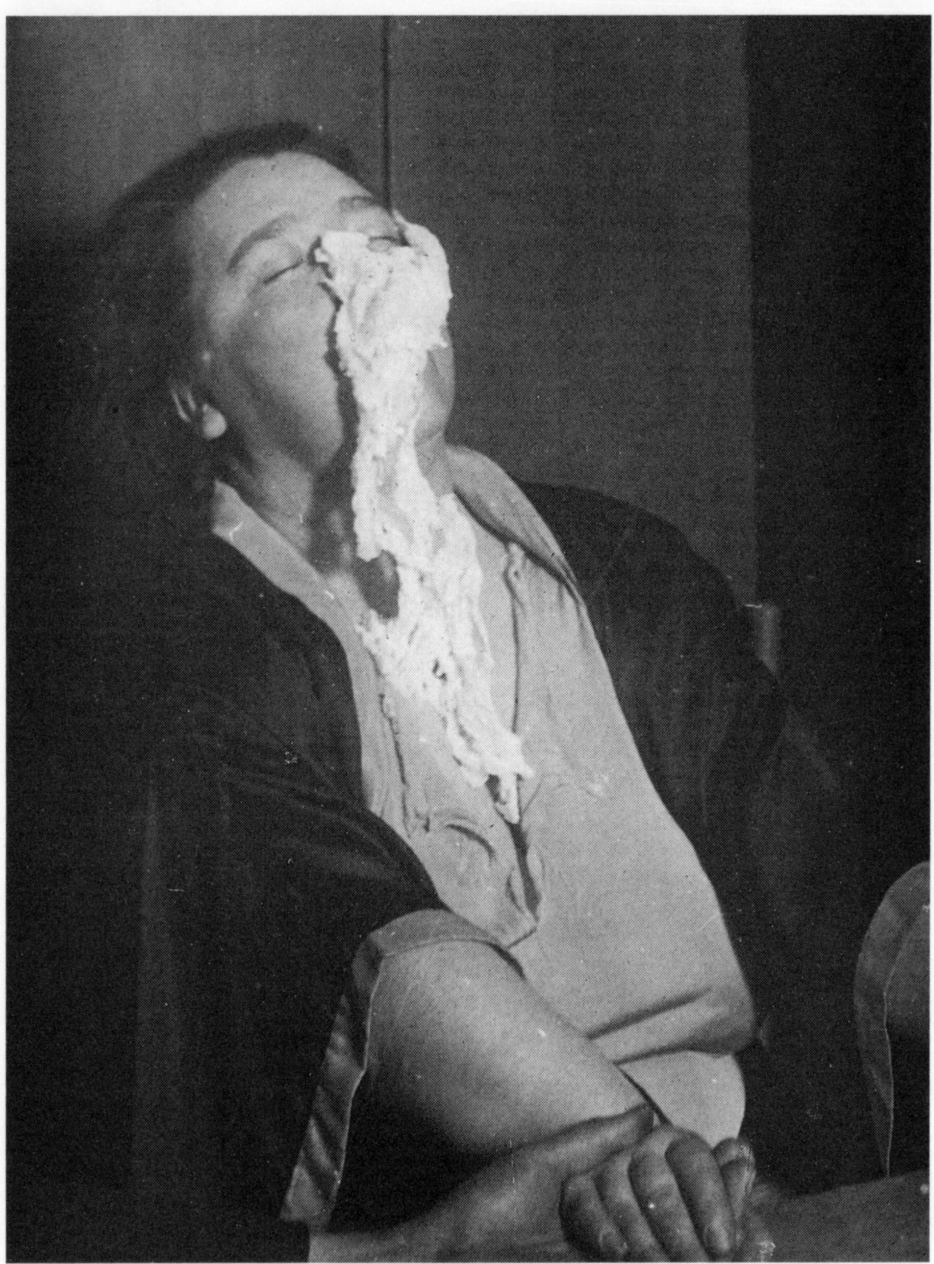

An amorphous mass identified as "teleplasm" is attached to the face of the medium, Mary Marshall, 1929.

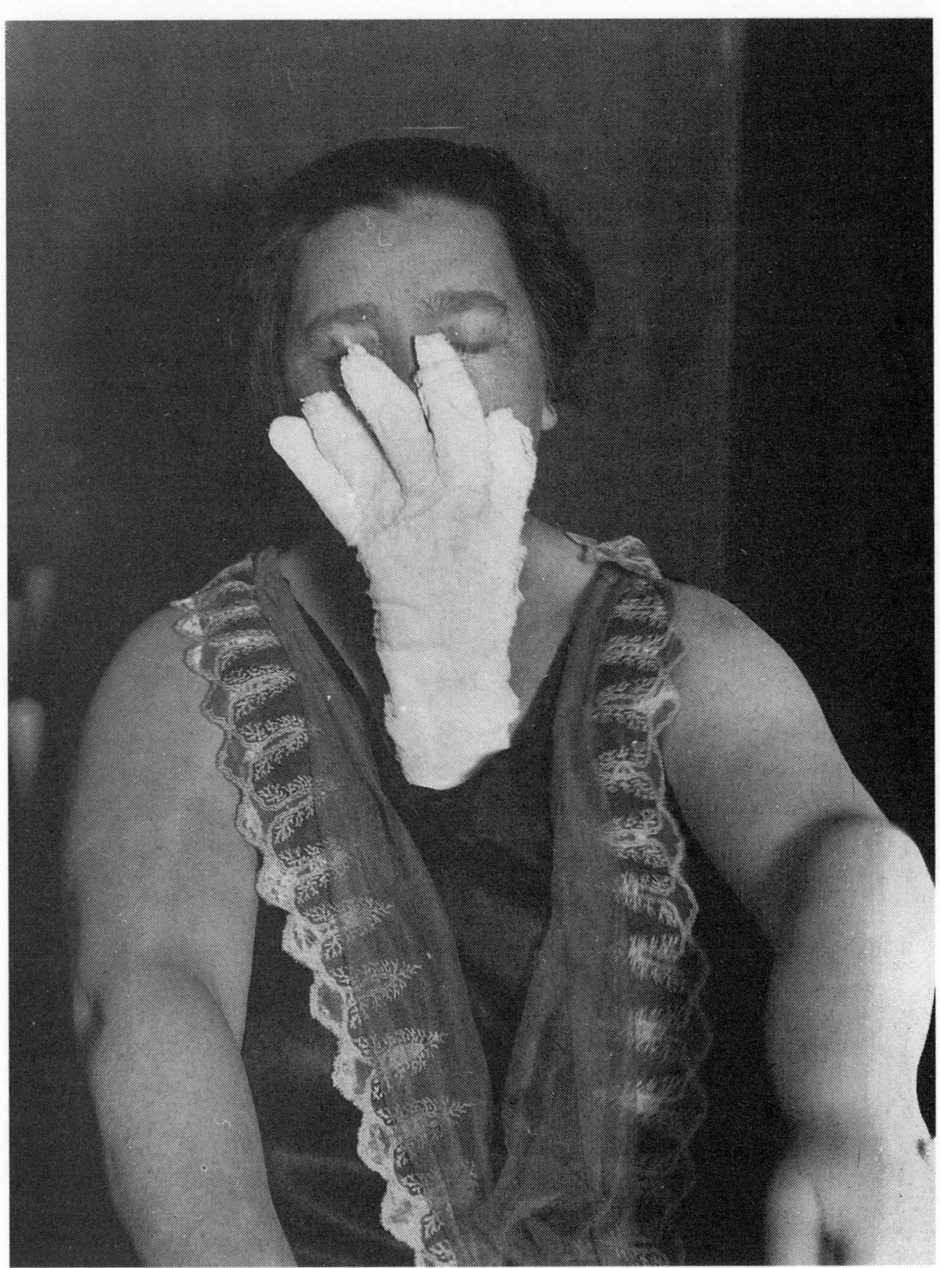

Another mass, this time resembling a zombie's hand, issues from medium Mary Marshall's bodice, 1930.

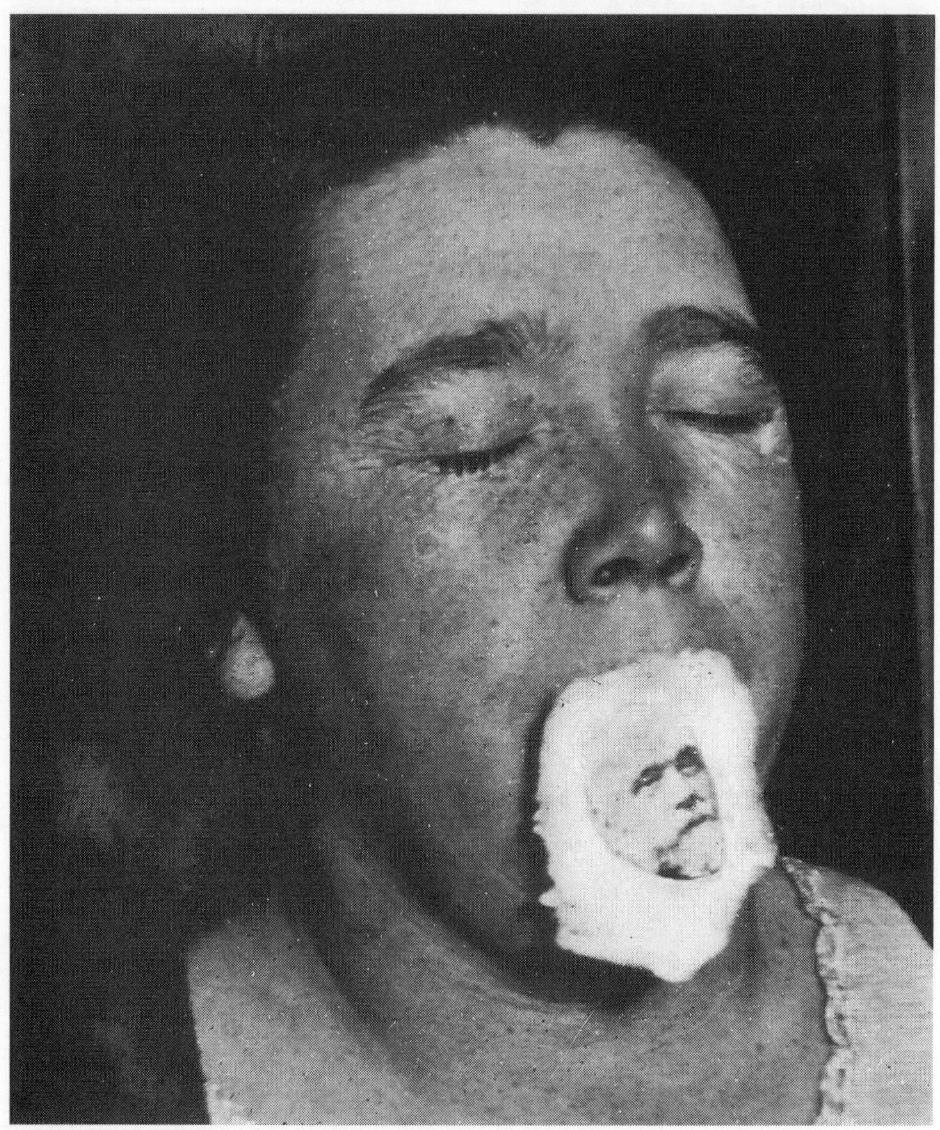

Mary Marshall produces "teleplasm" with the apparition of her father's image, 1928.

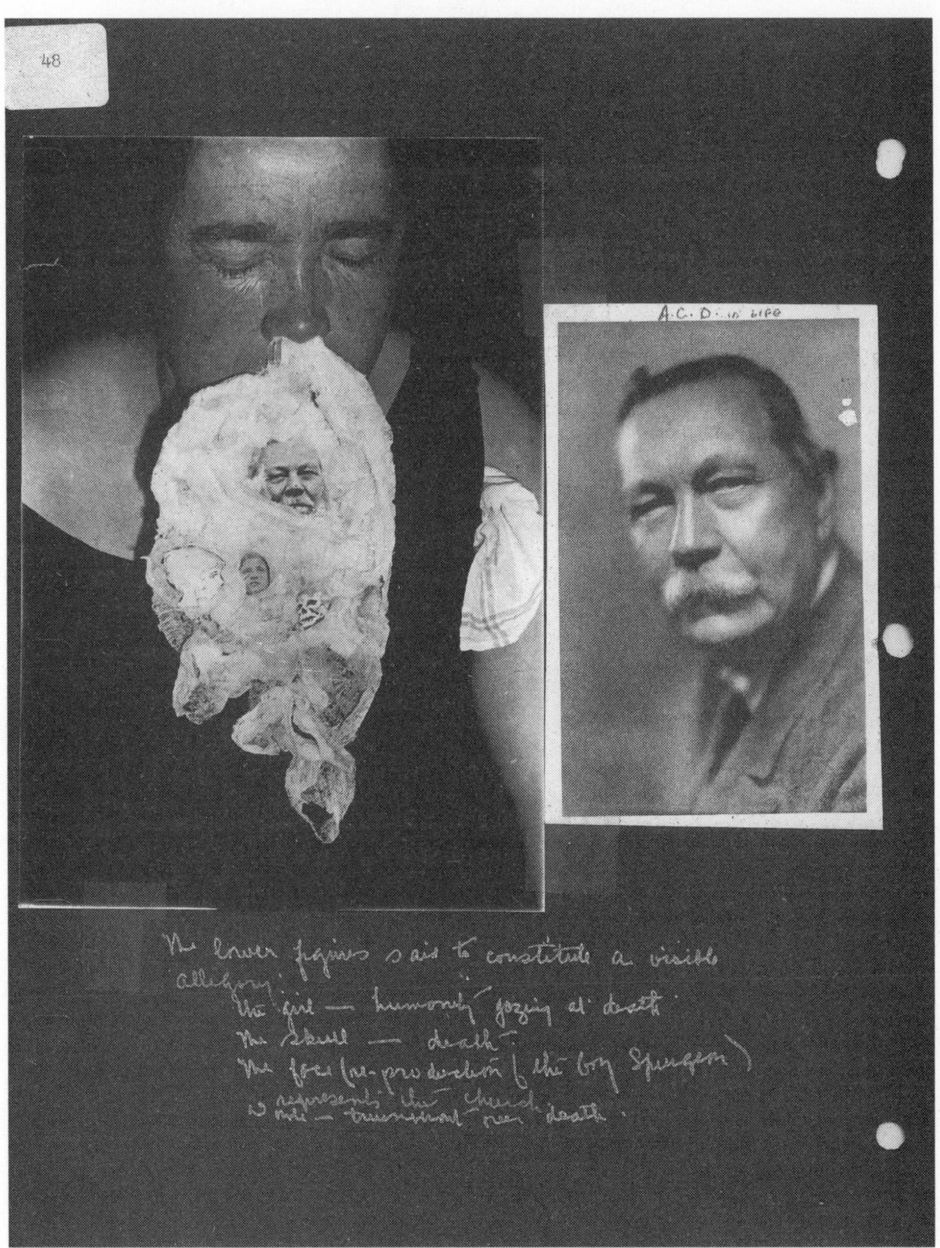

Here is an undated page from a photographic album with a photograph of Mary Marshall producing "teleplasm" with numerous imbedded images. A portrait of Sir Arthur Conan Doyle is also shown. The annotation reads (in part) that the images represent the "triumphant over death."

Directory of Predictions Page 3

Sept 8, 1929 Walter-MM: "The man's initials will be W.E.G."

Sept. 8, 1929 Re exposure: Walter-MM_"There is a small piece from each of MM's eyes." (Just after flash) "I would like you to place your hand on the medium's chest." TGH & JAH do so, and report it is very cold.

True. See exposures of this date.
Walter-MM says they have many "pictures" in preparation.

Sept. 22, 1929. Walter-MM: "The person I told you about is here." The teleplasmic mass is large and manipulated, revealing humour. A small face in the centre of the bow-like mass reveals a likeness of W.E. Gladstone. True.

Sept. 29,1929. Walter-Ewan gives signal. states 2 masses appeared one on medium's breast, one on left side of face. True.

Sept. 29, 1929. Walter-MM states he will give one more "picture" (a face-bearing teleplasm), and will then stand aside. He hints at new work.

Oct. 20, 1929 Walter-MM says he is working to put through two people. Lucy-Mercedes says that the coming mass is very very important.

Oct. 20, 1929 Black Hawk-MM states that the teleplasm photographed is in a rude unorganized state -"thick in one part, ragged in another". True. Fairly good description of mass exposed and photographed on this date.

Oct. 27, 1929 Walter-Ewan states that a mass has been photographed; that it lies across her face & neck; that thre are 3 faces in it, and that these will be recognized. True that position of mass correctly indicated; True that 2, not 3 faces are seen. These 2 faces eventually identified.

Some questions as to the third face. Walter-MM later said they had tried to give a third face, but did not have enough teleplasm at the spot just to Raymond's face. (Study the enlargement). Presence of 3rd face doubtful. We rest on what the cameras reveal. The faces were identified as Raymond Lodge, and Jack Barnes.

Oct. 27, 1929 Just after the extrustion of the 2-face teleplasm, Walter-MM states his intention of "building a material body in the cabinet" independent of Mary Marshall. It will be life-size. It will be a part of the body. The form will be on Mrs. Marshall's left. He hints that Lucy's face will appear. The form will have a mechanical aspect. There will be no more teleplasms for some time. 21 sittings may be needed to bring this "form" into reality.

Dec. 1, 1929 Walter-MM hints "Pull the string and the form will stand. It will be nearly as large as Mrs. Marshall.

Dec. 2, 1929 Walter-MM:"New friends are coming to help."

Dec, 29, 1929 Walter-MM:"We will try to give you a picture at your next meeting. It will be a small one; it will be part of the body - something funny.

Following the sitting, Ewan (normal) told LH that he had the impression that the next teleplasmic picture would show---he held up his hand.

Detailed records were kept, like this page from the "Directory of Predictions." The typescript discusses among other matters the production of a "teleplasm" and it notes "21 sittings may be needed to bring this 'form' into reality."

Here is the home of Dr. T. Glendenning Hamilton and his family, where the seances were held. The house is located at 185 Kelvin Street, Winnipeg, 1930s.

GHOSTS OF THE PRESENT

In the main the told-as-true ghost stories that were written and published in the 1870s, 1880s, and 1890s harken far back to the spirit of the 1840s, so far removed from us are they in tone and style. After all, most of these stories are more than a century old. Their age lends them an air of charm and extends an aura of innocence. To the reader today what is most apparent and endearing about those stories is their nostalgic value. They suggest days when wonders never ceased, when all things were possible. As well, their appearance in print has attested to — and attests to — the average person's continuing interest in "singular" events and experiences. Our ancestors were captivated with these odd and seemingly inexplicable events and experiences. We ourselves are also captivated; captivated too will be our successors.

One hundred years ago the public was as concerned with the unknown as are we today. They may have used words that are different from the ones we now use, but we recognize in these words some common meanings. We know their mesmerism to be our hypnotism. Today what was called phrenology is an exploded discipline, but we are familiar with palmistry and reflexology and similar, quasi-medical disciplines and modalities of treatment. Indeed, neuroscience is bringing back into vogue the "location" theory of the emotions.

Mediums may not have us sit around little tables in big parlours — whatever happened to parlours?— but they now visit Christian prayer halls and prayer palaces in the country's larger cities where the pastor-medium will ask, "May I come to you?" and if you say "Yes," he or she will give you an instant, public "reading." Faith healers with miraculous cures may run afoul of the Physicians and Surgeons Act, but one does not have to wander far to find a psychic surgeon or a fundamentalist preacher who will "call upon the Lord" to effect a seemingly miraculous cure. In the distant past, witches and warlocks dressed like menacing or dominating figures, robed with conical hats; but the present-day Wiccan is indistinguishable from the business man or business woman who passes you on the street carrying a black briefcase.

Jupiter, Minerva, and the rest of the gods and goddesses of Ancient Greece and Rome find few worshipers, when they find any at all, but they are still alive, for as Carl Sagan amusingly noted in his essay "The Ancient and Legendary Gods of Old," in *The Cosmic Connection* (1973), the gods and goddesses of Olympus may never have lived, but they are still alive, albeit according to one of his correspondents, they reside in their Pantheon in a mental hospital outside Ottawa! Hardly anything that is described in the pages of this book is truly a being or a thing of the past. The mysteries continue into the present and will presumably press into the future as well. Whether for good or ill, human preoccupations remain constant across time and space.

It is a good thing, on the whole, that they do. I am prepared to argue that the continuum of the sense of wonder which extends across the ages is what gives mankind its opportunity to surpass its previous efforts through technology and to transcend its previous levels of being through spirituality. Evidence for the drive to extend or transcend the senses may be found in mankind's earliest oral and written expression. It is present in the rites and rituals of shamanism, in the earliest mythologies, the so-called sacred scriptures, in descriptions of fallen and risen deities, of miracle-mongers, and of world saviours, in legends with their larger-than-life heroes and villains, in fables, fairy lore, folklore, traditional tales, tall tales, urban legends, movies, television, tabloid-like accounts of sightings, alien encounters, and conspiracy theories.

A "sea-change" overtook our sense of wonder in the early decades of the twentieth century. It became necessary for the incredible to be credible or, more precisely, creditable. There had to be an explanation to account for a wonder or a mystery. In keeping with our material-minded, mechanistic, and somewhat unimaginative age, it became the fashion to accept the fantastic in the guise of "the real." Reality has to be defined in terms of the rational and the scientific. Change and transformation are in the air. It was not enough to see lights in the sky; by mid-century, they had to be flying saucers. Faith healing was the result of remission, suggestion, or the placebo effect. The contemporary reader should waive some of these "tests" of reality in order to appreciate the news stories collected in these pages and read them as fiction, if necessary. Yet these "wonder tales" were told as true.

The strongest influence on the "wonder tales" that are preserved in the columns of old newspapers is the tradition of the ghost story. Telling ghost stories is an activity that is as old as the hills. Our ancestors, around campfires, shared spirit tales about the sprites and powers that inhabited the natural world, especially the nearby hill, the nearby dale, the glade, the plain, the lake, the river, the cave, and the "ley lines" that connect the sacred sites.

The ghost story that we know and enjoy so much has tap-roots that go back to those days around the primitive campfires, and their tendrils are found in all periods, climes, and cultures. Yet the story as we know it bloomed only in the late nineteenth and early twentieth century. Its growth was tended by writers and collectors like Andrew Lang and Elliott O'Donnell. Like the Brothers Grimm but a half century later, Lang and O'Donnell reworked the traditional stories of haunted castles and manor houses and retold them in our own time.

The late twentieth century has witnessed a terrific and terrifying widening of the sense of wonder to embrace not only our planet but also worlds unknown to us located in space — outer space and inner space. Encounters with angelic beings and alien beings — perhaps they are all members of the same supernal or extraterrestrial species — are discussed like everyday experiences.

In these pages you will find ghosts and wild talents, but no strange creatures of the sea, the land, or the air. Alien beings from space are a global or interplanetary phenomenon; ghosts are local phenomena. The accounts here come from specific sources and locales. All the newspapers of the period were first and foremost local newspapers. As yet no national press syndicates existed, wire services were in the future, and while there was the unregulated reprinting of non-exclusive stories, it was done on a "Dutch treat" basis. Hence the columns were filled with a lot of local news, little national news, and scarcely any international news that was not completely out of date by the time it was published.

Perhaps an advertisement best offers the contemporary reader a sense of the period. You are not expected to believe everything that you read in the columns of a newspaper. You must be especially wary of the display advertisements, like the one reproduced here. It appeared at the bottom left-hand column of the St. John *Daily Sun* (Saint John, N.B.) on 29 November 1901:

> Wood's Phosphodine,
> *The Great English Remedy*
>
> Sold and recommended by all druggists in Canada. Only reliable medicine discovered. Six packages guaranteed to cure all forms

> of Sexual Weakness, all effects of abuse or excess, Mental Worry, Excessive use of Tobacco, Opium or Stimulants. Mailed on receipt of price, one package at $1, six, $5. One will please, six will cure. Pamphlets free to any address.
>
> *The Wood Company, Windsor, Ont.*
> Wood's Phosphodine is sold in St. John by all respectable druggists.

The universal cure-all! One size fits all! If only the nostrum could deliver 1/100th of what the Wood Company says it can do! Advertising, from whatever period, is the true "wonder tale."

It is well to remember that the veracity of the account turned on the respectability of the informant. There was a willing acceptance of the fact that people of good background always told the truth, and only those people who had something to hide or something obvious to gain told lies. At the same time, practical jokes, leg-pulls, stunts, etc., were tolerated. Stories were written and published with an eye on their entertainment value, especially when the events being described had taken place far away and affected the lives of no subscriber!

The reader will find that these accounts are often quite long and detailed, unlike today's news stories which are generally short and specific though often lacking in relevant detail. The earlier accounts offer the reader a sense of atmosphere, often a carefree quirkiness, but they seldom satisfy the journalist's questions: who, what, when, where, why, how.

These are the stories that entertained readers of newspapers across Canada before the Great War. One of the casualties of that war was the *naïveté* that is characteristic of the newspaper coverage characteristic of the reporting in these pages. What went with *naïveté* was length. The postwar stories are invariably shorter. What was also sacrificed was the sheer entertainment value of the tales. Modern communication techniques — including the telephone — rendered stories from remote parts of the country susceptible to proof.

So here are articles, news stories, and columns — not to mention present-day emails — from the turn of the twentieth century to the early years of the twenty-first century. Each contribution is complete in itself. No editorial changes have been introduced. Some spellings have been corrected and regularized. Punctuation at the time reflected rhetoric rather than grammar; this has been largely retained. Obvious typographical errors have been corrected. Subheadings, which reflect layout rather than content, have been deleted.

1

SCEPTICS AND PSYCHICS

You will find in this section some scepticism and some acceptance of paranormal phenomena. I am pleased to present for the first time in a Canadian context the views of one of the world's best-known showmen: P.T. Barnum. Here in his own words he makes light of the famous — or infamous — Fox Sisters. More than anyone else in their day, they founded the Modern Spiritualist Movement and instituted the fashion of conducting seances in which the spirits of the dead communicated with the spirits of the living. Barnum was having none of it! Since Maggie and Katie Fox, as well as their brother Daniel, not to mention their sister Leah, were born in this country, their spirits clamour to be recognized in a book of Canadian ghost stories!

Barnum was sceptical if not cynical. Incredulous might be the word to describe the attitude of R.E. Knowles, a lively personality who interviewed the great men and women of his time for *The Toronto Star*. Knowles was one of the great eccentrics; he often claimed he was at least as interesting as the people he interviewed at length, in fact, sometimes exhaustively. That would be so except for the fact that some of the people he interviewed included Albert Einstein, H.L. Mencken, etc. Knowles was after "good copy," so he sidestepped or suspended all value judgement when spinning tales about people whom he deigned to interview. Dr. Jean O'Grady compiled the liveliest of his interviews for her amusingly titled collection *Famous People Who Have Known Me* (1999). She notes that he was, in addition to being the newspaper's "Special Correspondent," a Presbyterian minister. In this series of *Star* articles, Knowles describes at length a travelling psychic named A.M. Langsner. He is intrigued with Langsner and cannot keep his eyes off Mrs. Langsner. It is difficult to know what to make of Langsner, as I have come upon no other references to him. He seems not to be world famous at all. Marcello Truzzi, the sociologist who specialized in "the blue sense" (that is, the supposed use of psychical powers in criminal investigations), had never heard of Langsner (nor Knowles) until I brought the two of them to his attention. In the end, it matters little. What matters here is that Knowles casts his spell and entertains us effortlessly.

I have not met the next contributor to this section, though I assure you that he is alive and well in the Maritimes. Alan Hatfield defines himself as a medium; he is accepted as such by his clients and those in the media who interview and write about him. He admits to the existence of spiritual forces or energies, if not personalities. Indeed, he writes that he works with them or on their behalf, so it is only proper that Alan should have a role to play in this book. Physicists state that the world we know is but a small part of the world we do not know. There is all that "dark matter" to deal with; there is also that "grey matter" in the human brain that has no function. Perhaps the "dark matter" and the "grey matter" are related. Perhaps they have something to do with the world of ghost and spirits. Who knows?

THE SPIRIT-RAPPING AND MEDIUM HUMBUGS

Everyone knows the name P.T. Barnum, the great American showman. But not everybody knows that the favourite word of the nineteenth-century showman and circus-master was "humbug." More than Ebenezer Scrooge from the pages of Charles Dickens's *Christmas Carol*, he used "Bah, humbug!" to characterize and dismiss in all its forms nonsense, fraud, deception, pretense, fake, falsehood, swindles, lies, and even advertising. He was in a good position to know about the power of "humbug" and "humbugging" and "humbuggery," if only because fame and fortune flowed from the extravagant claims that he made for the attractions that he displayed in his American Museum. He was a master of advertising and promotion. Between 1842 and 1868, his museum in New York City attracted an estimated 82 million paying customers. There is no evidence that Barnum ever uttered the words "There's a sucker born every minute." But that statement could well have been his maxim, at least in his early years; in his later years, he busied himself exposing "humbug" wherever he found it. Thereafter he co-founded of the popular Barnum & Bailey Circus, which later became the Ringling Bros. & Barnum & Bailey Circus and which still delights audiences across North America.

Barnum was not much impressed with mountebanks who wore clerical collars. He wrote, "Religion is and has ever been a chief chapter of human life. False religions are the only ones known to two-thirds of the human race, even now, after nineteen centuries of Christianity; and false religions are perhaps the most monstrous, complicated, and through-going specimens of humbug that can be found. And even within the pale of Christianity, how unbroken has been the succession of impostors, hypocrites and pretenders, male and female, of every possible variety of age, sex, doctrine and discipline!"

Barnum wrote the book *Humbugs of the World* (1865) to expose deceptive claims and fraudulent practices. The lively and outspoken publication has been reprinted by Kessinger Publications of Montana. In Chapter X, he takes some time to tell the early years of the story of the Fox Sisters, the "world's first spiritualists." Indeed, they are regarded by historians as the founders of the Spiritualist Movement. Maggie and Katie were their names of these famous or notorious sisters, and their birthplace was the village of Consecon, in today's Ontario. When they were young the Fox family moved immediately across Lake Ontario and settled into a cottage in Hydesville, west of Rochester, N.Y. From at cottage they introduced the Spiritualist Movement (in essence today's New Age trance-channelling *à la* Shirley MacLaine!) to the modern world. Their subsequent history — involving exposures, confessions, disavowals, alcoholism, etc. — is worthy of all the pens Barnum ever owned, if only he had known of it. It is too long to tell here, but a detailed account does appear in an earlier book, *Mysterious Canada*. Barnum had no hesitation in denouncing spiritualism — today known as "channelling" — as humbug. Here he does not spare his pen on the subject of what he regards as the self-evident deception of the Fox Sisters:

> The "spirit-rapping" humbug was started in Hydesville, New York, about seventeen years ago, by several daughters of a Mr. Fox, living in that place. These girls discovered that certain exercises of their anatomy would produce mysterious sounds — mysterious to those who heard them, simply because the means of their production were not apparent. Reports of this wonder soon went abroad, and the Fox family were daily visited by people from different sections of the country — all having a greed for the marvellous. Not long after the strange sounds were first heard, someone suggested that they were, perhaps, produced by spirits; and a request was made for a certain number of raps, if that suggestion was correct. The specified number were immediately heard. A plan was then proposed by

means of which communications might be received from "the spirits." An investigator would repeat the alphabet, writing down whatever letters were designated by the "raps." Sentences were thus formed — the orthography, however, being decidedly bad.

What purposed to be the spirit of a murdered pedlar gave an account of his "taking off." He said that his body was buried beneath that very house, in a corner of the cellar; that he had been killed by a former occupant of the premises. A pedlar really had disappeared somewhat mysterious from that part of the country some time before; and ready credence was given the statements thus spelled out through the "raps." digging to the depth of eight feet in the cellar did not disclose any "dead corpus," or even the remains of one. Soon after that, the missing pedlar re-appeared in Hydesville, still "clothed with mortality," and having a new assortment of wares to sell.

That the "raps" were produced by disembodied spirits many firmly believed. False communications were attributed to evil spirits. The answers to questions were as often wrong as right; and only right when the answer could be easily guessed, or inferred from the nature of the question itself.

The Fox family moved to Rochester, New York, soon after the rapping-humbug was started; and it was there that their first public effort was made. A committee was appointed to investigate the matter, most of whom reported adversely to the claims of the "mediums"; though all of them were puzzled to know how the thing was done. In Buffalo, where the Foxes subsequently let their spirits flow, a committee of doctors reported that these loosely constructed girls produced the "raps" by snapping their toe and knee-joints. That theory, though very much ridiculed by the spiritualists then and since, was correct, as further developments proved.

Mrs. Culver, a relative of the Fox girls, made a solemn deposition before a magistrate, to the effect that one of the girls had instructed her how to produce the "raps," on condition that she (Mrs. C.) Should not communicate a knowledge of the matter to anyone. Mrs. Culver was a good Christian woman, and she felt it her duty — as the deception had been carried so far — to expose the matter. She actually produced the "raps" in presence of the magistrate, and explained the manner of making them.

Doctor Van Vleck — to whom I referred in connexion with my exposition of the Davenport imposture — produces very loud "raps" before his audiences, and so modulates them that they will seem to be at any desired point in his vicinity; yet not a movement of his body betrays the fact that the sounds are caused by him.

The Fox family found that the rapping business would be made to pay; and so they continued it, with varying success, for a number of years, making New York City their place of residence and principal field of operation. I believe that none of them are now in the "spiritual line." Margaret Fox, the youngest of the rappers, has for some time been a member of the Roman Catholic Church.

From the very commencement of spiritualism, there has been a constantly increasing demand for "spiritual" wonders, to meet which numerous "mediums" have been "developed."

Many, who otherwise would not be in the least distinguished, have become "mediums" in order to obtain notoriety, if nothing more.

Communicating by "raps" was a slow process; so some of the mediums took to writing spasmodically; others talked in a "trace"— all under the influence of spirits!

Mediumship has come to be a profession steadily pursued by quite a number of persons, who get their living by it.

There are various classes of "mediums," the operations of each class being confined to a particular department of "spiritual" humbuggery.

If the fact could be definitely determined, I think it would be discovered that in this "wide awake" country there are more persons humbugged by believing too little than too much. Many persons have such a horror of being taken in, or such an elevated opinion of their own acuteness, that they believe everything to be a sham, and in this way are continually humbugging themselves. [Chapter VI]

What power there is in spiritualism!

I shall be glad to receive, for publication, authentic information, from all parts of the world in regard to the doings of pretended spiritualists, especially those who perform for money. It is high time that the credulous portion of our community should be saved

> from the deceptions, delusions, and swindles of these blasphemous mountebanks and impostors. [Chapter XII]
>
> Whether superstition is the father of humbug, or humbug the mother of superstition (as well as its nurse), I do not pretend to say; for the biggest fools and the greatest philosophers can be numbered among the believers in and victims of the worst humbugs that ever prevailed on the earth. [Chapter XXXIV]

GHOST CASE

Just when you think you have heard and read "everything" there is to hear and read about ghosts and hauntings, you come across a case that is outlandish and in a way ridiculous. Such a case is the one that appears here. It concerns the real estate value of a property that is said to be haunted, no mean consideration if the "price" of a ghost is a drop in its monetary value. One hundred years later real-estate personnel refer to a property as "scarred" if its value is in any way threatened by oral or written remarks. Apparently the reputation of a property may be "scarred" if it is reputed to be haunted. This account was published in the columns of the *Winnipeg Free Press*, 9 April 1907. It is long and detailed, it reveals a lot about real-estate transactions, and it has some points to make about the justice system and human nature.

> ***$1,000 for a Ghost Story — Court of Appeal Grants Appeal of Plaintiff and Gives Her Damages***
>
> The following is the copy of the judgement in the "ghost case" delivered by the court of appeal yesterday morning:
>
> Nagy vs. Free Press Co.
>
> Richards, J.A.:
>
> A reporter employed by the defendant company discovered the following entry in what is known as the "occurrence book" at the police station in Winnipeg:
>
> "Second house east of Main street on St. John's avenue is believed by some people to be haunted at night between 11 and 12 midnight.

There are parties of men hanging around the house, also in basement, awaiting the appearance of the spook. This house is at present unoccupied. The Northern Fuel company are the agents of this house."

He then wrote the following for publication in the *Manitoba Free Press*, a newspaper published by the defendant company:

"A North End Ghost."

"There is a ghost in the north end of the city that is causing a lot of trouble to the inhabitants. His chief haunt is in a vacant house on St. John's avenue, near to Main. He appears late at night and performs strange antics, so that timid people give the place a wide birth.

"A number of men have lately made a stand against ghosts in general, and at night they rendezvous in the basement and close around the haunted house to await his ghostship, but so far he still remains at large."

The article so written was passed upon by one of the defendant's sub-editors and allowed by him to be printed in the defendant's paper, and it was printed and published in the morning and evening editions of Oct. 23, 1905, and in the weekly issue of Oct. 25, 1905.

An article somewhat to the same effect as the one published by the defendants appeared in the Winnipeg Telegram newspaper, and it appears that there were rumors of some kind to the same effect before either of these papers published anything concerning the property, though it does not appear to what extent such rumors had existed prior to such publication.

Closely following the publications by the defendants a number of people congregated in the evenings, and at night, about a house owned by the plaintiff, which is the house described in the above article. The crowds so assembled did damage to the house, and the plaintiff was compelled to employ people to stay in the house to prevent greater injury being done. This continued for several weeks; a crowd of people assembling every evening. Finally the plaintiff herself moved into the house for the purpose, she says, of protecting it.

At the time of publication of the article in question a physician named Kelly had agreed to buy the house for $11,000, intending to use it for a private hospital. He had paid down $250 on account of the purchase money, and had agreed to pay $4,750 more in cash on Oct. 24, 1905. He saw the article in question in the evening edition of the defendants' paper, and then refused to make the payment of $4,750, or complete the purchase. He broke off negotiations and forfeited the $250 already paid.

The plaintiff brought this action claiming damages for injuries alleged to result from the publication of the article in the defendants' paper.

In dealing with this case unusual questions have to be considered. While there are many people who have no belief in ghosts, there are many superstitious people who do believe in them, and many such, including especially many domestic servants and children, are likely to be terrorized by the thought of phantoms being in their neighborhood.

It is claimed by the plaintiff that the publication in question was malicious. I see nothing to support that contention. On the contrary, I take it to be evident that the publication was meant to be merely jocular, and I have no doubt that neither the reporter nor the sub-editor for a moment thought that the article would be taken seriously by anyone.

It seems to me further that we must assume that men of education, such as the reporter and sub-editor must have been, would know beyond a doubt that ghosts do not exist except in the imaginations of superstitious people, and, therefore, would know that the publication was untrue. In a case where a party publishes an article knowing it to be untrue, it seems to me that he takes the risk of such consequences as will naturally arise from that publication.

The evidence shows that the report of the house being haunted did attract the crowd of people that did the damage, and did put the plaintiff to expense in connection with guarding the house.

Part of the claim is for damages for loss of the sale to Dr. Kelly. In his examination as a witness the doctor stated that, but for this report he would have completed his purchase. In his cross-examination he made several statements which if not explained by other parts of his evidence, would appear to mean that his real reason for abandoning the purchase was not because of the story that the house was haunted, but because he wanted to go to Vancouver, and had changed his mind about buying the house. This learned trial judge took that view of his testimony.

I have carefully read Dr. Kelly's evidence, and with much deference it seems to me that the learned judge misapprehended its meaning as to the cause why the doctor refused to complete his purchase. What Dr. Kelly meant, I think, by the expression relied on by the learned judge, was only that he had no belief in ghosts, and therefore so far as he himself was concerned he was not influenced one way or the other by the thought of such phantoms; but his evidence does seem to me to show that what really influenced him in abandoning the purchase was the thought that, owing to the large percentage of people who were superstitious, and to the fact that the minds of sick people are easily influenced, he might lose intending patients for the private hospital which he meant to carry on in the house, because of such patients being afraid to live in a house said to be haunted. The evidence of the doctor was in no way discredited or contradicted, and therefore following the cases of Coghlan vs. Cumberland, 1898, 1 Ch. 704, and Creighton vs. the Pacific Coast Lumber company, 12 M.R. 546, it is the duty of members of this court, sitting in appeal, to review that evidence, and to deal with it, as regards its effect, as fully and freely as the trial judge has done.

It is contended by the defendant that an action of this kind does not lie; and apparently neither side has been able to find any law report of a similar action having been brought. It seems to me, however, that under the statute of Westminster, 2, 13 Ed. I., chapter 24, there is no doubt of the right to bring the action. It has been further contended that if such an action does lie the plaintiff must prove three things: first, that the statement was false; second, that the article was published with actual malice; and third, that special damage resulted which is attributable to the article complained of and to it alone.

As to the first point, it is urged that the plaintiff has not proved that the article is untrue, and that the house is not haunted. It is, of course, impossible to prove such a matter by evidence in the ordinary way. The very nature of a ghost, as understood by superstitious people, is that of a phantom appearing at rare intervals. Unless, therefore, we hold that courts should take judicial cognizance of the fact that ghosts do not exist, the falsity of the statement could never be absolutely proved. I think that the members of the court may, and as educated men should, assume that there are not such things as ghosts, and that therefore the statement is necessarily false.

I do not agree with the contention that malice must be shown to enable the plaintiff to succeed. It seems to me that people who publish an article knowing it to be false, as I assume that both the reporter and the sub-editor must have known it in this case, must be held to have done so without reasonable justification or excuse, and to render their employers, the defendant company, liable for the natural results of such publication, even though, as in this case, that result was quite unforeseen by those causing the publication, and though no malice whatever existed.

In using the word "malice" I refer only to what is ordinarily understood by that expression. Judges have in many cases used it as meaning only the absence of reasonable justification or excuse, and have attempted when so using it to distinguish it from real malice by calling it "legal malice." I see no need for its use in the latter sense, as such use only creates confusion.

As to the third question, I think special damage is shown in two respects; first, as to the physical injury done to the property, and the cost incurred by plaintiff in protecting the house from injury by excited superstitious people. The fact that superstitious people would be likely to assemble at the house; and when so assembling would be likely to make trouble, is something that would have occurred to the reporter and sub-editor had they taken time to remember that, while they themselves and other people of the educated class, would only treat such a report as jocular and harmlessly contemptuous, the more ignorant of humanity would through reading it be naturally and readily aroused to commit such overt acts as happened in this case. Secondly, as stated above, I also think that the effect of the article was to cause Dr. Kelly to refusal to complete his purchase of the house, as a result of which plaintiff lost the sale for $11,000. That result also seems to me a most natural one, and one which a reasonable man starting such a report would readily have foreseen had he known of the intent to buy the place for a hospital for sick people, or even for a dwelling house, and had he further taken a moment to think of the effect of the article on ignorant people. It is well known to everyone that many children, servants and others are particularly affected by stories of this kind.

A great deal of the real value of a house is that its use may be enjoyed as fully and with as little hindrance and annoyance as possible. Anything real or imaginary which interferes with that enjoyment is therefore a serious drawback to the value. It is to be expected that a man who is himself entirely free from belief in disembodied spirits will refuse to buy an otherwise acceptable house which is reported to be haunted, because though he would have no fears, he knows that it will be difficult to get servants to live in it, and that young children or sick people living in it would be terrorized if the report came to their ears.

The reasonable and inevitable result of such a publication seems to me to be, to greatly decrease the desirability of the house for purposes of habitation, and thereby to lessen its selling value.

With regard to the quantum of damages I find it difficult to arrive at an opinion. It is one of the many cases where they could be estimated more satisfactorily by a jury than by a judge. Still in this case the trial judge was, and, the members of this court are, in the position of a jury, and though the quantum of damages cannot be accurately arrived at by any course of reasoning, we must, as far as we can, put ourselves in the position of jurors and deal with the question in some such way as we think a jury of reasonable men would. It is not shown that all members of the crowds who used to be at the house did so because of the publication in the defendants' paper, but there is evidence that some of them did, and a jury would therefore be justified in holding that at least a portion of the damage resulted from the publication in question. As to Dr. Kelly's refuse to complete the purchase, the evidence seems to me, as already stated, to show that it was caused by the publication in question.

On thinking the matter over carefully as to the amount that should be assessed for damages, and allowing some part of the loss to be due to the publication in the Telegram, and to rumors otherwise started, it occurs to me that $1,000 is the nearest that I can come to the sum at which a jury would assess such damages as should be given against the defendant.

No case for a new trial has been made out. In my opinion the appeal should be allowed with costs, the judgement for the defendants in the court of King's Bench should be set aside, and judgment entered there for the plaintiff for $1,000 with costs of the action.

This is eminently a proper case to be appealed to the supreme court, owing to so much that is involved being new in law. If the defendants decide to so appeal there should be a stay of executions till one month after that appeal shall be finally disposed of.

Mr. Justice Phippen delivered a judgement agreeing with Mr. Justice Richards, that the appeal should be allowed and judgment entered for plaintiff for $1,000 and costs. Mr. Justice Perdue delivered a dissenting judgment, holding that the judgment appealed from should stand, and the plaintiff's appeal should be dismissed with costs.

Judge Perdue's Decision — Appeal in His Opinion Should Be Dismissed and Judgment Stand

Judge Perdue's decision was as follows:

"The plaintiff alleges that she was the owner of a house on St. John's avenue, Winnipeg, and that the defendant falsely and maliciously printed and published concerning that house the following article:"

"A North End Ghost."

"There is a ghost in the north end of the city that is causing a lot of trouble to the inhabitants. His chief haunt is in a vacant house on St. John's avenue, near to Main street. He appears late at night and performs strange antics, so that timid people give the place a wide berth. A number of men have lately made a stand against ghosts in general, and at night they rendezvous in the basement and close around the haunted house to await his ghostship, but so far he still remains at large."

By way of showing special damage, it is alleged that sales which were being negotiated with several persons were broken off by reason of the article. The plaintiff's cause of action is alleged in the statement of claim alternatively in several different ways, but they all come down to practically the same thing, the wrongful publication of a false statement concerning the plaintiff's property resulting in damage to her.

There is no direct precedent for this action to be found in the English or Canadian courts. It is an action on the case akin to slander of title and to actionable disparagement of goods. These actions are well known and frequently discussed in reported cases. It is well settled that an action will lie for written or oral falsehoods maliciously published concerning a man's goods, where such falsehoods are calculated in the ordinary course of things to produce, and where they do produce actual damage.

"When a defendant either knows or ought to know that special damage will happen to the plaintiff if he writes or speaks certain words, and he writes intending that such damage shall follow, or recklessly indifferent whether such damage follows or not, then if the words be false and if such damage does in fact follow directly from their use, an action on the case will lie." Odgers on Slander and Libe., 4th ed., p. 73.

If an action will lie under such circumstances, where a man's goods are disparaged, there seems no valid reason why an action should not lie where the false statements are made in regard to his house or his real estate, which cause direct damage to him by preventing him from selling or leasing the premises. Since the argument of this appeal, the attention of the course has been drawn to the report of a case of Barrett v. Associated Newspapers (Limited), which appeared in the *London Daily Times* of 7th and 8th March. That action seems to have been brought in respect of a statement in the *Daily Mail* newspaper that the plaintiff's house was haunted. Mr. Justice Grantham, before whom the case was tried, allowed it to go to the jury, apparently directing the jury that if they thought there was evidence of malice, they were to assess the damage plaintiff had suffered. The jury returned a verdict for the plaintiff, and judgement was entered for him.

Assuming that the plaintiff has disclosed in her statement of claim an actionable injury, it will be necessary to consider what she must establish in order to succeed. The present action is analogous to one of slander of title. The same necessary elements must therefore be established as would be necessary in an action for slander of title, before the plaintiff can succeed in this action. By authorities extending over a very long period, it has been established that to succeed in such an action the plaintiff must prove (1) that the statement is false; (2) that it was spoken or published maliciously; (3) that special damage was occasioned.

It would be difficult to establish conclusively the falsity of the statement complained of. One witness, Pugh, who passed a night in the house, said the statement was false, but on cross-examination he said he would not swear that there were not ghosts there. Upon the argument, the plaintiff's counsel asked the court to assume that the statement was false. But the court could do so only upon the ground that such a statement is repugnant to common sense and common knowledge, so that no proof of its untruth would be necessary. If the statement were admitted to be of that nature, it is difficult to see how anyone was deceived by it. The article complained of is not defamatory per se. It can only be actionable if it was intended to be believed and was believed by some third person who was influenced by it to the detriment of the plaintiff. This has an important bearing upon the consideration of the question of malice, which I shall next consider.

In some of the earlier cases it was held that to support an action for slander of title, actual malice must be shown. This view, however, has long been overruled. In Pater vs. Baker, Maule, J., expressed the opinion that there must be an intent to injure the plaintiff which might be inferred by the jury, and this view seems to be supported by the subsequent cases relating to slander of title.

It is distinctly stated by Coleridge, C.J., in Halsey vs. Brotherhood, that there must be in such an action an element of mala fides and a distinct intention to injure the plaintiff. The ingredient of mala fides or intent to injure may be described in various ways, but its presence is always necessary in one form or another and constitutes legal malice as referred to in the cases.

In view of the many decisions in which the word "malice" and "maliciously" have lately been discussed and criticized and the old meaning and effect of these words so greatly modified, one must approach with some diffidence the discussion of the meaning now to be given to these words as used in the reported decisions relating to slander of title and analogous actions.

In Bromage vs. Prosser, 4 B. & C. at p. 247, it is said that "malice" in its legal sense means a wrongful act done intentionally without just cause of excuse. This definition is approved by Lord Watson in Allen vs. Flood (1893) A.C. at page 94. He goes on to say: "In order to constitute legal malice, the act done must be wrongful, which plainly means an illegal act subjecting the doer in responsibility for its consequences and the intentional doing of that wrongful act will make it a malicious wrong in the sense of law."

In Brown vs. Hall, 6 Q.B.D. 333, Brett, L.J., with the sanction of Lord Selborne thus expressed his view: "Wherever a man does an act which in law and in fact is a wrongful act and such an act as may, as a natural and probable consequence of it, produce injury to another, and which in the particular case does produce such an injury, an action on the case will lie." In Mogul Steamship Company vs. McGregor, 23 Q.B.D., Bowen, L.J., said "'maliciously' means and implies an intent to do an act which is wrongful to the detriment of another. The term 'wrongful' imports in its turn the infringement of some right." These last two statements of the law are approved in Allen vs. Flood and in South Wales Miners' Federation vs. Glamorgan & Co. (1905) A.C. p. 250.

Now, I take it from these various definitions of legal malice that in so far as it relates to actions like the present, the conclusion may be reached that the statement complained of must be wrong, and it must be made with the knowledge that it will cause, or is likely to cause, injury to the plaintiff. There must be some mala fides, or improper motive, whether it be one of positive intention or of mere recklessness, coupled with a knowledge such as a reasonable person should possess that the statement is calculated to cause injury.

It cannot be pretended that the defendant in publishing the article in question intended or contemplated any injury to the plaintiff or her property. It is not as if the statement were that the house was badly constructed and unfit for occupation. if it was untrue to the knowledge of the party making it, it must properly be held to be a wrongful act, and an intention to injure might be inferred. But nothing derogatory to the house is stated in the article in question. To speak of a house as being the chief haunt of a ghost, or to speak of the house as haunted, would not, in the minds of reasonable men living in the present age, be considered as likely to produce an injury to the owner. There was evidence produced to the effect that some persons still believe in, or have a fear of ghosts. But the number of those actually affected by such a fear must be small, and we must consider the effect of the words with regard to the way they would be received by men of ordinary reason and intelligence, and not by the ignorant and superstitious. I think that any man of ordinary intelligence who read the article in question would see that it was an attempt to treat humorously an absurd rumor that had already got abroad.

It is said that in any event there was no justification or excuse for the newspaper publishing the statement. It may be that the falsity of a statement that is injurious implies malice, but in such a case the falsity must be distinctly proved. The Court cannot be asked to assume the falsity of the words, and from that to deduce the malice. That would be to assume two out of the three necessary elements, and nothing would remain except the consideration of the damages. It is true that in some of the cases we find the expression "without just cause or excuse" used as equivalent to "maliciously," but such use has occurred in actions for disparaging him in his trade. A disparagement of goods or a statement damaging a man's trade are acts calculated to do immediate injury by interfering with the sale of the goods or the profitable carrying on of the trade. If the statement was not unlawful, as, for instance, puffing one's own goods and comparing them with another's to his disadvantage, no wrongful act has been done, and the presence or absence of malice seems to be immaterial. But if the statement is prima facie injurious, as for instance where persons are warned against buying a certain patented article, then it is for the defendant to show that he had just cause or excuse for making the statement. I cannot, therefore, come to the conclusion that absence of "just cause or excuse" is equivalent to "malice" in the present case. The article which the plaintiff complains of is not prima facie injurious, or likely to cause injury.

If the statement is harmless on the face of it, it is for the plaintiff to show how it became harmful and she must also show that the defendant when publishing it knew it was calculated to prove harmful, and that it was published either with intent to injure, or recklessly, whether injury would be caused or not.

It appears to me that intention to injure must be established either directly or by reasonable inference to support an action like the present. Intention is not an element in civil actions for slander or libel, for it is not necessary in such cases to allege malice or to prove it unless the defendant claims privilege. But this is not an action for slander or libel in the ordinary sense and is not governed by the same rules. In actions on the case for wrongful injury, motive or intention is an essential element.

If the defendant must show "just cause or excuse," was there any such? The defendant company is engaged in the business of printing and publishing newspapers. The publisher of a newspaper undertakes to furnish its readers with news respecting current matters of interest. That is an important part of his business. Shortly before the publication of the article in question a rumor that the house in question was haunted appears to have been started. The house was unoccupied at the time and some persons hearing the rumor visited, or hung around, or went through the house, moved by idle curiosity to ascertain the cause of the alleged manifestation, or possibly to see if some trick were being played, and to detect its perpetrator. The police became aware of the rumor and of the actions of these persons, and an entry of the matter was made in the "Occurrence Book" kept at the police station. A reporter on defendant's staff read this entry and reproduced it in the form in which it was published, treating it in a quasi-humorous or serio-comic style. In publishing the article the newspaper only repeated as a matter of news the rumor that had already been circulated, that was evidently rather widely known, and to which the attention of the police had been directed. A newspaper would be justified in publishing under these circumstances such an occurrence, as a piece of news, first guarding against publishing anything defamatory. In the article in question nothing improper is said about any one, nothing improper is said about the plaintiff's house, but only incidentally and inferentially is it brought into the article in describing the vicinity where the alleged ghost was seen, and where persons had been congregating to watch for it. It is clear that there was no intention on the part of the defendant to do a wrong to the plaintiff and that it never entered into the mind of the reporter, or of anyone else concerned in the publication, that the article would be likely to injure any person.

I think the plaintiff also failed to prove that she sustained special damage resulting directly from the statement complained of. This she is bound to prove. In the statement of claim plaintiff averred special damage in that the publication of the article caused the breaking off of negotiations for sale of the property to three separate persons. The evidence failed completely in respect of two of these. Mr. Hodgins' offer had been declined by the plaintiff before the occurrence complained of, and in any event it appears to have been contingent upon his selling his own property. Mr. Hagel does not appear to have ever opened negotiations for the purchase of the house. The only evidence of importance in respect to his branch of the case is that referring to the transaction with Dr. Kelly. After reading the evidence of that gentleman I must confess that I consider it very contradictory and too inconsistent to justify the finding of damage upon it alone. Dr. Kelly had purchased the house and had paid a deposit of $250. He refused to complete the purchase. In his evidence in chief he stated that his main reason for refusing to complete the transaction was the report in the Free Press. But in cross-examination he stated that that was the reason he gave for not buying, that the real reason was he had changed his mind. He admitted it was not the ghost that prevented him from buying, but it was the change of mind. Then he said the cause of his change of mind was the report about the ghost and the other cause was that he wanted to go to the coast, that he could not say which was the real cause. Then immediately afterwards he stated that if it had not been for the report he would have completed the deal. He also on cross-examination made several admissions that were damaging to his evidence in chief and which cast much doubt upon his whole testimony. He admitted having said that the reputation the house had of being haunted did not influence him.

Upon evidence such as this it would not be safe to found damages, where damages are the gist of the action. The learned trial judge refused to believe the statements of the witness that were favorable to the plaintiff, and to disbelieve those that favored the defence. He saw the demeanor of the witness, and refused to find upon his testimony, that the statement in question had caused the breaking off of the sale. In this I think he came to a proper conclusion, and this Court should not interfere with his finding upon such evidence. His finding under such circumstances should be treated in the same manner as if it were the verdict of a jury. It rested upon the plaintiff to establish by clear evidence that she had suffered damage directly caused by the article in question, and in the opinion of the trial judge she failed to do this. The other claims for damages for wages guarding the house, buying extra furniture, maintenance of house, car fares, etc., are not such as could, under any circumstances be recovered in an action like the present.

The trial judge also points out that the rumor in question was current before it was entered in the police court book, and that it was published in another newspaper. This adds to the difficulty of finding damage directly traceable to the defendant's publication.

Evidence was put in to show a general depreciation of value by reason of the publication of the article. Damage is the gist of an action like the present. "The necessity of proving actual temporal loss with certainty and precision in all cases of this sort has been insisted upon for centuries." "Where the special damage alleged is that the plaintiff has lost the sale of his property, it is necessary for the plaintiff to prove that he was in the act of selling his property either by public auction or private treaty, and that the defendant by his words prevented an intending purchaser from bidding or completing": Odgers on L. & S. 4th ed. p. 76, citing Tasburg v. Day, Cro. Jac. 484; Law v. Harwood, Sir W. Jones, 196. In Ratcliffe v. Evans, which was an action brought for maliciously publishing an untrue statement about the plaintiff's business, proof of general loss of trade was held to be admissible to support the action. This was upon the ground that a general loss of business had resulted as distinct from the loss of this or that known customer. Such reasons can have no application here. It must be shown that an actual sale was prevented. Evidence of opinion as to depreciation of value, caused by the statement, is not sufficient. No lasting injury was shown to have been caused. A rumor like the one in question is soon forgotten in this community.

In my opinion the judgment appealed from should stand and the appeal should be dismissed with costs.

PSYCHIC AND SPIRIT MEDIUM

Readers of this book will be interested in checking out Alan Hatfield's webpage (*alanhatfield.com*). It is well illustrated, it is easy to read, and it is fully professional, despite the fact that it describes events and experiences that many readers (especially sceptical ones) will find well-nigh incredible. It does so in "high spirits," if I may risk a pun!

The website holds particularly interest because Mr. Hatfield is an experienced, accomplished, full-time medium. Indeed, he describes himself (below) as "a professional Psychic and Spiritual Medium." I have discussed with him (via email) his use — or misuse — of the word "Spiritual" in this designation. My sense of the language is that the proper designation is "Spirit Medium," using the convention established more than a century ago by the Society for Psychical Research. My argument is that he is not necessarily either "spiritual" or "non-spiritual." He connects with the "spirit-world," not the "spiritual world," hence the adjective to use is "spirit." (The same sense adheres to the word "psychic," thought not to the word "psychical." The former word refers to something or some action that *is itself* psychic; the latter word, to something or some action that *relates to* the psychic, as, for instance, a "psychical researcher" who is like a scholar — but not to a "psychic researcher" who would be a "sensitive" or "psychic detective" or "medium.")

Such quibbles to one side, I am intrigued with Mr. Hatfield and his series of evident successes. So I have included here, with Mr. Hatfield's permission, two extracts from his website: the introduction which appears on his homepage; the entire "FAQs" (Frequently Asked Questions) section. They make lively reading.

Additional note: Nomenclature is quite important and usually sheds a lot of light on approaches and attitudes. When Mr. Hatfield read over what I wrote above, he added some interesting comments for me to read, and again with his permission, I am able to share them with my readers. Here is what he wrote on April 17, 2005:

> Hi John.
>
> I received your letter and reviewed what you would like to present concerning myself in your new book. I feel that you have done a good job in conveying what you have observed from your own perspectives, and yet have also presented for your readers some very real paradoxes to consider for themselves in relationship with the paranormal!

In lieu of the question as to why I prefer to adhere to the title "spiritual medium" as opposed to "spirit medium," it is based on my Mi'kmaq ancestry, in that I use prayer before every undertaking which includes all Spiritual Readings, haunting investigations or recording E.V.P. (electronic voice phenomena). I connect myself to the Great Spirit when I do this, asking for Divine intervention and guidance, and speak in my Native tongue. I am considered a Spiritual elder in my community, which is why I have preferred this particular adjective.

John, please visit here to understand more about the term: "spiritual medium." *http://sm-pi.com/pages/services.html.* John Edward, James Van Praagh, George Anderson and Sylvia Browne also identify themselves as 'spiritual mediums' as opposed to "spirit mediums." Anyway, this is probably not any big issue to be concerned over, John. I think that you have done justice anyway!

If you have any further comments … please get back to me.

Have a great weekend!

Sincerely,

Alan Hatfield

Introduction

Since 1988, ALAN HATFIELD has been a professional Psychic and Spiritual Medium. He has conducted thousands of Spiritual Readings throughout Canada, the United States, and the world, bringing comfort and closure to many people who were able to hear from their loved ones in Spirit! He has also spent many years of research in the field of E.V.P. (Electronic Voice Phenomena), and has a very impressive track record over the years with his dedication to offer the most substantial evidence of LIFE after DEATH.

He is indeed the true pioneer of successfully recording the Voices of Spirit on audio tape in Eastern Canada; and bringing this discovery to the attention of the News Media with his first newspaper article being featured in *The Truro Weekly Record*, in the summer of 1992! Alan has been requested many times in the past to investigate Haunted Homes and dwellings in both Canada and the United States, and has had most of these events well documented in the News Media. He is also the only person who has ever recorded the Spirit Voices of the victims of the RMS *TITANIC* GRAVE, clearly onto audio tape; while under the scrutiny of all the News Media and a professional sound engineer! Over the many years of dedication to his profession, Alan has been the guest of Radio and Television Talk Shows as well, both in Canada and the United States. Since his first one-hour Television documentary *TALES of a PSYCHIC MEDIUM*, a World-Premiere, was released by VISION TV of Toronto, Canada, Alan has been looking forward to the filming of new documentaries in 2004, which are currently engaged throughout North America and the United Kingdom. The number-one mystery pondered by mankind: IS THERE LIFE AFTER DEATH? Please feel free to explore the possibilities as you view this site, as Alan has proven his sincerity, dedication, and expertise throughout a long career as a genuine Psychic and Spiritual Medium, helping to bridge the gap between our World and the World beyond.

Dave Hatfield

Alan Answers Your Questions

Over the years, I have been asked a multitude of questions, related to my profession as a Psychic and Spiritual Medium. I have compiled some of the more relevant questions and how I have answered these, on this page. It is hoped that it will bring understanding and perhaps a different perspective, in dragging the whole realm of the Paranormal out of the "dark ages," and into the light of acceptance and a new vision!

ALAN HATFIELD. Psychic Medium. April 14, 2002

Q: *What is exactly a Psychic or Spirit Medium?*

A: I would like to address this question, in the following manner. First and foremost, a Psychic or Spiritual Medium is a person who was born into this physical world, with a special gift and mission. Often he or she will try to fit into this world and live a life of normalcy, but this is quite difficult to do, because this person instinctively knows that somehow, there is a Divine purpose for their very being. Often they will attempt to work at everyday ordinary jobs, but always led back by Spirit and reminded who they are. It finally becomes evident, that this person must follow their Higher Guidance, and submerge themselves within this. Once this resolve is realized, and then they are able now to move forward into the profession and role as a Psychic or Spirit Medium. This is to become a "bridge" between the Spiritual and Physical world, and to help those in both of these dimensions to communicate with their loved ones, giving hope and bringing comfort for those who are grieving a loss of a loved one, or to bring closure to unresolved issues. There are many genuine Psychic and Spirit Mediums who have dedicated their lives to doing just this, as myself and others like George Anderson, John Edward, James Van Praagh to name a few. All of us have began with what we had thought to be an ordinary life… … only to be "re-positioned" into a life of what science calls paranormal, but as we consider to be quite normal and natural to us.

Q: What is the difference between a Psychic or Spirit Medium and a Fortune Teller?

A: The most distinct difference between a Medium and a Fortune Teller is the method in which information is received and given. A Fortune Teller may commonly use Tarot cards, tea leaves, palmistry, astrology or some other form of divination, to describe to you, what they "see" according to these structures. If this makes any sense to you, it also probably makes sense to others as well. This information is very generalized, and would suit a wide array of the general public. It is commonly labeled "for entertainment only" when in the media. A genuine Psychic or Spirit Medium would never portray their gifts as something that would fall under the category of "entertainment"! Communication to and from Spirit is a very serious matter, often very emotional and emphatically understood by those who need an answer from the Otherside.

These messages from Spirit are received by the Medium through "energies" that have been manifested, and through these energies, words and sentences are formed by Spirit, and quite often flash visions are given by Spirit, which enable the Medium to convey these particular messages to their loved ones. A genuine Medium has no need or desire to rely on external means such as Tarot cards or tea leaves, nor astrology, or any other form of divination. We believe that God has presented us with these gifts, to glorify Him in helping other people.

Q: Where is the "OTHERSIDE"? How can I understand this in relation to where I am at this moment, living in this physical world?

A: I will explain to you, how Spirit described to me, where the Otherside is. The physical world and the Spiritual world are neighbors, living alongside each other! Now to help you with putting this into perspective, suppose you had a table fan, and you were to turn the switch on, to "low speed." You would have no difficulty in seeing the blade of the fan, as it was turning. Now let us assume that at this low speed, that this would represent the Physical World. Now, if you were to turn the switch on the fan to "high speed," the blade would be turning so fast, that it would almost appear that it was not there, for not only do you not see the blade at this speed, but indeed you can see the wall right through the fan! Of course, rest assure, the blade is indeed there! Now suppose that this high speed would represent the Spiritual World. Like the blade of the fan on low speed, the Physical World, we are able to see our surroundings, but however, like the blade of the fan on high speed, the Spiritual World, we still see our surroundings, and we mistakenly assume that there is nothing more around us. Like the high speed blade, the Spiritual World although you may not see it … it is indeed all around us! An etherical dimension, or neighbour to us here in the physical world. That is why Spirit always says that they are but a mere thought away from us, at all times!

Q: Are there good Spirits, and bad Spirits?

A: Here in this physical world, we must use some common sense and logic, to what people we would want to embrace and trust to be associated with. We can come to call some of these people "friends," while others we may keep at bay, as perhaps acquaintances. Still, there are others sometimes we would not want to have anything to do with! We must also, when communicating with Spirit, use this same approach, because like here in this physical world, there are those whom you would rather avoid. This in itself does not imply that the so-called good vs the so-called bad. It is with prayer and compassion, do we draw our lines, here in this Physical World, and likewise in the Spiritual World.

Q: According to the Holy Bible, is it not wrong to consult with a Medium? Are Mediums doing the work of the Devil?

A: As can be expected, this question is a favorite to pose by those who follow man's translation and concept of the Scriptures. However, I do feel that I must address these kinds of questions, in spite of the fact of my Native ancestry with having their own beliefs, culture and language. I certainly would not imply that the Christian faith is one that should not be followed, but rather make some reference as to the early translations into the English language of the Scriptures. If one was to tell a funny story in English, then those who understood English perhaps would find the humor in that story. However, if this same funny story was now translated into another language, word for word, then a problem now presents itself! Somehow by doing this, the humor and understanding becomes lost! In the same manner, the Holy Bible could not have been translated word for word from the ancient scripts, without confronting this problem. Some compromising with translation had to be rendered, in order to have understanding. What I am stating here is the fact that the Old Testament and some of its teachings were the result of human concept of what was acceptable to God, and in their own judgment, what was not. It is often said that the Holy Scriptures are the inspired Word of God. Yet with the advent of Christ, even Jesus condemned some of the Old Testament teachings, and presented us with the New Testament teachings! One certainly could debate this whole topic for a life time, but in reality, I feel no need to do so. The very same God that I pray unto, and the very same God that the Holy Bible speaks of is OUR CREATOR. We could not be a separate entity from this Creation, no more than a river could be a separate entity from the sea, it is all water! A few years ago, Spirit sent me to a church, to offer help to a girl. As the church service was already in progress, I announced to an usher, that I had been sent here, to help a girl. At the time, Spirit did not tell me which girl, nor in what sort of way did this girl need my help. After about 20 minutes, a young girl jumped up from her seat, flailing her arms and legs about, and shaking rather violently about. This was the one who Spirit said needed my help! I will not go into details here, but an exorcism occurred, and all the Glory, was certainly given to God for this opportunity to use me in setting this girl free of diabolical entities! Consider the question now; would Satan have me go to a church, to rid a girl of his demonic agents, giving all the Glory to God? The truth is that God works with people in different ways, and if Our Creator has designed this path for me to follow, then I do not question this. Does not your dog have love and bonding for you? Your dog has no concept and understanding of the Scriptures however. God is Love and Light, and we all are part of His Creation, as Spiritual Beings having a human existence! If you are in the total darkness, and you were to light up a candle, then you would now have light and hope! It matters not the colour of the candle, red, yellow, black or white! They will all give this light, as God will give His Love and Light to all of His Creation, if only we remember to share this with others. Let those who have faith follow this path, but should those people meet others along the way who are following their own paths, greet each other with the same Light that dissipates all Darkness, for only then will you find your peace and have God lovingly smile upon you!

Q: Should a Ouija board be used for contacting the dead?

A: Absolutely No! The Ouija board is not a "harmless toy" that gives you hours of innocent fun and entertainment, but can indeed be a "portal" or doorway to the Spirit World. Would you allow complete strangers to come into your home, and fully trust them while there? What if amongst them, unknowingly to you, that one of these strangers that you have invited into your home, happened to be a child killer, or a rapist, or some unsavory person, could you now feel confident and in control of this situation? Far too often, when one consults a Ouija board for the purpose of communicating with Spirit, unsettling circumstances follow. The reason that this occurs, is the Ouija board is a doorway to the Darkside of the Spiritual World. In this dimension, we find very negative and troubled entities, that will respond to you, sharing their misery and havoc, and certainly their lies and will always in time, betray your trust! Be prepared to have uncertain events, with sometimes terrifying results that you may not be able to handle in your home, and more importantly, in your life, should you play with a Ouija board. I have seen the aftermath and consequences many times over the years, to strongly advise you against making use of a Ouija board for any purpose whatsoever!

Q: What if a loved one commits suicide?

A: Suicide of course is a tragedy that leaves a deep scar in the souls of the families left here on this physical plane, to not only cope with deep sorrow of this event, but also far too often, they carry the burden of responsibility that they must have failed this loved one somehow, they continually ask themselves what went wrong? I have had many instances whereby a person who crossed over by suicide, and who now has returned to Spirit, ask me to ask their loved ones for forgiveness, and always requesting prayers from them, to help bring them up to the dimension where other family members and friends await them. The suicide victim resides in a Spiritual dimension, just below where they need to be. This is a place of deep sadness, because this person is amongst others who have likewise, taken their own lives. I believe that God is a loving and compassionate Creator, and has the capacity to forgive, and through our prayers for these suicide victims, He responds by His Majestic Grace, and allows this person, to be lifted up, and be comforted by loved ones who have been waiting for this miracle to take place.

Q: Is there a difference between a Ghost and a Spirit?

A: Yes. A ghost apparition is similar in many ways to a photo-copy of an original picture. It is made up of energies of emotional "residue," which have been sort of trapped in an etherical dimension, often having to do with a tragic crossing over. A murdered soul for instance, may leave behind their highly charged emotional energies that form into an apparition. These apparitions are most often in a vicinity where a tragic event had occurred. A ghost may be seen here one time, or re-occur and be seen many times over an indefinite period of time. Although a ghost may appear sometimes as being terrifying to you, there is nothing to be really afraid of, as this image will usually fade away very quickly. Now, on the other hand, a Spirit is able to communicate, reason, and "physically manifest" at certain times, in order to get your attention to convey a message or to give you a sign of their presence. I have recorded their voices clearly many times on audio cassette tape in the past. A Spirit who is connected to you by a bonding of love, is always nearby, and will at most times give you subtle signs of this, but sometimes, if you do not recognize these signs, a Spirit may knock over something, turn a light off or own, cause a faucet to run, or find another avenue to "wake" you up! Spirits do indeed have a sense of humor as well! Always remember, that "like attracts like", so if you are kind and loving, and are inclined to be a prayerful person, then you have nothing to fear with Spirit, as you will attract those who love you to your side. Please understand, that if you prefer to "dabble with the Darkside" in your life, then you can expect to have some company! The more intensive you become with this, the more is the real possibility of having unknown entities, and their cohorts confront you, with sometimes very unsettling and frightening results. I have been called upon in a few of these cases, whereby an exorcism had to be done to restore this situation. Be very careful that this does not happen to you!

THE DEVIOUS ART OF IMPROVISING

"Massimo Poloidoro is an investigator of the paranormal, author, lecturer, and cofounder and head of CICAP, the Italian skeptics group. His website is www.massimopolidoro.com." That is a description of the writer of this column which first appeared in the May–June 2007 issue of *Skeptical Inquirer: The Magazine for Science and Reason*: This busy man has given me permission to reprint this column which was one a series devoted to how sceptics go about the business of turning the tables on psychics and (in this instance) on a non-critical promoter of psychics. After all, we read a lot about how psychics work; we should learn a little about how sceptics work! The participants are Allen Spraggett, at the time host of the weekly Global television show *ESPecial People,* and James Randi, the illusionist and psychical debunker known professionally as the Amazing Randi. Both men are one-time residents of Toronto. Randi is the author of numerous books that expose the practices of self-styled psychics like Uri Geller; Spraggett, journalist and broadcaster and former church minister, has written numerous books about psychicism, including critical ones about mediums like Arthur Ford and exposés of "the Psychic Mafia."

As an investigator of the paranormal and a psychologist, with a background in magic, I am intrigued with the art of improvising seemingly paranormal feats. Here is one of the most ingenious and extraordinary stunts that I have ever heard of.

In November 1974, when Uri Geller's comet was still burning bright, Randi was invited to be a guest on a Canadian television show titled *ESPecial People* on the Global Television Network. The host was journalist Allen Spraggett, a strong believer in the paranormal, and the main subject of the talk show was the hottest psychic topic since the times of Margery: Geller, of course.

Spragget was convinced that Geller was the real thing and that Randi, claiming that he could duplicate Geller's feats, was only a bragging skeptic, unable to really do what he claimed. Randi agreed to be on the show, but only on the condition that he would not be asked to perform.

It was clear that, to prove his point, Spraggett would never allow Randi the friendly atmosphere and relaxed conditions that Geller received almost wherever he went. And, since these easygoing manners were essential in order to "prepare" fr the wonders that would later be shown on camera, it was pointless for Randi to even try to demonstrate anything.

Spraggett accepted Randi's caveat and invited him only to chat about the paranormal. Or so it seemed ….

Tricking the Trickster?

The day of the show, Randi arrived late, accompanied by his assistant Moses Figueroa. They were both soaking wet from a heavy rain and were immediately escorted to the control room, where they dried off a bit. Walter B. Gibson — a friend of Houdini and the author of the famous *Shadow* detective stories — was present in the control room, along with two other program guests.

An interview was already underway, so Randi waited for his turn. "I was not particularly apprehensive," he said, "since I was not under any pressure to perform, and was there only to be interviewed."

Randi was soon introduced in the studio, and the interview started. They were only a few minutes into it when Spraggett started pressuring Randi for a performance. If he was so good a magician, Spraggett said, and if Geller was using magic tricks, Randi should be able to do the same things right on the spot.

Randi was quite furious; though he had said that he would not perform, Spraggett was demanding Randi do so under quite impossible conditions. Suddenly, Spraggett took two oversized, sturdy spoons from his desk and challenged Randi to bend them. They were not at all similar to the spoons that Geller had bent for Spraggett.

Without ever letting them go, Spraggett held the handles of the spoons and Randi lightly stroked the bowls. Then, the journalist discarded one spoon and they concentrated on the other. Spraggett agreed that at no time did Randi put undue pressure on them. After a moment, the spoon suddenly seemed to beome like plastic, sheared off, and broke into two pieces. Spraggett lost some colour in his face.

"The spoon," Spraggett said, trying to find an explanation for what had happened, "was bent as you were picking it up … uh, and, uh … this is a phenomenon, of course, of … in previously bending it so that there is a stress point, and then with a little bit of leverage, it separates quite neatly."

In fact, as can be seen on the video recording of the show, Randi never had a chance to hold the spoons in his hands and never picked them up: Spraggett held them the entire time, and Randi only stroked the bowls. Spraggett's explanation makes no sense.

Next, Spraggett produced a nail from his pocket, but Randi "passed" on this test. The journalist got some colour back on his face, but it wasn't there for long. There is a technique that's used in con games in which the con artist wins a little, then loses, and then seems ready to lose very big in order to reel in the victim. On the nail, Randi appeared to be losing his edge, but, in truth, he was getting ready to pull the fish into his net.

Backfire!

Spraggett reached into his inner jacket pocket and extracted an envelope, sealed with transparent tape. He explained that he had made a drawing twenty-four hours before, in the privacy of his own home, and then sealed it in the envelope, which he had kept in his jacket pocket. Geller had been able to reproduce a drawing under these conditions. "Now," he said to Randi, "let's see you do that!"

"And if I could do it, what would you say?" asked Randi.

"I would be very impressed. I'd be extremely impressed."

"But would you be impressed enough to say that I'm a psychic?"

"I don't know. I would have to consider that. But I would certainly say that you're a hell of a lot better magician than I think you are!"

"Wait a minute," Randi countered. "You say that Uri Geller is a psychic because he did this. Now, if I were able to do it, would you say I'm a psychic?"

"You do it, and I'll say that the Amazing Randi has amazed me."

Spraggett evaded the question and allowed Randi to hold the envelope between his hands for only ten seconds, as he had allowed Geller to do.

After the ten seconds, Randi asked for a pad and felt-tip marker and made a drawing, allowing the camera to peek in order to show that he was really making the drawing at that time. When he was finished, he placed it face down on the table and asked: "Would you like to open the envelope, Allen?"

Spraggett did so and removed and unfolded a small sheet of blue paper, revealing a drawing of a tugboat with two decks, on the waves, with a single smokestack billowing smoke to the right.

"Am I a psychic if I've reproduced that, Allen? Yes or no?" asked Randi.

"If you've reproduced it, you're quite extraordinary."

"But I'm not a psychic?"

"You're extraordinary. I'd have to consider —"

Randi showed his drawing, identical in every respect to the one Spraggett had drawn twenty-four hours earlier.

The journalist turned pale again. His attempt at debunking Randi had backfired on him.

"Am I extraordinary, Allen?" Randi asked.

"That's … quite extraordinary, Randi."

"Have I proved anything to you?"

"Look, we have to take a break…. "

And when the break was over, Spraggett claimed he could easily figure out how Randi had done it, and in fact he would probably have the answer in an hour. However, he was never able to do it. Not in an hour, a day, or thirty-three years. And now, for the first time in print, here is the secret of that quite extraordinary trick.

A Solution, at Last

When I first met Randi almost twenty years ago, one of the first things I asked him was how on earth he had been able to pull off that stunt on Spraggett's show. I had read about it and had seen the interview when it was shown on Italian television during a series on parapsychology by Piero Angela. I could not think of any trick used by magicians that could allow such an incredible feat. Learning how he had amazed Barbara Walters with the use of his "belly writer," as described in my previous column, only added to my confusion. For it was clear, by watching the tape, that he was not using any kind of hidden writer.

"Well, Massimo," he said, "I knew Spraggett quite well, and I was quite sure that he was not going to play by the rules. If he said he was not going to ask me to perform, I could quite confidently expect that he was going to play some tricks on me. Then, I had to be prepared."

Along with his assistant Moses, Randi went to Toronto, where the show was to be taped. Even though the taping was scheduled for 5:00 p.m., Randi showed up at the reception of the Global Television Network several hours earlier.

"But, sir," the guard had said, "you are expected to be here later this afternoon!"

"Of course, I knew that," Randi told me, "but I acted surprised. I asked the guard if he would personally tell Spraggett that I had been there but had gone away to get something to eat. The guard informed me that he would be done with his shift in about thirty minutes but he would leave a note behind for the next guard who took over. When he told me that, I asked if I could go down the hall to give my message in person to Spraggett. I left Moses behind to distract and chat with the guard while I went down the hall, but we didn't officially sign in at that time."

Thus, Randi got inside the building and found Spraggett's dressing room — Spraggett's name was on the door.

"I tried the door and found that it was open! I quickly went inside. I found briefcase there. I opened it and found a couple of big spoons and an envelope."

As expected, the journalist had decided to play some dirty tricks on Randi. However, he could not imagine the trap he was putting himself in.

"I took the spoons and prepared one of them, then, I carefully peeled the tape from the envelope, opened it, and saw the drawing of the tugboat. I replaced everything as I found it, quickly left the dressing room, and closed the door."

All was ready, now Randi only needed to make it look as if he never had a chance to get close to the studio before the interview.

"I hurried back to the guard's desk and told him that Spraggett was inside the studio taping — which was quite true. I told him not to bother about leaving a note, and Moses and I headed for the car out in the parking lot."

They waited outside, and, very soon, they saw the replacement guard arriving — it was raining hard, so the guard didn't notice them — he went inside, and the other guard came out, got into his car, and drove away.

Randi and Moses waited until very late, then stood in the rain to get wet and made their entrance. "Of course, this guard had never seen us before, and we both signed in and gave the exact time of our arrival. In fact, we met Spraggett coming toward the reception desk as we went down the hall; he was coming to see if we'd arrived. He saw us all wet, which was a 'convincer' that we'd just arrived at that moment. From then on, it was just acting."

And quite good acting, I must say.

"When Spraggett first produced the spoons," said Randi, "I allowed my expression to change and tried to look dismayed. Spraggett's face had a big smile. He was satisfied that he had cornered me."

When his plan backfired on him, right after Randi did the drawing, Spraggett called for a commercial break, and, as soon as the camera was turned off, so was the artificial smile he had on his face.

"Spraggett left the set," Randi explained, "and went outside into the hall, where we heard much shouting. I looked at the control room, where Walter Gibson was in hysterics laughing. All of the people, including the engineers and cameramen, were giving me the 'thumbs-up' sign of approval. They really didn't like Spraggett at all."

Of course, as Randi usually did when he intended to prove his point (in this case, that a television reporter is no match for a good magician), he left a chance for his puzzle to be solved. There was at least one way to get a clue as to how Randi did it. Someone may have questioned the guard who had been on duty when Randi arrived in order to find out whether Randi had been at the studio before. If so, the guard could only have said no. However, had someone asked the morning-shift guard as well, Randi's trick might have been discovered. The fact is that no one ever questioned that guard.

If Spraggett never checked all of the possible trails, in order to find a solution to the mystery that had baffled him, one can be pretty sure that he never even bothered to look for alternatives to the paranormal "explanation" when he met Uri Geller. He didn't think he needed to; he had already decided that Geller was the real thing. How easy it must have been for Geller to fool Spraggett!

Not surprisingly, the show with Randi was not broadcast on the day that had previously been announced. It was delayed by a week, and, two weeks later, the station suddenly cancelled the entire *ESPecial People* series. It seems that just one *special person* had been sufficient to knock ESP off of that network.

2

PECULIAR OCCURRENCES

In this section there appear accounts of bizarre events that lend themselves to supernatural interpretation. Other explanations are possible, inevitably, but the witnesses themselves will always be haunted by what happened to them, despite any rational interpretation.

"I NEED YOU"

H.R. Stevens, a native of Cameron, Ontario, contributed an account of an unusual Second World War experience which reverberates in his memory and also in mine and I am sure in the memories of my readers. Harry Stevens's life has been characterized by a series of unusual experiences — from the early years to close to the present. The following "extraordinary experiences" were described in the letter he sent to me on 16 April 1990:

> I believe whole-heartedly that there are unknown beings in our midst. I have had many small things happen in my life that lead me to believe in the supernatural. Or whatever. Who knows?
>
> I will tell you of some of them.
>
> When I was three years old, my two sisters and I lost our

Mother. Consequently our Dad hired a lady to look after and raise us children. This lady was named Mrs. Nel La Pierre. She was well known among our friends and neighbours as a tea-cup reader. She was so good with her predictions that many people came to her for tea-cup readings. Her predictions were accurate and it was uncanny how they frequently came to pass.

The most memorable thing about her was the following incident, which happened one winter's evening in the kitchen of our farm-house at Highland Creek, Ont. The kitchen windows were almost completely covered with frost. Mrs. La Pierre was sitting and staring at the frosted window. She jumped up quickly and remarked to my Dad that her close friend, Helen Reid, who lived on a farm a mile away from us, was calling out to her. She said she had just had a vision of Helen's face which was peering at her through the small opening in the frost on the window.

Dad tried to calm her down and convince her that she had been dreaming. This took some time and much conversation. The conversation was interrupted after a short period of time by the ringing of the telephone. It was Mr. Reid who was calling to inform Dad and Mrs. La Pierre that his wife Helen had just passed away and that her last words were "Nel, Nel, I need you."

Now, that story is as true as my name is Harry Stevens.

I STARTED TO DESCRIBE THE TOWN

John Fairley and Simon Welfare are the authors of *Arthur C. Clarke's World of Strange Powers* (London: Collins, 1984), the book based on the popular Yorkshire Television series. They devote a chapter in the book to reincarnation, the notion of "life before life."

Many present-day men and women maintain that under regressive hypnosis they remember being some of the great men and women of history. "But not everyone who feels themselves transported in time manages a brush with history's high dramas," the authors wrote. As one of a number of instances, they interviewed Mrs. W. Barnard of Kenton, Middlesex, England, who had a strange experience while motoring in Ontario:

> As we approached Smiths Falls, I started to describe the town. My husband knew I had never been in Canada before, so he was surprised when I described a part of the main street, a grocer's shop, name of Desjardins, on one corner opposite a Royal Bank of Canada branch on the other corner. Our surprise was complete when we drove up the main street and saw the bank on one corner, and a grocer's shop on the other, exactly as I had said, except that the name on the grocer's shop was not Desjardins. My husband stopped the car and went into the grocer's shop. There he was informed that the last owner's name was Desjardins — thirty years ago.

A GENUINE ROYAL PHENOMENON

"Have Your Say" is the title of a regular editorial feature that used to appear in the *Toronto Star*. Readers were urged to write and submit letter-length accounts of their opinions and experiences. One reader recalled an unusual experience that occurred to him in the palace at Versailles in France. He related it to the notion advanced by Hollywood director Oliver Stone in his revisionist film about the possibility of a conspiracy surrounding the death of U.S. President John F. Kennedy that history is a "hall of mirrors." The reader was Edward L. Bowman of Newmarket, Ontario, who contributed the account titled "Who Was that Naked Man in the Hall of Mirrors?" It appeared in the *Star* on 19 April 1992.

> In the spring of 1976, while touring Europe, I visited Versailles Palace, outside beautiful Paris. In one of the halls, possibly the Hall of Mirrors, trailing closely behind my tour group, I thought I saw in one of the mirrors, peripherally, an imposing, rather obese figure, *in puris naturalibus* (stark naked), observing me from across the hall. When I turned around to investigate, no one was there. Peering into the mirror once more, I saw him again, straight-on, although this time his bearing drifted off centre and he shrank in dimension, appearing more distant.
>
> Optical illusion? I immediately surveyed the opposite wall for paintings, or other items, which might project this strange countenance in my direction. I noticed none. So when I turned

around again, most perplexed about this fading human configuration, I promptly raised my camera and snapped a picture of its departure. Then, oddly enough, as though everything was normal, I completely forgot about the whole affair, until now.

Cutting a long allegory short, Oliver Stone, the director of JFK, said the film challenges the archaic notion of reality and asks, "Isn't history a distorted hall of mirrors …?" His question triggered an astonishing flashback and instant insight.

My hasty snapshot succeeded in capturing a brilliant flash of intense light. Obviously, the blinding illumination was caused by the exploding flash bulb. Consequently, the impressionable, ephemeral scrutinizer — if impression is, in fact, an integral part of "reality"— failed to register on my film. The individual titillating my mind's eye, whoever or whatever he was, escaped enlightenment.

Upon reflection, I now conclude: I witnessed something extravagantly irregular and portentous inside Versailles. Indeed, perhaps I observed a genuine royal phenomenon, the mansion's guardian spirit.

And perhaps I captured its "essence"— dazzling radiation — on film, after all. I say there, wasn't corpulent King Louis XVI also known as the Sun King?

THE POWER OF SUGGESTION

The following article was written by Dr. Peter Steele, a physician who practises in Whitehorse, Yukon. It appeared as "A Testament to the Power of Suggestion" in the *Medical Post*, 30 May 1995.

I'm a very conventional doctor — no iridology, a touch of homeopathy, little chiropractic — but I have had remarkable success with charming warts. My apogee of success was a child of nine who had forty-seven painful verrucae on the soles of his feet.

We went through my routine, with the essential connivance of the parents, of going to the bank to withdraw one new penny for each wart, going down to the Yukon River and throwing each of the pennies over the shoulder while saying the magic word: *Tikkitikkitembonaseremboberiberibushkidankerwallamannapannakofemaskoshotz* (which I have printed out on a label stuck on a wooden tongue depressor for the child to learn at home).

Since I started, I have had at least fifty successes, mainly with children between the ages of six (when they can understand my mumbo-jumbo) and twelve (after which they think I'm a jerk). I attribute this to their suggestibility in a matter I think is mostly attributable to self-hypnosis.

I find it marvellous that in these days of hi-tech science the charming of warts is so completely inexplicable. But I have a theory, completely empirical. Warts are small tumours caused by the human papilloma virus. Tumour behaviour can be modified by the immune system, and the immune system can be triggered by hypnosis.

I suggest that in charming warts we are inducing a state of self-hypnosis, whether it be by juice of celandine, frog legs under a full moon, or by my magic word. It is interesting that the only adults with whom I have had success are highly suggestible.

The mundane scientific fact is that it doesn't matter what your incantation, potion, or sacrifice, you must believe to trigger your immune system to alter the metabolism of the papilloma virus in your skin. Then, Presto! — Dr. Peter Steele, Whitehorse, Yukon

WE WERE GOING TO WORK SOME TELEPATHY

Roger Burford Mason taught in the school system in England for twenty years before coming to Canada in 1988. He settled in Toronto, worked for a community newspaper, and eventually founded *The Danforth Report*, a community newspaper. Over the next decade he published two collections of stories, *Telling the Bees* (1990) and *The Beaver Picture* (1992), then *Somewhere Else* (1996), a book of travel sketches, the biography of a book dealer, and finally *A Grand Eye for Glory* (1998), a life of painter Franz Johnston. One day Mason told me about an unusual incident that occurred during his teaching career. It involved telepathy or chance. I asked him to write it down for me. He did. Here it is:

I was teaching at a comprehensive high school in Luton, about thirty miles north of London in the early 1970s.

One morning, the period before lunch, I was covering a class for an absent colleague, and since there were no class notes, I was left to temporize for thirty-five minutes with a class of twelve-year-old students. Having finished whatever class work they had outstanding, and whatever homework they had already been assigned for the day, they still needed to be shepherded through the last fifteen minutes of class, so I decided to play a game with them to while the time away.

I sent a boy out of the classroom and then told the others that we were going to work some telepathy on him. Writing "eggs and bacon," or it might have been "bat and ball," on the blackboard so that everyone could read it, I then cleared the board and asked the boy back inside. He stood facing the corner while I told the class to try and think the brief phrase into his mind.

Nothing worked with this boy as I recall, and we had patchy luck with the next two or three children, but then a girl answered five or six correctly in succession, and as far as I could see, without cheating or being given help or clues.

As the bell rang to end the period, the girl had become tearful and frightened, and subsequently, I learned, had been unsettled and unable to sleep that night. Her mother complained about the game to the school principal. The educational psychologist for the school board was called in, and I was told not to conduct games or experiments of that kind again.

THE SHADOW OF THE CROSS

The parish church of San Francisco de Asis in Ranchos de Taos in New Mexico is a wonderful structure that combines the traditional architecture of Spanish New Mexico with the Modernism of Le Corbusier. It lies just off the highway that goes from Santa Fe to Taos, and one summer day in 1997 my wife Ruth and I drove to visit it. It was a memorable experience. The bright exterior of the church, freshly painted plaster, makes a stark contrast with its dark interior which makes use of wood. Next door is the Parish Hall where we were able to join a group of tourists and pilgrims to view "The Shadow of the Cross." This is a portrait of Jesus standing on the shore of the Sea of Galilee. With a group of twenty other people we entered a room where the larger-than-life painting has a niche all to itself. The painting is viewed twice: the first time by ordinary electrical illumination; the second time in the dark to see its glow. It was painted by an obscure Canadian artist, Henri Ault of Cobalt, Ont. How it ended up in New Mexico is a story by itself. I found this account contributed by John Winston titled "The Shadow of the Cross" on the Internet on 14 June 1995:

> As I have mentioned in the past, while I was in Taos, New Mexico, investigating the mysterious Toas Hum, I also checked out a weird painting. Here is the information about it.
>
> Of interest to many tourists is the mystery painting, "The Shadow of the Cross," by Henri Ault. After more than fifty years of exhibition in galleries in all parts of North America and Europe, this painting has found a permanent home in the Parish of San Francisco de Asis in Ranchos de Taos.
>
> What makes this painting so unusual is the fact that, while in daylight it portrays, on a shore in Galilee, the barefoot Christ, in complete darkness the portrait becomes luminescent, outlining the figure while clouds over the left shoulder of Jesus form into a shadow of a cross.
>
> It was first placed on exhibition at the St. Louis World's Fair in 1904. Later for many years it was exhibited at the Doré Galleries of London, and taken on tours of the Continent during the summer.
>
> Mrs. Herbert Sydney Griffin of Wichita Falls, Texas, and Ranchos de Taos, presented the painting to San Francisco de Asis Parish in 1948, along with several other historic and valuable objects of art.
>
> With the lights turned off for about ten minutes the figure changes posture, a cross appears over its right shoulder which is not visible in the light. The sea and sky behind the figure glow. The glow shades from light blue to green and has a quality of light that suggests moonlight. It is not a constant light: varying in brightness and appearing to be at its brightest at midnight.
>
> The artist disclaimed any knowledge of the reason for the change, saying that he thought he was demented when he went in the studio at night and discovered the luminosity.

> The picture was painted in 1896, several years before the discovery of radium. No luminous paint has so far been developed that will not darken and oxidize within a relatively short time. On one occasion flood lights were put on the portrait to induce fluorescence with negative results.
>
> From the time it was first observed by Sir William Crooks, British chemist and physicist of note, to the recent Geiger counter tests, no explanations of its marvelous change when exposed to light or darkness has been found.
>
> So there you have it folks. It is one strange painting.

HAUNTED OAK ISLAND

An Internet newsgroup conducted by a webmaster known as Obiwan offered its subscribers the following story of Oak Island. More news stories and feature stories have been generated by Oak Island in Mahone Bay, N.S., than any other mysterious site for some two hundred years. At one point in its long history, Franklin Delano Roosevelt bought stock in the company that was formed to explore for the island's buried treasure. Or should I say its *reputed* buried treasure? To this date there have been innumerable excavations but not one excavation has found anything of any value. If Oak Island is haunted, it is haunted by St. Dismus or St. Jude, the Patron Saint of Lost Causes. Lately the island was owned and operated by a Montreal-based investment syndicate which periodically engages in excavation. The island has proved to be a bonanza for the syndicate as a tourist destination. As a rule of thumb, the site of any buried or forgotten treasure is haunted by someone or something. Apparently Oak Island is no exception to this rule. John Coldrick filed the following account of his thoughts and experiences on 10 December 1994:

> I watched an old "In Search Of" a few weeks back and they talked about Oak Island. Apparently a pirate (I forget which one) buried treasure on it. Someone, somewhere, someday will be able to figure out a way to keep the water out of the shaft and get the gold.
>
> Nikki, I've been to Oak Island a few times — also an old relative of mine in the 1800s used to own a small hovel on the island! I've done a fair bit of reading about it and have always wondered

about it. However, it's got more exaggerations and mis-told stories about it than Bigfoot. It's been associated with not only pirates, but ancient civilizations and UFOs! Hardly surprising, I suppose.

Also, many of the "minor" details like gold being embedded in the teeth of a drill have been enhanced or possibly created by various people on the periphery of the mystery. The fact is that many, many people have thrown their hand into trying to solve the mystery over the years and each has small parts of the puzzle. Even the mighty beast that is the 20th century industrial age couldn't get to the end of the tunnel. It's rather sobering to realize that with all this power, time, blood and sweat that the hole still holds its secret. The fact is that the hole may have no true secret after all.

It was "discovered" in 1795 on Oak island (said by locals to have been haunted by witches, etc.) by a man named McInnis, one of the first settlers on the island. He found evidence of something unusual having been done at the base of a lone, old oak tree in the midst of what otherwise was a cleared area with a few young oaks sprouting up. On one large branch there hung an old tackle block, and under it was a depression in the ground, inferring that there was some sort of old well underneath that someone had been raising and lowering heavy things into. Right from the very beginning he thought he may have found pirate's treasure — thus the mystery has been associated with that ever since. After digging for some time he was able to find a layer of flagstones (unlike any other kind of stone on the island), a platform of oak logs at 10 feet, and earth settled 2 feet below that. After digging a further 15 feet he gave up because the earth became too difficult to dig in.

Since then, over the years, many people have dug very deep, finding several layers of oak logs, spruce, and metal in pieces. Some of the more recent drilling has been kept secret because it's being done privately by the owners of the island. However, word has it that there was found a 45-foot-high chamber with a two foot wooden roof and possibly an iron floor at 139 feet. Even more amazing is the existence of at least two tunnels that angle in from the side directly from the ocean. On more than one occasion they had thwarted attempts to go deeper due to flooding. The saddest thing about all these ambitious attempts is that they were very destructive. There's probably large amounts of useful information that could have been gleaned from some of the earlier discoveries — now all we're left with is descriptions of the logs being in a state of "advanced decomposition."

It appears that someone constructed all of this in order to protect something very valuable. It's unknown how they would have expected to get at it without killing themselves in the process, but it's always possible that a previously clever "back door" to the item(s) may have collapsed over the years and is all but invisible now.

There's still no guarantee that this has anything to do with pirate's treasure. For one thing, many mysteries in the past that appear to be incredibly complicated and deliberate have ended up being the combination of a simple thing that has been mis-interpreted over the years, possibly complicated by natural forces with no agenda but that with which they have always operated. Just ask anyone who lives near the sea about how powerful nature is and the incredible things it can appear to construct.

There does appear to be some human intervention here, though. The assumption of pirates is natural, since at the time of its discovery and for some time after treasure hunting was an extremely popular pastime for many people living in the new world. There actually was a fair number of hidden treasures discovered. There have been several artifacts discovered in the Oak Island area that associate it with William Kidd. However, there are numerous date conflicts with those theories. Also, there have literally been *no* tools found on the island, apart from that mysterious original tackle block, long since disappeared. With the vast amounts of work that were done you would expect numerous tools, or personal effects to be buried in the area surrounding the Money Pit (as it's come to be known).

There is a natural arrogance with Western culture that assumes that only European society in the last 500 years has been capable of truly awe-inspiring engineering feats. Thus the favoured pirate theories. However, as we now know, the pyramids in both Egypt and Middle and South America were truly incredible accomplishments that were done when Europe was a collection of hunters and gatherers. Also, Stonehenge, Easter Island, and other incredible feats were accomplished in "pre-history." Could Oak Island have been done by an ancient civilization — not necessarily burying gold, but possibly religious artifacts? Who knows?

Anyway, as you can see — I'm quite interested in the Pit. Pardon me for burbling on. My old relative used to tell ghost stories, apparently, of when he lived all alone on the island. He probably contributed to a lot of the myths of the area If anyone wants to hear them — they're short, but I know them….

3

HAUNTED HOUSES

As a species we bond with where we were born or where we live and we are lucky if these two locales are the same place. That was an easier accomplishment in the past than it is in the present because these days people move around a lot, not just from one region to another but from one country or continent to another. Yet as a species we feel the burden of the past as the promise of the future. Here are some accounts of haunted places, but as you read them, bear in mind that it is not just places that are haunted but the people to identify with them who may be described as haunted.

THREE GHOSTLY EXPERIENCES

One Thursday morning I was the guest of Steve Madely on his phone-in show on CFRA Radio in Ottawa. We chatted for a while about real life ghost stories, and then Steve opened the lines to hear from callers. Thirteen callers shared their experiences with us on air. A good many listeners wanted to tell their stories but didn't get the opportunity to, so some of them contacted me directly.

Here is a letter dated 18 February 1994 from Joan E. Skidmore of Gloucester, Ontario. She was born in Ottawa in 1941. "I am a third-generation Canadian," she wrote. "My ancestors were German and British. I am a homemaker and mother of five grown sons, and we have two grandchildren. My husband and I will be celebrating our thirty-fifth anniversary this coming October. I sew, knit, crochet, garden, read, write poetry, and love camping."

Dear Mr. Colombo:

I am writing after hearing you on radio station CFRA this morning. The topic was ghost stories.

Here are three of my ghostly experiences.

1. The first experience occurred in 1955, when our family was living at 20 Chamberlain Avenue in Ottawa.

My Aunt Annie, my maternal grandmother's sister, had lived with us the previous year. Her health was not good but when it improved she moved to Pembroke, Ont. Then she took ill again, and my grandmother travelled to Pembroke to stay with her.

My mother, my sister, and I were in the kitchen washing the dinner dishes when we heard footsteps on the back porch. The steps sounded as if someone was entering the room beyond the kitchen. We searched high and low but there was no one there.

A short while later my grandmother phoned us from Pembroke to say that Aunt Annie had passed away. Aunt Annie had always sat on the back porch.

2. In 1976 my husband was transferred to Kitchener, Ont. We bought an old brick house at 100 Moore Avenue. The house was situated quite close to a cemetery.

Shortly after moving in we realized that we were not the only occupants of the house. We apparently had the company of several ghosts. The ghosts were seen or heard by all the members of our family. We had five sons who at the time ranged in ages from six to sixteen years. It was a fascinating experience.

The original owners of the house, the Beerwagon family, had spent their entire married lives in the house. The land had been given to Mr. Beerwagon by his father. Mr. Beerwagon was a stone mason and he built the house in 1911. He brought his bride to their new home. They raised seven children and departed the house in death. We were told that they had the services of a live-in housekeeper named Mary.

My first ghostly encounter in the house was with an older woman in the upstairs hallway. She seemed to float past me. I was sure she was carrying laundry over her arm. I saw her several times, but for some reason I did not mention her appearance to the other members of the family. One day my eldest son came and told me about a woman he had seen in the upstairs hall. He described the same women whom I had seen, and he said that she appeared to be carrying something.

Our next visitor was an older gentleman. My oldest son told me that this gentleman had sat on the edge of his bed. He also said that he had gotten into the car with him. My husband suffered a serious injury, so we set up a bed in our living-room. A leather chair stood near his bed. My husband told me about an older gentleman sitting in the chair. He said he thought the gentleman was smoking. My son had also mentioned that the gentleman smoked.

My husband had renovated our attic, turning it into a large bedroom. We were startled to hear someone pacing back and forth in this room. The floor was carpeted yet we could hear the sound of footsteps on bare wood. One day, when I was the only one in the house, I was sitting in the room on the second floor near the stairway. I could hear footsteps come down the stairs. My hair felt as if it was standing on end.

Once the footsteps on the stairs started up, they were heard again and again by our family. Often the steps would be heard descending the stairs from the second to the first-floor landing. These stairs were carpeted; the stairs from the attic were not. However, all the footsteps sounded as if they were on bare boards.

Our third son slept in the attic bedroom. Every so often he complained that I was calling out his name to wake him. But I had not called him.

At times the window at the back of the attic room would open by itself. My husband had installed a new Pearson window that slid sideways and was difficult to open or shut. One day I closed the window and then sat down, only to watch the window open all by itself. There were no high winds and the room was electrically heated.

Our house was often filled with the delicious aroma of baking, usually chocolate. This occurred when I had not been baking.

There were no baking odours coming in from outside. When my sister came from Ottawa to visit us, she also mentioned the smell of baking. While talking to the next-door neighbour one day, she began telling me about Mrs. Beerwagon's love of baking. After her children had grown up, she used to bake cupcakes full of nuts, which she placed outside for the squirrels.

We had a bathroom off the dining-room. Originally the dining-room was the kitchen, and the bathroom was the summer kitchen. The bathroom door kept opening to the point that we had to install a chain lock on the door for privacy.

One evening my husband and sons were downstairs watching television. I was upstairs in bed reading, when a woman started sneezing. I searched the bedroom and the entire upstairs but found no one there. I was the only one upstairs.

We had decided to take out the dining-room windows and install patio doors and build a deck. We called for estimates. Three contractors came separately. The house seemed to come alive, especially upon the arrival of the third contractor. Lamps shook. There was banging in the basement. The house seemed so unsettled. This was the one time we felt nervous about our ghost. As a result, we decided against undertaking the renovation.

Once in a while we would hear things being moved about in the basement. When we checked, everything was always in place. I later learned that Mr. Beerwagon had placed a cot in the basement and he took naps behind the furnace. He also puttered around down there.

Our second son's girlfriend, who is now our daughter-in-law, maintained that our house made her feel nervous.

Before we bought 100 Moore Avenue, it had been rented to students. It was then purchased by a family of four and they undertook extensive renovations. After we sold the house, it apparently changed hands several times.

In all, we spent five years with ghosts from the past wandering through our rooms. This was the first home that I was glad to leave. On moving day, we never looked back, and never shed a tear.

Throughout all these ghostly experiences, for some reason or other, we never spoke about what was happening to anyone other than my sister and her husband.

3. My third ghostly experience came about in 1984. We were again living in Ottawa. Around 3:00 a.m., I was awakened by the sound of my Great Aunt Myrtle calling out my name. At the time Aunt Myrtle was in the hospital in Pembroke. She was very close to us. She was ill with cancer. Later that day we learned that she had passed away. Upon talking to my sister that day, she told me that she too had heard Myrtle call out her name, around eight o'clock that morning.

My maternal Grandmother had very strong intuition. She would always know when something was wrong. She would call me to say she had not slept all night because something was wrong at our house. She was usually right.

This gift was passed down to me. Sometimes it almost frightens me.

Possibly these stories will be of interest to you. It feels good to tell someone about them.

Sincerely,

Joan E. Skidmore

NIGHT SOUNDS

Here is an unusual account, dated September 1995, and written by Sanford Brooks, a young Toronto writer whom I have yet to meet. "Night Sounds" was published in the October 1995 issue of *Toronto Voice*. The account is unusual, for the present collection at least, because it is really someone else's story, not really the author's. However, it is a good yarn, one that smacks of verisimilitude. Brooks has an unusual, lively, and haunting tale to tell....

There is an old saying: "If you listen to the October wind you can hear the cries of a thousand souls."

A few years ago I went to a Halloween party held at one of Danforth Avenue's local bars. As I sat at the bar waiting to be served, I looked up to see that my bartender was Viki, a woman whom I knew from when she used to be a waitress at another bar in the area. We smiled and exchanged our greetings. After she brought me a beer, we engaged in some small talk. Our conversation soon shifted to the crowd of people, all of whom were attending this evening's Halloween festivities.

"Check out how many people are here tonight. This placed is packed!" I observed.

"That's for sure! I'll get some good tips tonight," Viki said, as she scanned the room.

"So, how come you aren't wearing a costume?" I inquired, as I sipped my beer.

"I'm not really into Halloween. It kind of gives me the creeps."

"Halloween is supposed to give you the creeps. I mean, after all, that's part of the fun. Right?" I replied.

"Well, a couple of years ago I had a really weird experience that's sort of left me with bad vibes," Viki said in a dour tone.

"Sounds like you've got a ghost story to tell. I'm listening."

"The last bar that I worked at," Viki began, "had an apartment for rent above it. My boss saw the ghost of one of the tenants who apparently lived there many years ago. That incident is why I'm not too keen on Halloween. I quit shortly afterwards."

Viki's story began the night of October 30th, 1990. Viki and her boss, Martin, were closing up the bar after a long and busy evening.

"Martin, I'll lock up," Viki said as she placed the last of the stools on top of the bar.

"Do you mind? My feet are killing me," Martin asked as he slipped on his jacket.

"No. Not at all. You go home," Viki assured.

"Thanks, love. Remind me to give you a raise," Martin said, flashing a smile.

"Promises, promises," Viki replied in a mocking tone.

"Well, good night. See you tomorrow," he said as the door slowly closed behind him. Viki reached behind the bar and retrieved a spare key-ring. Buttoning up her coat, she grabbed her purse and headed for the back door. Turning off the lights, the bar was plunged in darkness.

Outside, the cool air pricked her skin. Flipping through the keys, she eventually found the one that would lock the door. Viki was about to lock the door when she suddenly froze. Listening intently, she thought she heard the sound of a moan coming from inside the darkened bar. Unnerved, Viki hurriedly locked the door. In her car driving home, Viki dismissed the sound as probably being just the October wind.

The next day, October 31st, Viki wasn't due to start work until 6:00 p.m., when she would begin her evening shift. Viki was surprised when she received a phone call from Martin.

"Hello?" Viki answered.

"Viki? It's me. You left the door open. This morning, as I was about to open up, I found the door open."

"No way! I absolutely locked the door as I was leaving!"

"So you didn't leave the door open?" Martin stressed.

"No," Viki replied firmly. "Don't tell me you've been burgled."

"I don't think so. Except…" Martin's voice trailed off.

"Martin. What?" Viki sensed something was not right.

"It's crazy. I thought it was my eyes playing tricks." Martin sounded shaken. "After I found the door open and I looked around I started to take the stools off the bar…."

Tense, Viki urged, "And?"

"I heard this moan," Martin continued, "and saw this old woman in her nightgown, with dark, hollow eyes and flowing white hair moving towards the back of the bar."

Viki was relieved. "Did you call the police?"

"Viki, the woman was floating above the floor. She had no feet! When she reached the door she just … disappeared!"

Viki's stomach was in knots. Realization set in as she knew that the moan she had heard was from the ghost of that woman….

I remained silent for a moment before I spoke. I was stunned.

"That's a creepy story. I understand why you quit."

Viki paused, then slowly answered, "That incident made me a true believer in ghosts."

THE ENERGIES OF THREE SPIRITS

Eloise Y. is the name by which a medium who lives in the Parkdale district of Toronto wishes to be known. She contributed a brief account of the haunting of her apartment in that district in the city's west end. Eloise Y. is active in the city's pop musical scene with an arts organization called Magickal Pig Productions. She is interested in spirits and has collected her impressions for a "Ghost Crawl" which she planned to release in time for the annual Mariposa Festival.

Eloise Y. has decided views about the Parkdale district. "My own theory about Parkdale and the lower annex of Queen St. West is that the preponderance of alcoholism and cocaine addiction (the former a given, the latter predominating in the Rock scene, early 1980s) is a subconscious psychic response to the vestiges of activities from an earlier time. Simply put, many people act out in some way similar activities done by others who have crossed the veil."

When Eloise Y. wrote this account, we had yet to meet. We met, in a sense, as subscribers to Obiwan's ghost-story mailing list. Thereafter we met (as will be apparent in the account that follows this one). The following account came from her email communication, "Ghosts of Old Toronto," 4 October 1995:

> On a personal note, we live in one of the oldest sections of Toronto, the section known as Parkdale. Founded in 1810 and incorporated in 1856, it was settled by the French and English military stationed across Lake Ontario during the 1812 war (the one between the Americans and the British, not Tchaikovsky's.)
>
> Two important covert enterprises operated frequently: bootlegging and selling freed slaves back to Louisiana French. Our apartment, situated at the foot of the lake (a common site for spooky happenings), held the energies of three spirits.
>
> One, Genevieve, a mulatto Creole woman, stays with us and makes herself known almost daily.
>
> Her mother-in-law, on the other hand, made life a living hell for us, when we first moved in here. A sick-room smell constantly came from the master bedroom; when I was alone in the bedroom, I constantly felt under attack physically; when looking in the mirror above our dresser, I could not see my reflection, but rather the shadowy mists of an elderly woman. Both our children reported feelings of someone approaching them while they were sleeping.

The people helping us to paint the bedroom had their knuckles cracked straight on with a stick from a paint-roller, as if someone intentionally slammed them. The stick at the time was a good ten feet away from them.

Finally, since I have a particular openness to these kinds of energies, one final evening before we decided to call in the ghost-busting troops, my husband found me cowered in a corner of the bedroom, snarling and repeating, "Leave my house!" with a voice decidedly different from my own.

THE GIBRALTAR LIGHTHOUSE EXPERIENCE

Life changed in a small way for Eloise Y. after we first met. Producers at TVO, Ontario's educational television channel, asked her to act as a medium on camera. Eloise Y. was charmed and succeeded in charming the producers and producing a great show. She kindly shared with me an account of her experience in 1995.

Dear John,

What a delight to have been graciously recommended by you for the TVO children's show "Off the Hook." I am truly honoured. The producers of the show decided on the Gibraltar Lighthouse on Hanlan's point. Originally they were to have met at the Keg Mansion. However, we all agreed that the Keg might prove to be much more disquieting then the Island just in case the legends of rape and murder surrounding the old Mansion might be more validated. It was a lovely experience at the Lighthouse for me. I had hoped you might make an appearance there yourself. I would have loved you to see what I saw.

Speaking of what I saw, the following paragraphs are an account of what transpired for me on a psychic level. I had made a point not to research anything you or anyone else had written about the Lighthouse before going; quite a difficult thing to do for an old magpie like me. Nor had I the luxury of growing up in Canada where I might have heard school-day whisperings of the debacled and debauched goings on there. My approach, then, was fresh and untainted. Here then my Gibraltar Lighthouse experience:

Early last week I received a phone call from the researcher for a TVO children's programme called *Off the Hook*. The show is aimed at the 11- to 14-year-old ages with a mixture of fun and problem-solving expeditions called "Missions." The researcher explained that, since Halloween was approaching the producers would like to do a light-hearted piece on the pros and cons of the existence of ghosts. They were looking for a psychic who has had some experience with sensing spirits in alleged haunted places, and, since I had been referred to her by you, an accepted and respected authority on the subject, asked if I would be willing to take part in a small segment of the programme where the "mission" was to go and seek out a real live (?) ghost. Being a theatrical sort myself, I jumped at the chance, but not before agreeing on two conditions. Under no circumstance would I agree to taking a youngster on a haunting that would have possible malevolent vibrations without exploring it first, and that the spirits and the workings must be viewed with some respect. These being agreed upon, we set forth on the particulars of the day of the shoot.

On Thursday last, accompanied by my husband, we left for the ferry dock at Bay Street Quay to board the last ferry of the day to Hanlan's Point where we would be met by private shuttle to take us to the Lighthouse. Since we arrived almost forty-five minutes early for boarding I took the opportunity to psych out the area. I had no idea in which direction the Lighthouse stood, but began sensing some sort of pull from the southwest of the Island. Now, normally, I try not to do preliminary research or meditations on a haunting, rather personally preferring to save the pieces of research for later, then piecing information together in a puzzle-like fashion. In fact, when the TVO researcher asked me if I needed any special preparation I replied in my usual piquish manner that a walk around the outside of the building along with a strong cup of coffee and a cigarette will be just fine. I am grateful to report that this time I was most obliged.

Standing just a few feet from the turnstile where I was observing other ferries coming in to shore, I noticed two men debarking from a boat that had just landed. They were both fairly tall and painfully slim, lanky perhaps, dressed in identical bluish Navy P-coats, khaki coloured pants and long rubber boots. It struck me ever so clearly that these two must be deck hands. On their heads were caps that I can only describe as those worn by fishermen or sailors in the Maritimes, perhaps a hundred or so years ago. These caps were touched ever so lightly toward me as to say "Hello" as they sauntered away. From one of these men I got the clear message of "They're waiting for you on the other side, Miss." I was both dumbfounded and delighted that these two spirits, friendly in an understated manner, heralded what was to be an interesting evening.

Though it had been raining the entire afternoon ever since our departure, for a brief moment the sun peeked out from behind the dull slate clouds as if it was guiding me. I turned to my husband and said, "White with blue and red, now it is all red but it used to be blue and red and John, John wants to tell his story." Bless his heart, my psychically dead husband is used to these little outbursts from me and enjoys the adventures as if he is watching an episode of Miss Marple. I said nothing further until we reached the lighthouse.

The five-person crew, the young cast member, and several members of the Parks and Recreation from the Island were there to meet us. I was then informed that neither the cast member nor I was to go inside the Lighthouse until after dark as they wanted to catch the surprise element on camera, so I walked around the outside of the building and in surrounding property for a while. First I was shocked to notice how very small the structure was and that it was completely landlocked. I sensed a great deal of frustration emitting because of this fact but could not as yet tell if it was coming from the spirit of a person or from the building itself. Walking up the dirt path around the building the first thing I said was, "Drunken brawls, men, aggressive drunken men." I wouldn't know until much later how important that feeling was to the legend of the lighthouse keeper himself. At one point soon after I had inquired of the Parks and Recreation manager if there had been any small structure behind the lighthouse, say a meat-smoking pit, or an outhouse perhaps. He told me astonishedly that, there indeed, had been a small one room house about seventy or so feet from where we were that at one time had been used as a home for light-keepers. It had been demolished about forty or fifty years ago, he replied quite astonished. I knew it had been there because I smelled cooking flesh on the very spot where it stood.

What intrigued me next was the small grassy patches behind the lighthouse, toward the canal, and what is now some brush and landfill. I saw someone wounded, crawling toward water, bleeding and disoriented. Next I had a vision of a canoe, perhaps made of Native origin, some soldiers passing through on the thickets to our left and the soft rustling sound of someone trying to hide in the thicket. Only a few of these things noticed me at all, and nodding their heads for me to go back to the front of the lighthouse, they carried on with their business. By dusk, I heard no sounds at all and felt very clearly that the soldiers had aborted their tasks, retreating into the silent night. The crescent of the moon could be seen climbing overhead as I received my instructions for the after-dinner-break shoot which would be my entrance into the lighthouse for the first time.

We were driven over to another section of the Island to have a supper break inside the offices of the Parks and Recreation Dept. The TVO crew, much to my delight, had their own stories and beliefs of ghosts to share with me. All of them were believers in one form or another, all of them sharing the latest inside scoop about ghost and other paranormal activities being the current darling subject of the television industry. By the end of the hour we were calling this episode the "EL FILES." My one concern was the young man, LaVel, whose mission it was to enter the lighthouse and find a ghost. A bright and personable young boy of fourteen, he was visibly frightened and kept asking me if everything was going to be fine. He and the rest of the crew had heard all the legends of the lighthouse keeper. I had asked them not to tell me until I was done with my exploration. The director, a wonderful woman named Kathie Lee Porter, and I took LaVel aside and promised him that I would enter first with the crew in tow and without him. If I sensed anything at all remotely unnerving or frightening, I would tell Kathie Lee and she would cancel the shoot and take the story to a different angle. What I didn't tell anyone but Terry, my husband, was that I had already begun communicating with "John" and had told him I would not tolerate any ghostly theatrics coming from him. The sense I got at first was that he just wanted to finish up his work for the night and settle into a nice evening with a meal and a pipe. What he couldn't understand was why all these people milling about didn't "just bloody well come in already" and get about their business to leave him alone. What amused me greatly was his confusion about my presence. He could sense as well that I had come for a "secret purpose." The purpose, so "John" thought, was that I had been sent over by an inn keeper from the mainland to keep him "company" for the evening. Apparently, he thought I had been selected for this work since I was a mature and buxomly woman with a "bloddy fat ass" which would warm him quite nicely on a chilly October evening. I kept this information for the adults alone. We were, after all, taping a children's show.

Upon returning to the lighthouse I realized something about the structure. I believe it was built not to guide ships to a safe harbour, but rather to warn and send signals to the mainland, possibly by runners, of approaching enemy ships. I did not sense at all that this was a particularly honourable job and that our ghost friend "John" had somehow been promised a job that had not lived up to its expectations. Throughout the entire evening's experience was a nagging feeling of despondence and sadness mixed with some sort of anger at being duped somehow.

Now it was time for me to enter the lighthouse. It was completely dark outside save for the glow of a beautiful first quarter moon shining down on a clear sky and the invasive intrusive lights of a video crew. Just before knocking (I always knock or announce myself in some way) I saw our ghost come down the stairs and wait just inside the door for me. "Come in if your comin' in," is what I heard from him. I could feel what he looked like but at this point I could not see what he looked like. I was sure I would after a while spent with him.

The stairs leading up to the top of the lighthouse are small triangular wooden steps with unannounced treacherous turns. The walls are brick white wash with cob webs and insect exo-skeletons hanging like cotton floss from every imaginable crevice. I did not sense anything but physical decay and sadness until I made my way to the third of five small landings on the stairs. I was beginning to have some difficulty in seeing the physical stairs and began experiencing some psychic vertigo, both first clues for me that I am near something. Anger, frustration, anger and great loss is what I felt. The poor man is prevented somehow from doing his work. Perhaps there is here a discussion about being laid off, concerns about money and management, future employment and the future itself. I heard voices with foreign accents and tempers flaring, complete consternation over conditions and the overwhelming sense of frustrations a man feels when all he wants to do is work hard at the only job he knows and cannot. As I approached the top of the last landing leading to the metal door above, the door which leads to the actual room where the light was kept, I could not only see and feel "John" very clearly but the two companions with him. "There are three men here," I said on camera, "two English or Upper Canada and one is dark and swarthy, possibly Spanish or Portuguese," since I heard that accent being spoken. Here were three highly intoxicated disgruntled old seafarers who, because their services were no longer required by the government, were losing their jobs. What we had here was 19th-century down-sizing! At one point the anger was so pervasive that I believe I uttered an audible "Yech!" on camera. I began hearing the same words over and over again and seeing the repetitive actions of this ghostly trio picking up and putting things down on an invisible table, spitting, drinking and smacking each other's backs in an aggressive but congenial way. It was very clear to me now that I was seeing an event that was stuck in a loop. Although I saw muskets and knives, pistols and daggers, none had yet been used. I could see the energy of the anger going toward the weapons but it would rise just above it and then wane. Again, I was given a nod of a head and I knew it was time to descend the rickety stairs. I felt for this lighthouse keeper. I wanted to stay and speak with him. I wanted to encourage him to manifest deeply and clearly so I could aid him in some way in his dilemma. At this time the TVO crew was a little unnerved and was quickly agreeable to my suggestion that it was time to leave. On the descent, with a camera and audio crew behind me I received the loveliest moment of the evening.

About the fourth or third landing down on this 50-odd foot tower, I happened to stop and gaze out the little windows and touch some of the brick around it. Something drew me to a part of the white wall opposite me. I looked up and saw, as clear as any photograph or perfectly painted portrait outlined in a cameo frame, "John." Handsome and seasoned and in his very best, as if reading my mind, he was showing me exactly what he looked like. I was so pleased as I gazed at this gift from a ghost. He was more handsome than I imagined, with a facial structure I likened to that of Gregory Peck, with a full dark moustache, large dark eyes, a strong bottom lip, and a determined chin. Neither smiling nor frowning, but rather saying, "Here it is, girl. You wanted to know what I looked like. Well, here I am." I pointed it out to the camera man and audio man behind me. "Look, look, there he is!" I tried outlining where he was on the wall by first curving my finger and then describing every brick piece by piece until I was sure they too would see it. "Don't you see him?" I asked with great excitement. "Well, sort of, I guess," was the response I got. When I reached the bottom I ran outside to where Kim the researcher and Terry were waiting for us. I was so gleeful at this point that I went for another run with them up the stairs to the lighthouse to show them my wondrous gift from a very willing and co-operative spirit. At first I thought I had been mistaken as to which landing this apparition made itself known. I arrived at the very top of the lighthouse, stopping at each landing I thought was the spot, before I realized, much to my sadness, it was gone.

When all the excitement had waned, the crew, the Parks and Recreation workers, and Terry told me all the versions of the missing Lighthouse keeper and the terrible hauntings of Gibraltar Point Lighthouse. I had heard them for the very first time. This is what I think happened:

There was no murder on that dreaded night. Poor John and his card-playing cronies, probably seamen with no jobs, engaged often in roughhousing, arguing over ships, armies, and women. Their hopelessness drew others with similar fates to the company of the Lighthouse keeper. One fateful night, with some new invited men, the unknown variables, the drunkenness and despair escalated to the point of no return. Worried about money, John and his friends were either caught cheating or accused the newcomers of cheating. A fight began, weapons were raised, John ran down the stairs, possibly braised from a wound. Being very intoxicated he fell down at the entrance to the lighthouse. His friends, though I would hardly refer to them as such, and the newcomers left him for dead. Fearing for their own lives or fearing punishment, they fled in terror. John, in a drunken stupor, headed for the canal out near the lake, fell and was discovered by either some friends disguising themselves as Natives, or Natives found him, and quietly and secretly took him somewhere to be healed of his wounds. John never recovered. His friends concocted a story of his "mysterious" disappearance to the authorities, who sent out soldiers as a search party for him and would-be assailants.

Nothing was ever found. The human bones found near the Lighthouse? Relics that were placed there I think, perhaps a cruel prank, but more likely, someone buried John where any hard-working keeper would want to be…near his beloved Lighthouse.

The time loop I saw was nothing more than John's wish to right a wrong; wishful thinking if you will to undo a foolish but costly deed. Oh, he is there, alright, wanting to work, tired of the tourists who bother him and in need to clear his name and find some friends. But what he mostly wants is a bottle of stout, some pipe tobacco, and a roast pork sandwich.

There it is then, John Robert. Thank you again for making the referral which allowed me this wonderful experience.

Let's get together soon. I am anxious to share my most recent findings about the house at the corner of Jarvis and Gloucester.

Terry sends his regards.

Happy Samhain.

Eloise

THE POSSESSION

Every year thousands of people visit the Stephen Leacock Memorial Home on Old Brewery Bay outside Orillia, Ont. The site is one of the country's leading "literary shrines," perhaps second only in attendance and importance to L.M. Montgomery's

Green Gables in Cavendish, P.E.I. At Old Brewery Bay, the knowledgeable tour guide leads visitors through the fine old house, drawing attention to its peculiarities and to the foibles of its long-time owner, Stephen Leacock. In his day he was Canada's best-known writer and the sole Canadian humourist known in the United States and throughout the British Empire. Even today, more than half a century after his death, he has more books in print than any other Canadian author. Leacock was a Professor of Economics at McGill University in Montreal so he was able to spend only the summer months on Old Brewery Bay. Here he completed many of his articles and essays, as well as his classic collection of linked stories *Sunshine Sketches of a Little Town*. As far as I know, Leacock held no views on the subject of the afterlife, though in a number of sketches he spoofed the pretensions of spiritualists. In one essay he asked the rhetorical question, "What lies 'back of beyond'?" On a number of occasions I have joined the guided tour of the Memorial Home, and each time I learned something new about the man and about human nature. On each visit I sensed the presence of Leacock's spirit, the good spirit of bonhomie and mischief, but never that of a malicious sprite. Could it be that the malicious sprite is the legacy of the humourist's sole child, young Stephen Lushington Leacock? "The Possession" was written by the Toronto journalist Kathryn Newman for the Halloween issue of *Midtown Voice*, October 1994. It was declared one of the winning entries.

> Stephen Leacock's home in Orillia is a fine sprawling old mansion stocked with memorabilia from Leacock's life.
>
> In the Spring a group of writers met to learn more about Leacock, the humourist, and to bask in the literary inspiration that oozes from the grand old house.
>
> I had no idea that the house was haunted. However, when I first appeared on that fateful morning, I had a strange sense something was awry.
>
> I stood outside the house and peered up at the bedroom windows. I felt I was being watched.
>
> The moment I stepped across the threshold, I knew my instincts were right on. This house was haunted, and whoever, or whatever, was interested in me.
>
> I was led through to the rear of the house where the kitchen is situated.
>
> Luckily for me, I was standing next to a writer who just happened to be psychic.
>
> I began to feel dizzy, and the whole room began swirling. The

floor was moving right under my feet. "You have to protect yourself. Build an imaginary wall of mirrors," she said.

I was aware of someone, or something, intensely evil watching me.

Something touched me. It was cold, unhuman, and the hairs on the back of my neck stood up straight. I wanted to run from the house, but I am a writer, and I just had to find out what this thing was.

I was determined to get to the bottom of this ghostly mystery.

The main hall felt cold, and I felt those unseen eyes on me once again.

I walked into Stephen Leacock Jr.'s bedroom, and I froze. A fine mist hovered over the bed. Staff had reported footsteps on the stairs...doors opening, and closing, and many other unusual happenings. But I had never heard anything about mists.

It seems that Stephen Leacock Jr. was a person of small stature. He was known to have a rather nasty disposition, and stories tell of how he took pleasure in butchering goats on the pool table and the kitchen table.

I felt that the spirit was that of Stephen Jr., and he was angry, and haunting the bedrooms and halls of the house.

I should have left well enough alone. I should have made my very quick exit and left while I still had time.

The moment I crossed the threshold I felt a grey mass envelop me. I could not breathe. I was paralyzed. It seemed the ghost was waiting for me.

I don't remember coming down the stairs. But I was told later that I was leaping down three steps at a time. I ran out of the house and pointed an accusatory finger at my psychic companion.

"Hey you, look at me," I screeched. I was definitely not myself.

I returned to another building on the grounds where the seminar was underway. The psychic sat next to me. She was watching me all the time.

"All right," she whispered under her breath. She grabbed hold of my hand very tightly. Then she began to drive the spirit out of me.

It was a most unusual experience.

I felt the mass of evil being pushed down through my body, and a light coming in through my head.

At one point I remember an intense light entering into my body and driving the spirit out through the ground.

The psychic was mentally chasing the spirit back into the house. He was intensely angry, cursing up a storm. I felt much better after my experience. However, I was still very shaken.

I returned to the house once more that day to use the washroom before I left for the journey back to Toronto. The floor and walls began to move and to ooze a greenish substance. I ran from the house vowing never to step into Stephen Leacock's house again unless an exorcism was performed.

I was so unnerved by my experience that I slept with the light on in my room for a week.

Until recently I could not bring myself to talk or write about this incident. I felt that the ghost of Stephen Leacock Jr. might still be listening in to my thoughts and listening in on my conversation. Is he?

GEORGE OR HELEN?

Janet Warfield is the pseudonym I have given to the writer of this letter. Central Oshawa is the generalized location of her house with its resident spook. Whether it is called George or Helen, the spook is a specialist in the production of effects that seem silly and mischievous. Perhaps the spook is best described as a poltergeist.

I took part in a phone-in program on the subject of ghosts. Janet Warfield heard the show and later phoned me and described these occurrences. I urged her to describe them in detail in a letter. Here is that letter, dated 3 March 1994. It is carefully written and remarkably detailed. She apparently kept of log of the poltergeist-like occurrences in her home.

Dear Mr. Colombo:

Further to our telephone conversations of February 21st, 1994, I have made note of the occurrences of oddities that have taken place at our residence in Central Oshawa.

As I stated, we moved into the house in June of 1992, and after approximately three weeks, in the early morning hours, we were awakened by the sound of dishes tinkling. We immediately called out, "Who's there?" and rushed downstairs. We checked both doors, which were soundly locked. After checking the main floor and basement level, we noticed the buffet door in the dining-room was open and the dishes which had been stacked inside on the bottom shelf (including plates, glasses and vases) were sitting on the floor, placed as they had been in the buffet. My husband and I both expressed our surprise, returned the dishes to the buffet and returned to bed.

The next occurrence was 6–8 weeks later at, I believe, approximately 11:00 p.m. during a week night. I was ironing in the basement while watching TV. My husband was in bed, two levels up, at the time. The remote control for the television was on the desk close to the edge of same but not hanging over. The remote control turned over, and fell off the desk and when it hit the floor, button side down, the TV shut off. I immediately pulled the plug on the iron and raced up to bed. Many, many times over the years we have dropped the remote control on the floor button side down, but never has the TV shut off.

After this point in time, while entertaining friends and discussing these incidents, their children nicknamed our mysterious being George. Later, however, noticing the interest George displayed in the dishes in the buffet, and based on a dream that I had that I was talking to the ghost, I insisted it be called Helen.

My dream occurred while we were at our cottage in the late summer of 1992. I could see myself sitting at the table talking to a young woman of 30 or so who was dressed in long skirts and an apron and I recall she had brilliant blue eyes. She stated her name was Helen. She said she met her husband during the Civil War when she nursed his wounds, and following the war they wed and came to Canada to settle. She stated her husband was killed in a freak accident while building their homestead. Following the death of her husband, she left to return to her home state, got lost and never reached home. She asked me if she could stay with us. I replied yes and then woke up. I found myself sitting on the edge of the bed. I immediately woke my husband and told him about the dream.

We have never performed a search of the title of our property, other than the usual forty-year search undertaken when we purchased the house and property, so we have no idea of the status of the land prior to the time the modern house was built.

Several things have happened between about September 1992 and June 1993, which I will list below:

1. There was a loud knocking on the closet door in the basement, heard by my husband and immediately reported to me. We checked and found nothing in the closet that could have fallen and produced a knocking noise. Later that same evening, loud knocking on the closet door was again heard, but by me this time. My husband and I joked that we had accidentally locked George in the closet and he was trying to get out.

2. My father-in-law stayed overnight, sleeping on the pullout in the basement. He was awakened in the night by a voice. The voice was very low and he was unable to ascertain whether it was a male or a female voice he heard talking. He insisted he was awake at the time. He said that the stereo was on at the time so he didn't bother to listen carefully to the words being spoken. He added that the stereo was on because the red power light was on, but the power light is always on. Upon checking, we ascertained that the stereo was not on.

3. One morning, at approximately 4:45 a.m., when I was in the bathroom getting ready to go to work, I distinctly heard the sound of someone next to me scratching an arm or a leg. That sound and the thought that something or someone was standing next to me made me feel rather uneasy.

4. One evening in the Winter of 1993, we arrived home from work and discovered that the toilet-paper roll was partially unrolled. It had unrolled across the bathroom floor and out into the upstairs hallway. On another evening in May of the same year, I believe it was, we arrived home from work to find that the Kleenex box in the upstairs bathroom had been emptied (it was only half full at the time) and clumps of two or three tissues were lying around the

bathroom and hallway. It appeared that they had been scrunched up in a person's hand.

5. On Mother's Day, 1993, we were visited by my parents, and we discussed the fact that nothing had happened since early Spring of 1993. The following Tuesday, we arrived home from work and that was when we discovered the Kleenex box had been emptied. That same night, my husband got up early in the morning to go to the bathroom. Sitting on the toilet one can peek around the corner and see into our bedroom. When we had moved in, we tore out the wall between the two adjoining bedrooms in order to enlarge the master bedroom, thereby leaving a trench in the walls and the floor all the way around the room. As the floor was not yet covered in and was somewhat hazardous, my husband had turned on the light in the bedroom. The switch is located near the door. While sitting on the toilet, he noticed that the bedroom light had gone out. He asked me why I had shut it off and I informed him he could see I was in bed and hadn't gotten up to shut the light off. He stated the bulbs must have burned out or they were loose, but when we checked the switch, we found it had been turned to the off position. We joked about George having done it. In the morning, when the alarm went off at 5:30 a.m., we didn't immediately jump out of bed, as is usual, but instead, lay there for a while. After seven or eight minutes, the light turned on by itself, at which point we got up and stated something to the effect, "Knock it off, George, we're getting up."

6. A couple of times, while watching TV in the basement and doing laundry at the same time, the door between the laundry room and the family room has shut by itself, as if to say, "Shut the door, I can't hear the television." This has not happened recently.

7. The last occurrence took place on the evening of December 25th, 1993. My sister-in-law was scraping food off the plates into the garbage, when she heard a "growling" sound coming from the corner where the stove is located. When she looked around upon hearing the sound, the upper cupboard door just to the left of the stove was in the process of closing, at which point I walked into the kitchen. She mentioned the noise to me and said she hadn't

touched the cupboard door, which had obviously opened prior to her seeing it closing.

To date, all remains quiet. We often joke that we eagerly await the next occurrence.

For resale reasons, etc., I would appreciate it if you did not mention our names or address in the book, should you choose to include these details. Our location in Oshawa is best described as Central Oshawa.

We shall await your response.

Yours truly,

Janet Warfield

MUCH TO MY HORROR

Discovery Harbour (or Havre de la Découverte) is one of the components of the reconstructed Historic Naval and Military Establishments at the head of Penetanguishene Bay, Ont. The Officers' Quarters here are interesting for psychical as well as historical reasons. Few people are in a better position to talk about both of these reasons than Rosemary Vyvyan, historical planner with Discovery Harbour. In response to one of my queries — and some good-humoured goading — she prepared a personal account, dated 21 September 1995, that brings to life some of the distinctly odd events that have occurred here.

The Officers' Quarters at Discovery Harbour in Penetanguishene has a curious past. Completed in 1836, the building has had an almost continuous history of use. Today the building has been restored to the 1840s period and is furnished to reflect the genteel living quarters of the officers who once lived there.

I have worked at this historic site since 1979, and over the years our costumed interpretive staff have spoken to me about the uneasiness they experience in the building. Many of these people have said they feel a presence in there with them. On several occasions, staff have reported an item (wine glasses seem to be a favourite) missing from the building, only to find it moved to another location therein.

There have been a number of incidents that have happened to me that have been puzzling. I say puzzling because I am very much a sceptic when it comes to believing in the presence of a spirit or spirits in a building in which I work. The most consistent occurrence has been the impression of someone sitting on one of the beds in the building. There is one bed that always looks as if someone has been sitting on it. I cannot count the times I have straightened the blankets on the bed, only to return the next day to see the impression there again.

Another incident occurred several years ago when I was instructed to turn off all the heat in the building to help freeze-dry a humidity problem over the winter. I did so. About a month later I had a team of restorationists come to the site to look at the building and give me further advice on its restoration. I explained to them about the deliberate non-use of the furnaces. Much to my horror, when I took the group into the building, the furnace was blasting out nice warm air. To this day I have no idea who turned the furnace on and why.

It was during this same time that I removed all of the fragile furnishings from the building. In the spring, when I went to refurnish the building, I was missing one box of furnishings. I searched the site for the box of things. All efforts were to no avail. You can imagine my complete shock when I went into the Officers' Quarters one day and the box, full of the artifacts, was sitting in plain view at the top of the stairs.

We attribute these strange goings-on to Private James Drury, who froze to death on New Year's Eve in 1839, at the back kitchen of the building.

IT HAD TO BE A DREAM

This letter is a lively account of nocturnal disturbances that occurred to Karen P. Colautti, a college student, soon after she moved into Apartment 3A at 425

Sherbourne Street in Toronto. The letter, dated 14 September 1995, is reproduced here with minimal editing. Today Ms. Colautti still lives on Sherbourne Street, but not at the apartment building in which the disturbances occurred. There must be a reason!

What to make of her experience? Psychical researchers and channellers talk about pools and whirlpools of psychic energy. Psychologists and parapsychologists discuss hypnagogic and hypnopompic states of consciousness, "borderline" experiences that occur between sleeping and waking or between waking and sleeping. Folklorists have documented visits of the "old hag," a form of succubus or incubus that ravishes sleepers. Everyone has an intuitive understanding of nightmares and the terrors of the night. One interesting feature of Ms. Colautti's account is that it is open-ended. It comes to no conclusion. If someone devoted the time to research the occupant history of Apartment 3A, it might be found that an event occurred between those walls that places these nocturnal disturbances in some credible — or incredible — perspective.

Dear John,

I have owned a copy of *Extraordinary Experiences: Personal Accounts of the Paranormal in Canada* for a few years now. I am writing to relay one of my extraordinary experiences to you. Perhaps you will wish to use it in one of your future works.

In 1989, I was nineteen years old, in my last year of college, and I had just moved into a bachelor apartment at 425 Sherbourne St. in Toronto. The building I had moved into was once, I assume, some sort of boarding house that had been renovated into an apartment building. There were two entrances into my unit. One was from within the building itself, and one from the wooden fire escape — yes! wooden! — that led up from the ground. I shared the escape's landing with my neighbour. We have our own doors that led into our separate apartments.

For two years I had been living outside of my parent's home, so I was used to "being on my own." I had adjusted to new sounds and bizarre shadow-formations, etc. (As a student I made many changes of residence.) The first few months I lived there, nothing seemed to be out of the ordinary. The fourth month or so, I was awakened very late at night by what sounded like footsteps coming up the wooden fire escape. (Yes, wooden!) I thought at first that it must have been my neighbour returning from a late night out, but I did not hear him unlock and open his door, nor did I hear any footsteps retreat down the stairs back into the night. Thinking that it surely must be some lunatic out for blood, I got a knife from the kitchen and I put it under my pillow. Then for some strange reason — stress induced narcolepsy? — I promptly fell back to sleep.

Over the next couple of months, this happened many times. I never really gave much thought to it during the day. Actually, after putting the knife back in the drawer the morning after, I didn't even remember it had happened, until it happened again.

Over the next few months things progressed. I started to hear footsteps coming up the escape, enter my apartment, and then stop. Then they would come up the escape, enter the apartment, go through the living area, then stop. The next time they would come up the escape, enter the apartment, go through the living area, pass into the hallway, then stop. Then they would come up the escape, enter the apartment, go through the living area, pass into the hallway, go back into the living area, turn in circles, then stop.

I would be paralyzed with fear every time I experienced one of these "episodes." I would try to scream, "No! No! Get out — stop!" But for the life of me, I could not get the words out. I would be thinking to myself, "Please, Karen, just go back to sleep. Just go back to sleep and everything will be okay." Then I would fall back into a deep sleep.

Convinced that what I was experiencing had to be dreams, or games that my mind, sound asleep but conscious, was playing on me, I told one of my close friends that I was having some really odd dreams, and I explained them to her. She said that these did not sound like any dreams to her. There was too much order to them. They progressed too smoothly. She reminded me that I had never reported recurring nightmares in the past. Still, I was convinced that they had to be dreams. It was all so terrifying to me. I did not want to believe that this could be happening in my reality.

Still, I kept her up to date on what was happening. She would ask, "So, have you had any more of those dreams?" Yes, indeed I had. The footsteps continued. They did not stray from the aforementioned routine, until one night. That night, after the footsteps turned their circles, I heard them approach me. Then I sensed something was sitting on the edge of the bed. I felt panic. The time after that, they followed the same routine, but instead of something sitting on the bed, it felt like something was lying down beside me. Again I felt panic, extreme panic. I prayed that I could just fall back to sleep, and I always did, quite promptly. Except for relaying these occurrences back to my friend, I didn't think about them during the day. Since nothing odd happened during the day, I figured that it had to be a dream.

The next episode was the most frightening episode of all. In fact, it was the most frightening thing that I had ever experienced in my life. Again, the footsteps followed the regular routine. But this time, after turning in circles, they came towards me, and it seemed they stopped, as though someone was kneeling at my bedside. I sleep on a mattress with a box-spring that sits directly on the floor. I could hear breathing, very loud, deep breathing, as if through a nose rather than a mouth. My hands were resting on the pillows, up over my head. The next thing I remember was my wrists were being grasped in someone's hands. That did not seem to bother me as much as the breathing, which was so loud. I remember thinking, "Stop breathing! Just make that breathing stop!" It felt like someone's head was right there behind my own. With my hands still being clutched over my head, I decided the best way to stop that horrible breathing sound was to place my fingers up the nose of whoever or whatever was making the noise. I remember making an attempt to do this, thinking, "Stop the breathing, just stop the breathing, go back to sleep, and all this will stop." Then I fell back to sleep.

I called my friend the next day to tell her about this development. Apparently she had told her boyfriend about my experiences. I could hear him in the background yelling, "That's it! She's moving out of that place! Get her out of that place!" They scared the pants off me with stories about people being raped by ghosts, etc., so I agreed that I would move. And I did move away shortly thereafter.

I'm still not fully convinced that what happened to me was real. But I never experienced anything like it before I lived in Apartment 3A. And since I've moved, I've yet to experience anything like it again.

I've meant to do research on the building and the area, but I've never gotten around to it. I guess, perhaps, I'm afraid I may discover something to confirm my fears that none of it really was a dream.

THREE NIGHTS OF HELL

"Three Nights of Hell" is a riveting account of a haunting. It was written by Linda W., as she prefers to be known, and included as part of the article "Ghost Stories" in the *Hamilton Spectator* on 29 July 1995. The account was prepared for publication by the journalist John Mentek who kindly extended permission to me to reproduce it here. I also have the permission of the former private duty nurse who recalled these scary three nights. The house where all this occurred is located in the Hamilton, Ontario, area.

> About fifteen years ago, I was on private duty, nursing an old woman. She lived by herself in this old house. It's still out there. My husband and I drove by it this summer. It's been fixed up now, but it's still old and its brick is covered with ivy. The house is set way back from the road. It has those Amityville eyes on top, two kinds of rounded windows.
>
> When I drove up, I got this overwhelming feeling that I didn't want to be there. I was almost sick to my stomach. But at the time I never thought about ghosts. I went in and met the old woman. She wasn't the nicest person, but it was a job. She was very old and sick.
>
> That night, the weirdest things started happening. The tap turned on by itself. The doorbell would ring and nobody was there. Doors would open by themselves. I thought, "It's just an old house. It's got … problems."
>
> As I was getting ready for bed that night, she told me to put a chair under each window and leave the windows open an inch. The whole front of the house was windows. She said in the morning all the chairs would be moved and the windows would be closed.
>
> I thought, "She's trying to scare me." But I did as she said, got her into bed, and went up to my room. I was upstairs, she was downstairs. The house had never been fixed up. It still had the old feather mattresses and everything. I went to sleep.
>
> In the middle of the night I heard footsteps and heavy breathing, like moans and sighs, coming up the stairs. I'd left the hall lights on in case I had to get down the stairs to her in a hurry. The lights were out, and I thought, "Gee, she's up and is trying to scare me." I was always trying to find a way to explain it, you know.

So I got up and put the hall lights on and I looked around, but I didn't see anything. I went downstairs to check on her, and she was sound asleep, so I figured she had been up and had got back into bed. In the morning, all the chairs were moved and the windows closed, just as she had predicted.

Later that morning I went home and didn't want to go back. I called the agency, but they didn't have anyone to replace me. Later I found out that nobody wanted to go to this house. I went back the next night, and it was a little worse. There was a door in the kitchen that led to the basement. Every time I went near it, I thought I was going to throw up, the vibes were so bad.

So that night I got her to sleep, and I went through the same routine, leaving the hall light on. In the middle of the night, it was the same deal again, the heavy breathing, moaning, the foot-steps up the stairs and the light going off. I thought, "Geez, this is really stupid," so I put on the light in my room, and then I went to the bathroom.

The bathroom is right at the top of the stairs. I just sat in there and could hear something coming up the stairs. But I looked and looked and didn't see anything. So I started talking, saying, "I can't get out of the assignment now, but I'll try in the morning." All of a sudden, downstairs, one of those big brass serving trays crashed to the floor and started to spin around like a coin. I went down and checked her. She was sound asleep. I sat up the rest of the night.

The third night, it was all I could do to get myself back into the house. It was a hundred times worse. The doorbells were ringing every five minutes. The grandfather clock was going bong, bong, bong, not even on the hour. Doors were opening, and the tap was running by itself.

"She doesn't seem to notice," I thought. So I got her into bed and told her, "Now, don't get up in the night. If you need me, just call." I was still looking for a logical explanation. I thought it was just tricks she was playing.

After I put her to bed, I put the hall light on and went up to my room. When I turned on the light in my room, the whole room was covered in moths. Thousands of moths, just covering the ceiling. The closet door was open a crack, so I figured they had come out of the closet. I wasn't too happy, but I went to bed.

I woke up later that night with an awful charley-horse in my leg, and that's the only way I know one hundred percent that what happened next is for real. As the charley-horse settled down, I heard a scratching sound coming from a three-drawer dresser under one of the eye-shaped windows. I thought, "Oh great, I've got a mouse in there."

I got up — the moths were gone by then — and kicked the dresser, thinking to scare the mouse away. A drawer flew out at me, the light went out, and I heard, "Oooooooooohhhhhhhh," and footsteps rushing up the stairs.

I grabbed my clothes and ran into the bathroom. The door was open and I was sitting in there, when this thing, this presence, just charged at me. And I started talking aloud, saying, "I will not be back after tonight. Don't worry, I'm leaving."

Coming down the stairs, I felt something breathing on the back of my neck. I checked the woman, always the loyal nurse, and she was sound asleep, totally conked out. I went into the kitchen and called my Mom. It was four in the morning, but I said, "Mom, you've got to come and get me out of here. I can't take this."

Later my Mom said she actually heard moaning and breathing behind me over the phone, and her hair stood on end when she heard it. She said she couldn't come till daylight. So I talked to her for five minutes and then said, "Okay, I'm going to sit in the living-room until you come." I got dressed in the kitchen, went into the living-room, and sat with my back to the wall.

I piled a bunch of books around me to throw at it. There were footsteps pacing up and down the living-room, heavy breathing, and the grandfather clock was going bong, bong, like crazy. I pleaded with it, "I will not be back, I will not be back. Don't hurt me."

I was sitting against the wall and a couch to my left lifted up and turned around. There were two hours of this. It was awful. I had all the lights on and just sat there till morning.

The housekeeper came before my Mom got there, and she told me all kinds of strange stuff had always gone on in the house. Apparently even the old lady was terrified living in the house, and that's what the business was with the chairs under the windows. She always thought spirits or whatever were trying to come in through the windows, and she was trying to block them.

When I got home, I called the agency and told them I had a cold. I never went back.

WE HEARD ODD NOISES

I met Flavio Belli when he served as the suave curator of the Joseph D. Carrier Art Gallery at Columbus Centre in North York which is now part of the Greater Toronto Area. He combines the temperament of the artist with the talent of the showman. In 1972, when Flavio was twenty-one years old and an arts student at Sheraton College, he shared quarters with a friend named John, a student of photography at Ryerson Polytechnical Institute. They lived in the basement of an old house at 56 Huron Street, Toronto. They may well have shared their quarters with a poltergeist. Here is what happened when they moved in, as Flavio recalled for me at Columbus Centre's Café Cinquecento on the afternoon of 27 January 1998.

> In 1972, I was an arts student at Sheraton College. For about six months, I shared quarters in the basement of an old house at 56 Huron Street (below College) with my friend John, a student of photography at Ryerson. Both of us were twenty-one years old at the time.
>
> As soon as we moved in, we heard odd noises. The house was old, but it was new to us, so we felt the noises were explicable. But we soon realized the noises were not explicable, and they were soon followed by disturbances. There were knocks at the back door. We would open the door within ten seconds of hearing knocks, but there was never anyone there. If we shut the door, the knocks would persist. The knocks were not caused by the kids in the neighbourhood because at the time of the knocks they were nowhere in the vicinity.
>
> The superintendent and his wife occupied the flat on the top floor and felt that any noises or disturbances were caused by the tenants of the house. The flat on the main floor was occupied by two female violinists who admitted to us that they were hearing odd noises now and then. But they made noises of their own — violin sounds! They moved out and were replaced by some people,

who wore odd scarfs and explained that they were members of a commune in the Yukon. The cultists had no prior knowledge of any poltergeist in the house or of any explanation for its activities. Some time later, employing an Ouija board, they claimed to be in contact with the spirit, and even gave it a name.

Then a truly bizarre incident occurred while we were entertaining some friends. John and I were laying out a table of food, including cookies and half a watermelon. Without any cause or warning, the watermelon-half on the table began to eject its seeds, wildly shooting them into the air! Seeds were zipping across the room and landing everywhere!

Everyone was astonished. John got up to leave the room and a number of seeds shot through the air in his direction. Peter, a friend from the main floor, on impulse, yelled out, "Stop it! You're going to hurt someone." Abruptly the seeds stopped shooting out. Some of the seeds that were on the floor rose up and down of their own accord, taking a few seconds to settle down. It was an odd experience.

Some incidents occurred during the summer weather. In the evening, using masking tape, John and I would tape the lever of the thermostat on off. In the middle of the night, the lever would be turned to high, causing the furnace to go on. Yet the lever was still tightly taped. No one else had access to the room but John and me, and neither of us had readjusted the lever. There was no mechanism for the thermostat to turn itself up.

One night we returned from a concert. It was about two in the morning and the house shook. We feared for our lives. We were standing in the hallway before going into our rooms, when we heard an immense explosion! Our immediate thought was that an airplane had crashlanded in the front yard of the house and that the house would catch fire. We raced out the door we had entered but outside the house we found everything to be quiet. We re-entered the house to find that nothing at all had been disturbed.

On another occasion, at night, I saw a globe of light glowing in the darkness of the room. I started to wake up John to point it out to him, but as he was waking up, the globe was slowly shrinking in size. By the time John was awake, the light was extinguished.

On yet another occasion, I was entertaining a Lithuanian nun in the living-room. On a window-sill sat a small piece of tile, about the size of toonie, that had been used to burn incense. No windows were open. No wind was blowing, no curtain was flapping, but on its own accord, the tile simply flew across the room in the direction of the nun, narrowly missing her, but crashing into the print of Caravaggio's "Mother and Child" on the far wall. The print was hit but unharmed. Tile dropped to the floor behind a bookshelf. We were astonished. Later I fished it out and placed it back on the window-sill, where it regularly resided, and forgot about it for some months. Then we decided to move out of the flat. The day we were moving our furniture from the flat, the tile turned up, behind the bookshelf.

To this day John and I are puzzled by the inexplicable things that happened at 56 Huron Street.

THIS HOUSE IS HAUNTED

Most of the accounts I include in my collections of ghost stories come from friendly strangers. I received this story by email on 4 August 2007, but it did not come from a friendly stranger but from a friend, Ed Butts, who is a fellow researcher and author. Ed has family roots in Cape Breton, although he himself was born in Ontario and is a resident of Guelph. He often shares with me jokes and anecdotes, stories and legends that have the flavour of the Maritimes. Ed's most recent book is *Running with Dillinger* (2008), the story of the country's "forgotten Canadian outlaws." Ed has never seen a ghost, but in this email he tells of an unnerving experience that he had at a cousin's "haunted" house in Cape Breton Island.

In the summer of 1992, I and other members of my family went to Cape Breton. One day we were at the home of my cousin and her husband, near Sydney. We were just finishing supper, when my uncle asked my cousin's husband if they'd had anymore visits from their "guest." My cousin's husband began to describe some strange occurrences. After listening to him for a few minutes I asked, "Are you guys talking about a ghost?"

My uncle said, as matter-of-factly as if he were talking about the weather, "Yes, buddy. This house is haunted."

I know that people in my family are great storytellers, and I thought my uncle and my cousin's husband were pulling my leg. I said, "Oh, c'mon!"

One of them said, "No, b'y! This is no lie. This house is haunted."

Then my uncle, my cousin, and my cousin's husband started to tell me — and everyone else at the table — about things that had happened there. The house was an old one, to which some new parts had been added. The strange occurrences happened only in the new parts. Ordinary objects would disappear, and then be found in unexpected places. At night there would be loud noises, like the banging of pots and pans. A room would suddenly become cold and there would be a bad smell.

My cousin and her husband had two kids, both boys. One was a teenager of about sixteen; the other was just a little guy, about kindergarten age. My cousin said that both of her sons had experienced "visits."

The little boy often told his parents that "the lady" had been in his room at night. He was not afraid of her. My cousin believes this was her mother, my aunt, who had died some years before.

The older boy had very different experiences. He would wake up in the night and see a horrible face hanging above him. His mother said he would sometimes run out of his room, screaming.

I listened to these stories, not really sure what to believe. We were all drinking beer, and before long I had to go to the bathroom. The bathroom was in the part of the house that was supposed to be haunted!

All of a sudden my logical disbelief gave way to an unpleasant feeling of anxiety. I did not want to go in that bathroom. First I thought I could "hold it" until we left that house and I could use a different bathroom. But it didn't seem that the visit was going to break up soon. Then I thought I might sneak out and have a pee in the yard. But if I did that, everyone would think I was chicken, afraid to go into the bathroom.

So I headed for the bathroom. I poked the door open and peeked inside, just in case there was a ghost in there. After I went in and closed the door, I peeked behind the shower curtain. No ghost.

Then I went to the toilet and peed. I tried to pee really fast, because I wanted to get out of that bathroom. When I went to the sink to wash my hands, I did not look at the mirror that was directly in front of me, because I was afraid I might see something that wasn't me looking back.

Nothing unusual happened while we were in my cousin's house. That night I was in the home of another cousin who was putting us visitors up. I told him about the stories I'd heard that day. He said it was all true. The house was haunted.

He told me that one night he had been awakened when a brother of the cousin with the haunted house knocked on his door. This man was from Cape Breton, but he worked on the lake boats, and lived in Ontario. He was in Cape Breton to visit family. I should add that he was a big, tough man who certainly was not known for being timid.

When the cousin who was my host saw this other cousin on his doorstep in the middle of the night, he was very surprised. He said, "I thought you were staying over at ____ house."

The big cousin was shaking. He said, "There's no f...f...f... friggin' way I'm ever going back in that house." He would not say what had happened. The cousin who was my host learned a day or two later that our big cousin had indeed been at his sister's house, expecting to stay the night. He went to bed, but in the middle of the night he ran out of the house.

To the best of my knowledge he never told anybody what he had seen, and he never went back to his sister's house. He has since passed on, and I never did get a chance to ask him about it. I doubt very much that he would have been willing to talk about the experience.

There is a postscript to this. My uncle — the one who was talking to my cousin's husband about the ghost — lived just around the corner from his sister, the aunt who my cousin thought was "the lady" her little boy spoke of. In my uncle's house there was a large metal cross hanging on a wall in the parlour. I recall seeing it there when I was a kid.

According to my uncle, on the night my aunt (his sister/the lady) died, that cross — which had been hanging in the same spot for years — suddenly fell. It actually cracked the baseboard. A few moments later the phone rang, and my uncle was told that his sister had just died. As far as my uncle is concerned, that falling cross was a "forerunner"— a premonition that the death of a loved one was about to occur.

4

SPECIFIC SPIRITS

Spirits are sometimes little more than sparks of energy. At other times they have definable personalities with recognizable traits and characteristics. In the main this section consists of descriptions of encounters with specific spirits, *post-mortem* personalities that are recognized by the living to resemble the personalities of the deceased. No one knows why the dead appear to the living — if indeed they do so appear — but if the spirit has a personality, the chances are that it has the personality of a person newly dead or long dead. Here are some accounts of recognizable entities believed to be dead and … if not gone, then … away.

A GHOST CALLED MATTHEW

I was the guest of Bill Carroll on the radio show "Toronto Talks" on 8 February 1994. The show heard on AM 640 and Q107 has a wide listenership. Bill and I talked with seven people who phoned in to report on their ghostly experiences. So anxious were listeners to talk with us, we could have talked with seventy people, as the switchboard was lit up with incoming calls like a Christmas tree! About a week later, 10 February 1994, as a follow-up, I received the following letter from Jim Young, of Barrie, Ont. At the time of the incidents described in this account, Jim was working as a data processing operations manager and Shirley was a lab secretary in

Barrie. Then they moved to Eganville and then back to Barrie. The account speaks for itself. And it speaks volumes!

Dear Mr. Colombo:

Yesterday I tuned into the Bill Carroll show and was disappointed to discover I had missed the first part of the show featuring you as the guest. The topic, as you know, was ghosts and poltergeists. This is the reason why I am writing to you.

I am submitting our "ghost experiences" to you for your evaluation and possible inclusion in your new book about ghosts in Ontario.

It started here in Barrie in 1990, shortly after my wife Shirley and I purchased a home on Wilson Court. In the beginning, of course, we were unprepared. We didn't make any connection between what was occurring and we didn't anticipate future incidents. So we didn't make careful notes as to the dates or the order of the events. They are described here the way they happened, though not necessarily in this chronological order.

At our house on Wilson Court, when we were in the master bedroom or the main bathroom, we would often hear music. It was usually a little louder in the bathroom, which was in the middle of the house. It did not have an outside wall. The music wasn't clearly distinguishable, but sounded like the faint signal of a modern radio station or stereo without any commentary. On a couple of occasions we tried to trace the source of the music by going outside or opening windows to see if a neighbour was playing music loudly nearby, but we could hear nothing, even though we could hear the music inside these rooms before and after checking outside.

We used the middle bedroom in our house as a small study in which I had my computer set up. One evening the lights and power went out in that room. After checking the panel box, we discovered no switches had been tripped. Even more peculiar was the fact that the TV in our bedroom, which was on the same circuit as the computer, would still work. I mentioned this to my brother-in-law who is an electrician and he suggested there might be a short somewhere that should be checked out. We didn't follow up on his recommendation. After a couple of weeks the power mysteriously returned to the room, and we had no further problems with the power for the rest of our stay in that house.

The "spookiest" event, however, happened one night when I was not home. I was working on a special project at work that required me to stay there all night. In the middle of the night, Shirley was awakened when she felt someone leaning on her pillow and pulling her hair. At first she thought I had come home early, but when she turned to look, there was no one there. Shirley immediately called me at work to tell me what had happened, as it had given her quite a scare. When she spoke to me, Shirley told me that she had a creepy feeling that someone or something was there.

In 1992 we moved to a small home near Eganville where most of our "ghostly" experiences have happened. Shirley had a ceramic doll in the shape of a little girl who was lying on her side praying. Its mate had been broken by her abusive, common-law husband in her previous relationship. On two different days, we returned home to find the doll on the shelf turned 180 degrees and facing the wall. The first time this happened I assumed she had turned the doll, perhaps while dusting it, and Shirley had assumed that I had done it for some reason or other. When we talked to each other about it, however, we both confessed that we had not touched the doll. The only explanation we could come up with was that it had been done by the ferrets. During one of their runs out of their cage they might have disturbed the doll. We couldn't really comprehend this happening, as there were several other figurines on the same shelf, none of which had been moved. Anyone who has ferrets would quickly realize that, clumsy in their investigations, some of the other figurines would certainly have been moved if not knocked off this narrow shelf.

The second time this happened, however, we noticed the dust on the glass shelf on which it sat had not been disturbed and the outline of its proper position was clearly visible. We were now certain it was not the ferrets, as we had checked the shelf frequently, particularly after their last run, so they could not have moved the doll without disturbing the dust.

Shortly after we had moved into this house, we painted the back doors and door jam. As it was summer, we left the inside door open at all times, except at night. On the way out one day, I noticed deep scratch marks on the inside of the jam that had recently been painted. The scratches were inside the two doors and therefore could not have been caused by an animal from outside. At that time we had not only the two pet ferrets but also a cocker spaniel puppy. It would have been impossible for any of them to have caused these scratches, as they were far too deep for even the puppy to have caused it. He just simply didn't have the weight or strength to dig that deeply into the wood. Furthermore, the scratches were probably too high for even the puppy to have reached. In fact, there are scratch marks on the door that our puppy did make, which are hardly visible on the paint. There is absolutely no comparison of these two scratch marks. We have not repaired the door jam, and the scratch marks remain there to this day.

Around this time, one of our two canaries died, for no appartent reason. I buried him in a shallow grave in the backyard. A couple of weeks later, his mate also died, and I decided it would be appropriate to bury them together. I returned to the spot where I had buried the first canary to discover he was lying on top of his grave, although there was no evidence the ground had been dug up or disturbed since I had dug his grave there. Although it was starting to decay, the bird did not appear to be mutilated, as it would have been had a wild animal or neighbour's cat or dog dug it up. It would have eaten the dead bird or carried it off.

I have a bad habit of often being excessively neat and organized, to the point where I will face the canned goods in our cupboards or the beer in our refrigerator. One morning I noticed the loose change that I had left on our dresser a couple of days earlier, neatly lined up in rows of pennies, dimes, and nickels. It was something that would not be out of character for me. However, I had not done this. In fact, if I had lined them up, I would have placed them in neat piles, as opposed to laying them out side by side as they were. When I asked Shirley why she lined the coins up, she told me she had noticed them but thought I had done it.

On the top shelf in our bedroom clothes closet, we keep a box of massage oils that I use to give Shirley back rubs. Upon noticing one of the bottles sitting on Shirley's dresser, I assumed she was hinting that it had been a while since I had given her a back rub. However, when I confronted Shirley about this, again she had assumed it was I who had got the oil out.

By now we realized that we had a presence in our house. We affectionately named our ghost "Matthew" for no particular reason other than that it was a name that just popped into my head.

As I slept in one morning, I woke to hear my name whispered very clearly in my ear. I had been awake earlier and knew Shirley was already up, but I had fallen back to sleep. I assumed Shirley had come back into the room but I rolled over to find myself alone. I immediately got up and went to the far end of the house where Shirley was and discovered she had not been even close to that end of the house since she had risen some time earlier.

I began on occasion to see Matthew as small "wisps" of white light floating across the rooms. Most often, these sightings were made from the corner of my eye and disappeared as I snapped my head around for a better look. One night, however, as I lay awake in bed, I clearly saw Matthew float past the clothes closet. Our house was isolated in the country where it is very dark at night. No cars were travelling down the road at the time and there was no light source that I could find that would have caused a reflection. Matthew did not appear to look like I would have imagined a "ghost" should look like, based on what I had read up to that time. However, a short while ago, I saw a television program about some people who had captured some ghosts on video. Their ghosts were very similar to Matthew, with the exception that theirs moved very quickly. There were a number of them and they were slightly larger than Matthew.

Our cocker spaniel, during this time, would often walk around the house with his nose in the air, as if following some aroma around the room.

In the bathroom, I once heard scratching coming from some spot nearby. The ferrets' cage was right beside the bathroom, so I first thought they were awake and making the noise. When I left the bathroom, however, I discovered both ferrets sound asleep. Yet the scratching continued. I didn't mention this to Shirley at the time because I was afraid we might have unwanted rodents in the crawl space, although before that time and any time since I have never found any trace of anything other than insects in the crawl space, a space that is well sealed with a concrete foundation and close fitting doors.

Shirley has often felt a tugging on the covers at the bottom corner of the bed on her side of the house and occasionally still does. (Although we have since moved to Barrie, we continue to visit the house in Eganville whenever we can.)

In July of 1993, we moved back to Barrie to a basement apartment, where we are presently living. This Christmas past, we had a few candy canes hanging from various places, including a cardboard box which is temporarily serving as a filing cabinet for me. Shirley got up one morning to discover a candy cane, the only one different from all the others, lying in the middle of the floor. We no longer have our dog and the ferrets are locked in their cage and only allowed out for supervised periods during the day.

About a month following this incident, I got up one morning and found one of Shirley's negligees, which usually hangs on a hook in the bedroom, lying in the middle of the living-room floor, not far from where Shirley had found the candy cane.

I discussed this with a friend once, who told me that ghosts didn't normally follow people from house to house. Another friend, however, asked, "Who makes up the rules for ghosts? Can't they do just about anything they want?"

I am not suggesting that there is not a logical explanation for some of these occurrences. Furthermore, they may or may not be related to each other. I have merely made a note of them for interest's sake.

If you have any questions about these incidents, please don't hesitate to contact me at any time. Should you wish to include them in your new book, please feel free to do so.

Sincerely,

Jim Young

ELEVATOR RIDE

Liv is short for Livia. Livia M. Pravato lives in Weston, Ont., and submitted this true story to the Halloween issue of *Midtown Voice*, October 1994. The scary piece was a prize-winner.

It was three o'clock in the afternoon and a Monday. I was feeling fatigued and hadn't had a full break all day.

The garment company where I worked was undergoing some renovations. These were on the second floor where the main showroom and offices were located. The age of the five-story building was evident from the chipped paint on the ceilings and walls from the old factory windows that didn't open and had been greased by companies past. The floors and stairs creaked with every step; old wood and the smell of mold surrounded you as you walked in. The elevator had a single grey door that jerked open to a view of brown panelled walls made to look like real wood. The square-shaped buttons on the control panel showed signs of use. There was a clinging brown film which encompassed clean white spots where thousands of fingers must have poked the keys to get to each floor. And as with other things that have aged, this elevator took its time and you could almost sense its "I'll get there when I'm ready" attitude.

The third and fifth floors were vacant. We were using the fourth floor as a storage area for some of our merchandise until the renovations were finished. I was the sucker who had the grand job of fetching whatever was needed from the fourth floor. It was usually quicker for me to walk up and down the stairs rather than wait for the elevator. I was so tired by the hundredth trip I couldn't help but take the elevator down. I pressed the outside key and a green light illuminated the downward arrow. I could hear the wheels and cords of the elevator slowly working to get to the fourth floor where I waited. The grey door jerked open to show the small cubicle of brown paneled walls. I stepped in and lazily leaned against the side that faced the control panel. The number two button glowed a pale yellow as I pressed it. The doors closed and I awaited my descent. I thought to myself that if this elevator had broken down right now it would be a great excuse to have a break and maybe take forty winks.

The door clumsily slid open. I started to step out when I noticed that I was still on the same floor. I jumped back in and thought to press the button again, on the off chance that I hadn't pressed it hard enough the first time. The door closed. Nothing happened. The door opened. I repeated my actions and the door closed again, then opened, then closed. It wouldn't stop! I was so confused I started pressing all the buttons for all the floors. The door wouldn't stop opening and closing.

"I was just kidding!" I yelled. "I didn't really mean for you to break down!" Finally I came to my senses and pressed the "Door Open" button. The elevator door opened and stayed that way to give me just enough time to get out. I was breathless, as I watched the elevator door quietly close and the square lights about light up, one after the other, as the elevator slowly made its way down to the basement.

I ran down the stairs, thinking that now I would surely be fired because I took so long. I planned to answer questions of why I was yelling and who I was yelling at upstairs. I walked into the showroom. A couple of customers were browsing. The manager looked up as I walked in. She said nothing.

Quickly I said, "Sorry it took me so long."

"What do you mean?" she asked curiously. "You were only up there for a few minutes."

"I was?" I said with a surprised look on my face. It had seemed like an eternity.

Nobody even heard me yelling. It was as if I had been the only person in the building at the time. I had such a strange feeling. I couldn't help but think of why the elevator would do that, right at the moment when I thought of it breaking down. Was it my imagination? Or did it really happen? Anyway, I wasn't going to take any more chances.

At five o'clock, I saw people getting on the elevator. It was working normally now. I took the stairs. There was no way I was going to go back onto that elevator. Especially since I came to the conclusion that it probably knew … what I was thinking.

THINGS THAT TWITCH IN THE NIGHT

I have never met Debbie Ridpath Ohi, but I know that she lives in Toronto and that she is the author of this memoir. It was written in 1995 and reads like fiction. By that I mean it reads so smoothly it feels more like fiction than it does fact. But it is a true-life memoir. I wonder what the answer should be to Ms. Ohi's question. I wonder if she will ever be able to answer her own question.

When I was six years old, my babysitter and her friend told me about the giant rabbit who lived in the forest near our house.

"It eats children," Rebecca told me solemnly.

I was horrified, of course. My parents had never warned me of the monstrous predator in our vicinity, and had even taken me for walks on the trail. Perhaps they didn't know.

"Everyone knows about it," added Rebecca. "Three kids have been eaten, just this year. All that were left were their bones and their hair."

My lower lip trembled. "I don't believe you," I said, even though I did.

The next day Rebecca and her best friend Genevieve took me for a walk.

"What are those for?" I asked, apprehension stirring. Both Rebecca and Genevieve had a carrot in their hands.

"In case we run into the rabbit," Rebecca said matter-of-factly. "So he'll eat the carrots instead of us. I would have brought you a carrot except my mom only had two."

"Anyway, you said you don't believe there's a rabbit," added Genevieve. I didn't like Genevieve very much.

She was right, though; I had expressed disbelieve in the existence of their giant child-munching rabbit. So I didn't say anything and pretended not to be scared to death as we started on the trail.

The trees rustled with the wind as we moved deeper into the forest, and I struggled to keep my eyes on the trail, away from the shadows beneath the trees.

"What was that?" Rebecca gasped.

"I don't know. Maybe it's following us," Genevieve spoke in a whisper.

Panicked, I strained to hear. "What? What?"

"Ssshhh," whispered Rebecca, and we kept walking. I was numb with fear, and I kept looking around the forest behind us.

The giant rabbit knew I was here! I pictured its huge pink nose twitching malevolently as it caught my scent. I wondered how long it had been since it had eaten.

A few minutes later, Rebecca and her friend stopped. I was not happy about this, of course. All my instincts were screaming at me to run home as fast as my little legs could carry me.

"We've got something to show you," said Rebecca mysteriously.

They knelt, and motioned for me to come closer. I did, and glanced down at where they were pointing.

It was a giant rabbit footprint.

I gasped and took a step back.

"See?" said Genevieve. "Rebecca told you it was real. You didn't believe her."

Panic-stricken, I started looking around us, my head turning in jerks. "I wanna go home." It was here, I could sense it. Somewhere in that shadowy forest lurked an evil child-devouring monster with a twitching nose and pink-rimmed eyes.

Then I screamed.

To this day I swear I saw something, behind a clump of trees. What exactly, I cannot say. It was more a fleeting glimpse, a flash of raggedy fur perhaps, a single twitch of a giant whiskered nose. Whatever it was, the glimpse galvanized me into action.

Without waiting to consult Rebecca or Genevieve, I ran down the path towards home, screaming at the top of my little lungs all the way.

Rebecca managed to catch up with me two-thirds of the way back. The incident must have unnerved her, because she immediately took me to the ice cream store and bought me a cone (pralines and cream, my favourite) with some of her baby-sitting money, warning me not to tell my parents about what had happened just in case it scared them, too.

Years later I still go over the entire event in my mind and wonder. The rabbit footprint could easily have been created by Rebecca and her friend, as "proof" to me that the creature existed.

But what did I see in the forest that day?

IT WAS AN AMAZING EXPERIENCE

Perusing the "X Archives" on the Internet on 5 November 1995, I found this unusual story. It was untitled so I have given it the title "It Was an Amazing Experience." I know nothing about the author, who signed himself "Ekin," but I secured permission from the moderator of the newsgroup to run his story in this slightly edited form. For readers with internet access who are interested in reading more personal accounts of hauntings of this type, the address is as follows: < *http://www.crown.net/X/Stories/GSGhost.html* >

> I am new to this and I liked the info on paranormal activity, so I thought I would share my own experience.
>
> About a year ago, while working at a gas station known as The Beehive here in Sarnia, Ontario, CA, I came across various stories on the history of the building. Most notably were the painted-over sign that read "Methodist Church, 1886" and the fact that the place used to be a hotel (one of our customers was born there). However, the site has been a gas station / variety store for many years now.
>
> One story that stood out was that one of the original owners of the Beehive practically lived in the back room of the building with his cot, stove, etc., till one day he had a heart attack and passed away. Since that time, there have been a couple of owners, but I did not come into employment till after the new owner took over. Many renovations have been made, including the relocation of one on the doorways. (You can still see where the door was.)
>
> One evening, while working with another co-worker, standing side-by-side, cleaning shelves, we witnessed something that made me ever so excited. From the spot of the old doorway, we both happened to witness an image of someone walking through the doorway and behind the counter before vanishing. When it was gone, we both looked at each other, pale as (excuse the pun) ghosts. I became excited and intrigued and ran over there. My co-worker just stood there in shock. She quickly denied the whole thing, but I truly do believe I saw a ghost, possibly of the old owner. I have yet to see a photo of that person to compare it to what I saw.
>
> It was an amazing experience, no matter how short. I hope it occurs again.

NO ONE WANTED TO SLEEP IN THE ROOM

I found this story on the Internet on 6 November 1995 and communicated with its author who kindly gave me permission to reproduce it here. Ron Sandler posted it to the moderator of the newsgroup called "X Archives." The story is a good instance of the kind of haunting that has a history and is happening also in the present day. The history is the fact that an uncommon event took place in the past, usually without the prior knowledge of participants today, and that it continues to influence the present in a manner that is probable (though impossible). The haunting is the "anniversary" of the historical event, the reverberation or echo of the past event into the corridors of the present. There are many stories like this one in the "X Archives." The internet address is: *http://www.crown.net/X/Stories/TDRoom.html*

> I've told this one several times, and it is true. It is partially folklore, and partially a personal experience for I have witnessed the paranormal phenomena. So here it is.
>
> Amherstburg, Ontario, is a love, sleepy, old community on the Detroit River. It is an hour away from a large metropolitan area, and it still seems to be caught in an era from a previous century.
>
> One of my best friends at the time, Patti H., still lived with her parents while she was attending the University of Windsor. Her parents bought an old, turn-of-the-century farm house with a store-front to house her father's jewelry shop. Patti owned two very large sheep dogs, and the move to a large house in the country was welcomed by all of them.
>
> At first, the phenomena was viewed as an annoyance. There was a back bedroom that was always cold. No matter an addition space heater was added, the room remained bone-chilling cold.
>
> Then, Patti noticed that neither one of her sheep dogs would enter the room. When forced, they would growl, put their ears back, and leave as soon as allowed.
>
> I was over, once, for dinner, and they asked me, without explaining why, to enter the bedroom and tell me what I thought of the room. (I had been part of a psychic experiment at Wayne State University in Detroit, and had been considered somewhat sensitive. I am an identical twin with an empathic link to my twin and have experienced visions on occasion). I obliged them, and

was, "on edge" after I entered the room. I was chilled, and felt sad. I reported this to Patti, and she responded that was how they all felt about the bedroom. No one wanted to sleep in the room, or if they did, they had nightmares of a terrifying death.

Coupled with that, Patty reported that the bedroom door wouldn't stay closed but that it wouldn't drift open. The door would slam open with a bang on occasion, when no one was around it, and the windows were closed.

Sparked by curiosity, we contacted the local historical society and found out that a woman had been brutally murdered, knifed to death by her jealous husband, in that room, before he cut his own wrists and bled to death on the floor!

Needless to say, after that, if the dogs didn't want to go into that bedroom, they didn't have to.

The room is now being used for storage.

AN AREA KNOWN AS SALEM'S LOT

This story was submitted by someone with the username "Abbadon" to Obiwan, the webmaster of a site devoted to the paranormal. She received it on 25 March 1996 and posted it to the three hundred or so subscribers to her ghost-story list on 27 April 1996. I am pleased to be able to report that "Abbadon" is otherwise known as Robert Hedley of Whitby, Ont. Although I have called this account "Salem's Lot," a catchy title, he is anxious that it be known to all that Salem's Lot is a reference, not to a novel by Stephen King, but to Ontario's Salem Road. He subsequently explained to me: "We called it 'Salem's Lot' in high school, but a lot of other people do not know it by that name. The area where my experience took place was east of Salem Rd. in Ajax / Pickering, in the area we called 'The Lot.' There are lots of local stories associated with this particular road, many of which I heard after I had my experience. It can be easily found if you wish to investigate it first-hand. Take the 401 eastbound to Westney Road in Ajax. Head north on Westney to Rossland Road, and proceed east, past Harwood, to Salem Road. Salem Road starts at Rossland on the north side of the road. If you continue east, past Durham Auto Wreckers, you will see a cornfield on the north side. Stop at the top of the hill, at the cedar tree line. There is a path on the north side of the road, which heads into the bush. It is easier to walk through the cedar trees until you come to the footpath. I will show it to you if you wish. The hole we dug is still there (we checked it out this past summer). If you drive up Salem Road from Rossland, past Taunton, you will see a castle on the east side of the road, just south of Highway 7 (Winchester Road). There is also a graveyard that covers both sides of the road, north of the castle and south of the highway. I have heard other stories associated with both the castle and the graveyard (both of which are rumoured to be haunted)." The story of the hijinks of two grown men and the repercussions of their deeds leads me to believe that Salem's Lot is well named!

Here is a story I have been meaning to send to the list.

My name is Robert Hedley, and I live in Whitby, Ontario, in Canada. When I was in high school, we used to party in the woods north of Ajax (the next town over) in an area known as Salem's Lot (like the Stephen King novel). The area was located north of Rossland Road, a little east of Salem Road (hence the name). There were many stories associated with the place (not many which we believed), ranging from ritual murders and Satanic activity to ghosts that walked the woods at night. I thought that these stories were made up to scare the girls who went with us on these excursions, until one night three years ago.

I had been telling a friend of mine, Jay, about these stories I had heard in high school. Since I had just recently got my own car (an old '77 Malibu), we decided to go see if we could find the old party spot. We had a gym bag with us, with the following items: a double-edged knife, a can of lighter fluid, and a dime-store copy of Abdul Alhazred's *Necronomicon* (not that I believe the *Necronomicon* is real, but we had it just the same). We drove up to the place where the old road used to take us into the spot, to find it … gone. Within the five or six years since I had last been there, the road had disappeared. We parked the car and proceeded to walk through the woods. As we got farther into the woods, we found a path that led through two trees with arcane symbols painted on them. We followed the path through the trees and kept walking until we came to the old dam that I remembered from my high-school days. The path had a fork in it, one leading over the dam, and the other leading northwest.

It was around this time that Jay got this idea to carve a symbol out of the *Necronomicon* into the ground. He thought that it would scare any kids who came up there (he has a strange sense of humour). We chose the symbol of Pazuzu (coincidentally the same demon that possessed Linda Blair in *The Exorcist*). We started to carve out the symbol on the ground, and noticed that someone had poured asphalt and then buried it under about one and one-half inches of soil. We wondered about this, and asked ourselves who would go through all the trouble? Instantly, the stories of satanic cults came to mind. Yeah, we thought, there must be a body under the asphalt! We started digging and lit two fires on either side of the hole, so we could see what we were doing. The asphalt came up quite easily, but work was slow, as we were only using our hands and the knife.

By now it was getting dark. We decided it would be easier to go back to my house and get a shovel and flashlight before we continued. We picked up handfuls of the dirt from the hole, and threw them onto the burning embers of the fire. As the last bit of fire was extinguished, we started to hear what at first sounded like a large dog about a mile away start barking. Between us and this "dog" was a very large cornfield that the path ran parallel to. The rows of corn also ran parallel to the path. And it was within about fifteen seconds that the sound grew from sounding like one dog to a pack of dogs tearing something apart that just refused to die. And it was getting closer. Within another ten to fifteen seconds, what had sounded like it was a mile away sounded like it was fifty feet away, coming through the cornfield. And above all the howling, screaming, and snarling was a sound that was not unlike what a loose fan-belt sounds like on a cold winter day. It is very hard for me to describe the exact quality of the sound, but considering it travelled about a mile in less than thirty seconds (maybe less than that), and the closer it got, the louder and faster it squealed, I was quite terrified. By now it was about fifteen feet from us, and the noise was deafening. I turned to Jay, and he bolted down the path. I followed. We were tripping and falling over branches and undergrowth (it was dark by then), but we still ran in a complete panic.

Jay is about 6'1" and 180 lbs. and I am 6'8" and 220 lbs., and normally we aren't scared of anything, but that night we ran like the hounds of hell were after us! The next thing I was aware of was the fact that the noise had stopped. We ran back to the car and floored it out of there (after a few seconds of sitting there and realizing the lights wouldn't work; they did after about a minute).

To this day, I have no idea what caused that noise, but I am sure if had we stuck around, I wouldn't be here to tell the tale. I have heard wolves, coyotes, and bears before, and this sounded like none of them. Later we realized that the "asphalt" was the remains of the old road we used to drive down, but I have no idea who took great effort to ensure it wouldn't be driven down again.

There are a few more stories about the 'lot, and maybe later I will post them as well. Please refer any questions to

Thank you.

Zodiac

I COULD SEE A HUMAN FIGURE

In late March of 1997, Tony Hawke, friend and proprietor of Hounslow Press, the company that published my book *Ghost Stories of Ontario*, forwarded some letters that were addressed to me care of the publisher. One of the letters, signed by Vivian Hartley, is reproduced below. It was handwritten on lined paper, and it makes quite engrossing reading! As they say, it speaks for itself. Here it is:

Dear Mr. Colombo:

First off, let me tell you how much I enjoyed your book *Ghost Stories of Ontario*. Some of the stories really gave me the creeps! Now let me tell you about something creepy that happened to me.

I live in Toronto, and in July of 1996, I was on vacation in New Brunswick. My husband and I rented a small cottage in a tiny village called Barnesville. It's a tiny place, on the grounds of a huge mansion, but set back in trees so there is no view of the main house or the road. The cottage is constructed of stone and over a hundred years old. We stayed there for a month.

The first incident occurred when we were there for three days, and I almost discounted it as imagination, though it scared me.

I was taking a shower after a long day at the beach. The bathroom was filled with steam. After I pulled back the shower curtain and was drying myself, I saw something out of the corner of my eye. The steam was swirling around, too fast, and was forming a shape. I stood there in shock and I could see a human figure, even shorter than me and I'm only 5'1". It dissipated and the water in the shower that I had just turned off came back on.

Over the next few days nothing happened, but I felt constantly watched. Then I was lying on the couch one rainy afternoon. I was definitely not falling asleep. I was propped up reading, and suddenly all my energy drained away. I felt drowsy and hypnotized, and a paralysis came over me. Strangely I was not afraid. I couldn't move a muscle. Then a boy walked out of the bedroom and sat down on the edge of the couch and stared intently at me. He was wearing suspenders, about his dress, that's all I can recall. He had dark hair and a pale complexion, and light grey eyes. He was perhaps ten or eleven years of age. He placed his hand on mine and it felt cool and dry. While I could not see through him exactly, he looked insubstantial. I felt like I was having an asthma attack and began to gasp for air, and panic, struggling to move. He faded slowly and looked pained that I was so afraid. When he was gone I found I could move again and promptly sat up and screamed my lungs out. My husband came running from the kitchen. For some reason I told him I had a bad dream.

I decided that since we still had three weeks in the house, I was not going to be in it alone. I did not feel threatened but I did feel nervous and could feel a constant presence. I had a very vivid dream that I spoke to the boy and he was crying and trying to clutch at me. He was pathetic, but I woke up sobbing and terrified. I felt his name was Warden.

I went shopping for the day and when I returned to the cottage my husband was driving up the driveway toward the cottage and he saw a white face at the front window. The face had a shock of dark hair. It was only then I told him about what I had seen in the previous days.

On a Saturday night we invited another vacationing couple and their two daughters, aged nine and five. The five-year-old stayed in the house playing while we barbecued in the backyard. After she was out of sight for a while, her mother called out, "What are you doing in there?" The girl replied, "Playing with Warden." We had said nothing regarding the boy to these people!

For the remainder of our stay the only thing that happened was the taps would turn on. I felt depressed sometimes, and my husband felt sad for no reason as well. I feel that the boy is trapped there and was trying to communicate. We spoke to a Protestant minister in the village, and I think he thought we were nuts, but he agreed to go to the cottage and pray for the spirit to move on. I hope it worked.

RADIO GHOSTS

Here is an interesting communication from a former employee of the Canadian Broadcasting Corporation in Toronto whose name is unknown to me. It consists of an unequal balance of personal experience and word of mouth (another word for rumour!). I owe the account to Matthew Didier, one of the founders of the Toronto Ghost and Hauntings Research Society, who posted it on his website. The original posting is dated 28 October 1999. It is slightly revised for inclusion here. The former employee is quite right: various CBC buildings in Toronto have been described as being haunted not only by ghosts but by the spirits of such broadcasters as James Bannerman, Lister Sinclair, etc.!

Back in 1989 I worked for the CBC as a Security officer. I was given the job to patrol and check on other guards at 14 CBC buildings around Toronto.

My experience at 90 Sumach St. was on the fourth floor. Near the stairwell the area was always cold. As you went up and down the stairway, you could feel the cold getting colder as you reached the fourth floor, and it was getting warmer as you walked away from the fourth floor. I knew one of the Commissioners who worked there and heard the stories.

One night he set up a voice-activated tape recorder to record what he thought was voices. I checked on him around 1:00 a.m. and that's when he told me. He was going to put the recorder on after I left. No one was in the building except for him after I left and until I returned at 5:00 a.m. I asked if he recorded anything and he told me that he had something or someone on the tape. He would not let anyone hear it until he was able to identify what it was.

Another CBC Building that was strange was the Annex on Jarvis St., the old white house in front of the TV building. At the very top floor there was a light that would keep coming on. At night, the only way to get into the building was with Security. A key and a combination was needed, yet this light would be turned on. I can't remember how many times I has to climb the stairs to turn the light off. (The switch would be turned on.)

If you worked the night shift in the Radio Building, and if it was quiet, sometimes you could hear a faint moan being made a girl. Rumour has it that it was once an all-girls' school and one girl hanged herself, and it was her ghost.

Another was the building at 1140Yonge St.The Commissioners would tell me stories of one of the dressing rooms.The door would close and lock, lights would go on and off, wall outlets would lose power for no reason.

Hope this info could be of help to you.

A FABLE TURNED FACT

When I was researching the book that was eventually published as *Haunted Toronto*, I realized I needed some photographs of the interior and exterior of the Church of St. Mary Magdalene. The church, which is located near the intersection of Harbord and Bathurst Streets in Toronto, has a notable musical tradition as well as a notable spirit, and both of these involve one man: Healey Willan. Members of the congregation cherish the memory of Dr. Willan, who was for much of his professional life their resident organist and choral conductor. Lovers of serious music across Canada respect his legacy as a leading composer and musician. It is no secret that Dr. Willan said that on a number of occasions he was astonished to behold "the grey lady" in the church when he knew no one was there!

My need for photographs led me to Tom Hyland, a long-time member of the gallery choir of the church and a close friend of Dr. Willan. Tom is a character in his own right. Until his retirement he was employed in the photography department at Eaton's downtown store. A skilled photographer, he showed me his sensitive black-and-white portraits of Dr. Willan and also a number of fine atmospheric shots of the church's interior. He allowed me to reproduce a group of these in the entries on the church and its organist in *Haunted Toronto*.

Tom and I established a rapport and after a while he shared with me the suspicion that he too had seen the ghost. At my request he prepared a narrative account of his experiences and sent it to me on 13 November 1997. I am very happy to be able to include that account here in his own inimitable style. Thank you, Tom.

A Fable Turned Fact

At this time of writing, I've lived almost seven years beyond my allotted three-score-and-ten. My rather mature age, combined with the problem that I write of an incident close to fifty years old, makes this narrative exercise a most taxing effort. But yet it affords me the nostalgic pleasure of reliving some precious moments of the past.

There seems to be an indignant consensus among young people — especially hard-rock enthusiasts, aspiring computer analysts, and other adolescent ignoramuses — that older persons lose their memories. Or, as they playfully put it, "marbles." This, of course, is completely false! After all, we've lived longer, have a great deal more to remember and, if we didn't discard the trivia, we'd burst our memory banks! Therefore we are inclined to remember the importance of the personal; treat the impersonal as excess; embrace the fact, but dismiss the inexplicable as coincidence. Thus, in order to put to rest any concern as to my mental stability, and to bolster your belief in the validity of this tale, I must meander through some of my personal history that has a direct bearing on your assessment of myself and my sanity.

I began singing, as a boy soprano, in the Anglican choir of Christ Church, Belleville, before my eleventh birthday. I soon became lead boy and soprano soloist. Then, with the onset of manhood, successively graduated through the choral ranks of alto, tenor, to bass. Also, for several years, I served as choir librarian for that parish choir. (You might say — with all that training and responsibility — I knew every piece of music from the top to the bottom and the correct alphabetical sequence of our complete repertoire!) The duties of that post gave me free access to the church, day and night. Quite often, I laid out Sunday morning's music in the choir stalls the Saturday night before, and became accustomed to being mortally alone in the building. The loneliness of those occasions gave birth to my lifelong addiction to test the acoustics of the empty church by the sound of my own voice.

In September, 1945, (my wife and I having moved to Toronto from our native Belleville in the summer of '44), I had the extremely good fortune to be accepted as a bass member in the gallery choir of the Church of St. Mary Magdalene by its eminent director and precentor, the late Dr. Healey Willan. The gallery choir consisted of sixteen voices in those golden days of liturgical music, and Willan left no stone unturned to achieve choral perfection. Time seemed to be expendable. Within ten days, preceding and including Easter Sunday, we sang two full-length rehearsals, several short rehearsals, attended and sang eight services! Nothing was left to chance — not even the simplest of hymns — and, from our busy schedule of rehearsals, services, recitals, it was easily imagined the average choir becoming so totally exhausted they'd "throw-in-the-towel" and quit!

At the beginning of my lengthy tenure of service in the choir, I was a fledgling photographer. When I became familiar with Anglo-Catholic rites, the fluent beauty of properly sung plainsong, and the precision with which all rites, rituals, masses, motets, processions, etc., were performed, I fell madly in love with the music and the uniqueness of the church: The austere solemnity of its architecture; the inviting refuge of its colourful appointments.

There was a mystical aura about the place that defies adequate description. I can only suppose it was generated by the dramatic differences in its contrasts. The entire interior of the nave was bare and grey — walls; pillars; arches … cold as death! Whereas the chancel and side chapels were alive with warmth. In the Chapel of St. Joseph, a children's altar: pink in motif; portrait of child in field of wildflowers, butterflies, and birds. In the Chapel of Our Lady: heavenly serenity; blue, vaulted ceiling; Virgin Mother and

Child looking down lovingly, forgivingly on all who came and all who passed by. In the chancel, sanctuary: aptly named high altar; massive canopy, seasonal trappings; candles; ever-present Host, and magnificent gold cross — resplendent — infinite — commanding reverence in the brilliance of its shining. And the huge rood suspended high above the entrance from the main, broad arch with its Christ seemingly saying, "This is the House of God." "Here is the Gate of Heaven." They all gave one a strange sense of feeling a part of antiquity, without being old, and a part of the present, without being blatantly modern.

Here, indeed, was ample opportunity for me to pursue the art, capture the mood, and make memorable photographs with permanent appeal. There were so many things and atmospheres in that building crying out to be recorded on film that I started toting my camera along with me.

Eventually, by trial and error, by investment in equipment and the sacrifice of persistence, my skill became quite effectual. The results of my painstaking efforts were soon rewarded by the friendship and confidence of the clergy, and I found myself in the enviable position of coming and going as I pleased at any reasonable hour of the day or night to photograph whatever I wished. Thereafter, I spent innumerable hours by daylight or incandescent light (and, sometimes, the near lack of either!) to satisfy my desire that the church, in its varied aspects of sanctity, should be visually preserved as a special environment for Christian worship. And I'm forever grateful that some of those prints have found their places in books, on record jackets and music covers, and in the homes of many individuals whose love of that church and its music was equal to mine.

The gallery choir never donned the conventional choir robes. To some, that may seem sacrilegious. But, if anything, it was the opposite, as well as unnecessary. Being seated high above the back of the nave, we were out of sight and hidden from the view of the congregation. The absence of those robes had three distinct advantages. First, it was economical, saving us the expense of upkeep and the wasted time of dressing and undressing before and after each service. Second, it was convenient, should we have to silently slip down the gallery stairs during the sermon and rush, via an exterior route, to the basement lavatory. Third — and perhaps most important — it saved us the emotional distress of feeling "holier than thou" along with the damnations of women's mortarboards and makeup!

Healey was kind and considerate to all people of good intent — especially the members of his choirs (there were two). But that did not deter his stern demand for their sincere devotion to both the music and the words. I can still hear his most oft-uttered critical precaution: "Any fool can sing notes!"

Our weekly rehearsals were held Friday nights between the hours of eight and ten, precisely, with a ten-minute "smoke and gossip" break approximately halfway through. The ritual choir (the other choir and an exceptionally capable group of men and cantor who sang [traditionally robed] in the chancel and responsible for all plainchant) held their rehearsal the same night, prior to ours, from seven to eight, and again, precisely. When we arrived, the two choirs joined forces to practise all music in which we had mutual or overlapping parts (hymns, responses, canticles, etc.) that was required for the following Sunday's services. They then departed and we continued with our rehearsal.

The rehearsal room was in the basement of the church, directly below the chancel and sanctuary. It was adequately large but had the advantage of "flat" acoustics which prevented echoes from masking errors. The outside entrance to that room and the basement was through a street-level doorway on the southeast side of the church and a landing for stairs that went up to the vestry, chancel, and nave, and down to our rehearsal room. When the members of the ritual choir made their exit, the last one out tripped the latch on that door, and any gallery member who dared to arrive later — without Healey's permission — would have to knock; be let in; come down those stairs and … face the music!

There were two petty annoyances that plagued the choirs, clergy, and congregation in those days, even though they were confined to frigid temperatures. That door to the basement, when opened, ushered in an arctic blast of air that came rushing down the stairs, flooding our rehearsal room with chilly discomfort. The other annoyance was caused by the heating system in the church. There were radiators spaced along the perimeter walls at floor level that made their presence known by their noisy expansions and contractions. One of those convenience eyesores, in particular, had the habit of infusing its off-key harmony right smack-in-the-middle of our motet, or punctuating a solemn, sermon sentence with a loud "ssss" and a "bang"! Also, the supply pipes for those radiators ran beneath the floorboards of the chancel and chapels, leaving those boards so dry they "squeaked" at the least of foot pressures. In short, we were all thankful for warmer weather!

But I remember it was in the cold of winter when this disturbing incident occurred, for there were overcoats, hats, and parkas hanging along the walls on hooks and hangers — one of the few necessities in our rehearsal room. The others being a piano, a music cupboard, an assortment of wooden chairs; a washbasin, one-seater toilet, and a table on which Healey placed his music; sat upon with one leg up and one leg down to conduct, or lecture us for our (thankfully few!) faux-pas and occasionally emphasize, by illustration, the proper pronunciation of ecclesiastical Latin … usually followed by a relevant witticism quoted from one source or another.

One Friday night, during our break, Healey called me aside: "Tommy, old man, be a good chap; run up to the gallery and fetch me my copy of.…You'll find it.… " (I honestly can't remember the title of the organ score, nor where I should find it.) Giving me his key for the gallery door, he explained his need of it the following day and expressed his frustration for not having had time to go get it himself. So off I went.

There were two flights of stairs from the basement to the main body of the church. The one on the south side, which I've already described, and another on the north with a passageway at its top, running parallel with the chancel to a doorway for entry to the nave. I opted to take those stairs for they were nearer to the gallery stairway in the northwest corner of the church. In the passageway, there was a single light bulb in a pull-chain socket hanging from the ceiling. This I pulled on, opened the door, propped it open, and made my way to the opposite end of the church.

Healey and I had become close friends. So much so that I welcomed the opportunity, and pleasure, to stay behind after mass or evensong, lock up the gallery, and accompany him down to the basement where a large pot of hot tea was waiting to lubricate the vocal chords of choir members … courtesy of a very kindly lady and parishioner, Mrs. Bailey. (I do hope I've spelled "Bailey" correctly. She justly deserves proper recognition.) On those journeys he might ask, "What did you think of the Kyrie this morning, old man?" or discuss a problem with the tempo in a certain hymn. (And you have no idea how vainly proud I felt at being asked for my personal opinion — sometimes advice! — from such a renowned musician as Healey.)

The path we travelled on those intimate occasions was the same as I followed in this instance, and so familiar I probably could have traversed it fully with my eyes closed, as in the unconscious sight of sleep. But the dim light from the open doorway partially lifted the eerie shroud of darkness from the unlit aisle and prevented me from bumping into a pew or two.

There was a high, spacious vestibule the full length of the west wall of the church for coats and hats and more silent and draft-free entry to the nave. It had three sets of double doors with the gallery stairway in the north corner. I opened one of the nearest set, switched on the vestibule light, and mounted the gallery stairs. At the top, I switched on the two lights in the gallery, unlocked the door, and went in. Unfortunately, the empty church proved too tempting for me to resist my youthful addiction, and I started humming, quite loudly, with a few bass "booms" thrown in to more enjoy the echo. Having found the requested score, I was about to leave the gallery when I noticed the effect of those gallery lights fading into the darkness of the sanctuary.

Always on the lookout for a different angle, different highlight, different shadow, I paused to analyze the photographic possibilities. I was standing near the back wall, and from that position could barely see the front row of pews in the nave as the gallery railing was table-top high and heavily draped to block the view of any obnoxious gawker from below. So I moved closer until I could scan the entire nave. Still humming, I looked down and caught sight of something so totally unexpected that I nearly fell over the railing in cardiac arrest!

There, below me, kneeling in a pew part way up the south side of the nave, was a woman on whom I'd never laid eyes before! I was so startled that my lungs forgot to breathe — my vocal chords ceased to function — and my eyes became fixed like a lifeless statue's! Her faded, grey apparel appeared to be more suitable for warm weather than for the frigid temperature outside, and, oddly enough, no protective outerwear was anywhere visible. I was so petrified by surprise and so mortified with embarrassment, my wits became so befuddled that I could not think straight, and could not determine whether to attempt a pleading apology for intruding on the privacy of prayer, or to vacate the premises as quickly and quietly as possible. But as she was an absolute stranger to me, and I, probably to her, I thought I'd better leave it that way and chose the latter option.

As I locked the door, switched off the gallery lights, descended the stairs, switched off the vestibule light, and retraced my steps to the passageway door, I kept thinking it also very odd that my considerable vocalizing seemed not to have disturbed her! I did not look back. There was little point to staring at the blackness of the nave. But as I closed that door, pulled off the light, and descended the stairs to our rehearsal room, I felt an immense sense of relief at leaving her and the church to the darkness in which I'd found them.

When I entered the room, Healey was poised to conduct the second half of our practice. So I took my seat, after laying the copy on his table, and my common sense suggested that I shouldn't report the unbelievable lest I be deemed a loony — if not called one! But through the remainder of that rehearsal, I kept one ear cocked for the sound of a squeaky board overhead, and one foot firmly on the floor for the feel of a cold draft … but I neither heard nor felt, either.

(There was a third oddity about that woman's appearance — a haunting enigma that's eluded my comprehension ever since that night. But now, in the poignant remembering of so many personal and related truths of the past, I've finally solved the mystery of her presence. And the motivation that's prompted my telling of this tale.)

I write this on the 10th day of November, 1997. Comes the 27th day of this month, my wife and I will celebrate our fifty-fourth wedding anniversary — God willing. On that Saturday date, 1943, we came to Toronto for our honeymoon. The following day, Sunday, the 28th, we attended High Mass at St. Mary Magdalene. The music of the Mass and motet that morning was exquisitely beautiful, and sung so clearly and devoutly by the gallery choir that I actually wept. (That, I think, is the greatest compliment that can be paid for a sterling, sincere performance.)

Shortly after I'd joined the choir, I learned of a particular area in the nave where the gallery choir could best be heard. A place almost in isolation with angels. It so happened, on that glorious Sunday morning of our honeymoon, my wife and I — by accident and because of its availability — sat, knelt, and prayed in that same area — perhaps in the very same pew where this grey-clad lady knelt!

The vivid recollection of that most precious time; that special place — that separate beatitude of beauty — had finally solved the riddle of the third oddity: It was her location! ....As if in anticipation, she occupied the exact spot, chosen by many an astute listener as the ideal ambience to fully experience the ecstasy of sound floating from that loft in an a cappella halo of faultless harmony — veritably enveloping all within our resonant House of God in a polyphonous paradise of immaculate adoration!

Healey used to tell of a ghost, dubbed "the grey lady," who interrupted his private organ practice in the church by her visual presence. Frankly, I never knew whether to doubt his sober sincerity or marvel at his clairvoyant sensitivity ... whether we had a female phantom in our midst, or a figure evolved in a spasm of indigestion! But, after putting all the facts of two and two (or twenty and twenty) together: the dark, unlit church; the late hour; the long-locked doors; the squeaky boards; the frigid temperature; the cold draft; her lack of outer clothing; her undisturbed composure, and the pew she occupied, I'm thoroughly convinced there really was a "grey lady," and I — most surely — had seen her!

Now this anecdote would still be a latent episode, locked for life in my own mind — straddling the fence of indecision with its facts, doubts, and possibilities — had it not been for a request from our local author, John Colombo, to supply prints of the church and Healey. These were gladly given and faithfully reproduced in two articles of his excellent book *Haunted Toronto* published last year

(1996) by Dundurn Press. Obviously, I've read those entries and the book itself, and would urge all those interested in the subject of "ghosts"— however remotely — to do also.

Colombo's request and that reading had revived my lazy memory, and my ostentatious ego suggested I could write of "ghosts" as well as he! And since I had witnessed a bona-fide visit of an apparition, I've given it a shot. And there it is … faults and all … and that's that!

Tom Hyland
The [yet] City of Scarborough
November 10, 1997

MY FIRST RECOGNIZABLE SUPERNATURAL EXPERIENCE

Ted Currie is a freelance writer and researcher who lives in Gravenhurst and contributes regular columns to the *Muskoka Advance* and *The Muskoka Sun*. One of his current projects is re-examining the mystery of Tom Thomson's death and burial.

In the 1970s and early 1980s, shortly after graduating from York University, Currie lived in a local landmark, historic McGibbon House, a three storey brick dwelling at 115 Manitoba Street that had once housed a local physician, Dr. Peter McGibbon, M.P. Rumour has it that in the 1920s Prime Minister Sir Arthur Meighen was guest at McGibbon House. In the 1970s, the building was converted from a single family dwelling into a mixed residential-commercial property. Finally, it was entirely demolished and replaced by a new mixed-use development identified as 111 Manitoba Street.

On 16 February 1996, Currie kindly sent me an account of his many experiences as a resident of McGibbon House.

My first and most profound experience of a spiritful nature while residing in the McGibbon house was in February 1978. I was in the habit, that winter, of working in the attic. I had a typewriter set up by the huge attic window looking down on Manitoba Street,

Bracebridge's main street, across from Memorial Park. It was writer's heaven and the perfect solitude for lengthy writing campaigns.

On this particular evening, just past midnight, I decided to shut down business and make my way downstairs to my main-floor apartment. At the time there was no one living in the abutting second-floor apartment, so I had left the connecting door open, and the hall light in this unit on to assist me coming down. At the top of the stairs, on the landing, I shut off the main overhead attic light (the switch was on the wall) and stepped slowly down the steep stairs toward the apartment light. When I reached this next level, I went into the doorway and clicked off this light. The only light on then was shining from my kitchen on the ground floor, a zigzag and twenty steps from the second-floor landing.

Shortly after stepping out from the apartment doorway, in the back stairway (at that point), I walked into what appeared a chilled, floor-to-head fog — mist, which momentarily blinded me, and I recall being worried I was about to fall down the stairs. I stopped and felt the coldness pass, like a push of air you often feel when shutting a door. It was subtle and the entire occasion — encounter — lasted for only several seconds. I can clearly recall thinking, at that precise moment, I had just experienced a ghost — had the peculiar pleasure of walking though one. I must admit feeling frozen to that spot where we had crossed paths.

I regained my composure, after a few seconds more, and headed back down the stairway toward the light. When I finally arrived at the bottom, I stopped and looked back as far as I could around the corner. At that point I was pretty sure I had participated in my first recognizable supernatural experience. Then came denial. I sat down on the bottom step, scratched my head as if to enhance rational thought, and tried to settle my heart-rate which the chance encounter had stimulated.

It was then I felt the chill again, a definite air current of cold air coming down the staircase, enough to move the hair on the top of my head. I turned and faced up the stairs, and I could feel it against my face. It continued for several minutes until I ended the encounter by backing away. This wind current should have been impossible, based on the rise of furnace-warmed air in the apartment pushing upward — as hot air indeed rises — and in fact there were no devious areas in that concealed stairway (excluding the sealed-tight upper window) where the draft might have entered. I was, after two particular incidents, wise to the notion a ghostly presence had been rightfully encountered.

Two days later, in the afternoon, I was tending the antique shop, when I entertained a group of visitors. They were dressed formally and I assumed they had just attended a funeral next door at the Reynold's Funeral Home. These people seemed more interested in the house than in shopping for antiques. In fact, one woman asked if she could look around the house, past the limits of the shop. I offered to show them the upper apartment (but not the attic). One lady in the group told me voluntarily that her uncle had died several days earlier. The deceased had once lived in the house. She even took me to his favourite room, on the ground floor, where she claimed he used to sit and rock in a chair while gandering out the large park-side vertical window. The uncle had passed away shortly before the time of my encounter on the back stairway. I didn't make any comment about this, as it didn't seem an appropriate moment to be discussing the possibility her uncle had made a final visitation to, I guess you could say, an old haunt.

Of many strange bumps in the night to keep me company in that historic Bracebridge house over a period of six rather comfortable and inspiring years, I never again experienced anything like what had passed — rather crossed — my path that February night when the very thought of ghosts was well down the list of hopeful encounters.

To this day, I do have recurring dreams about the staircase and attic — about four times each year — and unfortunately it has painted the attic as the hot spot for the powerful entity … if indeed the entity could be considered one that challenged trespassers. I never felt that way while I was living there, and some of my most prolific periods at the typewriter came in that attic studio. The dreams became prominent long after I had moved away and the building was torn down, to make way for a new office and apartment block. In each dream I push my way up the stairway, against the cold wind blowing downward, and prepare to challenge the entity lodging in the attic. I always fail before the top stair is reached, but I'm close enough to see the glow of the apparent nasty spirit, just beyond the blackened doorway. I wake shivering.

THE HAIRY MAN

For the following account of a ghostly man, I am indebted to Fred Habermehl of Niagara Falls, Ont. He mailed it to me on 28 May 1996 but he is not its author. The account was written by his daughter Cathy Craig who, with her husband Stuart and their children, lives in a duplex on Briarwood Avenue, south of Thorold Stone Road and west of Dorchester Road, Niagara Falls. Do they share their duplex with the "hairy man"? It is true that children are known to acknowledge the presence of "imaginary playmates." Is the "hairy man" an "imaginary playmate"? Or is it the ghost of some real person?

> In 1981, we moved into a duplex on Briarwood Avenue, next to Meadowvale Park, in Niagara Falls. Almost immediately, our eight-month-old daughter, Tabitha, started seeing something. I would pass it off as just my imagination, a glimpse of something passing down the hall, a presence in the room when you knew you were alone, or a baby laughing at someone behind you, when there was no one there.
>
> When she was old enough to talk, Tabitha and I were in the north end of the basement, when she began to have a conversation with something in the dark laundry room at the south end of the house. I asked her who she was talking to. She replied, "The man."
>
> "What man?" I asked, to which she replied, "The big, hairy man."
>
> I immediately dropped the conversation, picked her up, and went upstairs. I kept all the lights and the TV on. I always knew there was something there and that she sensed it too. Her blunt response, as if I should have been able to see him too, was too much. Since we were usually home alone and I tend to hear things that go bump in the night, I never told anyone. I didn't want them to think I was nuts. That was the most obvious and haunting incident with Tabitha, and eventually the hairy man faded away.
>
> In 1984, Deidre was born and the hauntings returned. The "hairy man" frightened her one day in the upstairs hall, when I sat within eyesight in the living-room reading the paper. Deidre was playing quietly in front of the hall mirror. I glanced at her just as she jumped up with a look of terror on her face. She ran right up over

my paper and onto my lap, screaming that the man was scaring her and he was going to get her.

Deidre's other memorable encounter was in the laundry-room. I was putting clothes in the washer, as she stood beside my leg facing the opposite way. She was talking to someone and I asked, "Who are you talking to?"

She answered, "The big, hairy man."

I looked to where she was pointing and asked her what he looked like, but she just lowered her head and stopped talking. I kept asking questions, trying to be calm and chatty, but she didn't speak of him again. I knew he was always around and she was aware of him. As with my first child, he seemed to appear less and less often as she got older.

In 1988, Michael was born and the man returned. By the time he was two, he had verbalized his sightings to his father and we discussed openly what I had known for years. On one occasion, at about age three, he had gone downstairs to sleep in our bedroom next to the laundry room. He wasn't down there long, before he came racing up the stairs, saying, "Daddy, the hairy man wants to talk to you." His father, refusing to play this silly game, told Michael to tell the man to come upstairs if he wanted to talk to him. Seriously, as if the man was truly downstairs, Michael leaned over the rail and bellowed, "My father says to come up if you want to talk to him." That night, because his son's reaction was so convincing, his father became a believer.

Two years after Michael's birth, our neighbours in the adjoining house, Chris and Roger, had a baby, Alyssa. Within the year, they had seen enough to speak openly to me about this presence. They had stories of their own. Roger was vacuuming the recreation-room one day, when he felt someone enter behind him. He began chatting with his wife. When she didn't answer, he turned around to see that no one was there. He later questioned his wife, who said she had not even been downstairs.

On another occasion, Chris was in the shower, when she sensed someone else in the room. She struck up a conversation with Roger. When he didn't answer, she pulled back the curtain and found she was alone. Later, he confirmed he had never entered the bathroom. As with me, they knew their baby could see someone else in the house. They also felt something moving about. As Alyssa got older, the man faded.

In 1992, Chris and Roger moved to the house on the other side of us. Since then they have had twins, but the man has never appeared to them in that house, even though there are only ten feet between the two houses. The hairy man seems to be only in the two homes of the duplex and only when there are young children present.

I FELT A CERTAIN PEACE

It has been said that the most haunted community in Canada is Niagara-on-the-Lake. If this generalization is true, it applies on a *per-capita* basis, though I know of no statistical records of hauntings by locale! But if so, it is a photo-finish with the even small community of Galt, Ontario. Perhaps what drew the ghosts and spirits to this picturesque community on the shores of Lake Ontario were its many beautiful old residences, homes erected by the United Empire Loyalists and maintained by their descendants to this day. Many of them have long histories as haunts.

Niagara-on-the-Lake is renowned as the home of the Shaw Festival. In fact, it is the only theatre in the world dedicated to the works of the playwright George Bernard Shaw. Now Shaw was a rationalist and he professed no belief in ghosts or spirits. Yet his innate curiosity was such that he read the books about psychical research that were current in his day; he even reviewed a number of them for the London press. In one review he made an amusing reference to the classic English ghost story. With his customary wit he wrote about "the classic — that is, untrue — ghost story." Shaw admitted that it was a characteristic human need to tell ghost stories, if only to account for the many strange and unusual things that have happened to people through the centuries.

Donald L. Combe is a descendant of the U.E.L. and he lives in an old house in Niagara-on-the-Lake. Knowing my interest in the supernatural and the paranormal, he kindly faxed me the following account of a peculiar disturbance. I have reproduced as I received it on 9 May 1996.

Dear Mr. Colombo:

I live in an 1838 house in the old town of Niagara-on-the-Lake. Shortly after I moved here, I noted some strange behaviour by my Scottie, Andrew. This normally rational and pacific animal, who never had ill-will toward anyone or anything, and who certainly never growled, took to sitting in the corner by the front door where he stared intently into a blank wall and carried on a low and rather disturbing growl. This behaviour of Andrew's went on from time to time and made no sense at all, but I felt certain he knew something that I didn't, but which he probably thought I should.

One night I was in the cellar immediately below the spot where the dog was used to growling, and I heard a dripping sound on the floor above my head. I concluded that I had overwatered some large pot plants that stood nearby, so I ran up with a rag expecting to find pools of water. To my amazement there was nothing on the floor. I looked about and decided I had imagined the event and returned to the cellar. In a few minutes the sound began again. Now I was certain that a water pipe had burst, so I dashed back up the stairs. Again I found no water, and look as hard as I might, there was no explanation of the dripping. I returned to the cellar and the dripping continued, but as I had no explanation, I ignored it.

There were no further episodes of the dropping sound, nor were there any further episodes by the dog with his mysterious growling.

Some time later I discovered that there had been a murder in this house and that the location of the growling and the dripping sound was where the hapless soul had died. He had been bludgeoned, and a trail of his dripping blood led to the front door as he tried to escape from the house.

The man who had been killed in December 1971 was a simple soul who had been murdered in hope of a few dollars. He was greatly liked by the townspeople and sadly missed. The date that I experienced the dripping sound was the anniversary of this poor mans' death.

There was a relief for me in hearing the story, as it explained the phenomena the dog and I had experienced. He never visited either the house of the dog and me again. I felt a certain peace that a troubled spirit had departed from the scene of its trauma, and I certainly experienced neither fear nor apprehension.

Faithfully yours,

Donald L. Combe

GRANNY'S COTTAGE

Some things take time to come to fruition.

One thing that took two years to bear fruit was the suggestion I made in a letter to Mrs. A.J. (Jeanette) Earp of Niagara-on-the-Lake, Ont. I had learned from a friend of a friend, who lived in this picturesque community on the Niagara River, that Mrs. Earp had a story to tell about her years living in "Granny's Cottage." So I wrote a letter and sent it to Mrs. Earp. The letter was delivered but, as happens from time to time, it was misplaced in a drawer and it disappeared only to reappear two years later. Mrs. Earp phoned me, somewhat chagrined, and inquired if I was still interested in receiving information about the haunting of "Granny's Cottage." I assured her that I was, so she wrote the letter which appears here. It is an extremely well organized response to a series of peculiar experiences. In her letter she refers to Ray and Eileen Sonin. Ray was a radio broadcaster with a booming voice and a weekly early evening program titled "Calling All Britons!" which was heard on Toronto's CFRB. His wife Eileen was the city's best-known sensitive. She was also the author of two popular books based on her ghost-hunting experiences: *Ghosts I Have Known: The Psychic Experiences of a Natural Medium* (1968) and *ESPecially Ghosts: Some True Experiences of the Supernatural in North America* (1970). It seems as if Mrs. Earp had a poltergeist in "Granny's Cottage." She kept careful notes of the disturbances. Here is her interesting letter dated 18 August 1998.

Dear Mr. Colombo,

As promised, the long overdue response to your April 1996 letter.

The few unexplained occurrences which I experienced while living alone in "Granny's Cottage," 240 Gate St. in Niagara-on-the-Lake certainly puzzled me but I never felt or heard any sinister or other presence in the house during my seven years there. The house was built circa 1818 with extensive alterations made in the late 1960s, a few years before I moved in. I should mention that at this time I worked in St. Catharines, returning home in the late afternoon or early evening.

The unexplained events, as I remember them:

(a) Books turned upside down

There was a long, two-shelf bookcase under a window in the

living-room which contained, among other books, my sixteen-year collection of hardcover Horizon magazines, filed chronologically by issue number and year. I noticed one evening that all, or almost all, of the Horizons were upside-down on the shelves; one would have to stand on one's head to read the spines. They were still in chronological order, aligned neatly at the shelf edge. None of the other books were disturbed.

(b) The moving vase

While watering house plants one morning before leaving for work, I topped up a vase of roses in my bedroom. Noticing that I had over filled it, I placed the vase on the mirror windowsill while I mopped up the spill on the dresser. Running short of time, I left the vase on the sill rather than return it to the still damp dresser top. When in my room that evening I noticed to my surprise that the vase was not on the windowsill but on the floor beneath it, the water level still at the vase rim and the roses undisturbed in their arrangement. I know for certain I had not placed the vase on the floor.

(c) Rearranged curtains

My little cottage had crisp, tie-back curtains on every window. Returning home from work one evening I discovered all the curtains on the garden side of the house had been drawn, the tie-backs and their securing pins laid neatly on the table or chest nearest each window.

(d) A curious cat

My cat, Theo (black, partly Siamese), liked to stretch out on top of the sofa back when I sat there evenings, reading or listening to music. The sofa sat in the middle of the room facing the fireplace. A number of times Theo would suddenly sit up straight and seem to follow with his eyes something descending the stairs behind and to the right of the sofa. He would then lean back as though avoiding whatever was passing behind the sofa, then crane his neck as he seemingly followed with his eyes that something as it passed through the doorway into the room beyond. Did Theo have repeated bouts of indigestion or was he actually "seeing" something?

As I understand it, the stairs were new with the recent renovations, the original stairs being not much more than a ladder rising from the kitchen area at the back of the house.

(e) An uncomfortable Eileen Sonin

Mrs. Sonin may have been known to you. She wrote one or more books on ghosts, spirits or things that go bump in the night. I knew her and her husband through a mutual friend in broadcasting. One evening I met friends for dinner at the Oban Inn. Ray and Aileen Sonin were at the next table with friends and we had a jolly time. I invited everyone back to the house for coffee and more conversation. Mrs. Sonin had been lively and cheerful through dinner, but once seated in the living-room it wasn't long before she began complaining of a headache and was clearly feeling some distress. The Sonins left shortly after.

I learned from our mutual friends a few years later, after I had married and moved to a new address, that Mrs. Sonin had not been physically ill but had experienced such distress from something in the house that she had had to leave. Apparently the next day she called my friends, asking them to urge me to find new accommodation: something very disturbing was in the house.

(f) More uncomfortable friends

Those friends to whom Eileen Sonin had expressed her unsettling feelings were occasionally overnight guests in the cottage. The husband stayed only once, but his wife visited frequently, leaving mid-morning the next day. (I would have left for work an hour or two earlier.) Again, kindly, nothing was said at the time, but apparently she felt most uncomfortable during those few hours alone in the house.

Even more remarkable was the husband's experience the one and only time he stayed the night. His wife and I went to a concert in St. Catharines after dinner. He planned to have a leisurely bath and settle down to watch a game on TV. We came back rather late and were surprised to find him sitting in the car in the driveway. He said he had changed his mind and had gone to the Oban to watch the game in the bar, had not been able to get back into the house, so had waited for us in the car. We thought his story strange, not least because of his appearance. What I learned subsequently was that while relaxing in the bathtub, he suddenly felt such dread; the room became chilled and he sensed such an overwhelmingly evil atmosphere that it was almost palpable. He fled the bathroom, threw on some clothes, and hurried from the house to his car. He felt foolish, frightened and distressed that he had not picked up Theo, the cat, and saved him from whatever evil was in the house. And this was a sensible, no-nonsense, successful businessman. I don't believe he felt anything untoward when we three joined Theo in the living-room a little later, chatting over tea and cinnamon toast.

Fortunately, none of these weird sensations troubled me during those seven years in the cottage. Whether the two subsequent tenants experienced anything I do not know. I doubt it, for surely they would have mentioned something to me — we are friends. The house has once again undergone major alterations. I don't know the current residents.

A wordy account, I fear, but I hope I have described the unexplained occurrences satisfactorily.

Sincerely,

Jeanette Earp (Mrs. A.J. Earp)

THE GHOST OF JOSEPH GILLESPIE

The days leading up to Halloween are always busy days for me, as I am often asked to appear on radio and television shows to talk about ghosts and spirits. I often agree to do so for two reasons: I might have a new book on the supernatural or the paranormal to promote and I enjoy chatting on open-line programs with callers who have strange experiences to share with listeners or viewers and with readers of my future books. I was the studio guest of host Maureen Taylor on TVO's *More to Life*, 29 October 1999, and we heard a series of stories about hauntings. The last story we heard was from someone with a rich voice who identified himself as Jeff. Jeff told the story of the ghost of Joseph Gillespie, a kind of guardian spirit, and Maureen and I were quite charmed with it. On air I asked Jeff to leave his phone number with the studio operator and I would contact him thereafter for further particulars. Later that day I phoned Jeff and it turned out that his full name was David Jeffery Essery, and that he was a graphic designer who had worked for the Canadian Broadcasting Corporation on the *Wayne & Shuster Show* and *Mr. Dress Up.* I interviewed him and then wrote up this account of living with a guardian ghost. He kindly read it and revised it. The revised version was completed on 15 November 1999. So here it is:

> The name Essery is Welsh. I was told it was once spelled with a d-apostrophe: D'Essery. The family of thirteen brothers disbursed from Devon so that any Essery you find nowadays is a direct relation. I myself was born in Toronto on October 11, 1942.
>
> I believe I am psychic. At least I am open to the idea of spirits. They don't frighten me in the slightest, but I didn't expect to cohabit with them in the flat over a bakery shop.
>
> The bakery was Rood's Bakery Shop at 2618 Yonge St., Toronto, across from Sheldrake Boulevard. I moved into the flat about 1974. You entered through a door on Yonge Street and climbed a flight of stairs to a hallway. At the rear was a porch and a bedroom. The kitchen and the bathroom were near the entrance and the dining-room and living-room, divided by an arch, were at the front overlooking Yonge Street. There was not a straight wall in the whole place.
>
> Within minutes of moving in, I saw something. Standing near the front windows, where he could peer out and yet watch me, was an old man. He was transparent and yet he had colour. He was wearing a brown suit and it was shiny. It was the kind of cheap suit that grows shiny with wear until it falls apart. He usually wore a brown suit but sometimes he wore a blue one. It too was shiny with age. He was of average height, slightly stopped, in his eighties, I would guess, and balding. He seemed very curious.
>
> At the time, I didn't think much of the sight of the old man. I acknowledged his presence and went on with my unpacking. That seemed to be enough. I didn't think much about him. There was an old gentleman who ran the Sheldrake Barber Shop a few doors south. He was the barber and being well into his eighties himself, he knew everything and everybody and I did need a haircut.
>
> Now when you're psychic, you get a sense of whom you can talk to about such matters. "So who's the old gentleman in the

brown suit that I keep seeing? He certainly seems very interested in everything."

"That's Joseph Gillespie," said the barber without any hesitation. "He used to own the building, the one with the store and the flat. He used to live around the corner on Craighurst Avenue. He lived alone and he was absolutely paranoid about theft. He liked to own and acquire property but he wouldn't own objects because they could be stolen from him. He wore a suit until it fell off and he lived quite simply, one overstuffed chair, ate out of cans and the like. I don't think he ever bought a newspaper; he always read mine in the store."

I believe that the spirit of Joseph Gillespie was attracted to me because I had a tremendous collection of masks, sea shells, prints, and puppets which lined the walls of the apartment. My Christmas tree had over three thousand ornaments on it. It was an artificial tree that sparkled with miniature objects that I had picked up on my various travels all over the world. Ghosts, as you know, are attracted to shiny things and the tree lights would reflect on these tiny detailed objects. He could enjoy looking at them for hours and, best of all, he didn't have to take responsibility for them. He could enjoy all my stuff. His "unfinished business" was, in fact, to learn to enjoy things for sheer pleasure; something he had never allowed himself in life. I came to feel that Joseph was a kind of guardian of my apartment.

He was a generally friendly spirit and the guardian of my things, but he was not always pleasant to have around. One Christmas, when I had put the artificial tree up, I allowed the branches to settle. While they settled, I lounged on some cushions on the floor listening to music. Suddenly I was sharply beaned on the forehead!

There was not a spare space on any of the walls, as things were hung everywhere. One of the masks, high on the wall, was from Mexico. It was a devil's head surmounted with a wooden carved blue bird. On its own, the wooden bird's head was torn off its neck, thrown past the Christmas tree about twenty feet and hit me square on the forehead! It didn't hurt much but it did register Joseph's complaint at the delay in erecting the tree. The rest of the mask still hung in place on the wall.

It was the only physical contact I had with Joseph, but he did move a lot of my stuff around. He loved to hide keys, those symbols of security. He would swipe them from the middle of an empty table where I would have placed them in plain sight. He loved to do this when I was in a hurry to leave. After just missing countless busses, I soon learned that if I swore directly at Joseph, he would put them back again. The funny thing was that when he returned them, the keys were always freshly cleaned and highly polished.

Once, he took the stopper from the kitchen sink, which was actually a deep laundry tub. When I couldn't find the stopper anywhere and couldn't do the dishes, I pounded my mist on the edge of the tub and yelled at him, "Joseph!" and called him a few things angrily. Suddenly, the large stopper appeared out of nowhere, hovering above my head! Then it fell into the sink. There were no shelves or ledges overhead so it couldn't have fallen off anything. I thanked him, placed the stopper over the drain, and did the dishes.

When I left the flat, I would turn off the lights and leave through the front door, making a big thing of locking up for Joseph's sake. Many times on returning later that evening, the front door would be ajar to Yonge Street and all the lights would be on. I would make a lot of noise climbing the stairs just in case. Nothing was ever disturbed. It was Joseph showing off. His authority inside the flat apparently extended to three steps up from street levee. To make things earlier for him, I hung a brass policeman's button from a string just inside the front door. Any visitor only had to touch that symbol of security on entering and Joseph would know you were not a thief.

Aside from being beamed with the bird's head, he never hurt me. He didn't want to take the chance of my banishing him from the premises. No one else ever saw him but they sure felt his presence. He would suddenly change the temperature in the room on entering. Some times he would sit down between two people and they would both shiver. You could then take a thermometer and record the sudden drop in temperature. Sometimes, when friends came to visit and were sitting around, he would freeze just the tips of their noses.

All that was about ten years ago. During that time, I lived alone. Guests would stay there once but no one would stay there alone. They were afraid.

A person did stay in the apartment for three weeks once during October when I was in Europe. He agreed to stay but Joseph didn't like the idea and at the first opportunity hid his keys. The friend decided to keep the front door locked for security and enter by the back door off the rear sun porch. Bad idea. He had to use a fire escape, the way a thief enters. Joseph was apoplectic. One night, when the friend was sleeping, he was awakened by a tremendous crash from the front room which shook the entire building. He raced there and saw that a fifteen-pound piece of slag glass, which usually sat on a corner cabinet over three feet high, was sitting on the floor. It had not fallen because it was not chipped or broken and the floor was not at all scuffed. One of the many masks on the wall had been lifted up off its nail from above and been placed carefully face down on top of a series of specimen sea shells which covered the rest of the surface of the cabinet. Not one of the shells was in any way harmed. The nail that had held the mask was still secure in the wall. Every picture in the entire apartment was tilted. The floor was freezing. It was so cold that one could see their breath. When you think of it, this was very strange because there was a bakery with ovens in use directly below the flat.

Yes, Joseph Gillespie was a hilarious old Scotsman with a wicked sense of humour. He had owned the building and when I moved in, he was reluctant to leave it. Everything in it was stuff for him to enjoy. He was certainly not ready to go yet. He had felt that time had been stolen from him even though he had lived to a ripe old age. I considered him a room mate and he was welcome to protect the flat and its contents. I like to think that we both learned something during our years together and we wish each other well.

I moved away when the owners sold the property. The bakery moved up to Thornhill, I think, and the barber is long gone. I now live in a condo in downtown Toronto. I consider myself psychic. I have heard voices, or part of me has. I psychically shop. People tell me that I should write a book about the things that have happened to me here and all over the world. I have collected many things, from Bali, Asia, the Far East. There, they live alongside their gods. There is a constant balancing between good and evil. I am totally at home with that. Some of the masks still have energy. There are some I would never wear.

One of the many incidents happened to me in that flat but it did not involve Joseph. During the Second World War, my father rescued an entire orphanage full of children in Sicily. He had an audience with the Pope because of it. At the time the priest in Sicily gave my father a rosary that he believed contained a sliver of True Cross. I had it and one day absent-mindedly hung it over the knob on the end of a hot-water radiator in the front room. Later that evening, I was watching television in the room and the rosary began to swing back and forth of its own accord, but I left it there and went to bed. Later that night, I awoke freezing with cold. The temperature in the bedroom had dropped. It really dropped, thirty degrees. Even my eyes were cold. I sat up. There were moving pinpoints of orange light tracing lines in the dark air at the end of the bed. The heavy smell of incense filled the room. I was seeing the lights from a censor. I could not see the censor itself, just the lights from it. I could smell the charcoal as it continued swinging. I got up in the dark and went down the hall toward the bathroom for a glass of water. The cold floor crunched beneath my bare feet. I ran the tap and glanced in the mirror. Instead of me was the image of a hooded monk!

Next day, I retrieved the swinging rosary off the radiator. I carefully fastened it to a brass hook in the bedroom wall. It did not move there.

I never saw the monk again.

5

THE POWER OF FEAR

QUEBEC CITY GHOST

Here is an amusing item from the front page of *The Globe* (Toronto), Thursday, September 26, 1929. Who was that "nocturnal visitor"? We will never know …

Unidentified Reporter — Axes Are Used to Destroy Ghost — Crowds Gather in Quebec City to Chase Spectre — But Nothing Is Seen — (Special Despatch to The Globe)

Quebec, September 25. — Rumours of a ghost being seen on Arago Street culminated last night in the gathering of a large crowd, armed with pickaxes, other implements for offence and defence, and even firearms, to solve the mystery of the nocturnal visitor.

On Monday evening the supernatural apparition is claimed to have been seen on the housetops of Chateauquay Street, while last night he chose a section of the cliff. Literally hundreds of residents gathered when the news was noised about that a spectre was in their midst, and excitement ran high. Traffic was temporarily stopped and the police were called from No. 11 Station to deal with the crowd and to maintain order.

No satisfactory solution was arrived at, since this particular ghost, like so many of his fellows, appears to have the annoying faculty of disappearing as soon as careful investigation of his movements begins.

Police patrolled Arago Street till after midnight to dispel the crowd and permit circulation of traffic.

SCARED TO DEATH?

The subject of the following letter to a scientific publication is a self-fulfilling prophecy; either that or it is a testimony to the power of a curse. The letter appeared in the correspondence column of the *British Medical Journal*, No. 5,457, 7 August 1965. It concerns the death of woman following routine surgery at North West River Hospital, Labrador. The hospital, founded in 1915 by the International Grenfell Association, has since then been closed. It was located at North West River, northeast of Goose Bay, Labrador. The physicians who signed the letter appealed to "any reader who has had experience of a patient dying under similar circumstances." Two replies were published in No. 5,461, 4 September 1965. The first was contributed by J.C. Barker of Shelton Hospital, Shrewsbury, Shropshire, England. Barker noted that "one is left wondering why a fortune-teller should impart such devastating information to so young a child which was to make such a terrible and lasting impression upon her." He wondered whether "it is possible that were she a hysterical manipulative type her psychological symptoms, stress incontinence and reaction to it, leading to surgery and its attendant complications, might have resulted from her own unconscious efforts to predetermine her demise at the appointed time, having reflected endlessly upon the admonitions of her soothsayer." He concluded, "Perhaps the boundaries of western psychiatry should now begin to be extended to include some of the phenomena of extra-sensory perception." The second reply was contributed by A. Fry, of London S.E.25. He noted that "the case may represent a version of voodoo death." He observed, "A persistent state of fear can end the life of man," and then drew attention to the influence of a persistent state of fear on the sympathetic nervous system and its role in the control of the patient's blood supply. He concluded, "'Scared to Death' is not an idle saying. A feeling 'I am afraid I am going to die' may actually result in death. The anxiety is not removed even when the patient is anaesthetized. Although asleep, the patient is still suffering from anxiety." I am pleased to be able to offer this verbatim account to my readers and I am a little relieved to be able to do so because the story has haunted me for some time! I learned about it in *Arthur C. Clarke's World of Strange Powers* (London: Collins, 1984). That is the book, written by John Fairley and Simon Welfare, that served as the basis or as the by-product of the popular Yorkshire Television series, one of the few programs on television that seriously considers claims of the supernatural and the paranormal, even to the point of examining what evidence exists, whether pro or con, and regarding it both sympathetically and un-sensationally. Then, at a reception in the 1990s, I met with a medical doctor from Labrador who had worked at the North West River Hospital in the late 1960s. I asked him about the incident. He said it was familiar to him and that everyone on staff at the hospital regarded it as deeply puzzling. But he had no further light to shed on the incident. Fairley and Welfare concluded intelligently: "It may be remembered in this connection that fear serves biologically as a defence mechanism which, among other effects, leads to an enhanced activity of the adrenalin glands.... The surgeons in the above case drew the conclusion that death was likely to have resulted indirectly from the stress created by the prophecy. While the present case hopefully involves a reaction of exceptional severity, the self-fulfilling pressure on those who profoundly believe in the fortune-tellers' powers is probably far from negligible; and the numbers of predictions that have been made to come true in this manner no doubt continue to swell the number of adherents."

Scared to Death?
A.R. Elkington, P.R. Steele, D.D. Yun

Sir, — We would like to report a case of an apparently healthy middle-aged woman dying with massive adrenal haemorrhage, following a relatively minor operation, who was subsequently found to have had forebodings of death.

Mrs. A.B., aged 43, mother of five children, was admitted to North West River Hospital, Labrador, on 18 March 1965. She had been complaining of severe stress incontinence for several months. She had been treated during the past three years for anxiety which responded well to reassurance and mild sedation with phenobarbitone, 30 mg three times daily. There was no relevant past medical history. On examination she was found to be in good health. Vaginal examination revealed a moderately large cystocele and urethrocele. On 19 March anterior colporrhaphy was performed under general anaesthesia. The premedication was pathidine, 100 mg, and atropine, 0.65 mg; induction with intravelous thiopentone, 400 mg, and Flaxedil (gallamine triethiodide), 40 mg; maintenance with nitrous oxide, oxygen, and a trace of trilene, accompanied by intermittent intravenous pethidine to a total of 80 mg. The operation, which lasted less than one hour, was straightforward with minimal blood loss. Her blood-pressure remained around 120/70 throughout the operation, and pulse and respiration were normal. She regained consciousness before leaving the theatre. One hour later she became shocked and her systolic blood-pressure fell to 70 mm. Hg. She remained conscious, but shortly afterwards complained of severe pain in the left hypochondrium. Methedrine (methylamphetamine) was immediately given, 15 mg. intravenously, and 15 mg. intrmuscularly, and the foot of the bed was raised. As the blood-pressure showed no response Aramine (metaraminol), 10 mg, was given intrmuscularly. An infusion of dextran, 500 ml, with hydrocortisone, 100 mg, was started. Despite continuous infusion with metaraminol and hydrocortisone no improvement was obtained and intransal oxygen was required as the patient became cyanosed. The pain was partly controlled by injections of morphone, 16 mg., given on three occasions. The E.C.G. was normal. Her condition deteriorated and her temperature rose to 103.6 degrees F. (39.8 degrees C.) by midnight, when she became comatose. She died at 5 a.m. on 20 March.

At post-mortem examination the adrenal glands showed extensive haemorrhage. Petachial haemorrhages were found in the stomach, ileum, liver, and in the skin of the nose. There was no other pathology.

Subsequently we learned that this patient had had her fortune told at the age of 5 years, when she was informed that she would die when she was 43 years old. She had told her daughter for many years that she would die at this age. Her forty-third birthday was one week before operation. On the evening before operation she told her sister, who alone knew of the prophecy, that she did not expect to awake from the anaesthetic, and on the morning of operation the patient told a nurse she was sure she was going to die. These fears were not known to us at the time of operation.

We would be grateful to hear from any reader who has had experience of a patient dying under similar circumstances. We wonder if the severe emotional tensions of this patient superimposed on the physiological stress of surgery had any bearing upon her death. — We are, etc.

A.R. Elkington.
P.R. Steele.
D.D. Yun.

Grenfell Labrador Medical Mission,
Ottawa, Canada.

A RETARDED, DEFORMED THING

Out of the blue I received a phone call from Jim Greenwood. He had been given my name by Mike Filey, the photo historian who publishes books on Toronto's pictorial past. Mr. Greenwood had a strange story to tell and a photograph that he wanted me to see. I listened to his account of his experiences and his description of the photograph and urged him to type out his experiences and send the script to me. Three weeks later I received the letter. Make of it what you will. I have limited my editing to breaking up some of the sentences and adding some punctuation.

Saturday, November 28, 1998

Dear John Robert Colombo:

The incident that I talked to you about over the phone three weeks ago, after talking to Mike Filey, who I thought did a program on the house but didn't. He wasn't interested in ghosts, but was helpful in giving me your name, knowing you would be interested.

This incident happened about twenty years ago, around 1978. The reason I am writing to you about this experience now is I was being visited by spirits last year after my Dad died. Incidentally, this is the second anniversary of his death. I don't know exactly what it means, other than it was a warning from God. These spirits visited me here in Toronto and on Lake Kashwakamak which, I think, is sacred Indian land. This visitation went on for four months, from June to September 1997, up north and in Toronto.

I want to iterate that these spirits were evil spirits because of what I've learned. I also want people to know there is a spirit world which I have proof of. I have a photo of a spirit. I will send a copy of it to you. The Indians recognize it as the Bear Spirit. I had it digitally copied by a photographer because I didn't have a negative. The picture was taken by one of my aunts. In it is the image of a bear, also my mother, grandfather, and one of my aunts. The person that this incident happened to at 21 Grenville, his wife develops film for a major photography firm. She said she has never seen a picture like it. Psychiatric letters from Westminster Hospital in London, Ontario (a war hospital for Canadian World War I and World War II veterans — he suffered from shell shock and was institutionalized from 1923 to his death in 1975) state my grandfather was having auditory hallucinations in English, French, and Iroquois. He was being visited by spirits, in my opinion. He was a captain in the First World War in France. Incidentally, this picture was taken in 1948. I don't want to delve to deep into the subject. I only want to know the truth. I was not in good mental or physical health when all this happened. I was going through alcohol withdrawal at the time in '97. I also had over one hundred Bible verses memorized, which means a lot, believe me. I also believe in JESUS CHRIST as my Saviour and Lord. So much for the introduction; Now on with the story.

We were renting a sound studio on the top floor of 21 Grenville Avenue, one block north of College, off Yonge Street, right behind Fran's Restaurant and across from the Coroner's building. A friend of mine had just got back from Florida from a win-a-week's vacation for the best costume at a Halloween contest in a local bar. His mother had made it. She was at one time a seamstress. He had a lot to do with it too. His character was Gandolph from Tolkein's *Lord of the Rings*. He and his girlfriend won. He was the drummer in the band. There were five of us in the room when this incident took place. All of us were childhood buddies. We were all around twenty-two at the time. There were two brothers who lived across the street from me, one a guitar player and the other a conga player.

One was a keyboard player who lived in the West End who was a high school buddy, and the drummer, the leader of the gang whom I knew all my life and still know. As I said, he just got back from Florida. We had just picked him up from the airport. His girlfriend went home and we went down to the studio from Keewatin Avenue where we all had grown up together. As the drummer said before this happened, he had a high sense of spirits that "this place is haunted." Climbing the last flight of stairs to the top floor, he said it "gave you the chills."

We all came into the studio room. I was the sound man, lowest in the pecking order, the one least daring. The room had a tape area which was about five feet wide and twenty feet long, with a window and a door. The room was fifteen feet wide by twenty-five feet long, with a vestibule going out to the stairs. The room had a table at one end, with four chairs, and a couch along the wall.

We were smoking pot that night. It was strange stuff because of its dark colour and strange smell, but that had nothing to do with what happened. I have never seen anything like it since, so the name we called it was "Demon Weed." I'm totally straight now. I go to church.

The drummer had a t-shirt on, I recall, with the Union Stars and Stripes flag and the Confederate flag crossed. He was setting up his drums when he cut himself on the high hat. I figure the month to be November. When he saw blood, he fainted. I don't know if it was jet lag or what, but when he saw his finger, he said, with an "oh, no" expression on his face, "See you later boys," and simultaneously he sat down on the couch.

All four of us were sitting at the table. His eyes went up into the back of his head and he started going into convulsions. His body would jerk forward violently and then he would become animate. Another personality had taken control of his body. The entity would stay long enough to show his or her personality, but everyone was animate. This happened with his eyes closed. After the spirit would show its identity, the drummer's body would lurch forward and come back again, but this time with a different spirit. This happened over a two-minute period. I figure ten spirits passed through his body. Everyone sat motionless as this was taking place. I didn't know who the spirits were because I didn't know them, but I could recognize male from female. I think there was only one female spirit. But the last spirit that entered his body was unmistakable because it was hideous. It was that of a Mongoloid child. Deformed, he became a Mongoloid, a retarded, deformed being, so animate it changed his whole appearance. It made your skin crawl. When this spirit left him, he died. His teeth dropped and his cheeks went back and he sat motionless on the couch, leaning to one side for two minutes. After one minute, I got scared because I knew he was dead. So did the others. So I got up and grabbed his arm and shook him, calling his name, and one of the brothers, the conga player, said, "Leave him alone." So I sat back down, talking to him. I can't remember what I said, I was in shock. So were the others. So we sat and waited another minute not knowing what next.

And all of a sudden he jerked forward violently and he was back in his body, but he was dead, I figure, for two minutes. For half an hour no one could talk to him. He was in a post-traumatic shock. He said after a while, "Leave me alone." Because I was so freaked out about what had happened, telling him what just took place, he was afraid he was going to go back into a fit. He was holding his head and was obviously in grief, and that was not like him, being a drummer. After a while, he started feeling better and we got into his car. We didn't jam that night, and he drove us home, up Yonge Street to Keewatin. He went for electro-cardiogram tests after this happened, but they found nothing abnormal.

He told me that during the experience he left his body and was going down the tunnel. He went into another fit later at a party, when a dog bit him. The guitar player was there. I wasn't, so the guitar player thought it was an illness. The guitar player didn't want to talk about the experience either because he didn't want to accept it or put it down to an epileptic fit. But his brother, the conga player, remember the Mongoloid child.

I lost contact with the keyboard player. He was an exceptional keyboardist, but he got a little mixed up with Transcendental Meditation and never was the same. He didn't say much about it.

Just a note. The drummer moved up north to Huntsville and bought a 102-year old house that I helped him to renovate. He's sold it since, but it was haunted. They called in a diviner, and this person said there were seven spirits in the house. I've talked to the guitarist recently. He now lives in B.C. with his brother, and he now knows what happened that night after all these years.

Yours truly,

Jim Greenwood

A NIGHT IN OLD CITY HALL

Here is an intriguing, gripping story of a night spent in Toronto's Old City Hall. The ghosts of convicted murderers are said to haunt the halls and chambers of the old building, particularly Courtroom 33. Agatha Bardoel decided to see for herself whether this was true, but she did not do so alone. She made sure she was accompanied by her friend Fannie! Agatha Bardoel's brave account appeared as "This Is a Ghost Story" in *The Toronto Star*, 27 October 1979.

We lie in our sleeping bags on the floor of Courtroom 33, terrified.

It is the middle of the night.

And ten feet away, in the prisoner's box where nearly twenty years ago two men were condemned to hang, a slow, steady knocking breaks the silence.

It is Old City Hall, one of Toronto's most haunted buildings, at 3:00 a.m. on a Saturday in October.

We came here, my sister Frannie and I, at 11:00 p.m. the night before with a photographer, hoping to get evidence whether the building is indeed haunted.

By 4:00 p.m. the unexplained events had driven us out in panic into the night.

Old City Hall. Five days a week during daylight hours, it teems with life. There are marriages. There is traffic court. There are minor criminal cases — women up on prostitution charges, men up for shoplifting. There are preliminary hearings for murder.

And until the mid-'60s, when a new court building opened on

University Ave., there were the great murder trials.

The memory of those still hangs in the air, casting shadows on the rich oak walls, the doors, the rows of spectator seats, the jury box — and the small, rectangular prisoner's box that still stands before the judge's bench in Courtroom 33.

Here, where we now lie in our sleeping bags, the last two men hanged in Canada stood before the judge and heard how they would die. Arthur Lucas and Ron Turpin were tried for murder in two separate trials and hanged at the Don Jail, Dec. 11, 1962.

"Tough break," Lucas told the court calmly when the sentence was read.

Ten years earlier, in September, 1952, Steve Suchan and Leonard Jackson, members of the notorious Boyd Gang, were condemned to hang for the murder of a Toronto detective. They, too, stood in that prisoner's box.

They were hanged Dec. 16, 1952.

Beverly Janus, a Toronto teacher of parapsychology and writer of a weekly syndicated newspaper column called "The Psychic," believes that the spirits of the dead linger around areas where they have suffered great unhappiness or stress, that they "sear" their emotion onto the environment. They have no intellect, she says. They stay and do the same thing repeatedly until one day, they disappear.

From 1900 to the mid-'60s, the courts at the Old City Hall saw several other murder trials that ended in death.

There were William McFadden and Ray Holtrum, hanged in 1921 for the murder of a druggist.

In 1942, Bill Newell was tried and hanged for the murder of his wife on Centre Island.

In 1948, Leslie Davidson was tried and hanged for the murder of Margaret Meredith.

Excellent credentials for a haunted building. And there have been many stories.

The night staff tell of cleaning women who have asked for transfers, unnerved by door handles turning, objects falling off shelves, groans in the night.

A night watchman claimed that his feet were rooted to the floor, held by unseen hands.

Judges have said they have felt their robes being tugged as they climbed the back stairs to the courtroom.

We took large sheets of film, taped to our bodies. Some psychics believe that apparitions will leave vague forms and shadows on the film, even in darkness.

We took a camera loaded with infra-red film which is said to be capable of photographing ghostly images in the dark.

And a tape recorder, with a blank tape, to record sound. Mrs. Janus said that when a tape recorder has been left on in an empty room, it has later been found to have voices on it.

None of it was any use to us. When the time came, we had no time for experiments. We just wanted to get away.

"You simply do not know what you're letting yourself in for," Beverley Janus told me the day before.

City Hall staff said more or less the same thing.

"We had to take one man off the night shift. He asked to be transferred, he was so frightened by the sounds he heard," said Jim Scott, superintendent of the building. "But you have to remember that this is one of the few large old buildings around with wooden joists.

"Of course the windows blow open, floors creak, doors close. Old buildings groan."

Maintenance worker Joseph Bonett insisted it is more than that. "When I'm alone on Sunday during the day, I won't move from my chair."

Bonett's office is on the ground floor. Above him, on the first, there are some courtrooms, some clerical offices.

"They start running, footsteps, and not just one or two. There are many of them and they run up and down the corridors, hard and fast."

Bonett says the sound of running feet goes on for a long time. He went up to investigate once, but there was nothing there. He has not been again.

Dennis McTernant, who was once maintenance foreman in the building but now works elsewhere, recalls one story he was told.

"One of our guys was up in one of the halls one night, walking around, about 2:00 or 3:00 in the morning.

"Suddenly he couldn't move. Something had grabbed a hold

of his ankles and he was rooted to the floor. For fifteen seconds or so, he couldn't get loose.

"Then, just as suddenly, it was over.

"He swears he couldn't move."

McTernant says many of the cleaning women reported similar mysterious events. They'd be going along the halls and the door handles would begin to rattle and they'd turn, as if they were going to open. When they went into the room, there was no one there.

"One watchman we had swears that one night, when he was going through the courtyard, he saw a man standing on the tower in the northwest corner.

"He was dressed all in black, just standing there.

"The women were complaining to that they'd put something on a desk or a shelf in one of the offices. Then they'd go back in half an hour and it'd be on the floor.

"A lot of them were really scared."

"Some of the women have asked for transfers out of there over the years. And we have transferred people," says John Carry, manager of operations. "They were upset by strange noises, doors closing after they had been propped open, that kind of thing."

Night watchman Charlie Dobrzensky led Frannie, photographer Doug Griffin and me up to the second floor.

"Some of the guys have been talking about it," Charlie said, "and some of them were making fun of it.

"But others said they'd heard things and they didn't think it was funny."

Dobrzensky opened the door; the photographer took his pictures and left.

We heard his footsteps echoing down the hall. Then there was silence. The darkness wrapped itself around us.

We pointed our flashlight at the clock on the wall. It was minutes after midnight. Suddenly the flashlight went out. I pressed down anxiously on the button. It flickered, then went out.

On the next try, it worked again. For what seemed like the first time inside the room, we breathed.

Of course it would go out, I thought. We're nervous as cats. I can hardly hold this flashlight.

In the centre of the room, illuminated only by the faint yellow light from the hall that filtered through the courtroom door, stood the small prisoner's box.

Our footsteps echoed as we walked over to it, opened the small swing gate and went inside. We sat down. Almost immediately, I felt very cold.

The rest of the room had been quite warm, so warm we already had taken off our sweaters.

"I feel terrible," Frannie moaned. "I don't understand it. I'm so anxious, like there's something awful that I've got to do, and I don't want to do it.

"And it's so cold, like you get by the lake at the cottage. There should be some water."

I had not told her I felt cold. And I had not told her that if there were ghosts, I was told we would feel cold. A drop in temperature, and a damp, clammy atmosphere often accompanies apparitions, psychics say.

We sat there for moments in silence. I asked her to stand and face the judge's bench, to grip the railing in front of her. Almost immediately there was a sharp rapping sound from the floor of the box under our feet.

It was then that I first began to feel uneasy.

We left the box and climbed into our sleeping bags on the floor, about ten feet away. We lay very still, talking quietly.

"We shouldn't have done this," Frannie whispered. Outside the window on Bay St., a siren wailed in the night.

To the left of the judge's bench is a small doorway that leads to a narrow hall and a small wooden staircase. It is the judge's private access from the street to the court chambers on the second floor. Then it runs on up to the third and fourth floors, where the attic is.

In the mid-60s, two judges reported strange happenings on the staircase. One, now retired Provincial Judge S. Tupper Bigelow, told a Toronto newspaper he had heard light footsteps on the staircase and, on one occasion, felt a tugging at his robes.

Another, Judge Peter Wilch, followed the footsteps up to the top floor, which was then untenanted (court reporters now use it). There was no one.

Frannie and I walked quietly through the door and into the corridor.

The air was cold and the light from a single overhead light bulb showed that it was also clear.

The wooden steps creaked under our weight. We descended, then ascended right to the top. We heard nothing. "This feels good," Frannie whispered. "Let's sit for a while."

We sat in a corner of the stairway, occasionally looking gratefully at the light bulb. "Has someone been through here smoking?" Frannie asked after a while.

"There's some kind of a smoke through here. Look, you can see it on the light bulb, around it."

There was. It was getting misty. And it was clouding up against the window to the courtroom.

Frannie did not know that, like a sudden drop in temperature, a mist or fog also often accompanies an apparition. Sometimes it is wrapped around the apparition itself, sometimes it fills the room and there is no other phenomenon.

I sucked in some air. "Let's go," I said. "If there's someone there that wants to meet us, it can meet us on our own turf."

It was just after 3:00 o'clock. We lay quietly. Frannie had taken a long wooden stick with an iron hook on the end used for opening tall windows, and placed it between us on the floor.

The room had grown very cold. Echoes, groans and sights that are part of an eighty-year-old building hung in the background. The sound effects were continuous. We had become used to them; we were interested in this room, but not afraid. Over in the corner, the pale window leading to the judge's staircase kept its eye fixed on us.

I began to tell her stories about the courtroom that I had found in old newspaper clippings. I told her the background of some of the trials, how Suchan and Jackson had show down Sergeant of Detectives Edmund Tong and Detective Roy Perry in a Toronto gun fight. How Tong had died, his spinal column severed.

And then, from ten feet away, from the prisoner's box, we heard it again. A steady rapping sound, not hard, not quick, but keeping pace with my words.

"Listen!" Frannie urged. I stopped talking, and as I did, the rapping stopped. "Did you hear it?" she said.

I resumed speaking, but very slowly, measuring out each word.

"Tap … tap … tap … tap … " came back the rapping, keeping pace with each word.

We froze. In the vast room, our hearts beat thunderously. The blood ran to our heads. Sweat broke out on our hands.

Fear, in small doses, can be pleasurable.

But we were terrified.

It was a matter of leaving immediately, or no longer being able to, I thought.

We grabbed everything, half dragging, half kicking it to the doorway.

Frannie looked to the right, into the judges' hallway.

"My God, look at the smoke," she cried, digging her nails into my arm.

In under minute, we were down the stairs and at the back door, then into the cold October night.

A few days later, I asked Building Superintendent Scott how the building was heated. I was trying to account for that fog in the hallway.

"Steam heated," he explained.

"Ah," I said, "that explains it."

I froze at his next words. "But we had not turned it on yet. Not when you were there."

I NEVER FELT COMFORTABLE ALONE THERE

Gloria Dove is the professional name of Gloria Dove Kavanagh who is a musician and singer of Country, Western, Bluegrass, and Gospel songs. She lives in the picturesque town of Elora, Ont. I sent her a letter of inquiry when I learned from the photographer Jack Kohane, who was photographing haunted houses in nearby Fergus for my book *Mysteries of Ontario*, that Gloria was known to have had some strange experiences in her house in Elora. She replied on 14 September 1998. I wrote back and encouraged her to write an account of her experiences, and this she did on 29 September 1998. I keyboarded this and wrote to her again and she replied on 10 November 1998. Here, finally, is her account of her experiences in different houses in Fergus and Elora. In its way it is a remarkable odyssey.

In July, 1980, my husband Bill and I purchased the house at 195 Barker Street in Fergus, Ont. It was built around 1826. At the time our two children were young, eight years old and six years old.

The large stone house was old and we started to renovate it that August. We ran into difficulty renovating the upstairs and ended up tearing most of the downstairs apart, as the joist had to be replaced to straighten the floors so we could do work on the upstairs.

In January of 1981, I was wakened up by coughing in the attic. I thought I was dreaming and went back to sleep. In the morning I got up and went downstairs, and the sound of coughing never crossed my mind, until my daughter came down and said, "Did anyone hear the coughing in the attic last night?" I didn't want to believe what I was hearing, but I told her that I had heard it. She wanted to know who was causing it. I just told her I didn't know.

Bill suggested we move the beds downstairs so we would not hear the coughing sound again. We did that and raised a curtain between our bed and the children's. A few nights later, I was awakened by the sound of boots walking in the house and the sense that someone was standing by the curtain staring at us. I was so frightened I could not move to wake Bill. Finally he stirred and I managed to tell him someone was in the house. We got up and looked around but no one was there. We went back to sleep.

The next morning, when Bill and I talked about what had happened that night, my daughter told us of her experience. She said that when she saw the man, he was already inside the house. He was standing in the back room and staring into the main part of the house. He was pointing a rifle ahead of him and not aiming it at her. She could see his hat on his head sideways. She said that he had come there every night since we had moved downstairs.

We started to tell some neighbours what was happening but they thought we were completely ridiculous. So we quit telling them and kept our experiences to ourselves.

We moved the children's beds back upstairs but kept ours downstairs near the back entrance to the house. Again we raised a curtain but this time along one side of the bed. That night I heard the sound of boots walking on the floor. They sounded to me like big army boots and I had no idea where the sound came from. The fan on our wood stove stopped of its own accord. A chair began rocking.

This time I woke up Bill and we got out of bed. The fan on the stove came on again, the chair quit rocking, and we heard the sound of someone running in army boots, fleeing the house. All this happened at the same time.

The next morning I got up and checked all the doors. The fan seemed to be in working order. We didn't have a rocking chair and none of our chairs had uneven legs. There was a chair near the stove but it was not a rocking chair.

It was time to find someone to help us. I called a lady in Fergus who had lived a few doors away back in the 1970s. Her name was Pat Mestern and I knew she had something in her house sometimes, and I asked her if she could tell me what to do as we were really upset. We told her everything that had happened. Everything had taken place over the last two weeks. She said to leave it to her for a few days and she would get back to us. She said I should talk to "it" with my mind and ask it what it wanted.

The next thing I knew, a night or two later, it was in the house again, shutting the stove fan off, rocking in a chair, and walking around the house in boots. So I asked it what it wanted. All that I could hear faintly was "you." I poked my husband to get up, "It's in the house again!" and I hollered at it to get out now because it was in my house. Everything happened the same as before. The fan came on, the chair quit rocking, and the boots whooshed by. My husband went to the door and opened it and our cat raced out meowing as if it was following someone. We could actually feel its presence at times.

I phoned Pat again and told her what had happened. She said that we could have someone like a psychic come to our house, but she added that she had found out something very interesting and said that we really didn't need to be afraid of it. She had contacted the previous owners of our house and learned that the grandfather had served in the Boer War. He had come home from South Africa in the wintertime, and he liked to sit by the stove and rock in his rocking chair. He had died in the house. She believed that he didn't like the house being disturbed with renovations. She believed that when we completed our renovations, the disturbances would stop.

The presence played tricks on us. Quite a few times we had to get up in the night and turn the television off because it would turn the set on full blast. One particular night Bill called to me to tell me to turn the hall light off, so I did. Part way down the stairs Bill said, "I thought I asked you to turn the light off in the hall." I told him that I had, but if it was still on, I would turn it off again. Before I got down the stairs, the light was on again. I hollered at my son to turn the light off. He did so and before my eyes it jumped right back on again. So I finally said, "You want the light on, we'll leave it on." The next morning Bill switched it off and it stayed off. We checked the switch and the socket but there was nothing wrong with them.

Sometimes Bill and our daughter would hear people eating and laughing in the old part of the house. He would holler at them to knock it off and it would be quiet. This happened many times with him and a few times with my daughter.

The years 1987, '88, and '89 were quiet ones. The house had been renovated by now and there wasn't much in the way of "the presence." In all, we owned the house from 1980 to 1989. I never felt comfortable alone there. Bill and I separated in January 1989 and I left the house for good.

Bill passed away in January 1987.

Dan, my common-law husband, and I moved into this very old home at 16 McNab Street in Elora on October 1, 1987. Within a few days of moving in, I sensed something was odd. I was upstairs at the time and thought someone was watching me from the back part of the house. I looked but nothing was amiss. I let it go at that and went about my business. But every now and again it felt like something was there.

One morning at the end of November, I was awakened by a very gentle knocking on the bedroom door. I thought I was dreaming and dismissed it. The next morning, I was awakened by the knocking again. This time I wasn't dreaming. The third time it happened, I knew I had a problem. About four days passed and I was in the bathroom in the early evening when I heard what sounded like a pile of books falling over. I ran into the back room but there was nothing there. There were no books there to fall over.

Four or five days passed and Dan went away on a trip. I decided to vacuum the upstairs, starting with the bedroom. I took the vacuum cleaner upstairs and set it up in the bedroom. Then I decided I would vacuum the room the next day, after I had sprinkled the rug with carpet cleaner. I had a package of Cow Brand baking soda on a shelf behind the door. I had used it on the carpet a few times because the cat that belonged to the previous owners had left its smell in the room. I decided I would use the baking soda the next day to deodorize the room and then vacuum it.

The first night alone in the house I was too nervous to sleep upstairs, so I slept on the couch downstairs. The next morning I got up and went upstairs to get dressed. I opened the bedroom door and there was the Cow Brand baking soda sprinkled all over the carpet. The box was sitting on the bed, not on the shelf behind the door. I was so shocked I couldn't even use the phone in the house. I went across the road to use the neighbour's telephone. I called Pat Mestern, the lady in Fergus, the one I had called years before. I told her what had happened. I thought perhaps the presence from the other house had followed me after all these years.

Pat asked, "Does it feel the same?" I said that it didn't.

She asked me what I sensed it was. I said that it seemed to me it's a child.

She said to go home and just say that you don't have time to vacuum but you'll clean it up this time. You're not to ask it its name.

Pat thought perhaps it was a child playing mischievous tricks. I feel that this is so because I have since learned that the original owners, when they lived in the house, had two young boys. The family was not sure what has happened to them. A relative is checking this out for me.

Also, when I talked to Pat, she asked me things about the house. She wanted to know the location of the room where the disturbance was coming from. Had it been ripped apart by the previous occupants? Pat figured if we got the room back together again, the disturbance might stop.

When Dan returned home from his trip, I told him what had happened. He said nothing. He just listened. Well, one night I was away and came home and he was sitting in the living-room with his arms crossed. On the table was a small rack from a planter that I had set up at the top of the stairs. I asked him what it was doing on the table, but he didn't answer me. I had to go to the bathroom rather quickly, so I ran upstairs. At the top of the stairs there was a clump of dirt from the flower-pot on the floor. I went to the bathroom and came back downstairs and asked why the dirt was up there on the floor. He didn't answer me. I asked him what was wrong. He said that the "thing" in the house had thrown the rack at him when he was coming down the stairs.

I believe that it wanted him to know for sure that it was there.

My daughter came back from Alberta early in the summer of 1998. She helped me put the bedroom back together. Since then we have had no more problems in our house.

6

EMAIL ENCOUNTERS

This section consists entirely of readers' responses to the invitations I extended in my books and media appearances to share with me and with future readers their experiences of the supernatural, the psychical, the paranormal, or the just plain weird. A few points should be noted. What might be called "extraordinary experiences" or "anomalous experiences" are not as rare as we might think. They seem to occur all the time, not rarely, only we might fail to make note of them or, if we notice them, we fail to ponder them and their implications. As well, the average witness or experiencer will, if pressed, admit to having had more than the single eerie experience that is being related. Witnesses with multiple experiences to record are known as "repeaters," and the sensitivities or acceptances of such phenomena and their interpretations may well run in families: seventh son of seventh son, etc. Psychologists have termed such people *fantasy-prone personalities*. One last point to make here is that people cursed or blessed with anomalous experiences to report do not necessarily believe they occurred: they believe something happened, but what precisely happened remains an open question. So here are the incredible emails that I have received, with some commentaries. After all, it was researcher Iris M. Owen who observed, "Parapsychology is people."

A CALL IN THE NIGHT

The following handwritten note is dated 26 January 2007. It was addressed to me care of Key Porter Books, one of my publishers, and was forwarded to me a few days later. Here is the note:

> Dear John,
>
> I read and enjoyed your book "Ghost Stories." I am sending my ghost story (or rather my mom's and dad's), hoping you may see fit to include it in a future book.
>
> Sincerely,
>
> Gusty

I am always pleased to receive mail and emails from readers of my books, and I make it a point to respond to all such communications. I certainly have to respond with gusto to a woman who signs herself "Gusty"! (This seems to be the familiar form of my correspondent's first name, Augusta, who is a resident of Regina, Saskatchewan.)

The hearing of voices is a widely reported phenomenon. Explorers in the Arctic have stated that they distinctly heard the sounds of their own names being pronounced in the wilderness — summonses in the solitude, so to speak. It is an oddly disorienting phenomenon. (From time to time I have heard my own name being sounded, when I was alone in a room, sometimes at dusk, sometimes at dawn.) It is rare that two or more people report hearing the same effect but it is not unknown. Folklore holds that such sounds act as "forerunners," vocalizations of preoccupations, concerns, and perhaps future events.

Ms. Chartrand's account is interesting in a number of ways. First, the vocal phenomenon is reportedly heard by two people in the same place at the same time. Second, when the voice is heeded and answered, the phenomenon usually ceases, as it does in this case. Third, in this instance, there is a direct connection between the audible effect and the author of this account. Fourth, the reader is offered a vignette of what pioneer conditions on the prairies were like in the early decades of the twentieth century, a period that is still (but not for long) within living memory.

If you hear a voice calling your name, listen. And then reply. Once.

In 1921 my pioneer parents, Fred and Rosalie Kurbs, had been married for 14 years and had a family of five children, ages 13, 11, 9, 7, and 5.

Dad had come to Canada in 1902 and his parents followed him three years later. Grandpa helped dad improve the homestead — digging rocks, breaking the land on the quarter-section, and building shelters for the animals. Grandma did the housework and found it very lonesome with no one to talk to during the day. So when dad finally found his wife, grandma was delighted, especially after the children started arriving. Looking after them became her priority.

When the youngest one was 5, grandma thought that must be the last one and the thought saddened her, as babies were so dear to her. (She had raised five of her own back in her homeland.) So, when in September mom told her there would be a new baby in mid-May 1922, Gram began to happily prepare for the event.

But, tragically, shortly after this announcement, Gram fell and broke her hip and become bedridden. The two oldest girls, 11 and 9, were a big help when they were home from school. The two younger ones also did their share, but mom was kept busy with cooking, housework, and tending to Gram. But Gram was very patient and never called for help unless the pain got too severe. This often happened during the night and mom would get up and turn Gram in her bed, fluff up her pillows, and massage her hip until she felt more comfortable again. This went on for three months. There was no other help. Doctors were 30 or 40 miles away. Mercifully, one night in early December, Gram passed away in her sleep.

For many nights after, mom would waken and get up to tend to Gram before she realized Gram wasn't there any more. After Christmas, mom was able to rest more often during the day and enjoy uninterrupted sleep at night.

Winter passed and spring was in the air. During the night of April 23rd, mom was awakened by Gram's voice calling her name. She was about to get up and go and tend to Gram, but quickly realized Gram was gone. Before mom got back to sleep again, the voice called, "Rosa," again.

Mom turned to dad, who was lying awake beside her, and asked, "Did you hear that?"

Dad replied, "Yes, if she calls again answer her."

Gram called one more time and mom answered, "Yes, what can I do?"

Silence. No more calls.

The next afternoon, April 24, at 4:30, I was born. Three weeks premature!

Go figure.

NINE EXPERIENCES

I have yet to meet Marion E. McKenzie of Medicine Hat, Alberta. But when I do, I expect we will have much to talk about.

I have long been fascinated with the name "Medicine Hat" because it is a reference to the Grand Medicine Society of the Native, Algonkian-speaking people of the Prairies. That society is also known as the Midewin, the secret circle of the Mide, practitioners of the arts and crafts of healing, conjuring, praying, charming, spirit-communication, etc. So it is not surprising that strange events and odd experiences should emerge from a city whose name recalls this background.

The Midewin may seem a far remove from the concerns of Mrs. McKenzie. But are they? Here are her emails to me. I find these nine experiences to be interesting in that they seem to be woven into the warp and woof of Mrs. McKenzie's everyday life and are understandable or interpretable only in terms of those daily experiences. The truest magic is the magic that is not recognized to be magic at all!

> *March 4, 2007.* Hello John — I have just finished reading of your awesome biography of accomplishments on your Internet site. Amazing, to say the least. I am currently reading your book *Mackenzie King's Ghost* and have found it very interesting.
>
> Having had several experiences myself, I was wondering if you were compiling information for another book, although you have written many on the subject of the paranormal. If so and if you are interested, you may e-mail me at [my email address]. If not, that's okay too.

Congratulations on all your good work. I look forward to reading more of your books.

Sincerely,

Marion E. McKenzie

Later, March 4, 2007. I was quite excited to have your e-mail reply pop-up so quickly while I was still at the computer. Thank you for your prompt reply. I haven't written my experiences out before, just told friends about them, so I will try to get them off to you as soon as possible.

Thank you for your interest and I really look forward to "Halloween 2008." Sounds great!

Sincerely,

Marion E. McKenzie
P.S. Sorry, yes I will e-mail them, one or two at a time. The first will be a bit about my life.

June 20, 2007. Dear John:
I do apologize for the delay in getting this to you. A family reunion, spring flower-beds and other stuff, got in the way. I am currently reading your book *Ghost Stories of Canada*. Being Canadian, the stories are easy to relate to. I find the book hard to put down!

A little of my history. My parents emigrated from Bridport, Dorset, in the South of England, with my two older sisters. They settled in Indian Head, Sask., where two of my mother's sisters had already come over and settled there. They lived there for about 4 years where my older brother and I were born, and then relocated to Regina where we were raised and educated. In 1942 my family moved to Maple Ridge, B.C. By this time my two older sisters were married and my brother was overseas in the Air Force. I moved to Calgary where I met and married my husband in 1948.

His employment, as a lab technician, took him to south-eastern Alberta, to the Suffield Experimental Station, and we resided in the Village of Ralston for 17 years. We had four children — 2 boys and 2 girls.

In 1969, the British Army Training Unit took over the Base and employees living there had to relocate to Medicine Hat, just 25 miles away. Meanwhile, my husband and I separated, and sadly he passed away a few years later. I found employment as District Director, Medicine Hat and South Eastern Alberta Unit, of The Canadian Cancer Society, where I held this position for twenty years until retirement. I remarried in 1973. My Husband, Bud, passed away in March of 2003, just after his 83rd. birthday.

Bud & I did a fair amount of traveling out of the country, England twice, the Continent, Japan, Soviet Union, Mexico, the Western States and the Maritimes. Bud retired in 1982 and spent his retirement reading, gardening, making beautiful wooden ornaments for the yard, crosswords and television. He had an extensive library, loved history and biographies. My hobbies were making porcelain dolls, clog dancing, and watercolour painting, which I still do.

We moved to this lovely brick bungalow in 1983. It was built in 1954. Before the houses were built in this area, there were the equivalent of 10 blocks of fields of corn and market gardens on both sides of the road which was a main artery into the city.

I haven't delved into paranormal experiences except for my own experiences. I hope this gives you some insight to the names and locations relevant to the stories.

I did pass on your e-mails to one of my younger sisters. Dorothy Kenworthy, who lives in Maple Ridge, B.C., and she is going to contact you as well with her experiences. I gave her your book *Mackenzie Kings Ghost.*

Thank you

Marion E. McKenzie

Later, June 20, 2007.
Paranormal Experiences No. 1: The Birth of Our First Baby

In our first married year in 1948, we moved from Calgary to Edmonton, where my husband was employed with a seismic crew. I was 4 ½ months pregnant with our first child. When I was very close to my 6th month, I began having symptoms in my pregnancy that indicated that my baby may be born 3 months premature. I was hospitalized and given hypos to hopefully prevent from going into labour, but it was not to be. I delivered a tiny little, 2 lb. baby girl on Oct. 21st, 3 months premature. The doctor did not expect the baby to live the hour, so he thought it better to tell me that she didn't live while I was still under a little anaesthetic. However, she did live quite miraculously for twelve days. The doctor explained the situation to me and he said they would not be able to save her and I would not be taking her home from the hospital. We were heartbroken and I hoped and prayed that she would prove us wrong. On November the 2nd· She passed away.

The point in telling this story is because while under the light anaesthetic during the birth, I had a dream. I was somewhere floating above. There was a man who was dressed in a robe and looked like all the pictures I have seen of Jesus. We were on a boat that was all finished inside in light varnished wood and he was standing at the helm. He was saying to me — "There are two things you can do — you can either turn the wheel this way and —" (I don't know what else he said) — "or you can turn it the other way and — " (I don't know what else he said), but there were two options. I hadn't heard about out-of body experiences at that time but have since. I have no reason whatever to think that I was near death, or if I was, I was never told, but I doubt it. I have wondered if perhaps I was hearing the doctor talk to his associates during the birth. I had never been on a boat in my life.

Further to this story, I was grieving for a long time. At Christmas, another young couple invited us over for Christmas dinner. We didn't have a car, so took the "street car" (remember — this was 1948). It was a calm but cold crisp day and it was about 5:00 P.M. so it was already dark. When we got off the transit and were walking down the street to the home, I happened to turn and look in the sky. There was quite a large white cross. It was quite unmistakable. In my heart I was sure that it was our little girl "Bonnie" letting us know she was all right. It stayed in the sky as we walked. The next day there was an article in the paper that someone else reported seeing it but there was no explanation.

Thank you

Marion McKenzie
P.S. I decided to send these in order of the sequence that they happened. You can use your own judgement as to whether they fit the criteria for paranormal experiences. All the best.

Paranormal Experiences No. 2: I Hear Someone Calling My Name

An experience I have had for many, many years is that I hear someone calling my name. I have had this happen since my young married years and maybe even earlier. It is so clear that it stops me in my tracks so that I look around to see if someone is there. It is always the voice of my parents, but most of the time, it is the voice of my father. My parents passed away when I was 26 and 30 respectively. At first I thought it was odd and I said to myself, "Oh, well!" but after my parents had passed away, I wondered if it was some kind of warning that perhaps I was in danger. So when I heard it, I would check over whatever I was doing for safety reasons, or check the kiddies if they were preschool or if they were home, or look out the windows. Always satisfied that everything was fine, I would just continue on with what I was doing. This always happened when I was at home. My parents had never been in any of the houses that we lived in. It is interesting to note, we had 8 children in our family, four have passed away, but of the remaining four, none of them have experienced hearing someone call their name. There isn't any reason for me to be singled out. I was one of the ones in the middle, not the youngest or the eldest. I wonder how many others experience hearing their names being called. It would be interesting to know!

Thank you,

Marion McKenzie

Paranormal Experiences No. 3: A Mysterious Phone Call

One Saturday evening in the spring of 1982, in Medicine Hat, AB, at close to 10:30 p.m., the phone rang. I answered saying, "Hello — hello," but no one answered. I listened and then I heard the operator say, "Ma'am, do you want to talk to this party?" Silence. "Ma'am?" Then I heard the woman caller say in a kind of despondent voice, "No — it's all right." This was the only call we had that evening. The operator then said to me, "I don't know what's going on. This caller has called you 3 or 4 times but she hangs up before I get the call through." She then told me the caller was in Victoria, B.C., and did I know anyone there who might be in trouble. I told her I didn't know anyone there, but it was the voice of my sister but she had passed away 19 years earlier. So the operator said she could give me the number if I would like to call there and she said she knew the location. It was a couple of blocks away from the beginning of a "seedy" area. Then I thought, well my youngest sister sounds just like her and she lived in Maple Ridge, B.C. I called her and they were fine, it was about eleven o'clock by this time and they were just going to bed. So then I did call the number the operator gave me. A young boy about 13 or 14 answered. I asked if his mother was there and he said, "No, she went out." I asked him what time she went out and said some people picked her up about 8:30 or 9:00 p.m. I asked if he thought she would have called my number in Medicine Hat and he said he didn't think so. This was when long distance calls were expensive and you just didn't pick up the phone and call long distance unnecessarily as we do so often now. I should have followed up a day or so later out of curiosity if nothing else. A person who claimed to have psychic ability said that it was my deceased sister just trying to get in touch with me. But whether it was some kind of coincidence or not I don't know.

Thank you,

Marion McKenzie

Paranormal Experience No. 4: A Very Strong Feeling or Intuition

This experience might be considered intuition, but nevertheless it was a very strong message. It was when we were living in Ralston, AB. In the summer of 1959, my sister, her husband and young boy and girl came to visit us on their way back to Chilliwack, B.C. For something to do one day, we decided to drive into Medicine Hat and have a tour through Medalta Potteries and buy a couple of bean pots. We had four children so that would make 10 people to fit into the car. This was before seat belts. We decided that my two boys 9 and 10 could stay home and go to the local indoor pool, which they did every afternoon for a couple of hours. And we would be back home shortly after they got home. The plans were all set, we would have lunch, take the boys to the pool and then we would leave. I was busy around the house and all of a sudden this strong feeling came over me that I shouldn't really go with them. So I told the others I was going to stay home. Well, that was met with "Why," "Oh, come on," etc. So I said, "Okay." Well, this occurred three times. The third time I said definitely that I was not going with them. I wasn't the slightest bit worried that anything would happen to them, it was just that I shouldn't be there. The boys went to the pool, the others went to the Potteries, had a great time and happily came home with their purchase of two bean pots and the boys were fine after swimming. Nothing uneventful happened to anyone. But I know I felt a lot better staying home. I wonder if had I been in the car that I might have caused some distraction and we would have had an accident. Or maybe I just had overly guilty feelings about my boys. It was a very strong feeling, one that I could not ignore.

Thank you

Marion McKenzie
P.S. The above stories seem to relate more to intuition, but the following stories in the next e-mail are more the paranormal.

Paranormal Experience No. 5: Oh, My God, I Just Saw that Woman!

It was in May of 1983 that my husband Bud and I purchased a lovely brick bungalow that was built in 1954. We remember when this house and the surrounding houses were built in this area because the road was the main artery into Medicine Hat at that time. Both sides of the road were fields about ten blocks long of corn and market gardens. There were two previous owners, the original owners who had built it, the second owners, who lived here for 6 years We were the third owners.

In our first years here, Bud, my husband, sometimes told me that saw an image of a young woman. He said she is all dressed up in a dress and high heel shoes and she is a fairly tall slim woman. He said, "I don't know who she could be," meaning that he didn't think she really looked like anyone he knew. When I ask him where he saw her, he said just anywhere around the house. He didn't seem to be very concerned about it, so I wasn't either. I never did see the apparition but I know that he did twice when I was with him.

One morning, in the summer, Bud came into the kitchen and I started talking to him about something. When he was going to answer me, he kind of gasped and said, "Oh my God, I just saw that woman!" But she disappeared and we went on with our conversation.

Another time on a winter evening about 9:30 p.m., Bud was doing his crossword and I was watching TV. The commercial came on so I got up to make a cup of tea. I asked Bud if he wanted a tea. Just then he looked up to answer he sort of gasped and said, "Oh my God, I just saw that woman!" It always startled him, as you can imagine it would. We always just let it go, she was here and sometimes Bud saw her.

Bud's description of her did not resemble the women of the family who had first owned the house and had passed on. The description did not fit the second owner either, and she still resides elsewhere in Medicine Hat. Very interesting and it makes you wonder!

Marion McKenzie

Paranormal Experience No. 6: I Saw This Beautiful Boy

One winter evening about 9:30 p.m., in about 1990, my husband Bud was downstairs working on some project. I was watching TV in the living-room. When the commercial came on, I glanced around the room, probably wondering what I might go to the kitchen and find to eat, when my eyes caught the image of a little boy sitting at the entrance to the hallway. I couldn't believe my eyes. He was looking at me, and when he saw that I had noticed him, he smiled and jumped up and ran to a lounger we had by the TV, folded his arms on the top of back, the and rested his chin on his arms and was smiling. And then he was gone. It was a very vivid experience and it still is very vivid in my memory. He was about 4 or 5 years old, had a round face with an olive complexion, brown eyes and curly very dark hair. He was wearing a hand-knit sweater with narrow, yellow, red, and blue stripes. He had medium blue cotton pants and I think I saw dark blue socks and no shoes. He was such an adorable looking little boy. I only saw the apparition once and always wonder who this little boy was.

At the time thinking about it, it had no relation to what I was watching on TV or to the commercial. Nor was it relative to our family. Our family are all blue-eyed blondes, nor were there any friends who looked like him. Both of the previous owners also are fair-haired and had blue eyes too. However, in the early days there were Indian settlements in this and the surrounding area. Our city's name is derived from an Indian incident. The South Saskatchewan River runs through the city just 2 blocks from our house. Reportedly, an Indian Medicine man in crossing the River (likely in a canoe) lost his head-dress in the river and thus the name of Medicine Hat. Could this possibly explain the origin of this adorable little boy?

Isn't it odd too that Bud never saw the little boy and that I never did see the woman that he saw? I guess we'll never know!

Marion McKenzie

Paranormal Experience No. 7: My Deceased Husband Appeared

It was in the spring of 1996 when I had this experience. My first husband had passed away nearly twenty years earlier. I had been remarried for many years. It was about 7:30 in the morning. Bud was still sleeping. I was attempting to eat breakfast, but I was very distressed about something that had been a problem for some time and nothing I said or did seemed to help. Feeling very despondent, I was just more or less playing with my breakfast and mulling over the circumstances and wondering why couldn't it be solved? etc.

In my pre-occupied mood, I suddenly heard a shuffling sound by my chair, just as if someone had just jumped there. I disinterestedly glanced down, but I immediately recognized the feet and legs of my deceased husband. He had one foot that was always turned out a little farther than most. I saw the familiar brown dress shoes and brown pants and the stance was definitely him. In my despair I remarked, "Oh it's you," and turned back to the table. At that moment I felt a hand close over my shoulder with a squeeze as much as to say, "Don't worry, it will be all right." That really got my attention. I was horrified at myself. It was my first husband after all these years, and he had appeared to give me assurance and support and I hadn't even said thank you! But of course, it was too late, he was gone. However, my mood lifted and I felt much better. It was an amazing experience.

Marion McKenzie

Paranormal Experience No. 8. Let's Push Her out of the Bed!

On a winter evening in about 1998, a weeknight, I had gone to bed, and had been asleep for about an hour and a half. It would be around 12:30 a.m. My husband hadn't come to bed yet and I was awakened with a dream. I suddenly felt something strongly pushing me in the back. I started to wake up and was wondering what the heck was going on! Annoyed, as I turned my head to look behind me, I distinctly heard a voice whispering, "Let's push her out of bed, let's push her out of bed," and as I heard it and looked, there I saw 3 figures at the side of the bed, like a young mother and two young girls about 8 and 12. It was as if they were in "pause-mode" leaning over the side of the bed. They were wearing what I think of as the Amish costume: large black bonnet with big brim, black blouse with puffy sleeves in the upper arms narrowing at the lower arms and long black skirts. I could only see about to their knees but presumed their skirts were floor-length. But they had blank white oval faces! As I looked at them I said in my annoyance, "Stop it!" and they were gone. I was fully awake and was not frightened, just annoyed at them. I wonder why they wanted to push me out of bed and I wondered if I hadn't wakened up if they would have succeeded!

As far as their appearance — covered wagons went over this land years ago.

Paranormal Experience No. 9. My Deceased Family Members Appeared

I believe this is my last story to relate to you. This is a dream I had about 1999 and it was about 1:30 or 2:00 a.m. It is quite nice, but I have to give you a few details first, to set the scene.

One of my sisters, who was 5 years older than me, passed away in November 1963, at the age of 43, of ovarian cancer. My mother passed away on May 11th, 1951, just two days before Mother's Day, also of cancer. I dreamed my deceased mother, my deceased sister and my eldest sister Claire, who is still alive, came to my bedside. They stood there looking down at me. My sister, who is alive, is the only one who spoke. She was smiling and said, "See, she's just sleeping," and then she said it again, just as if she had been asked to bring them to me to show them that I was all right. My mother and sister were smiling down at me but they didn't speak but they didn't speak. It was if they knew that I couldn't hear them. Then they turned and left and I woke up. My sister Claire lives in Chilliwack, B.C.

I believe a psychic would say they were wanting to check on me. I hadn't been thinking of them or anything, and it makes you wonder why you would dream something like that. I thought it was rather lovely and comforting!

Marion McKenzie

Medicine Hat, AB

P.S. I don't know what you will think of my stories. Some people don't seem to have any such experiences, or if they do, they don't place them as having any meaning.

I hope you find some of them worthy of printing. Thank you and best of luck with your new book.

Marion

I REALLY LIKE MY GHOSTLY HOUSEMATES

I received the following email on July 10, 2007 and found it so straight-forward and so interesting that I immediately emailed Ms. Moodie and asked her for some biographical particulars. I also asked her to send me those accounts of "even more ghosts" mentioned in the last paragraph!

There are indeed some families that do seem to possess "a strong psychic streak that goes back many generations." Quite often people of a Gaelic background (Scots, Irish, Welsh, etc.) will boast of the same, and then relate a series of family stories to illustrate what it is all about. I call these stories "memorates," using the folklorist's term for first-person narratives meant to be told in close or family circles. Ms. Moodie has a wealth of them!

Dear Mr. Colombo,

I just finished reading *True Canadian Haunting Stories* and really enjoyed it. I like hearing about other people who have seen and experienced the same sort of things I have. I also enjoyed reading about haunted places in cities close to my own, Stratford, Ontario.

My family has a strong psychic streak that goes back many generations. My aunt Jo Ann is a very talented medium who has conversations with spirits as easily as you or I speaking to a living person and has daily interactions with ghosts. Jo Ann lives in Kitchener, and we talk quite often. She has taught me so much. As such, I grew up with this sort of thing being seen as just part of life, not scary or weird. Jo Ann is the most pronounced psychic in the family, able to do many amazing things like leave her body, predict some future events, get impressions of people from objects they recently touched, and see/interact with spirits. She is amazing. I am nowhere near her level, but have still had many experiences with ghosts.

The first major one came when I was about 12. My grandmother moved into a little wartime Ontario Cottage here in Stratford. It was a pretty, tidy little house that Nan fell in love with instantly and bought the same day she first toured it. Though Nan loved the house, Mom, my aunt JoAnn, and I felt that something in that house was very wrong. Whenever we entered, we instantly felt unwelcome, that something was hating us. It certainly wasn't Nan. She had helped raise me when my Mom was sick during my infancy and early childhood, and we were incredibly close. Our whole family were close.

Something else in that house wasn't right. We didn't tell Nan … she was so happy, and we couldn't find any logical reason for our feelings. I just stopped spending as many nights and weekends at Nan's. The first few freaked me out so much that I left the comfortable spare room bed to sleep on the hardwood floor beside Nan's bed, in a sleeping bag. That was the only place I felt secure. At that point, I hadn't seen or heard anything too weird, just felt that overwhelming sense of being hated.

The first real "appearance" happened to my uncle Paul. He and JoAnn were staying at Nan's and were sleeping in the spare bedroom. Jo had taken a sleeping pill and was very deeply asleep. Paul wakened abruptly at around 3 a.m. and saw the figure of a shortish, stocky elderly woman standing at the side of the bed. Her features were indistinct, but her eyes were fixed on Paul and were glaring fiercely. She had both hands wrapped around his throat, trying to throttle him. The pressure against his neck and encumbered breathing had wakened him. My poor uncle launched himself out of the bed and ran to the living room, scared out of his wits. He spent the remainder of that night on the couch and refused to spend any more nights at Nan's. He didn't tell Jo, Mom, or I about this for about 5 years. There was no one in the house who looked anything like what Paul saw. Nan was 5' 8" and about 90 pounds, Jo took after Nan in build and height and was asleep beside Paul. There was no one else in the house.

A few weeks after Paul's experience, I brought my new kitten, Mump, over to Nan's. Mump, never a nervous kitten before, howled if separated from me for even a second, and kept staring and hissing at the doorway to the spare room and places in the living room and kitchen. He would only sleep if he was in physical contact with me.

We kind of got used to Nan's ghost … we got so that we could tolerate being there and more or less ignore the feeling of being hated. Things were going o.k., until Nan got sick. She'd been having problems with increasing dementia, which was aggravated when the doctor gave her Prozac. Prozac can cause this reaction in some elderly people. She was delusional and having panic attacks, forgetting that she took her meds and taking them again, leaving stove burners on. Our family doctor decided to admit Nan to the hospital and told Mom and I to go to her house and take any meds she had out. Nan had pills squirrelled away in the oddest of places, a testament to the dementia. While we were there, the feeling of being despised was stronger than ever. So strong that we had to leave and would not come back until Jo was with us.

That night, the house was struck by lightning again. That house, despite being the smallest house on the block, was hit by lightning incredibly often. This strike took out the 220 fuse in the 1940s era electrical panel. Mom went in alone the next day to do some laundry for Nan. The dryer wasn't working well because it ran on the 220 phase and currently had only 110 available … it was limping along and taking forever. Mom was standing in front of the dryer when something made her turn around. Just as she moved, a box hit the wall in front of where she had just been standing, hard enough that the glue holding the box in shape let go. The box had flown (been thrown) from the storage room shelves. This room was at a right angle to the main room of the basement and had no straight path between the shelf and Mom. Needless to say, Mom was incredibly scared. She unplugged the dryer, leaving the wet clothes inside, and ran out. She waited until Dad and I got home to get us to go back with her to get the laundry. After Mom told Jo about this, Jo decided to do a purification / exorcism ritual. After that, the house was tolerable … not pleasant, but not hostile.

I decided to look into the house's history and went to the city archives. I found out that the first owner of the house had been an elderly Eastern European woman who had died in the spare room. Since she had no family or friends, and her neighbours had not liked her, her body was not found for a few weeks. She had been a lonely, bitter, sour old woman. Jo felt that this elderly woman had liked Nan because she was another elderly widow, but had been jealous of Nan's relationships with family and friends since she hadn't had these positive relationships herself. Nan sold the house about 3 months after Jo's ritual. Nothing incredibly odd had happened in that time. We were very relieved when the house sold. When we were packing Nan's belongings, I walked through the house, talking to the ghost. I suppose I had to make a certain peace with it before I left for good.

I now live in a very old house that has its own resident ghosts. None are nasty like Nan's resident spook was. I have had numerous visits by the household ghosts, all previous residents or owners of the house. Toby wakes me out of nightmares (and only nightmares) by pounding on the walls or ceiling in my room and sometimes appears as a glowing red or white floating orb beside my bed, Stella physically lifted me off the sofa and shoved me into the laundry room to avert a dryer fire, Amos appeared as a shadow man when I was nervous during a very violent storm and power outage and calmed me right down, John sent a message to his daughter through me (we became friends when I bought the house she grew up in) and I always know he's around by the smell of Old Spice cologne, and the last "regular" is a young man named Walter who likes listening to the radio, turns lights on and off, and loves to flirt. He has touched my leg, tousled my hair, and gently kissed me. I have been told by a medium that they all like me. Sometimes they talk to me, but I just know what they're saying in my head rather than hearing it with my ears.

The spooks in my house do many things. Sometimes they turn on an old 1950s-era radio on my kitchen table to listen to baseball games or music. That radio is not plugged in and has no batteries, but it plays when they want it to. Sometimes they open and close doors, and have even taken doors off their hooks to open them. They turn lights on and off, especially my bedroom and stairway lights. Sometimes they tap on walls. Joe sometimes sits with me on the couch, and I can feel the sofa cushion sink under him beside me. I often smell his cigarettes and cologne.

I really like my ghostly house mates. I think they're neat.

I have met even more ghosts while on the job. I work as a security guard, often on night shifts, and I am usually alone for my entire shift. A prime situation for ghosts. But I will make that the topic for another email. I've gone on long enough, this time!

Sara Moodie

THIS EXTRA DIMENSION

A reader of one of my books of ghost stories sent me this email which arrived on 21 February 2008, after being forwarded by an editor at the Dundurn Group, one of my publishers. I am always pleased to receive emails, like this one, that give accounts of ghostly events and experiences! The reader is Daisy Morant and she explains what happened to her more than thirty years ago, an event and an experience that have affected her and her husband to this day.

I want to share an experience my husband and I had in the 1970s; I was family editor of the *Oshawa Times* until spring 1973; we moved to Toronto (my husband is an artist) and bought a motorcycle; in the summer we decided to go to a festival being held at Port Perry.

We took Hwy 7 out. It joined Hwy 12 for a while and then 7A turned off to the east — I no longer remember what roads we took to get over there, except that we turned at a light where there was a gas station on the northeast corner. (I think this was the 7A turnoff but can't be sure.)

At this point we were flagged down by several other motorcyclists. We pulled up on the south side of the road and when we couldn't answer their question *re* directions, we pointed them to the gas station. We watched idly as they drove across the road, pulled in, and spoke to an older man who came out of the station. Then we got onto our bike and went to Port Perry and enjoyed the day. After a few hours we returned homeward.

At the corner there was no more gas station, only a pile of smoking rubble, with a man poking a stick through it and an ambulance standing by. We were both shocked. All the way down Hwy 12, I kept looking back, expecting any moment to be passed by the ambulance but none came.

Being the good journalist that I was — and am — I called it in to Canadian Press.

Some time later (maybe 45 minutes later?) I got a phone call from Tom MacKay, who was city editor at Oshawa and whom I knew well. He wanted to know what was going on so I told him. I also told him that we were still shocked at the extent of the devastation. We wanted to know whether any of those cyclists had been hurt, etc., etc., etc. I assumed he was making notes for a news item. Well, Tom told me, that gas station had blown up two weeks previously. If it had been my experience only, it would have been bad enough. But this was experienced by both of us at the same time; we neither drank nor smoked nor took any other drugs; we weren't stressed out — neither of us could then — or now — think of any explanation for what happened to us. I think it has affected my husband more over the years. I do know that when we talk about it — as it still comes up from time to time — we get a sick sort of feeling in our stomachs.

Neither of us has returned to that area. We don't want to go.

A bit more about ourselves:

My husband is one of those show-me-then-I-might-believe-it types. Canadian-born, he did have a previous experience as a young man in a boarded-up school in Etobicoke which he put down to suggestibility on his part.

I was born in Europe. The women in my family have always had this extra dimension, though I am not certain quite what to call it — I could tell you stories — and I hate it.

My sister once called mother in Sacramento in hysterics, begging her not to take a return flight to L.A. — she gave her the flight number and it was the one mother had intended to go on. Because my sister was so distraught, mother decided to change to a later flight and was glad she did, as the earlier one went into the Bay at L.A. — don't know if you remember that one (also in the 1970s), it went down too steeply and "undershot" the runway. People were killed. So I was not — and am not — happy to have this dimension.

I am a writer/journalist and a Mensan. Rational thought is supposed to be our supreme achievement but there is this other way of being that intrudes....

Thank you,

Daisy Morant

SANDY'S GHOST

The afternoon of the day of Halloween 2007, radio listeners in Victoria, British Columbia, could hear me discussing ghost stories on Joe Easingwood's very popular daily program. Now Joe is an "easy" guy to listen to, and to speak to, and his listeners often became his callers, phoning in to share their own ghostly experiences with all of us. I encourage radio listeners to contact me if they are willing to have their weird stories included in some future collection of eerie stories. On this occasion a couple of listeners accepted the invitation, and Ron Armstrong is one who did.

I am glad he did. I received his email on 15 December 2007 and it makes for "easy" reading. It also poses some interesting question. Are there psychical forces?

Do the dead yet live? Are some people inherently "sensitive" to these "entities"? Does the Ouija board really work? Where did the information about the name of the house's earlier inhabitant come from? As Bertolt Brecht once wrote, "Questions, questions!"

Dear Mr. Colombo,

I told this story on Joe Easingwood's show on C-FAX here as part of the run-up to Halloween. You asked me to send it to you for inclusion in your next book about "Canadian Ghosts."

In the early seventies I left home to share the upper floor of an old house with two fellow University of Victoria students. The layout was unusual, with a big kitchen, two medium bedrooms, a small bathroom, and a very small living room.

It was a time of new encounters, many fueled by curiosity and even more by drugs. One encounter was Sandy, a genuine, if troubled, free spirit. Tall, beautiful, and blonde, she had the largest doe eyes I'd ever seen.

She fetched up at John's invitation, needing shelter and support until her latest crisis resolved. We were happy to oblige and gave her the spare bed in the kitchen. For a few days all went well. Then she started to complain of restless nights. As her sleep declined she became more aware of "something," a presence in the room.

One night this presence took form. Sandy awoke in the middle of the night to see a man wearing an old-fashioned brown suit and fedora standing in the middle of the kitchen. His face was in shadow while his body was surrounded by a shimmering yellow light.

Still not having alternative arrangements, Sandy felt compelled to stay, despite her mounting dread. She did ask us never to leave her alone in the suite at night. We agreed.

Sandy's ultimate terror came when she awoke, labouring to breathe. She was sure the presence was lying full-length on her! It was too much. She wanted to flee. Before she did, she agreed to an "investigation" of the ghost haunting her.

The next night we gathered in a circle, armed with a Ouija board and liberal amounts of "demon weed." The latter was necessary to prevent any human manipulation of the spiritual forces, if any, that might come our way.

After all had a suitable buzz, we lightly held the wooden triangle and asked direct questions.

"Who are you?"

The triangle spelled "C.H.Thompson ."

"Why are you here?"

"To see my wife."

"Do you mean any harm?"

"No, I love her."

"When did you die?"

"1936."

"Is your wife here?"

"Yes."

Sandy was the only female in the room and it was too much for her. She somehow found other quarters and left.

The other guys were very quiet, without the usual dopey remarks. In the days following they dropped the subject.

But I pursued it. Through some research, I found the startling facts. "C.H. Thompson" really did live in the house when it was a single family dwelling. His master bedroom was the site of our kitchen. Thompson's beautiful blonde wife was the spitting image of Sandy.

In a jealous rage he had killed her in that very room. For the crime he had been hanged … in 1936. Ironically our living-room window looked across at the hill where the old gallows stood before the site became a junior high-school.

He had returned in spirit to try to make amends with the image of his wife.

SOME FRIGHTENED ME MORE THAN OTHERS

I received this email on 24 September 2007 from a reader who lives on the West Coast who has a whole series of eerie experiences to relate, beginning with those in childhood and advancing into those of early adulthood.

Victoria Hood, the sender, writes with great ease and fluency about her unusual experiences. They seem to me to lie on the "no man's land" between consciousness and unconsciousness. It is hard to know what to make of them, and that is Ms. Hood's point. The episodes do not horrify her, although they could, because she finds something that might be affirming about them. Where they are concerned, she emerges as neither a believer nor a doubter, neither a spiritualist nor a sceptic. She seems to me to be entirely level-headed about these experiences. She also strikes me as being entirely sincere and not interested in exaggerating her sensations, feelings, and thoughts. A psychologist might describe her as a person who is "fantasy-prone," that is, predisposed to confuse "marginal" encounters, but that psychological category fits so much of the adult population that it is probably meaningless.

Ms. Hood is a young woman with at least a half-century of life ahead of her. I wonder if she will find that the years to come will be made memorable by yet more appearances of these shadowy figures, forerunners or spirit-guides.

Dear Mr. Colombo:

I recently purchased *True Canadian Haunting Stories*; I very much enjoyed reading it and will be sure to check out your other publications! I thought you may be interested in hearing my experiences. Please feel free to contact me if you have any questions, comments, or would like further details. If you choose to include my account in one of your collections, please edit as you see fit. I know I tend to ramble!

I was always what one might call an imaginative child. Born the second of four children in the small town of 100 Mile House, B.C., I was the only one in my family to have an imaginary friend (although as an adult I tend to believe "imaginary friends" are something more like ghostly visitors, but that's another topic altogether). I was plagued by nightmares almost every night from a young age, something that has continued into my adulthood. (I also sleepwalk!) I remember many of my dreams as clearly as my actual life-experiences, and due to my acquaintance with vivid dreams, I am very comfortable with my ability to distinguish dreams from reality. However, such things make it easy for my family and friends to dismiss my experiences as the work of an over-active imagination, while I can assure you they are not.

When I was about three years old, I had a recurring nightmare that particularly terrified me. I guess I could hear my pulse while

I slept, because I would dream there was a pack of men in white clothes with dark hair marching down the street in front of our house to the beat of my pulse. I would hear or see them coming and somehow knew I had to get in bed and pretend to be asleep before they found me or something awful would happen. I never found out what that something was but I was very frightened every time I had this dream.

This particular nightmare is relevant because of something that happened when I was a teenager. One night I was getting in the shower, fiddling with the taps to achieve the perfect water temperature. In the reflection in the faucet suddenly one of the men who had marched down the street in my dreams appeared behind me! I let out a shriek and turned around quickly, but of course there was nobody there. I looked back at the faucet but the reflection was gone, and there was nothing in the shower that could have created this type of reflection. I saw the same man's reflection once again about two years later while getting something out of the freezer in our basement and I think that was the fastest I ever ran up the stairs!

Despite these experiences, if someone had asked if I had ever seen a ghost, I would have said no; that all changed when I was nineteen. I was renting a basement suite in Coquitlam while attending Simon Fraser University and my grandfather was very ill. I was taking it very hard because I hadn't seen him for two years and he was at the point where he didn't recognize the family members who visited him. I was carrying a lot of grief because of a lot of things I'd always wanted to tell him but never would get the chance. He passed away on March 3, 2001.

At some point during the days before his funeral, I was roused from sleep by a bright light shining in the corner of my bedroom. I stared at it, squinting and blinking, trying to figure out what was causing it. Slowly a figure emerged from it and started walking towards my bed. Despite the fact that the figure was unmistakably my grandfather, I screamed like I have never screamed before, terrified at what was happening since I had never seen a spirit before. Both my granddad and the light disappeared in an instant while I was screaming and I have regretted my fear and the scream ever since. I sincerely believe my granddad was coming to visit me because once on the other side he knew how much I had wanted to talk to him, but I don't think he will ever come back again because of how scared I was.

After that, my suite became a hotbed for ghostly visitors. I suspect that in his haste to leave because of my fright, my grandfather somehow didn't close the door to the spirit world properly, leaving a portal open to any spirit who wanted to use it. On a regular basis I would be awakened by the light in the corner of my bedroom, and various shadowy figures would appear from it and roam my room. At first I was terrified at such occurrences but then I got used to it and even had a little fun with it.

I went online to see if there was a way to summon specific ghosts; I found a set of instructions but was unable to inspire my granddad to return. However, one of my favourite musicians, Bradley Nowell (from the band Sublime), had passed away several years earlier, so for fun I thought I'd see if I could get him to come visit me. To my surprise, he came! He emerged out of the light one night and began talking to me. I eagerly and fearlessly sat up at the end of my bed to see and hear him better. This was the only time I've heard a spirit talk and it was very distorted and hard to understand. I was straining to hear what he was saying — it sounded like he was giving me instructions to do something. He then began to fade back into the light, and I cried out, "Wait! I have so many questions to ask you!" He responded by saying, "First, get the —" but because I couldn't understand what he was saying, of course I could not follow his instructions and have not seen him since.

I should also mention that of the ghostly visitors I had in that suite, some frightened me more than others. I remember one that crawled up my wall and across the ceiling over my bed (*à la* Spiderman), then paused and stared down at me for a moment — he scared me out of my wits. Also, during the day my cat would often seem to be watching something that I could not see. Furthermore, the family that lived in the house above me had a little boy who slept in the room above mine; I would often hear him start crying and screaming in the night so I've wondered if these visitors were showing up in his room as well.

I moved around a lot during my early twenties, and after

leaving the basement suite in Coquitlam did not have any more paranormal experiences until I was twenty-four. I moved into an apartment building in New Westminster, where I continue to live now at the age of twenty-six. The first few months living here were uneventful. I always sleep with my bedroom door open so my cats are able to wander freely through the apartment during the night; where my bed was positioned at the time I could see straight down the hallway to the entrance door of my suite.

At some point I began to wake up and see a tall, shadowy man (somehow I know he's a man) standing by the entrance door. At first I was scared, thinking someone had broken into my apartment, but then as I stared at him he would vanish. It was startling to wake up and see him but due to my experiences in the Coquitlam basement suite I quickly came to the understanding that he meant me no harm and therefore I was not frightened. However, that did not stop me from becoming annoyed that he kept interrupting my sleep! One night I woke up to see him standing there, and in frustration I charged down the hallway at him; he sort of wisped away into the living room. I ran after him and flicked on the light, only to find myself standing in the middle of the room, alone. After that he did not return for about two months, but then continued his habit of visiting regularly.

Several months ago my boyfriend moved in with me, and as a result the furniture in the bedroom has been rearranged so I cannot see the entrance door from the bed. It was quite some time after my boyfriend moved in before I saw The Man (as I call him); I actually had somewhat hoped he would no longer visit due to my boyfriend's presence, or that I just wouldn't see him because I couldn't see down the hallway anymore. However, now The Man stands at the bedroom door, just watching me as I sleep. (My boyfriend has not seen him, but he is a very sound sleeper, so even if The Man started jumping up and down on the bed, I don't think he'd notice!)

It is still a little startling to wake up and see him there, but I have grown accustomed to him and am not bothered by his presence. I comfort myself by telling myself he's my Guardian Angel or Spirit Guide, or, although I do not recognize him, perhaps he is a deceased loved one checking in on me and reassuring me that life does in fact continue after physical death.

With utmost sincerity,

Victoria Hood

MAYBE I IMAGINED THESE THINGS

I received this email from Anne Finney who had read a recent publication of mine called *Strange but True: Canadian Stories of Horror and Terror*. In that volume there is an invitation to readers to write down their eerie experiences and then, if they so wish, to share them with me and my readers.

Here is what Ms. Finney wrote on 7 January 2008. It is apparent to the reader that she is very much a family-oriented person. Perhaps there are psychic connections between the members of her family and that these attachments offer premonitions and reminders that there is some form of life after death. Ms. Finney's strength is her courage and her willingness, even eagerness, to accept the reality of these states of mind and emotion.

I corresponded with Ms. Finney and asked her for a few more biographical particulars. She replied, "As I mentioned I grew up on a farm in Millbrook, Ontario. I have always had a vivid imagination which certainly helps me when I write my stories. I work in retail which I love as I am very much a "people" person and enjoy talking with all types of people. I have three grown children and one grandson who I absolutely love to bits. What other types of information would you like to know? I appreciate the interest you have taken."

Dear Mr. Colombo,

My name is Anne Finney. I just finished reading your book *Strange but True*. I really enjoyed it. I have had a few unique experiences over the years that you may be interested in.

First, a little about myself. I grew up in Millbrook, Ontario, on a farm with my parents and two older brothers. I have always had an interest in writing. I write personalized books for children and enjoy it very much. I love children and I love to see their faces when they read about themselves. It gives me great satisfaction. I have written approximately ten stories and would love to have one published some day.

My Mom died suddenly at age forty-five, which was a shock to us all. The first occurrence happened in my kitchen about ten years after she died. I was listening to the radio. A certain song came on (I have no idea what it was now) and I felt a hand on my shoulder. I looked around to see if someone was there, but there wasn't anyone there. I had a feeling it was my mom.

The second incident happened on my twenty-first birthday. Before my Mom died we had gone to a cattle sale. She bought me a musical doll. I didn't know this at the time. She died on Dec. 6. My birthday was Dec. 10, and when I opened my gift up, there was the doll which she had bought for me. You make think this isn't unusual, but my doll plays the music on its own. The song is what the world needs now.

One time in particular I was coming back into bed. It was around six in the morning. I had just got nicely into bed and was startled by my musical doll playing on its own. It was loud enough that it woke my husband up. We both were amazed and a little scared that this happened. Occasionally it will start playing on its own.

I firmly believe that it is just my mom saying hello. What do you think?

My Grandmother (Mom's Mom) had a strange thing happen after my Mom died. We used to pick morels (like mushrooms) every year. The year after my Mom died a single morel started to grow beside my Grandmother's house. There had never been any there before. I think it was a sign from my Mom.

My aunt (Mom's sister) had something happen after my Mom died. She was very upset and would go for nights without sleeping. She was constantly thinking of her. One night my Mom visited her and said she was fine and not to worry about her. She was with my other Grandmother and Grandfather. After this happened my aunt was more at ease. I guess she just needed to know that everything was alright with her sister. I believe my aunt is very sensitive to unknown things and maybe this is why she had this happen.

I wonder if sometimes we are so anxious to know that our loved ones are okay that we do actually have things happen. I would like to believe that there is a way that this actually is possible.

I guess the experience that still upsets me the most is this one: My Mom died before I had my kids. I remember one night having a dream that I took them up to heaven to meet her. This is still emotional for me. I would like to think that this really happened. Whether it did or not it still makes me wonder.

The next happenings are about my Dad. My Dad died ten years after my Mom. There are three experiences that I had concerning my Dad.

Lying in bed one night I heard a voice saying, "Everything will be all right." It was so clear, as if it was in the same room. I called downstairs to my husband to see if he was calling me. He wasn't. That was at a time when my husband was out of work. We had three small children and were worried about what would happen. After that things improved. My husband found work again and things did work out. I think it was my Dad's way of saying, "You'll be okay."

The second thing that happened was this. My kids were down for their afternoon nap so I decided to lie down as well. As I was on the couch, my heart started beating so fast I thought it was going to come out of my chest. I sat up startled wondering what was wrong. It really scared me. My husband came home early that afternoon, which was very unusual. He told me that my Dad had had a heart attack. It was at the same time that I had my racing heart. Coincidence? I don't think so. Maybe it was his way of preparing for me later.

Shortly after my Dad's heart attack, I was obsessed with thinking about the Twenty-third Psalm. It was always on my mind, where it got to the point that I couldn't think of anything else. This continued for over a week. I always associate this psalm with a death, as they always read it at a funeral. Approximately two weeks later my husband came home early again. This time it was to let me that my Dad had died. I wasn't shocked. Everyone was surprised that I wasn't upset with my Dad's death. As a daughter and only girl, I was very upset but I felt I had had two previous warnings to prepare me for what was going to happen.

I still have dreams of my Mom and Dad.

My musical doll still plays on its own.

Maybe I imagined these things, but I firmly believe they are signs that my parents are still with me.

Please feel free to contact me if you would like.

Anne

WE KNEW VERY LITTLE ABOUT THE HOUSE

Over the last quarter-century I have published a good many books about mysteries. Two of these books focus on one province. *Ghost Stories of Ontario* is a collection of largely traditional tales about haunted places in the province. *Mysteries of Ontario* is an illustrated guidebook to sites in the province associated with strange events and weird experiences of the past and the present.

M. Marlene Beyer, the contributor of the following account, holds a Master of Arts degree and is a very keep observer. I am grateful to her for writing this account of her haunted house and emailing it to me. It arrived on 15 August 2007.

It is true, as Ms. Beyer says that there are reports that upon the passing of a loved one, scents are discerned. No one knows why. Departed spirits are associated with sights, sounds, and disturbances of one sort or another. So why not lovely, lingering scents? Why not indeed!

Dear Mr. Colombo:

I have enjoyed reading (and re-reading) your accounts of hauntings in Ontario.

In 1999, my children and I, my daughter, Aryme, who was twelve and my son, Simon, who was nine, moved into a small, two-story, wood-framed home at 1027 Wellington Street East in Sault Ste. Marie. We knew very little about the house, but I was drawn to the fact that it had been built in the early part of the 20th century and had been nicely renovated.

Since it had only two bedrooms, we immediately began our own renovations by splitting one of the bedrooms into two smaller rooms. One evening, shortly after we had moved in, I heard a knock on the door. I happened to be looking at the kitchen clock and it was 6:10 p.m. When I went to answer the door, however, no one was there. I logically assumed it to be pranksters.

Since the house was not equipped with a doorbell, I installed a battery-operated one. The next morning at precisely 6:10 a.m., the doorbell rang. Like the night before, no one was on the other side of the door. This continued for several mornings (and evenings) until I decided to remove the batteries from the door bell. I was astonished the next morning to hear the door bell ring as it had the previous morning, without its batteries!

I travelled quite a bit during that time on business and often found myself sleeping in hotels. More often than not, without being set, the alarm clock radio would go off at 6:10 a.m. Once, exhausted from driving, I had fallen asleep in my hotel room, only to be awaken at 6:10 p.m.

I had asked my girlfriend, Julie, and her boyfriend, James, if they would watch my cat and two dogs while I was away on business. The next morning, Julie called me to inform me that James had refused to stay over night in the house, since the door bell had gone off (still without its batteries) at its scheduled time.

I would often come downstairs in the morning to find that both front and back doors were wide open, but that no one had entered and that my animals (particularly my Husky who was constantly running away) had left the house.

One evening, I awoke in the middle of the night, hearing a slight disturbance in the room. I clearly saw the outline of a tall man, and, believing it to be my boyfriend, rolled over and went back to sleep. When I awoke in the morning and called to ask him why he had left so early, he told me that he had been on call at the hospital the night before and not been able to come over.

While I was at work one day, a case aid entered my office and mentioned to me that she had seen me raking leaves in front of my house. She said, "Do you know that that house is haunted?" She continued on to explain that friends of hers had briefly lived in the house and that they had "sensed" benevolent spirits.

About five years later, I was having dinner in Kitchener with my friend Jeff, when, for some reason, the topic of ghosts came up in the conversation. I told Jeff the story about the house and he was fascinated. We discussed what the possible significance of 6:10 a.m. or 6:10 p.m. might have been and the fact that my "ghost" seemed to have been following me. When I moved from "the Sault" two years later, no further unusual incidents occurred.

As I was sleeping early the next morning (it was still dark outside) I was awakened by the sound of the laundry-room light being turned on. I was apprehensive since I was alone in the house at that time. I went into the laundry room and turned off the light, running back into the bedroom. I chastised myself for telling my friend Jeff about the "ghost." As I was drifting back to sleep, I happened to notice the time; it was just after 6:10 a.m. Perhaps my "ghost" was letting me know that I was still in its thoughts ….

Nothing unusual occurred following that incident, although from time to time, Jeff and I did speak about ghosts and of an afterlife.

In April of 2005, Jeff was diagnosed with stomach cancer which quickly metasticized throughout his body. Over the next month, I telephoned Jeff and spoke to him from his hospital bed. On May 5th, 2005, my 44th birthday, I telephoned Jeff around 9:30 a.m. to see how he was feeling. We spoke only briefly, since he seemed preoccupied. I remembered that he was scheduled to see his oncologist that morning and I contributed his aloofness to that. Shortly before 10:00 a.m., my boyfriend called to tell me that Jeff had passed away. We were both devastated, as Jeff had been a devoted friend. During the funeral, I found myself speaking with Jeff's ex-wife, and I happened to mention to her that I had spoken to him the morning of his passing. She snapped at me, telling me that Jeff had died around 7:30 a.m. and that I couldn't have spoken to him almost two hours after that. Over the last five years that I had known him, I had spoken with Jeff numerous times on the telephone as well as in person. I was certain that it was Jeff to whom I had spoken that morning.

Later that day, my boyfriend and I decided to spend the evening on our boat. I spent the early part of the evening going through pictures of the three of us, since we spent so much time together both on (and off) the water. I must have fallen asleep, since I was awakened in the early morning by the most amazing smell; it was so beautiful! It was as if someone had taken all the smells and scents that I have loved throughout my life and had placed them in one room. It wasn't until I began to read your books that I discovered that (sometimes) loved ones who have passed on communicate with the living clairsentiently.

Perhaps these experiences only exist in my imagination, but I know what I have heard, sensed and seen.

Thank you.

M. Marlene Beyer, M.A.

FOUR STRANGE ACCOUNTS

Dreams, hooded figures, ghosts, revenants … we have strange experiences and share this world with even stranger beings, entities, and forces.

Deborah Black's four experiences are exemplary in the sense that she reports them with clarity and a sense of bewilderment. She dreams about the appearance of the babies that she is bearing. Such experiences are often reported. Perhaps pregnancy is close to prophecy! Her uncle is a rationalist and sceptic, yet he repeatedly sees a "hooded figure." Her high school friend takes comfort in the fact that the spirit of her deceased mother may be watching out for her. And her daughter witnesses an elderly woman's account of a dead man's spirit that appeared in her room. The ghost of the mother and the ghost of the man are revenants, spirits that return from the dead.

It is difficult to know what to make of these accounts, which Mrs. Black composed and sent to me on March 17, 2007. Perhaps they are not meant to shed light on knowledge, but as experiences they cause us to pause and wonder about the gulf between the living and the dead which may, it seems, at times, be bridged….

1. My Prophetic Dreams

My name is Deborah. I am forty-nine years of age and I work in the field of professional fund-raising. I have been fascinated by unusual phenomena since I was in my teens but I had no strange encounters until I entered my twenties.

My first incident was not a supernatural one but it was

profoundly awesome to me. I married at the age of eighteen and was pregnant with my first child at nineteen. However, before I met my husband, I had a dream. Two nights a week this dream came to me. I met a man with black hair, black moustache, and he drove a dark green car. He would come to pick me up at my house each day and a small child would be seated in the back seat. This child was about the age of three and had sandy brown hair and was thin. I could not distinguish either the child's face or the man's. I did not realize the significance of the dream until I gave birth to my first child. Oddly enough, my son had sandy brown hair and was thin as a child. My husband had a dark green car when I met him and he also had black hair and a black moustache!

My second child was born four years later. I had only one dream before her birth. I dreamed that she would have dark brown hair and dark eyes. Seven months later, I produced the exact baby of my dreams. They do say women may be psychic during pregnancy.

2. My Uncle's Hooded Figure

My uncle had a terrifying experience with a ghost in his apartment. He is retired and lives alone in an apartment above a convenience store in Acton, Ontario. The building was rebuilt on the site of an old rooming-house that used to be a home for transient workers employed at the old tannery in Acton, since demolished. The rooming-house apparently burned to the ground in the 1960s.

My uncle is not a believer in the supernatural. To him it is only nonsense and the work of idle minds and / or overactive imaginations. However, what he witnessed in the summer of 2004 and thereafter changed his mind somewhat. His first encounter with the spirit-world happened one hot, summer evening as he walked into his apartment around 9:00 p.m. He had been out playing a round of golf at one of the local clubs and was tired and sought the comforts of home.

Above the convenience store there are three apartments, and my uncle's is the one directly above the store. It faces the fields where the tannery had once stood. There was only one entrance and it opened into a large kitchen. This connected to a short hallway that led to the single large bedroom. The bedroom had only one closet at the far right-hand corner of the room. This was the extent of his living quarters, except for the small bathroom off the kitchen.

He entered his apartment by unlocking the one entrance with his key and relocked the door behind him. Grabbing a cup of coffee, he settled down in the easy chair in the corner of the bedroom and watched a half hour of television, then retired to bed. My uncle sleeps soundly, but around 2:30 p.m. he awoke to the shadow of a man looking down at him from above his face, just an arm's length away. The figure had on a black jacket with a hood, which obscured my uncle from seeing his face. It startled him so that he reached a fist towards the intruder to grab him and yelled, "What the ....!" His fist closed on nothing and the shadowy figure backed away, turned, and walked into the closet. My uncle, thinking this was a burglar, jumped from his bed and followed the stranger into the closet. No one was there!

Needless to say, he didn't sleep that night and spent most of the night searching the apartment to make certain that all of the doors were locked and that there was no way anyone could have entered. He also spent some of the time questioning his own eyesight and sanity. When he realized the apartment had not been entered by anyone, he sat up trying to rationalize what he had seen and make some sense of it all. He did admit that more than a few shivers ran up his spine that night.

Since that evening, there were two more incidents with the hooded figure. One night, about seven months later, my uncle awoke for no apparent reason to see that the lights were on in the kitchen. He knew for certain that he had turned off every light in the apartment before he had gone to bed. Nervously, he peered down the short hall to the kitchen. There sat the hooded figure on a chair at the kitchen table, with his back to the bedroom. My uncle yelled something to him, and the figure stood up and walked out of sight. My uncle went into the kitchen to check, half expecting to see him disappear from around the doorsill, but the kitchen was completely empty, and the doors and windows were securely locked.

All of us tell him to move into a new apartment, but he just says the ghost has not harmed him so he is getting used to its being there. Jokingly, he said that the next time the ghost appears, he will offer him a beer. Maybe this entity is one of the roomers who used to board in the old rooming-house that was lost in the fire. He may be trying to discover who this stranger (my uncle) is that is living in his room!

3. My Daughter's Experience

My daughter is the only other person I know who has had a supernatural experience. Here is her story.

I will call her Jane for reasons of personal privacy. Jane works as an admittance administrator in a nursing home in Burlington, Ontario. She has heard many stories from staff and residents alike about peculiar and unexplained events that have happened in her home for the aged. Of course this is the ideal place for such things to happen, as each day residents pass away to another life.

In the early spring, a resident of the facility died. This gentleman was ninety-two years of age and was quite a distinguished-looking man with silver hair. He had been a tall man and had been given to outbursts now and then. His room was his home and he treated it as such. As is customary, a week after his death, the room was given to one of the new residents who was entering the facility. She happened to be a mild-mannered woman who was quiet in all matters. I will call her Emma.

Each day, the nurse would ask Emma how she liked her new room, and each day Emma would answer by shrugging her shoulders and saying it was okay but cold. This she complained of even though extra blankets were given to her and the thermostat was checked and adjusted each day. By the end of the week, Emma's children arrived to visit her. They sought out my daughter and asked that Emma be moved to another room. She just wasn't comfortable in Room 103, so Emma and her belongings were moved to a room down the hall. No sooner had Emma arrived there that she began to feel more at ease, warmer, and pleased with her new surroundings. This sat well with everyone, so this is where Emma stayed.

The next day, the nurse, once again, asked Emma how she liked her new room. Emma replied, "This is much better, thank you. I'm not cold any longer, and that tall, silver-haired man hasn't been back. He made me nervous. Every night he would walk into my room and tell me to get out of his bed! So I like this new room much better."

My daughter and the nurse looked at each other in utter disbelief! Emma had described the previous resident of Room 103, despite the fact that she had not known him and had not even heard of him.

My daughter has stated that she believes that there is more to life than what we can see. With the many incidents and stories that go on in the facilities that are a home to the aged, she no longer questions. "They are lambs while they are here, so I see no reason to be afraid when they pass on," she states, so much wiser than her twenty-seven years.

4. My Friend's Mother

One spring morning, a friend of mine, who was also a neighbour of ours, came across the street for coffee. We — my family and I — lived in Milton, Ontario, on a quiet crescent, in the centre of town. I was born and raised in Milton and knew many of the members of the community. Our visitor was an old friend from highschool and we were busy raising our children together. The year was 1984. I will call her Anna.

Anna's parents were also from the Milton area and Anna was particularly close to her mother. Unfortunately, in 1983, Anna's mother had passed away, suddenly, of heart failure. She had been a widow for the last twelve years of her life.

As soon as Anna entered our foyer, I knew she had something important she wanted to tell me. She appeared as if she hadn't slept very well. "Come on in," I invited. "You look tired. Did you sleep well last night?"

"I'm okay, but I didn't sleep very well last night. I woke up around one-thirty. All of the lights came on in the house and we don't know why. We thought there was something wrong with the wiring, so Barry and I stayed up half the night looking for the problem. We checked everything, but we couldn't find a thing! I know for sure we turned the lights off before we went to bed." She looked back at me, wide-eyed and disbelieving.

"You know what I did notice?" she said.

"What?" I responded.

"The date on the calendar … it was May the 10th … exactly one year from the day my Mom died," she stated with sudden realization. "It must have been her!"

My jaw dropped and I led her in for a strong coffee.

I don't know if this has ever happened again, since Anna and her family have moved away and I've lost touch with her. She seemed comforted by the experience, and I hope that it continues, as she thought her mother was coming to say hello to her.

Who knows?

These are all of the true accounts I know of. If there are more to come, I will certainly write to you. I enjoy reading your books and would like a copy of the book you print my accounts in, if you choose them.

Thanks for reading them anyway!

Sincerely,

Deborah Black

YOU NEVER HAVE TO WORRY

On June 21, 2007, I received the following email. It had no greeting, but it did have a signature. The correspondent, Dorothy Kenworthy, was a person unknown to me. Here is what she wrote:

> I would like to tell you what I experienced at a funeral of a friend named Giles. I did not know him well, but I met he and his wife when they were running the Centre for Light in Surrey, B.C.
>
> Every Friday night they would invite a guest who would bring information about all things spiritual.
>
> Giles died of cancer and had a very peaceful passing. The church was filled with people of all beliefs. Beside the coffin I saw the outline of a man, surrounded from head to thighs in the most vibrant green light, just gently floating up and down.
>
> Around the person conducting the funeral were orbs of brilliant light, and every person who came up to speak or to sing had brilliant auras.

I looked around at the audience, trying to see if anyone else was as astounded as I was (even though I have had many profound experiences). I kept testing my eyes to see if I was really seeing these auras. Each aura was not a fleeting glimpse, it was a steady image.

I remembered hearing from somewhere the statement that if you ask a question you will get an answer. I asked, "If I am really experiencing this, please send me a message." The response came immediately, "You never have to worry." It was so reassuring and peaceful and real: the thought I live by now.

When I got home, I drew a coloured picture of what I saw, and after telling Giles's wife that I thought Giles was there, she said other people had said that too. I gave her the picture I drew.

The experience is very clear in my mind, even though it was about six or seven years ago that it happened.

If you are interested in hearing about other experiences I will be happy to tell you about them.

Good luck with your new book.

Sincerely,

Dorothy Kenworthy

GHOSTS OF BOTH OF MY GRANDPARENTS

I received this intriguing account of ghostly apparitions by email on 15 November 2007. The account is intriguing because it is written in a straight-forward manner that transports the reader right into the heart of the family in question. Here are stories that are told by members of the family —"memorates" about loved ones who do not seem to fully depart the family circle.

I have no explanations for Ms. Boudreau's experiences, other than to describe them as "crisis apparitions," that is, ghostly resemblances of well-loved people that are reportedly seen around the time of deaths. They are commonly reported (as proof of love and loss), or commonly not reported (out of fear of ridicule), by family members.

In her first email, Ms. Boudreau identified herself as C.B. In a subsequent email, replying to mine later the same day, Ms. Boudreau identified herself, her sister Patricia

Ellingwood, and her mother Polett Boudreau. "I did not mention them before as I did not think you would be interested in my story," she wrote. "The haunting took place in the house in which I am living in Halifax. The first haunting happened in 1981, the second in either 1993 or 1994. Things still continue happen to this day."

> I have been trying to decide if this story would suit one of your books. I have decided that you shall be the judge.
>
> My mother has witnessed the ghosts of both of my grandparents; we have lived with my grandmother my whole life in the house my grandfather built. When my sister was small my grandmother used to take her to bed with her and when my parents would get ready to go to bed for the night my mom would go get her and put her in her own bed.
>
> My grandmother had been very sick one night (my sister was about three) when my mother had gone in to get my sister. There stood my dead grandfather at the foot of her bed arms clasped behind his back looking very worried. As my mom opened the door he turned and looked at her sadly. She claims all the hair on her neck stood on end and she just backed out of the room to let him do what ever he had come to do and when she had returned a while later to get my sister he was gone. My mother swears it is true and that she has never felt a more peaceful feeling then when he looked into her eyes. She also swears that he was as solid-looking as someone standing there in the flesh. My grandmother was diagnosed with cancer and a few years after that she passed on. Which leads me to my mother's second encounter.
>
> My grandmother was an avid watcher of the "Shopping Network." It was always playing when I would get home from school. One day while my mom was preparing supper in the kitchen she heard the front door open and the TV turn on to the "Shopping Network." Assuming that it was me returning from school she came in to tell me "homework before television" (one of her famous lines) but I was not there she was alone in the house. When she looked down the hall in the direction of nanny's old room (occupied by me at the time, and a room to this day despite renovations and a double layer of insulation is still cold even on the hottest of summer days) she saw the back of my grandmother

in her favourite dress turn the corner into her room but when she went in to look she was gone.

My grandfather passed before I or my sister was born so neither of us knew what he looked like but when my sister was young she used to spend hours on her little toy phone "talking to granddad." One day she hung up her toy phone and said granddad is coming to visit. My mother laughed and said he had better not dismissing the incident and sent my sister to her room to play. A short time later my sister came out screaming and crying that a man was in her room. My mother assured her she was wrong and upon my sisters request did a thorough check of the house showing her there was no man to be found. But my sister still claimed she was right so out of curiosity she pulled out a photo album and asked my sister to see if the man she saw was in the album. A few pages later sure enough my sister said look mommy there he is. Sure enough it was my grandfather and he indeed had came for the visit he had promised on the little toy phone earlier.

I swear that everything I have written is true and has not been embellished at all.

Yours truly,

C.B

THERE WAS BLOOD ALL OVER THE LIVING ROOM

I received this email on 4 September 2007, just after the long Labour Day weekend. The weekend was a hectic one for me, but this account of living in not one but two haunted houses in Toronto "takes the cake."

Seldom have I read an account that is so horrendous. (I was going to describe it as *horrific*, but there is a slight difference between those two words, though they both descend from the word horror. *Horrendous* events are multiple and follow one other in a seemingly endless chain, whereas a *horrific* event is a unique occurrence, one so bad it is never repeated.) Seldom have I read an account of horrendous events that is as well and as movingly written as this one. I do not know what Ms. Atherstone does for a living, but she might consider taking up writing … fiction … horror fiction!

But this account is not fiction but memoir. The area of the city in which the houses are located is the Parkdale district, and I have accounts of hauntings of dwellings in that west end part of the city, but none on Gladstone or Delaware Avenues. Quite the opposite: I associate Gladstone Avenue with Beatrice Lillie, the vaudevillian who rose to fame "on two continents," where there is a library named the honour of this Toronto native. I associate Delaware Avenue with W.W. E. Ross, the poet who wrote his imagist poems in a modest house there. Now I associate them with the problems faced by Ms. Atherstone.

The reader, like me, will sympathize with Ms. Atherstone for the pain behind this series of disheartening and frightening occurrences. The scary part of it is that there is no *known reason* why all of this — why any of this — should have happened. Maybe the Talmudic scholar knew his stuff and had an answer or two.

Dear Mr. Colombo:

I am not in the habit of writing celebrities as I know it can be a bother to respond, but after reading your book, *Ghost Stories of Canada*, I thought I would dare inflicting you with a couple of questions.

I would like to know if you have any recorded hauntings on Gladstone or Delaware Avenues in Toronto, two houses I have lived in, and the only two places I have lived where supernatural events occurred that had nothing to do with the people residing there, *i.e.*, my family.

In 1982-1983 we lived in a large old house on Gladstone, a few houses north of Dufferin Park. We got used to "the ghost" residing there as events were so frequent. The front door had a large glass pane in it, so we could see who was knocking at the door. Frequently we would hear, then see the doorknob turn, but no-one would be there.

We would also hear footsteps up the stairs and down the upstairs hallway, often passing us while we were in the bathroom with the door open, but would see no-one as the sound of steps continued to pass us. It was sometimes annoying that I would hear my husband in the next room, or my niece coming up the stairs, only to learn I was talking to "no-one" yet again.

The only real problem in that house was that my niece, in her late teens at the time, began being "attacked" in her sleep, once waking up to a heavy weight on her chest and in fear, and we did visually perceive mist spontaneously appearing, then fading as quickly, in her bedroom. These occurrences were accompanied by a drop in room temperature and a bad feeling, but we did not believe the house ghost was the perpetrator; my niece, in fact, believed it was a relative who had hanged himself in jail, and was being drawn to her by a photograph she kept by the bed.

A few years later, I was living alone with my children in an old house on Delaware Avenue, on the second block north of Bloor Street, and had a female tenant in the basement. My husband had made it clear he would only refrain from disputing custody on the condition I had a house (difficult to rent on a secretary's salary), and this decrepit Victorian house was the only one I found that I could afford. This is why it took so long for me to find another more suitable house.

I found some newspapers stuffed in behind the huge and still working bulbs of an ancient heater that had been painted over in the living room; the dates were 1919, so the house had to be at least that old.

About a year before the event I shall describe (in 1985), my daughter had been hounded by a large and unusual Irish wolfhound, none of the rest of us could see (and which she remembers clearly to this day). Being a Christian, I had a problem with some of the ideas my daughter was starting to come up with that she attributed to the dog, so a friend arranged for a Talmudic scholar to come over and say some prayers, which made the dog go away. However, about a year later something happened that I have never heard the likes of before or since, and have not spoken of to many people.

One evening after watching the late news on CTV, when the sports came on, I left the small living room to go do the dishes before going to bed. While I was finishing the dishes in the sink, I looked over to our round wooden table to see if there were any I had missed, and noticed something about the table that looked odd, as if it were covered in molasses and dripping. I went over to it with the dish rag, and found it to be puddles of blood, some starting to thicken away from the edges of the puddles. There was blood dripping to the floor, over the handles of my captain's chair, and it seemed to be trailing back to the living room. The floor on the main floor is white ceramic tiling, so this showed up very well.

I followed the trail, thinking one of my cats must have been hurt, but confused as I had not seen the cats at all in the past while, knowing they preferred to be outside on hot nights. None of the trail had been stepped in, as it would have been had it been there when I came down the hall into the kitchen.

The blood led back into the living room, and was splashed all over the screen of the TV I had just been watching a few moments before. There was blood all over the living room, and a hand-print on the wall about six feet up, to the left of my piano. There was blood all over the foyer leading up the stairs, down the hall, and into my bedroom. The blood led up to a low window beside my bed, where there was another hand-print with splayed fingers. There was no blood on my bed or on anything other than the surface of the table, floors, TV, and walls.

I called the basement tenant up to see this. She looked at me strangely, but helped me to try to get the cats in. They would not come to the house; my one beauty stayed in the yard, but she would not enter. I felt numb and overwhelmed and went to bed without cleaning up the mess. My kids asked what had happened the next morning, but I gave them a hasty breakfast and shooed them out to school.

At work, I burst into tears in the ladies' room and told a colleague what had transpired. She told me to phone the police when I got home. I also phoned a trusted friend, a physician who was also a minister, and she arranged to come over after work to see this stuff for herself.

The police said it had to be a cat, that they could cut their tongue and bleed a lot. I pointed out that there was more blood splashed around the house than a cat could contain, and they said, oh, it just looked like a lot. I asked how the hand-prints would have appeared from a cat cutting itself, and they said one of my kids must have done it. (None of us had the adult size or shape of these hand-prints, nor were the kids awake when this happened; I had been completely alone.)

My friend looked at it all and observed that I really did not know how to react, and that no-one really would, but that this was definitely real. She said prayers throughout the house and comforted me. She also conferred with a psychic (I don't know who), who told her that there had to be a woman in my life who wished me evil, possibly the tenant, and this was probably what was behind the manifestation of blood, though there had been no human presence when it occurred.

My family and I continued to have unusual problems that seemed to come out of nowhere the whole time we lived in the house, from 1983 to 1989. I am not suggesting that the house caused such problems, merely that it was coincidental that so many problems would plague a woman and two children, almost non-stop (dire illnesses, suddenly being infested horrendously by cockroaches, attacks on the children by strangers, fires in outlets, extreme cold in the kitchen, etc.).

When I moved to the Beaches, all such badness stopped, only the effects of things that had been initiated while living in that house; even my ex-husband stopped coming over to stand on my lawn to yell at me, bad behaviour he had never engaged in before or after.

Though my children and niece, now grown, still show the effects of those years, very little has occurred in their families to compare with what they experienced as children.

If you have heard of such manifestations occurring on those streets, or anything like them at all, I would be most interested to learn of them.

Thank you for your time in reading this,

Ann Atherstone

FORT STEEL GHOST ROAD EXPERIENCE

For Halloween 2007, radio host Joe Easingwood invited me to be his telephone guest on his talk show for listeners in the Victoria, B.C. area. I have been on his lively CFAX show a number of times. I agreed because I like Joe. He is enthusiastic and talkative, but on this occasion it happened (as it sometimes does) that our timing was off, with host and guest both talking at the same time! Maybe it makes good listening!

I was not Joe's sole guest. John Adams, the local historian who organizes the city's "Ghostly Walks," was the other guest. This gave me the opportunity to remind Mr. Adams of how much I had enjoyed taking the walk he organized about seven years ago. I told him and radio listeners, "It is the second-best ghostly walk I have taken in numerous countries on two continents." Joe naturally inquired about the "first-best ghostly walk," and I replied, "It was in York, which is considered England's most haunted city, sometimes the most haunted community in Europe. The guide was very knowledgeable about local history and ghostly lore — just as Mr. Adams knows all about Victoria's older buildings and all the local ghost stories." I urged those Victorians who had not already done so to sign up for the early evening walk.

Joe's program is a phone-in show, so listeners were invited to call us and share their stories with us. Half a dozen callers did so. I was most impressed with one caller, Darren Skaalrud, who in a very organized and confident manner, told an incredible but fascinating story of what had happened to him in 1985. On air I urged him to email the account to me, but he confessed that he still used pen and paper! During one of the many commercial breaks, I gave him my mailing address. To my pleasure, there arrived a five-page, handwritten letter on lined paper. I read it with interest and then keyboarded the text. I reproduce it pretty well as I received it, adding only some punctuation. I am grateful to Mr. Skaalrud for sharing this experience with me and my readers.

What to make of it? I have no doubt that this account is a truthful one. Some people are more psychic than others and maybe Mr. Skaalrud is psychic. That sounds like a serious statement, but what are psychical properties? Sensitivity, intuition? Imagination, mirage? Who knows? I urge the reader to decide after reading this account of the phantom procession that crossed a gravel road in the dead of night. It was certainly scary!

Oct. 31, 2007
Dear John Colombo:

The 1985 Fort Steele Road Ghost Experience

Back in 1985 myself Darren A. Skaalrud age 24 at the time and my friend Brian Irving Shaw age 22 at the time were driving South in the Columbia Valley from Golden, B.C., Canada, and we decided to take a short-cut to bypass Cranbrook and turned east along the Fort Steel Road, a gravel road at the time. It was a very clear sky that night, in late June, with lots of stars visible, not a cloud in sight. Everything was normal for several miles, then all of a sudden there was a solid flat wall of fog standing about 20 feet high and spanning the entire road. As we passed into it, it soon mellowed to a very eerie flowing mist about 1 ft high spanning the road and sides. We slowed down to about 30 km and travelled about 1/4 mile or so, when all of a sudden there were several glowing white people coming up from the lower side of a shoulder on the East side of the road. They were all very well dressed in Victorian style clothes. Some of the men I remember were wearing long tail tuxedos, with frill-collar shirts and top hats and boleros. Some men had beards and or moustaches, and the ladies were wearing bell-style dresses and bowl hats with feathers. Some had umbrellas and canes. All of these people were adults. A very large group of at least 40 people emerged onto the road. We were about 200 ft from the place they were when we first saw them, and as we got closer, they turned and looked directly at us coming toward them as they continued to keep going across the road. As the pick-up truck we were in closed in on the group, we quickly locked our doors as we were escalating into a serious state of fear. Our eyes must have looked bugged out. The truck then made contact with the group and I remember clearly the front end of the truck didn't knock any of them down. The truck passed right though them. Some of the people looked and responded and lifted their hands in a friendly way and I remember one man with his top hat smiled at us. We got so freaked out I said to Brian, let's get out of here, right now. He agreed and we picked up speed even with the trailer we were pulling. We soon left the group of ghosts behind us, but we didn't know if any had climbed aboard. So we went down the fog-covered road and soon passed through a solid wall about 20 ft high of fog and the road was clear. We travelled for a few miles and agreed to pull over and have a talk. We quickly agreed to let one of us tell what he had seen without interruption and the other would listen to the story and we agreed not to change what we were going to say when it was his chance to speak. After we had both shared our sightings to each other, we agreed we both had seen the same thing, and we were both still experiencing that state of fear. We couldn't believe the clear visible look we had with these ghosts, and the clothes they were wearing. It made us have goose bumps all over. Then we got up the courage to unlock the doors and inspect the truck and trailer for any hangers-on. Thankfully it was all clear and we carried on to Fernie, B.C., and Sparwood, B.C., our final destination. Since this incredible experience we returned to the same road three months later and we encountered the wall of fog but had no sightings as we passed through the same eerie mist flowing across the road for maybe 2 km and passed through the final wall with no ghosts. On other trips me and Brian had visited the old ghost town of Fort Steele and checked it out really well all of it during the daytime. I'm not sure if I wanna be there at night time. Me and Brian have talked about our ghost group sighting of 1985 may times and we have shared our story with friends and even added we could call each other to let our friends spontaneously confirm the story right after one of us had told them, and I must say every time I talk about it I can always recall in my mind what I saw, like playing back a video file, and I still get goose bumps and sometimes I get tears just by talking about this event. It's been 22 years since the incident. I haven't seen a single ghost since 1985 and I'm happy about this. I still share my story for family and friends' 8 year old son Nazareth loves to hear the story and he asked me to draw a picture of them about 2 months ago, the picture is since gone in the recycle box. So its gone. You can call Brian Shaw in Edmonton at [phone number suppressed], me and Brian haven't called each other for several months. But he might share his story with you. This is a true story as told by B.C. resident Darren A. Skaalrud [mailing address suppressed], if you have further questions. Call me or write if you are gonna use my story in your book. Please contact both of us as this story hasn't been published before. O.K. Alright.

Sincerely,

Darren A. Skaalrud

JEWELLERY BOX MUSIC

Kevin Pickett sent me the emails that appear here. I have never met him but I feel I know him because he writes so well: direct, self-reflective, reasonable. He explains who he is and he has an intriguing story about an experience that occurred to him and some of his buddies at a summer camp in Ontario a decade or so ago. It quite puzzling, and as Mr. Pickett explains, "haunting." Make of it what you will. I find myself wondering, as does Mr. Pickett, why his buddies would not own up to being scared that night in the woods.

9 Aug. 2007
Greetings, Mr. Colombo,

I was just wondering whether or not you are still collecting ghostly accounts. I'm not sure if I believe in ghosts or any of that stuff, and have had few experiences that I couldn't explain away with a bit of effort. However, there is this one thing that happened to me and some friends when I was a teen that I have not been able to forget. Anyway, if you're still gathering, let me know if you'd like to hear about it.

Thanks, Kevin Pickett

13 Aug. 2007
Dear Mr. Pickett:

Yes, yes, I am still collecting.

Please send your account or accounts, in as much detail as possible, and I will respond quickly. (I was in Montreal when your email arrived.)

Best,

JR

14 Aug. 2007
Greetings once again, Mr. Colombo:

My account is attached to this email. If you've any questions regarding it, please don't hesitate to ask. I've noticed that you sometimes include a little something about the contributors in your books, so I think it's best that I tell you about me.

I am a graduate from McMaster University and hold degrees in philosophy, English, and History. Currently, I am a supply teacher with the District School Board of Niagara. I am twenty-seven years old and live in Hamilton, Ontario, with my wife.

Right now, I'm in a bit of rush, so I'll keep it short. This story is one of two strange things that happened to me at Braeside; I just remembered a second one that is not as long, but still weird. I've done my best to remember everything exactly as it occurred, and swear that this story really is true. I hope my transparency gives me some credit.

Cheers,

Kevin Pickett

When I was fifteen, something very strange happened to me and my friends while we were at summer camp. The camp is called Braeside, and it's out in Paris, Ontario, which is about three minutes drive from Brantford. Even though it's pretty close to the city, the camp is kind of remote, surrounded by a fair amount of forest and wilderness. In any case, Braeside has been around for at least sixty or more years, I think, and parts of the place seem to have been neglected and forgotten. The reason I know that certain places in the camp have been forgotten is because we (my friends and I) used to always break the midnight curfew by hanging out in "forgotten" places where the security guards never bothered to patrol. That's right, there were security guards at a summer camp for teenagers; the camp itself was the most boring place on earth, so breaking curfew to hang out was about the most fun we could get. There were a few places you could go, where you wouldn't get caught: there was the hill at the one edge of the camp, which was overgrown with thorn bushes and small, rotten-looking trees. Obviously, the hill wasn't the best or most comfortable place to hang out, so we only used it as a last resort (or if we were being chased by the guards, the hill was a good hiding place). Another option was to pass the fence on the other side of camp, cross the highway, and find this tiny clearing that overlooked the Grand River; the clearing was called "Lester" for some reason that I never figured out. The final place to dodge curfew was just left of the hill, at what may be called the very corner of the camp. When I was younger, there were all these abandoned shacks along a dirt road. I can't remember when they were replaced, but stories abounded that one or more of them were haunted. However, I never experienced anything more than an uneasy feeling when I looked at them that probably had more to do with imagination than the supernatural. In any case, these shacks and the road they stood on figures into this account geographically only.

It was late at night, past the midnight curfew, and my friends and I were out walking. We were all around fifteen or sixteen. It was a somewhat rainy evening and so we avoided the hill and "Lester" because the grass was wet. Our last option was to walk the back roads near to where the creepy shacks used to be.

As the five of us made our way along the dirt road where the shacks used to be (they were torn down by this point), we began to hear, very distinctly, the sound of music; I call it jewellery box music for lack of a better term. I'm sure there's an actual word for it, I just don't know what it is. The music sounded close. We were bored and decided to find out where it was coming from. I don't think any of us found it odd, at that point, that someone would have very loud, jewellery box music playing outside, past midnight. No one said anything about it anyway.

We turned off the dirt road and onto the paved one that led past the pool and eventually ran parallel to the wire fence that stood perpendicular to the camp's hill (essentially the corner of the camp). The music continued to play and we kept following along the wire fence until we noticed that part of the fence had been stamped down. Beyond this point, we noticed an overgrown, dirt road that was no longer used; it ran straight into the fence. With little hesitation, we past over the wire fence with ease, and began to follow the music along the forgotten road. This is about the point where I, and my friends I'm sure, began to feel wary. The only light out there came from the camp and we were slowly moving away from that. To make matters worse for us, a sweeping fog suddenly rolled in overtop of our company and within seconds we could barely see anything at all. Keep in mind the music; the music was still playing. I was genuinely afraid. In my pocket, I had what might've been the smallest knife on the planet; I doubt it could cut open an envelope. All of us, I believe, had this sense that something bad was going to happen to us. One of my friends noticed that I'd unfolded my minuscule blade; when I noticed that he'd noticed, I said, very seriously, "I'm ready." He laughed, and I felt pretty dumb until I saw him pick up a stick and smack it into his palm. Another one of my friends had taken out his admittedly better knife as well (back then it was cool to pack a knife).

In the midst of the fog, I think we moved on slowly until we reached a copse of pine trees. The ground was a bit hilly here and we managed to leave the fog behind as we past under the branches; we had to bend down a bit as we walked. I could see that we'd stayed on the overgrown road we'd started on, but couldn't see very much at all once we'd gone deeper into the trees. That was when one of my friends suggested we go back. Somebody laughed at him and that pretty much sealed our going on; we were teenage boys trying to prove that we were men. Really, added the peer pressure just meant that we were all afraid. Against all of our better judgment, we continued to follow the music; something of note here is the fact that I don't recall the music getting any quieter or louder. It seemed to be the exact same volume from the camp onwards until we reached its source; then it was very loud.

We stumbled through the trees for I'm not sure how long. I can't recall exactly who suggested (it might've been me), but we were soon all holding the shoulders of the person in front of us so that we wouldn't get separated. I'm sure it would've looked very peculiar or scary even to passers-by, out there in the country, to see five boys come marching out of the trees, in a line, onto the highway. I call it a highway, which it is, though it is nothing more than a small, two-way road that is usually quiet during the night.

The place where we exited onto to the road was still very dark. I felt the difference under my feet, but had to bend down and touch it with my hand before I realized that it was indeed the road. Across the highway was another line of huge, pine trees that hid a large house. We could see an outdoor light in the yard there, and we determined that the jewellery box music was coming from there. Together, we pushed into the wall of trees until we hit a solid, wooden fence.

As soon as I peeked through the music suddenly ceased. A woman, I think, dressed all in white was standing near a small table; I couldn't see her face and couldn't tell you much about her. Within seconds of our arrival, she darted away, into her house I guess. The light went out and we were in total darkness again. We made our way back out to the road, and found that we weren't exactly sure which direction along the highway led back to the camp.

Fortunately, one of us had a decent sense of direction and picked the right way. We walked along the grassy edge of the road until we reached the main entrance to the camp. The security guard didn't appear pleased to see us, but we were very happy to see him. He made us go back to our respective trailers and cottages, so we never got a chance to talk about everything that happened then.

By the time I was back at my trailer, everyone was asleep; I ended up in my sleeping bag, staring up at the ceiling, just thinking about the weirdness of the whole ordeal, wondering if there was anything miraculous or supernatural about any of it. Certainly, it was a strange set of circumstances and coincidences, but not impossible. I fell asleep rationalizing.

I woke up early the next day, ate, showered, did everything I normally do, and then set out to the tuck shop where I could expect to meet my friends. Sure enough, I found all of them there, sitting at a picnic table. Immediately, I brought up our nighttime adventure. Just as fast, they each went tight-lipped. I remember saying something like, "It was pretty freaky, eh?" Not one of them would even open their mouths to agree with this sentiment. They didn't want to talk about it then or later! Before we drifted apart, I tried to bring it up, at least once every summer; never, and I mean never, did any of them say a word about it. To me, this is the oddest part of the whole experience.

What occurred during that night that I might've missed? As you might've already guessed, I am the type of person that seeks, sometimes in vain, a rational explanation to everything. Fortunately, this is probably why I was attracted to and majored in Philosophy at university. Unfortunately, I'm afraid this tendency has imposed on me a reputation as an excruciatingly severe critic and tenacious logician. In other words, a joy-killer capable of coring the most basic of statements, heaping doubt on deeply ingrained and accepted beliefs, and, most importantly, finding the logical explanation.

Yet, I've never forgotten this incident. Too many coincidences of eerie occurrences, the music, the fog, the woman in white I couldn't quite see, does amount to a pile of circumstantial evidence for the possibility of the supernatural. However, the fact that my friends did not want to delve into the incident tells me, logically, that something substantial occurred that night that was unsettling enough, perhaps even supernatural, that they'd rather forget it altogether.

I haven't seen any of them for years. It's too bad (for them) that I will be bringing up this event the moment chance allows us to meet once again. For it would be accurate to suggest that this strange night haunts me still.

I forgot to mention that I did try to find that huge house a few days later, but couldn't figure out if I did. When my friends and I walked away from there, I guess I lost track of how far it was from the camp. Also, I believe a year or so later, somebody bought some land in that area to start up a canoe business on the Grand River. (I think this is has come and gone now however). The old road at the back, however, was still there the last time I visited Braeside, which was in 2002 I believe. Finally, I recall hearing a story, from my mother I think, that the camp had once been involved in some sort of drug ring a long time ago; unfortunately, I don't know anything more about this.

GHOSTS DO EXIST

I received this email with its attachment on July 29, 2007. The correspondent is unknown to me but, in a sense, I believe I know her, if only because the experience she describes is reassuringly similar to other experiences that have been described to me by otherwise unknown correspondents. What are being described are poltergeist-like events or experiences: no visible spirit, but mindless otherwise-inexplicable activity.

There are two schools of thought here. The first is that each paranormal experience or event is unique — no two are alike. The second is that paranormal experiences and events fall into categories — they have features and factors in common. I subscribe to the latter view, and so does Ms. Inglesi, I believe. If they have features in common, we can learn from them. If each one is wholly individual, the sense of reality and residual knowledge that it conveys cannot be communicated to anyone else: a loss, to be sure!

I do not know what caused the pictures to fall especially if the nails that hold them to the wall remain in place. In answer to Ms. Inglesi's concern about publication, her story "has enough spook"! It is reproduced here with the minimum of copy editing.

Dear Mr. Colombo:

I have recently started your series of books on Canadian hauntings. I find the stories fascinating — not only by the account of which they were written, but because I can imagine the truth behind them. I have been a firm believer in ghosts all my life, and have even tried to seek them out by visiting supposedly haunted places. Unfortunately, I haven't had much luck with that.

However, I have had a few unsought experiences of my own, and here I have attached an account of one that had taken place in the early 1990s in my childhood home. The first part of it is very similar to a story I just read in one of your books published in 2005. Actually, if I hadn't read that, I probably wouldn't have thought to write you this letter, but it was too similar an account I thought you would've had the pleasure of knowing.

I would love to see this story published in one of your books, if you feel it has enough spook. I also would just love to hear your comments.

Thank you.

Antonella Inglesi

Dear Mr. Colombo:

I write to you this letter by my own free will and am not ashamed to say that even though the world around me is a skeptic, I have believed and always will that ghosts exist; and, there may have been one or two in my very own childhood home.

I rushed to my computer this evening after reading a similar account of the story I'm about to unfold in your very own "True Canadian" series of books of which I am a fan. Upon reading the story I was truly convinced that our experience was more than just a case of "coincidence."

My family and I lived in a house in central Scarborough on Applefield Drive. My parents were the second owners of the home, and I don't know much about the first homeowner or his family except that a death had occurred either to a close family member or friend of his, or in the house itself.

My family ate dinners quite early in the evening. I was about 10 or 11 years old when the five of us had sat down for dinner. Our house was a bungalow built with two kitchens and two dinette areas, one of both on each floor. Also on the upper floor was a formal dining room, occasionally used. We generally occupied the basement dinette for informal dinners, and this was one of them. I don't remember the exact time, but it would have been between 4:30 and 5:00 p.m., when suddenly all of us were startled by the sound of a loud thud. We thought the noise was generated outside, but we investigated the house just in case. In the formal dining room, my mom had a collection of large floral paintings in their original solid wood frames. Well, the loud thud was made by one of the hanging pictures as it fell to the floor. Ironically, the nail was still intact.

The day after, we sat for dinner again. Although we were astonished by the picture falling, as no one had been in contact with it especially as the room was so rarely used, we thought nothing of it.

We began our dinner, and just as the night before, we heard another loud thud. I looked at the clock, and although today I cannot recall the time I saw then, I was certain the time was down to the very minute as the time when the picture had fallen the night before. We ran upstairs again to investigate that a new picture had taken a fall, but this one was a photo taken of me in Italy a few years before. The picture and the frame were left hanging. What had made the terrible noise was the falling of the glass that protected the picture and its impact on the furniture. The glass did not break.

I've used this story to tell to friends and family in persuasion that ghosts do exist. I didn't have many other accounts with this one though. However, I do remember one night going to bed after all the others, but not being able to sleep, so I just lay there. We were in the process of renovating our basement family room and we had boxes full of our junk sitting in the foyer, out of the way. Since my ears are like those of a bat, I could hear footsteps in the basement walking across that floor even with my door of my bedroom closed. And, we didn't have chains, but I could hear the sound of chains slapping against the floor as if someone had tied them around those tiles and dragging them.

My mom had relived some of her experiences to me, but for about ten years after that we didn't have any other stories to tell. I wonder if the current owners do.

THE SINGING WAS COMING FROM BEHIND ME

Theatre buildings are places where comedies and tragedies are staged and where the human emotions are given free range of expression. Those buildings that are the homes of theatrical and musical groups are often among the oldest buildings in the community. So it is not surprising that ghosts and spirits seem to linger in such precincts. They seem like "holdovers" from the past. But most of the stories of hauntings are simply that: stories that took place decades ago, traditions hoary with age. Readers of my earlier books may remember meeting with accounts of supernatural events reported to have taken place in theatres in Vancouver, Winnipeg, Whitby, London, Toronto, Montreal, Halifax, and other Canadian towns and cities.

Here, in contrast, is a richly detailed account of a hunting of a theater in modern times, reported by a woman who is observant and sensitive to her surroundings. What to make of her experience? It is hard to say. The building itself is described in fine detail. The fact that the singing and other sounds she reported hearing were also heard by her colleague, the producer of the show, and the fact that the two of them assumed the noises were caused by the set designer rather than a poltergeist or "noisy ghost," all add verisimilitude to the account. The uneasiness they experienced is easily shared by the reader. I know that I shuddered as I read the account.

It is a shame, in a way, that the former school house has been renovated. Ghosts seldom survive renovations! One wonders where the white-haired man now makes his home.

Sunday, May 06, 2007
Dear Mr. Colombo,

I have just finished reading *More True Canadian Ghost Stories* and noticed in the acknowledgements an invitation to readers to send in our stories to you. Are you still accepting stories, because I have one that happened to me in a small theatre on Vancouver Island that I could send if you are interested?

Let me know and I will send it to you right away. I really enjoy your ghost story books and hope there are more to come!

Thank you.

Sincerely,

Sophia Maher

Here is my account of the haunting I experienced in a small theatre in Nanaimo. I hope you enjoy it.

My name is Sophia Maher and I am a theatre artist and entertainer who lives in North Vancouver with my husband and very new baby son. I have lived in the Lower Mainland since 2001 and before that lived in Nanaimo on Vancouver Island.

I moved to Nanaimo from Edmonton, with my family, in 1995. My mother, sister and I have all had our share of strange experiences with the unknown, but we have never sought out such experiences, nor do we put much thought into the meaning of them once they have occurred. That is not to say that they are easily forgotten and they seem to live on in the "Well, that was creepy!" file in our memories.

One of the weirdest experiences I've had took place in September of 1997 at a small studio theatre in Nanaimo. The building belongs to the local community theatre group with whom I had been involved since moving to Nanaimo. I believe it used to be a small school house but has been owned by the theatre group since the '50s. There are many ghost stories attached to the building, with reports of entities having been sighted in the dressing rooms, the bathroom, on-stage, backstage and in the house. By the time this took place, I had already experienced a few hair-raising moments and was getting used to the obligatory cold spots, self-closing doors, lights that turned on and off at will, and all the other bumps and bangs that seem to come with a haunted building.

That fall I was stage managing a show at the theatre, and so was responsible for arriving early, unlocking the building, disarming the alarm, and setting everything up for rehearsal. I unlocked the main door and left it open, disarmed the alarm, then walked straight through to the kitchen door, leaving it open as I passed through, then into the lobby, leaving that door open as well. These three doors are all in a row so that if you are standing in the lobby and they're all open, and you can see straight out into the parking lot. I then dropped my bag in the lobby and passed back into the kitchen.

Suddenly, as I was making coffee, all three doors slammed shut in unison — not one after the other, but at exactly the same time. Needless to say, I jumped out of my skin at the noise and it wasn't until I had taken a few breaths that the eeriness of what had just taken place struck me. There was no wind that night, it was a calm still evening, but I was willing to entertain that it had been a rogue gust strong enough to blow through the entrance, kitchen, and straight to the lobby with enough force to slam all three doors, and so I continued with my coffee-making.

The coffee maker is situated on the bar and so the kitchen is open, over the bar, to the lobby. It was not long before I could distinctly hear footsteps squeaking across the lobby floor. I stopped what I was doing and really listened. Sure enough it was as though someone was walking through the lobby right in front of me, yet I was definitely the only one there. I listened for a few more seconds, the sound stopped, and I finished what I was doing and walked into the lobby to retrieve my bag and move into the theatre.

There is a long hall that passes by the theatre door and down toward the back of the theatre. If you follow it, you end up at the washrooms, and further back is a small hallway to the right for storage and the props room which is always freezing and smells like death due to the mouse traps, although you can imagine it adds greatly to the ambience! I paused at the entrance to the theatre long enough to turn on the light by the box office and to glance down the darkened hallway and decide to leave those lights off for now. I entered the theatre, propped the door open, and turned on the lights. As I walked toward my table in the front row, I could hear a faint singing. I thought it was coming from outside. I put down my bag and crossed to the emergency exit that opens to the parking lot. I stuck my head out and it was only then that I realized that the singing was coming from behind me, in the theatre! I knew there was no one else there because I had one of the only sets of keys, and even if someone else had come in, they would have had to have come in after me because I had disarmed the building, and therefore would have run into me. I stood in front of the stage and realized the sound was coming from upstage left. It would alternate with a mumbling, and then back to singing. I stepped onto the stage and slowly walked towards the sound until I came upon the spot it seemed to be coming from, very much hoping that someone of flesh and blood was hiding in the wings playing a trick on me, at which point the sound stopped and all I could hear was my heart pounding. I decided to continue setting up, and as I did I found myself desperately trying to explain the events that had taken place.

While I was unpacking my bag at the table, I had just about convinced myself that it was all my imagination. I glanced toward the door into the theatre and saw a man walk past the door and down the darkened hallway. He had white hair and was wearing a white shirt, and while the quick glimpse I had of him didn't afford me any more details about his countenance, I was certain that he was no one I had ever met. With the hair on the back of my neck standing up, I quickly walked over to the door and looked down the hallway, but no one was there. I called out but received no answer. I even went so far as to walk down the hallway, turn on the lights and have a look around. There was no one there; I was alone in the building.

At that point I felt I had reached my limit and so I left my set-up and decided to wait in the lobby for someone else to arrive. I would have liked to have waited in the parking lot, but as stage manager it is important to retain some dignity, so I parked myself on a couch in the lobby and waited. The next person to arrive was the producer of the show who is also a good friend of mine. He sat down by me and we had a cursory conversation about the weather or some such thing until I could take it no more and I told him all that had happened thus far. He had also had strange experiences in that building, so he suggested that we both wait in the lobby for a few more people to arrive. I thought that was an excellent idea.

It wasn't long, as we sat there, before we could hear banging and clunking noises coming from the theatre. These are not strange noises to hear at the onset of rehearsal because often the set designer arrives with some new set pieces and will install them for the rehearsal that night. He also has keys and will let himself in through the side door, straight into the theatre, and so would not have passed by us. The noises sounded exactly like wood being dropped off onto the stage and heavy footsteps walking around.

We were sitting by the door that leads to backstage and the noises were very clear and recognizable, so we were not alarmed. My friend said he would go and say hello and see if the designer needed any help, and he disappeared into the theatre. It was not long before he emerged quite quickly from the theatre and announced that there was no one there and that the stage was still bare. I went in and had a quick look, and sure enough there were no signs of the designer having arrived yet, and everything was just as I had left it upon my rapid departure. We looked out into the parking lot and his truck was nowhere to be seen, nor were there any signs of anyone around at all. We both decided that the parking lot was the place to be on such a lovely night and beat a hasty retreat from the building, pausing only to pour ourselves each a cup of coffee on the way out. We did not go back in until a few people had gathered, and by that time all of the spirits had seemingly gone back to sleep.

This is a true and unexaggerated account of my experiences that evening. As I've already stated, there are many other stories associated with the building, but interestingly all haunting activity seemed to stop there after a rather extensive renovation was done on the building a year or so later.

I hope this story has peaked your interest, as it has certainly lived on in infamy in my memory! Please feel free to edit it however you wish.

A MAN DRESSED ALL IN BLACK

This email arrived on a bright fall morning, 30 October 2007. Despite the warm weather in Toronto, where I read it, the events described in the email, which took place six or so years ago in Souris, N.S., sent shivers up and down my spine.

I am reproducing Ms. Holland's account the way she wrote it, with some routine copy editing. (For instance, she likes to refer to her boy friend as "bf" and readers are likely to find this abbreviation distracting!)

What to make of this account? Some psychical researchers and parapsychologists maintain that it is people who are haunted, not places. Is Crystal Holland — what a wonderful first name! — haunted? It does not seem so. Is the 110-year-old house she shared with her boy friend haunted? It seems so, and there is a tradition that it has been for some time, though its haunting seems not to bother the boyfriend (or his new girlfriend). Perhaps the disturbances occur only when Ms. Holland is in the house.

It is easy to ask questions, impossible to answer them to everyone's satisfaction. In the meantime, all we can do is read about these odd and scary occurrences.

Hello!

I just recently read your book *The Midnight Hour* and was amazed by all the stories. I would like to share my experiences with you I hope you will be interested in hearing. :)

It was about 6 years ago, November of 2001, when I and my boy friend bought a old house in the small town of Souris, P.E.I. It is located on a side road called Chapel Street. At the time the thought of owning this house was rather exciting but we knew it would need a lot of renovations as we had a baby due within a month. The price was cheap and we bought it through a friend of the family, I loved the fact that we had our own house and wanted to move in right away. Never once did we hear of any stories or anything bad about the house before we moved in, but the previous owners had simply just moved and left most of their belongings behind so we had to deal with a lot of old furniture and such.

Our first few months in the house were normal, at least until our son was born in December. The first strange thing I recall happening was hearing a baby cry in the middle of the night. This doesn't seem strange at all, except it wasn't my baby. This happened more then once but I didn't really think much of it at the time, My boy friend didn't really believe in ghosts and stuff, and he just kept on saying that it was our imagination. (He soon changed his mind.)

In our 110-year-old house, there was a doorway that lead from the master bedroom. If you opened this door, you would go into this small hallway, with barely enough room to walk in there, and you had to duck so you wouldn't hit your head. It was creepy and when you get to the end of this hallway you come to another door and in there was a bathroom and a wide open space (which we used for storage at the time). The first time I went into this space, or room rather, I had this really strange feeling that someone was in there, when obviously there wasn't. I wouldn't be able to stay in there for more then 5 minutes before getting freaked out, and I would run out of the room slamming the door behind me, The air was different in there, much colder then the rest of the house. I thought this was odd but of course my boy friend had an explanation for everything at that time. And once again I thought nothing of it.

Time went by and more and more strange things started to happen. My son was a little older then, and he got into a stage where he refused to sleep in his bedroom. I thought it might be just a stage he was going through, but he would wake up screaming in terror as if he had seen something. This happened every night, until I moved his things into a different bedroom and he slept fine again after that.

The strange encounters would happen more often and finally my boy friend started to realize that just maybe there wasn't an answer for the things going on. We started to give our ghost a name and joked about it often. It seemed that our "ghost" liked to trick us with the same objects, such as the washing machine. I would simply put the clothes in the washer and put the lid down with the washer going and leave the room. It usually happened that about 5 minutes after I left the room the washer would stop and the lid would go up. It only happened if nobody was in the room. Things like that would get very annoying and we knew that we had something or someone with us. The microwave would turn on by itself, TV's, radios … pretty much anything electronic. After a while we just got used to it. I can't explain it, but I wasn't scared, but I get goose bumps today as I write this.

Our relationship changed over time, and like any bad relationship there were a lot of fights and much anger every day. The "strange events" would be different as well. Eventually I was too scared to stay in the house by myself. It was a different feeling then than it was before.

I was almost scared to take a shower because I felt like someone was standing in the room watching me all the time. I would sit and watch TV and have the same feeling too. One time I was in the kitchen making lunch and felt a presence behind me and almost like a shiver going up my spine, kind of like someone was breathing on my neck.

The first time I ever saw something was the night I was lying in bed and couldn't sleep at all. Once again I had the feeling that someone was watching me all the time. I got up to get a drink and to watch some TV and was alone downstairs … I wasn't down there 5 minutes before I heard my hair dryer turned on in the bathroom. I ran in to find that it was, *yes*, turned on, but it was truly as red as blood, and hot to the touch too. I unplugged it and it went back to normal. I went back to bed after that to try and get what had just happened out of my mind. Finally I drifted off to sleep but I woke up to a noise that startled me. In my doorway was a man dressed all in black looking towards me. My heart jumped into my throat and I screamed and that woke up my boy friend. After that the "man" was gone. That did it for me, I started sleeping in the spare bedroom, but still had those feelings at night that someone was there watching.

Another day shortly after that I had a fight with my boy friend and he left the house to go to see a friend. I was pretty angry and decided to leave the house to go for a drive as well. Well, our fight didn't last long because we came home together and our house door was locked as usual and so was all of the house. But something was odd. When we walked into the kitchen, things were moved from their places. The most obvious was in the living room where pieces of our furniture were turned over on their sides. We checked all of the house for any break-and-enter, but it was impossible for someone to get in or out. The master bedroom was the most disturbed, The blankets on the bed were pulled off. All the clothes out of *my* dresser were thrown all over the room. The television was unplugged and on the floor upside down. As well, every electronic device was unplugged and on the floor. I stayed at my mother's that night I was too scared.

A few years passed by and we decided to renovate the house. We pretty much gutted out the whole place and did it room by room. And one day while we were working on the outside, a few elderly ladies stopped by to see the house. They had grown up in the house and were curious. One of the ladies told me stories of the house and one of the stories just happened to be about the room upstairs that I was scared of. Her sisters would be made to clean the room (which was used as a storage closet at their time) and they would be crying from fear of the room. I told her about all the things that happened in the house and she wasn't surprised at all. It ended up that nobody had wanted to stay over at the house for the night, as they would hear strange things in the night.

I could really go on and on about all the things that had happened there, but it would be too much because all these things happened everyday.

Every detail in this e-mail is true and not lies. To this day my (ex) boy friend and his girl friend live in the house, and I have given up my rights of ownership. I'm not sure if anything strange still happens or not.

I hope you enjoyed this true story. :) I look forward to hearing back from you.

Keep up the good work on your books.

Crystal Holland

STORIES FROM THE RESERVATION

Collecting and publishing true-to-life ghost stories is one of my interests. Another interest of mine is collecting and publishing Native lore. Among my many publications, I take special pride in "The Native Series," a uniform set of six separate volumes of traditional Canadian lore and literature. These volumes consist of folktales and poetry as well as specialized studies of the Wendigo and the mystery of the Shaking Tent. (The former is the Algonkian spectre of cannibalism, and the latter is the so-called Oracle of the Indians, a conjuring complex.) It is not often that I am able to combine my interests in ghosts and Native traditions. So it was with considerable pleasure that I opened the email from Nicholas R. (whose full name I know) on 4 April 2007 and read his graphically written account of his own eerie experiences and those of some of his friends and relatives on his First Nations Reserve. How to account for these events? I will not even try!

Hello:

My name is Nicholas R. I am 25 years old and have recently moved to Toronto. Originally, I am from Northern Quebec, from the Timiskaming First Nation Reserve. I have just finished reading *The Midnight Hour* … really cool!

I have some stories I would like to share with you … one of which happened to me … the others to some people from the reservation.

My Story

Summer of 2001 … summer job after high school … I was painting a porch for a senior in the community. I was painting with my friend "Mike." We had started that morning at 8:30 and it was a fairly HOT day … made all the more aggravating in that the old lady left us the wrong paint and when she returned at lunch … she demanded we start over with the colour she had originally wanted. That afternoon, after lunch, I had to continue alone because my friend had a dentist appointment out of town. So I took my time. The lady, before she left, told me she'd leave her door open so I can go in and get more paint, drinks of water, etc. … so it was all good. I painted all afternoon … then at around 3:30 p.m. … I started on the steps. I was fairly tired by this time. Now I had been in and out of that house all afternoon … I can say with 100% conviction … NO ONE was in that house. So a little while after I start the steps … I am sitting with my back to the window … the kitchen window, when I hear, right behind my head (I could feel the vibration) 3 LOUD bangs on the glass … then a voice said, "Get away from here." I went instantly cold … my hair stood up and I felt sick. I packed up everything … I did not dare look at the house nor that window … I left everything outside the side door and walked home. It was now almost 4:00 p.m. … I sat outside my house for about an hour calming down and thinking about it. Why was I so frightened? It had taken me a long while to calm down. Anyway … my mother came out to talk to me and she was wondering why I was so distant. It took me awhile to come around and I finally told her. She was quiet for awhile then finally told me that the old lady who lived there … the one living there still … when she was younger, she made a priest give up his vow … she seduced him, etc. … and he left his priesthood and married her. My mom said it's probably because of that. Now I am a very spiritual person … in the native beliefs. I have never gone back to that house since.

Other Stories

About 15 years ago … wintertime … this was told to me a local resident named "David" … he said his wife returned one night after driving taxi … completely shaken and frightened. It was late … foggy from the cold … it was the weekend. Anyway, his wife was doing the taxi rounds … to the bars mostly … and on one trip down alone … she saw someone walking … so she felt bad and pulled over … might as well give someone a free ride in this -30 maybe -35 degree weather … anyway … she waited and she looked into her mirror (on the door) and saw the person moving toward her … then she noticed that he had no lower half … was gliding fast towards the car … all black … no legs … she sped off … picked up her passenger at the bar and turned around … feeling a little better that she had someone with her … she went back and no one was on the road … there is a mile of road before you get into town again from the reservation … the incident happened about halfway … when she got home she told her husband right away and that was it … she doesn't think it was eye trickery … there was at least a good 10 minute walk before anyone could go into anyplace … and when she had returned with her passenger … 3 or so minutes had passed … the bar is nearest to the reservation, leaving town …

This next one happened in the '80s sometime. In the mid-to-late '70s sometime … a man drowned one weekend while out fishing with some people and they were partying too. Anyway, they never found his body. I will use the name of Jackie for the man who drowned. Anyway, in the '80s … one of Jackie's nieces … noticed a man waiting on the road outside her house … most of her family lived in the same area … anyway, after awhile she went out to ask the man if he needed help. The man said he was waiting for someone by the name of Jackie … that he had "dropped him off here 3 days ago" and he was to pick him up today … Jackie had told him he was here to "see family he hadn't seen in years"… ⋆shrugs⋆.

This story is from the '60s … my dad told me this story. He had uncles … lots of them … this was back when they were mostly still making there … living out in the bush … camping for most of the year, still living off the land. Anyway … one of his uncles had gone out once with some of his family to go camp and fish for a few days. While he was away, my dad's uncle's brother died. And the people were wondering if they should go out to try to find his brother and let him know his bro' had died or just wait until he returned. They decided to wait. A few days later, they saw them returning and prepared to let him know his brother was gone. Now … where my dad grew up, there is a big hill that goes down to the lake … and that is where people left their boats and canoes. The family had come up first and the uncle had stayed down there to pull the boat up and such … finally he came up and someone simply went up to him and told him his brother had died. He replied, "I know … he told me just now… at the boat."

I have more stories I will share later.

Stay well!

Nicholas R.

Invitation Extended and Accepted

Needless to add, I accepted Nicholas R.'s offer to email some traditional tales and individual experiences from the reserve, and he did so the next day. Here they are.

Wendigo Stories

I have a wendigo story… a *memegwesii* (little people) … have quite a few from my people … maybe take a couple of emails to send them.

First Wendigo Story

In about … 1980 or 1981 … on the reservation … it probably lasted over a period of a few days … very few people heard it at first … then one night pretty much everyone heard this noise. To my mother's recollection, she said it sounded like moaning, crying, but at the same time while these sounds were heard, someone twiddling there tongue through it … she can't reproduce the noise if she tried, only saying it was "awful." The sun was just going down when my family first heard it … my mom, dad and uncles and cousins who were sitting around outside my grandmother's house. The house is not there anymore. The police had showed up, the reserve police. They got some people together to go with them into the forest to see if they could find the source of the sound.

The dogs on the reserve were all quiet, under porches etc. … My uncle went, my dad and some others along with the police. Some turned back right away. The ones who went said they'd get close to the sound, it would stop, then it would start again seconds later, but on the other side of the reserve or further away. This went on until well after midnight. Never heard the sound again. No one had seen anything.

Memegwesii

Not sure of the spelling … but this is a story my dad used to tell me when I was a child, as his grandparents told him. Long ago … there lived little people. Small … maybe 6 inches tall. They had no noses and were "spikey" … as if there clothes were adorned with quills from a porcupine. Anyway … these little people would always steal fish from nets, steal food from storage and the like. And they were generally nasty little things. Finally, after enough of this … someone followed them back one night to there home … an old dried out stump … a big cedar tree stump. They went into this little hole and the man who followed stopped and listened. He could hear them talking, laughing, many of them. He returned home and brought back many others to help him get rid of this nuisance. They set fire to the stump and kept watch … if any came out, they'd promptly throw them back in. Morbid … but it sure gave me something to think about as I drifted off into dreamland. Ha ha. The people in Bear Island, Ontario still believe in these little people and some claim to still see them to this day. They've taken to living under rocks in rapids. Ha ha ha ….

Another Story

This is another story my dad used to tell me when I was a child. It's about Papshkoogahn … or Paguk the skeleton. It's rather humorous. He said some time ago, someone he knew was walking through the forest in the fall and saw Papshkoogahn stuck in a tree. He grabbed a long branch and had to nudge him free, and Papshkoogahn flew away. Ha ha. Oddly enough … I remember too when I was quite young, my Great Grandmother crying one morning, scared … saying that "He" flew over the house, she heard him.…

Another Story

In the early '60s … my Grandfather and uncle were moose hunting … in the bushes in Quebec … all within the area around Belleterre, Angliers, and such … and one night while they were either getting ready to go hunt or had just gotten back, they heard, from the mountain across the lake, someone or something shouting, "Heeeeeeeeeeeeeeeeeeeeeey!" as if in great pain. My uncle says it was probably Sasquatch … people used to see things like that in that area lots of times. People camping near Sand Point would have someone throwing sticks and rocks at there tents at night … fisherman saw a HUGE black "man" picking blueberries one summer on the edge of the mountain.…

Another Story

My father's relatives … in the late '60s or early '70s … went camping. They had set camp on some island … maybe in the 7 Rapids area … not sure … but they had their new baby with them … months old … still in his *katinagin* (a sort of basket for carrying your baby on your back) and they had gone to bed now. They put the baby near one side of the tent. And they went to sleep. Middle of the night, they hear the baby crying. But far away. The father had to unzip the tent, run out into the might to find the baby … found him on the shoreline, edge of the water, crying. Now I don't know of any baby who could unzip a tent, zip it back and crawl all the way through sticks and such to the shoreline, in darkness … needless to say, when sunlight came, they packed up and went home. That I find extremely creepy.…

Another Story

I believe this was around Grassy Narrows … people had set a fire at night where they had set there tents up. Weekend camping. Anyway, across the lake there, they saw a fire light up on the other shoreline. They had seen no one else that evening moving in to camp or anyone else on the lake. They called across to the other side but no reply. They put the fire out later on … a little while later, the fire on the other side went out too. The next day, they couldn't see if anyone was camping across the lake so they went across to look. No fire ashes, no sign of anyone being there … certainly nothing reflective anywhere as well.

Another Story

My dad told me this story, this happened to some family member … I will get more info on who it was … but he had been fishing or hunting all day … and it was getting too dark and somewhat windy to travel home. So he found an open little space along the shoreline along the way, pulled up his canoe and went to sleep in it. Twice that night while he tried to sleep, something pushed him over. Like the entire canoe. Finally, after the second flip, he moved his canoe to another spot and rested comfortably all night. Next day as he was getting ready to leave, he noticed that he had been sleeping on or too close to an old burial mound….

I have a few more, will send those tomorrow.

Nicholas R.

NOW I'M NOT SO SURE

I have the full name of the young woman who is known here as Tammy. She read one of my books on ghosts and spirits and to my pleasure sent me an email about the disturbances that have taken place in her family home and also in her present place of residence. She writes very clearly and I have reproduced her account with the minimum of editing. It is commonly said it is not places that are haunted, but people. Hauntings seem to run in families, or at least they are recorded in families. What Tammy reports — with good spirits, I might add! — is a series of poltergeist-like manifestations. A poltergeist is a ghost that is not seen. It is known by its deeds alone. In this instance the effects are innocent enough, but even innocent noises heard at night may be unduly alarming. I am grateful to Tammy for recording these experiences. I emailed her back and asked her for the further particulars offered in the original letter. These arrived July 27, 2007, and appear here following the asterisk.

Hey there, Mr. Colombo:

My name is Tammy, I'm 22 and I've just recently finished reading one of your books, *Haunting Stories*. I found a lot of the stories very interesting and some a little spooky.

On the last page you mentioned that if any of us readers had any supernatural stories to feel free to share them with you. Well, let me tell you, I have a bunch. Many of them personal to my family and me.

I live on Cape Breton Island, Nova Scotia, in a small fishing community. A lot of the stories I have involve my mother's house, and the basement apartment in my grandparent's house in which I now live. I also have experiences which involve me and a few of my friends foolishly going out to seek the unknown in some of the supposedly haunted areas in surrounding communities. The story I would like to share with you tonight is about a ghost that I believe dwells here in my basement apartment.

I first moved into this little apartment on Boxing Day 2005. Ever since I was a little girl I always promised my Grandmother that I would come and live with her. My Grandparents inhabit the upstairs portion of the house. The basement consists of the furnace room, a rec room, the laundry room (that has a walk-in shower), my living-room, and my bedroom. I share the upstairs kitchen and bathroom with them.

I didn't regret my decision to move in here. I enjoyed freedom from my parents, and at the same time I had the safety and security of having family close by. I have to say that I never really noticed anything *really* strange happening during the first year of living here.

A few things I did notice was that my dog, a little mutt named Dil, would not stay down here at all at night. He would always run upstairs and sleep in my Grandmother's room. I also noticed that I often couldn't sleep down here and would sometimes creep upstairs and sleep on their livingroom couch. There was a time when I woke up in the middle of the night, after hearing a loud banging noise, and when I sat up and looked to the side of my bed, I was certain that I had seen a dark figure standing against the wall of my room.

Naturally, I turned the light on pretty quick, there was nothing there, and nothing there that could cast such a human-like shadow. It "creeped" me out a bit, but I dismissed it as I was still half-asleep. Now I'm not so sure ….

There was one day I was sitting around watching TV. It was really overcast outside so I had the light on as well. I went upstairs to get a drink and when I came downstairs all the lights were off and the TV was off as well! There was no one in the basement but me. My Grandparents don't really come down here, it's too hard on their old legs.

Little things like lights being turned on and off seemed to happen more often. And as Christmas approached, I bought a tree and put it in the corner, and I would put all the gifts sort of in a semi-circle around the tree skirt. Well, on many occasions I would go upstairs for something, usually just for a few minutes, only to return to see all the presents I had laid out *pushed* to the very back of the tree, in the corner next to the wall where anyone could hardly reach! After this happened once or twice I decided to stop sleeping in the basement altogether. It seemed that all the activity was confined to the few rooms down here.

Now all of this happened last year. After moving out for a few months I'm now back and sleeping in the basement once again. Despite being "creeped out" sometimes, I have many more experiences concerning my little ghost in the basement and the strange things that happened in my mother's house as well

If you would like to hear more please let me know. I would be more than happy to share my stories with you. It's just that it's getting quite late here in Cape Breton and I have to get up early.

You can email me at I'll be happy to hear from you.

Tammy

I'm glad that you want to use my story and hear about more of my experiences, as I said before. I am happy to share them with you. I have had many experiences in the house that I'm currently living in, and in my parents' house as well. Since the first experiences I ever recall were in my parents' house, I figure I should start by telling you some of those rather than getting right back to my little ghost in the basement.

We first moved into the house when I was five and my little brother was just one year old. Both of my parents were only in their mid / late twenties. The house was what I guess you could call "average size." The upstairs included two bedrooms (which are right next to each other), a bathroom, the kitchen, and the living-room. There was a basement but it was mainly unfinished and had the furnace/laundry room (with both an oil furnace and a wood-burning stove) and rec room which my father converted into a third bedroom. The two bedrooms upstairs belonged to me and my brother, my parents slept down in the basement room.

Here are some of the stories that involve that house.

"Get Up"

This story doesn't really involve me. But I've heard it a lot over the years from my mother who still can't explain it.

It happened one night while mom was sleeping. She said she was suddenly awaken by somebody shaking her arm. She opened her eyes, expecting to see me because I used to have nightmares a lot and ask to bunk with her. But there was no one there. Shrugging it off, she rolled over and tried to go back to sleep. Again she felt some one shaking her. Again she looked, again there was no one there. And again, she tried to go back to sleep. The shaking started again, a little more violently this time, and she swears she heard someone say, "Get up … get up!" My mother did indeed get up and made her way upstairs. She just felt it was something she should do. When she got upstairs, she noticed that all the burners on the stove were turned on and red hot! She hadn't used the stove since dinnertime that day. And, with having two small kids in the house, she was always sure that the stove was turned off. She turned off the stove quickly and checked on my brother and me. We were both sound asleep.

Marbles

Another strange occurence that seemed to happen a lot in my parents' house was the fact that marbles could be heard rolling across the floor when there were none.

My father told me of one experience he had when he was home by himself on day. He was down working in the basement, when there was a large crash upstairs, and the sound of a mass of marbles rolling across the kitchen floor. At first the thought that my mother had come home with my brother and me and he yelled out, "Hello?" There was no answer, just the sound once again of marbles running across the floor. He left what he was doing and went upstairs. There was no one there. But sitting in the middle of the kitchen, perfectly undisturbed, was a basket that had been sitting on the top of our fridge, a good four feet away. There were no marbles, loose change, or anything that could make that strange rolling noise anywhere to be seen. And there was no way for the basket to just fall that far away from the fridge without being disturbed.

The Laundry Machine

This is one story that I can really account for. It happened when I was around eight years old and my brother was five. My mother had just put me to bed, but I couldn't sleep. There was a loud racket coming from the laundry room which was located directly below my bedroom. "Mom!" I called out. She came to my room and asked me what I wanted. "Are you doing the laundry?" I asked. She told me no and that she had done a wash that afternoon. "Well, it sounds like the laundry machine is going," I said, and she shook her head and said it wasn't. I insisted that I heard a strange noise coming from the laundry room, and finally she caved and went downstairs to check. A few minutes later she came running up the stairs and she was on the phone yelling at my father. (He was at Darts at the time this happened.) I remember her yelling, "You have to come home now! I swear this house is haunted! I'm not staying in it! Get home!"

What exactly happened in the laundry room I'm not sure. My mother won't speak of it. The only thing she confirmed was that the washer was going when it couldn't possibly be going. But there had to be more that happened down there because my mother doesn't spook easily.

Other Things

Other strange things happened in that house. Things would go missing and reappear in strange places. My toys, which would always be on a shelf or on the floor in my room, would be strewn all across the house. My mother and I had both seen figures standing next to our beds at night. My little brother often used to have conversations with something unseen as well. When we asked what he was talking to he said, "The ghost," which apparently he said was an older boy.

Other Stories

Those are all the stories I can recall involving my parents' house.

When it comes to the place where I'm living in now. Aside from the story I already told you about the Christmas presents, most things that happen are minor. Lights turning off and on … on their own accord … there are strange noises … things will go missing and then show up in odd places … that sort of thing. There was one incident that scared me quite a bit, though. It happened not too long ago.

I was just after getting home from work one night. Around 1:30 a.m., and after getting into my pj's, I threw my dirty clothes into the laundry room and went back into my living-room to watch some TV. After an hour or so, I got up and decided to head upstairs to get a drink of milk before heading to bed. To my surprise there, sitting at the bottom of the stairs, were the very clothes I threw into the laundry room. The laundry room is a good 15 feet away from the stairs. Quickly, I gathered up the clothes and threw them back into the laundry room and ran up the stairs.

Already I was shaken up, and as I poured myself a glass of milk, I was shocked to hear the sound of footsteps coming up the stairs. I didn't want to wait to see what was coming up. I knew there were only three people in the house. There was me. There were my grandmother and my grandfather, and they both went to bed shortly after I got home. I forgot the milk on the counter and darted to the bathroom and locked myself inside. (I know … I'm a chicken!) The footsteps kept coming and just outside of the bathroom door I heard a childlike giggle. It was very unnerving and it took quite some time until I gathered up the courage to leave the bathroom.

After that incident and hearing the little giggle, I sort of figured that my little ghost was that of a child. I told my friends about my experiences. One of my friends, an older gentleman that I worked with, said that he once had similar problems while living in Toronto. He told me that I should try leaving out a toy or something for it to play with. I thought it was a farfetched idea but, desperate to be able to sleep in my own room again without being scared witless, I found an old teddy bear and left it out in the rec room where a lot of things seemed to be happening. Since then things have quieted down but they haven't stopped altogether. Right now, I'm trying to do research on the old church that used to be where my house is now located, as well as the history of that particular part of the town.

"UPDUPTED"

Imagine being in communication with an alien intelligence and being able to quiz that intelligence: ask it relevant questions, receive reasonable replies.

That is the experience that is being reported by "Anne," not the real first name of a woman who is known to me through email correspondence but who wishes her full name and locale to be kept in confidence.

What follows is a transcript of this communication about the nature of life in the Universe, about clones, and about death. Call it inspiration, call it automatic writing, call it imagination, call it whatever you wish: Anne offers it in the spirit in which it was received: as revelation.

The back story: On 14 August 2007, I received the following email from a woman who identified herself as Anne. Here is a record of our correspondence.

> Hi there,
>
> I read *True Canadian UFO Stories* and thoroughly enjoyed it. It wasn't sensationalized and it had the "feeling of truth" in it.
>
> I had an experience of abduction that I wrote about. Would you be interested in reading it? Thanks.
>
> Email me at: ____.
>
> To: AnneSent: August 14, 2007
> Subject: For Anne
> Dear Anne:
>
> I would love to read the account of your experience and I will respond to it right away.
>
> Best, JR
>
> To: John
> Sent: August 19, 2007Subject: Abduction
> Hi John Robert Colombo,
>
> I haven't had time to write. I'm a lowly paid cashier at a big-box outlet and I get home half dead from my shift every day.
>
> Here is the attachment that I would like you to read.
>
> I called it "Updupted" because my youngest son asked me when he was 3 years old (and I was watching the *X-Files*), "Mom, what does 'updupted' mean?" I wrote all this when I was in a deep meditative trance.
>
> Anne

Naturally I opened the attachment and to my surprise I found myself engulfed in a question-and-answer session with an intelligent entity or maybe two intelligent entities. At no point could I predict what would be said next. As the scientist said, the Universe is not only stranger than we can know, it is stranger than we can imagine.

All I will say about the communication (which seems to be the result of three "sittings" in a trance) at this point is that it reads like … revelation!

There are passing references to Andy but his name too has been disguised.

"Updupted"

Why me?
Because you were the oldest one out of all of the kids, therefore, you retained more information. And you were also the most intelligent one.

How do you know that I was the most intelligent one?
By your aura. Intelligent people have a more brilliant aura than others who are not as intelligent. They read your life path.

How did they read my life path?
It's like a movie. The present is this second. The past is rewind. The future is fast forward. They already knew that you were going to be a writer. They abducted you because they knew you were going to write about it someday. It is a plot for this science fiction book.

Was I the only one out of all the kids who was abducted?
No.

Who else?
Andy.

Why him?
He was the most intelligent male.

What was his life path?
They knew he would die in a motor vehicle accident and that his spirit would come back and help you and that you would believe him.

How would he come back and help me?
Mostly through dreams but also though meditation.

What happened to us?
They only took you for a couple of seconds each. The other kids didn't even notice that they took you. They had no time to notice. They know that time is an elastic band. They can manipulate it. A couple of seconds to them is like a wormhole. That's how they got here, through a worm hole. You asked them how they got here and that's what they said. They said that there are worm holes all over the universe and that they are like highways for space crafts. Some are better than others. Like a country road for a donkey cart is not as advanced as a runway for a space jet. You need the right technology to get clearance to fly certain worm holes. You get to a toll booth and you have to punch in your info on a clearance security pad. An ID number which contained all your info. You only get clearance to travel that highway if you have the correct technology. For example, if you are meeting an asteroid. What do you do? Some would smash it to clear their path. Some would redirect it to clear their path and others would avoid it by going over it or under it. They are the most advanced ones because they did not change the course of the asteroid. When you smash it, you are changing the course of its evolution, which no one has a universal right to do. There are universally recognized rights and wrongs here. If you redirect it, you are again changing its course of evolution, although you are not destroying it. If you accommodate its right on its evolutionary path, then you are not changing its evolution. Every asteroid is a piece of a puzzle of creation. It is a part of a new star or sun or planet or it is the fragment of an old one. They have a right to "live" that is universally recognized and protected. There are worm holes that are dark and ruddy and old. There are others that are will lit and advanced superhighways and they go to more systems, like an interstate highway or Highway 1, the cross-Canada highway. There are some that are short and some that are long and some that are circular like traffic circles.

Did they do any tests on us?
Yes, but they were painless. They took a DNA swab from the top of your left hand.

What are they going to do with this?
Test it.

How?
They will clone you many times over and you will become a test subject in their galaxy. They want to see if your clone can survive on their galaxy.

Will my clone know that it is me?
No, but they will know that they do not belong there. Something will tell them that they have never belonged there and that they are from somewhere else. They will always have that feeling that they belong somewhere else and they will always want to go back there.

Was Andy cloned?
Yes.

Does his clone live in another galaxy?
Yes, many of him and many of you.

Do we live together on one galaxy or separate?
Some of you's are separate and some of you's are together.

What do you mean by together?
Don't worry, it's not to reproduce … you repel each other like that and you are always best friends wherever you are. You are attracted to each other's friendship through genetic memory. You recognize each other from another lifetime and you always maintain your friendship throughout eternity. True friendship lasts forever if that is how you intend it to be. It lasts through all kinds of worlds.

Do we ever know or find out who we really are?
On some planets, yes.

How do we find out?
Through mind control like hypnosis or dream therapy or meditation.

Tell me about this.
In one world called Myon —

How far away from Myon is earth?
Trillions of light years. This was a very advanced culture that took you.

Alright, tell me about it.
You met on a hill at twilight. There were many "people" there (these are clones from other planets and some "native" people). There was something going on like a fair or an exhibition of some sort. It was a beautiful twilight and you went for a walk to enjoy the evening by yourself. You've never been into fairs, it's a part of your personality, whether you're in Myon or earth. They do not interest you. Nice evenings always interest you more. You met Andy sitting on a hillside doing the same thing you were…getting away from it all. He was alone, too. You looked at him and he looked at you in exactly the same way… like, "Hey, don't I know you from somewhere? Haven't we met before?" You both laughed at these corny lines and asked each other for forgiveness for intruding on his/her space. That was the manners there. "People" asked for forgiveness for intruding in each other's space. It is known that everyone has their own space that is sacred and protected as a fundamental right in the universe. That is your aura. It is a very sacred space. It is your space that God gave you. This is still the same God that exists on earth and everywhere else, it doesn't matter where you go in the Universe, He created everything everywhere. Anyway, Andy asked you to sit by him and you did. You talked about everything the whole night, but never once talked about being lovers. It wasn't in your nature. It wasn't in your genes. But somehow, you felt that you weren't alone. You felt you were being watched and you were. Everything you did over there was being watched and recorded. You were, after all, a couple of test subjects from earth. There is a transmitter in the brain of every clone that sends back to the test center everything that is perceived by the mind, the smell, the taste, the touch, the sight, the sound … All of the physical senses, but not just that, the mental, emotional, spiritual and psychological senses.

We have other senses?
Yes (chuckles).

Tell me about these other senses.
Like what earth calls ESP, paranormal thinking / experiences. Your intelligence picks these up through your aura. Your aura is like your antennae. It picks up info from the universe before it "hits" your body's senses or your mind's senses. It acts as a filter. It protects you from certain evil sorts of information. It is spiritual protection. More enlightened people need less protection because they already know how to protect themselves. Their aura is brilliant light with some rays of all colours. Each colour has a different function.

Like what?
Red is a filter. It filters out a lot of negative universal energy for you. It warns the universal energy not to come in. If the energy chooses to come in anyway, the red rays surround it and take it out of your aura and take it somewhere else where it cannot come back.

And?
All the colours of the spectrum have a different function to protect you. One is not stronger than the other. They are all the same strength, they just have different jobs to do. Orange, for example, injects the entire being with strength, thus the vitamin C in oranges. Yellow is the power of all suns everywhere. It brings enlightenment and knowledge through this. Purple brings the knowledge of the obscure future, it is the colour that goes the furthest into the future universe. Green is the colour that brings abundance. When you want abundant growth in your life, you pray to the colour of the green spirit. This is the power of prayer flags. There are spirits which protect all these powers from any kind of abuse. That is how the power is maintained pure and unpolluted by other powers. They, therefore have the same power through time and space.

Tell me about the beings in the space ship and the craft itself.
The craft is designed to repair its own damage like a doctor. It is a giant computer. It diagnoses the problem and it repairs the damage to it by replication, like cloning. It clones itself when it is damaged.

The beings also clone that part of their body that is damaged and only that part. That way, they are whole for the whole voyage.

Do they ever die?
Yes.

Are they cloned after they die?
Yes.

How?
Before their voyage, they each give DNA samples and these samples are preserved.

Through freezing?
No. That is ancient technology. It breaks down when there is no power to freeze.

How are they preserved?
They are purified and isolated from being contaminated. They are put in a fool-proof container into their tiniest parts and these parts are reassembled to clone later. The parts are so small they cannot be seen by our microscopes but they exist. They are much smaller than atoms. They are assembled from small to big … parts smaller than atoms, atoms into molecules, molecules into tissues, tissues into organs, muscle and bone.

Does the info in the mind get transferred?
Yes. There is genetic memory.

How does genetic memory work?
Every experience that you have, every breath that you take is recorded in your memory. Your memory is always on. It cannot be shut off. You even store all of your dreams even though you don't remember them. This memory storage never stops because life never stops, so you never stop having memories of everything. Your memories continue after you die. They just occur in a different reality.

Where are these memories stored?

In your DNA. There is a storage "tank" of memories, like a black box that you know of in a plane that cannot be destroyed.

Why can't they be destroyed?
Because anything that has already happened cannot be destroyed by anyone. No one is empowered to destroy a happening. There is also a collective memory, two or more people remembering the same thing. They are different people, so naturally, their perception is going to be different. Each person's perception of reality is different. Their memory of the same event will be stored in their genetic memory and it will be slightly, although not totally, different from someone else's. Memory is like a hard-drive on a computer. Your mind is "programmed" to receive only so many memories, everyone's mind is like this. When your storage space runs out, it is time for you to die in this world. That doesn't mean that you are not alive in another reality, like you and Andy alive on Myon right now, but your realities don't connect with the one here. In the one here, Andy has died more than 20 years ago. On Myon, he still lives, but he is lonesome. He knows in his heart that Myon is not his home but he doesn't know where his home is. This is his clone that lives there. Clones have no soul of their own. Only God can give you a soul. Andy's soul is in what you call "heaven." His clone is in Myon and he will have many more clones because the DNA sample taken provided for many clonings for him as well as for yourself. These clones are always lonely because they are lonesome for their souls and for earth because that is where they originated from. Your clone is lonesome, too.

Can I connect with my clone?
Yes, because you are the host. If you were another clone, you wouldn't be able to connect with another clone. You can only connect with your real soul host. Clones never feel like a total person. They know that there is always something missing. That something missing is the soul and the planet of origin. Earth is so important if you were born here.

Why?
Because of the vibrations your body and soul were born into. Each planet has its own vibrations. These are the same vibrations that existed when you were a developing fetus. You felt them then and you

felt "at home" in your mother's womb. When you were born, your mother became the earth because she has the same vibrations. Your people knew this through spiritual contacts that told them this and that is how they knew that the earth is their mother, our mother. The earth has its own vibrations in the universe that no other planet has. It gets them from its position in the universe, the sun, the galaxy, the solar system, the star constellations ... the gravitational pull of the earth and the moon together. There is a unique energy centre here and it proliferates life here on earth.

Isn't that wrong? To have Andy's clone and my clone living and existing on another planet just be someone else's experiments?
It depends on your point of view.

That sounds wishy-washy. No strong values to stand on.
There are other more barbaric races out there that come to earth and perform horrendous experiments, very painful ones for the subjects, and they don't care. They just perform all kinds of painful tests and even kill some of the subjects and think nothing of it. They have no values. No respect for life.

That doesn't justify genetic experimentation with us.
They do not kill you. They do not harm you. They merely watch every move you make, every thought you think.

And you think there is nothing wrong with this? What kind of a value system do you have? Is it right to clone a person who has no soul and to let him/her live without one? Is it right to watch and record every move they make without ever telling them that they are under constant observation? How would you like it if it was recorded every time you used the bathroom and you didn't even know it? Like that Jim Carrey on the "The Truman Show"?
That's what you're doing to animals right now, isn't it? Some of them for purely cosmetic purposes, like whales. How many mascaras will it take before they become extinct?

We're talking human beings here. We're not exactly talking about whales.
We're talking life, all life, not just human beings or whales.

So, it's okay for you to experiment on human beings and to clone them to kingdom come, but it's wrong for us to experiment on whales. Where is the right and wrong here? Aren't they both wrong? Quit trying to say you're right when we are actually both wrong! I can't even imagine myself being cloned 300 trillion light years away and I have no soul and I am talking to my nephew's clone who also has no soul. What kind of an enlightened world does that to a human being or does that to life, period. How can you do that to us and justify it in any laws in the Universe? Are you allowed to do that? Who allows you to do that if you are allowed to do that? How can you go to other planets and take DNA and clone without permission from the host and get away with it? Do clones reproduce?

No. You wouldn't be asking that question if we didn't know the answer. We know it through experimentation. They can't reproduce. They are like mules. The cannot beget other mules. You need a horse and a donkey to get a mule. Two clones cannot reproduce. You need a host and a clone to get reproduction. And the clones only live as long as the host does. They die every which way, but they die at exactly the same time as the host did. For example, if the host is 31 when he dies on earth, then all his clones will die when they are 31. There is a time-clock in each of us that the Creator puts there and it tells us when we are born and when we die. We only have a limited number of seconds.

Seconds?

Yes, seconds. Time is precious and it is given out in seconds. You do not die on the hour, or the minute. You die the split second you were meant to and you are born the split second you were meant to. You have only a matter of seconds to live. That's how your life is counted. When the host dies, all the clones die.

Can you clone a clone?

Yes. But it is like the quality of pictures. Each successive cloning is of poorer quality than the one previous to it. The quality deteriorates with time if you use the clone of a clone. If you use the clone of a host, it is different. If the host is continuously used to produce clones, then you will always get a high quality clone. But if a clone is used to clone a clone, then the quality deteriorates. It's like photocopying a copy of a copy of a copy. Eventually, the quality of the copy becomes so poor that it is not worth copying anymore. The principle is the same.

Why do you keep cloning us?
Each lifetime that the clone lives is done for a different purpose.

You mean a different experiment.
How do you know your life is not an experiment? How do you know that your life here has a purpose? How do you know that your purpose is not an experiment?

Shut up. You're starting to bother me.
That's because I may be getting too close to the truth for comfort. You don't know for sure, do you? No one knows for sure, to tell you the truth.

*

You said for me to think of myself in a very nice thin long, white lace dress and to go to the side of a mountain in front of a cave and then outstretch my arms when I want to communicate with you. Why did you instruct me to do that?
So we would know when you wanted our knowledge. We would know that you were asking for our knowledge and we would open our doors to our intelligence.

Yeah, but why a cave on a mountainside?
Because this knowledge is for you alone and the mountain symbolizes the strength of this truth. The height of it symbolizes the inaccessibility of it except by you. The cave is someplace you can retreat when you have received enough into your mind for the time being until the next time.

Why the long, white lace dress?
Isn't that your very favorite way to dress? A wedding dress to wed yourself with this knowledge? You are married to this knowledge … until death do us part. In sickness and in health … you will have this knowledge?

Why did you pick me?
You are strong and beautiful and you will carry this truth strongly and beautifully.

What knowledge do you want me to have?
The knowledge of the Universe.

Which is?
Each person creates their own reality through their thoughts. Each person is a creator because each person is a part of God and that's the part of God that everyone is: the creator part. That is the gift that God gave each creature that He ever created.

Tell me about DNA. What is it exactly?
Your DNA is not just a map. It is a whole world, a whole Universe contained in a single cell. It is a library, it is a computer. It contains your whole heredity, not just of this world but of all other worlds from which you originated and once lived. All of your past lives are contained in your particular DNA. Some of your ancestors were aliens as you know them. The DNA tells your exact age right down to the last second. Each person is an infinity of years old.

Why is it in a double helix?
Because there is a duality of life everywhere. Everything has a mirror image, every plant, every animal, every person.

You mean there is a mirror image of me somewhere in the world?
Not necessarily somewhere in this world, but somewhere in the Universe.

Can I get in touch with my own mirror image?
Yes, but not physically. If you tried to get in touch with your mirror image physically, you would cancel each other out.

How do I get in touch then?
Psychically with the power of the mind. You sit in front of a mirror and burn a candle and stare into your own eyes and communicate with "yourself" and "yourself" will answer right back.

Is my mirror image the same age as me?
Yes. Your mirror image is born exactly the same time as you so the DNA is exactly the same age.

Will my mirror image die the same time as me?
Yes. Exactly at the same moment.

Of the same thing?
No, because you are of two different worlds, usually, and I'm saying usually because at rare times, it happens that your mirror image is in the same world as you and even rarer, still, in the same space as you. Some people "see" themselves and it scares them, usually. They get an intense feeling that they want to draw closer to this person but all their instincts tell them not to because if they touched, they would cancel each other out. They can look but don't touch.

Is my mirror image the same sex as me?
Yes, everything is the same: age, sex, height, weight, hair colour, because the genetic blueprint is the same for both. You are only one side of the double helix, your twin is the other side with exactly the same genetic blueprint. The strands are kept separate so that they won't cancel each other out, so usually, they are born into separate worlds.

Why is DNA made up of amino acids, why not something else?
Because amino acids can survive in many different environments, many different worlds and planets.

Are some planets more harsh than others?
Of course.

If that's the case, then why would my mirror image die at exactly the same time if she was born in a harsher climate?
The strands of DNA were designed to survive at exactly the same rate in both climates.

Does my mirror image age faster than me if she is in a harsher climate?
No. Every line is the same no matter where she is. She is conditioned to her environment the same way you are.

Can I dream about her?
Yes.

What is her name?
The same as yours and her birth-date is the same as yours. She was born at exactly the same time right down to the last second.

Is her mother my mother's mirror image?
No. Her mother, like all mothers, brought her into her world.

How do you read a DNA molecule?
Every "chain" on it is the life of one ancestor. All the dominant characteristics of that person are passed on to the next generation through reproduction … like the colour of the eyes and the hair and the height … but the memory of that person is also preserved, every second of that person's life is preserved in the genetic memory of the DNA molecule.

Where do you start reading it from? The top or the bottom?
There is no top or bottom, just ancient to modern. Ancient is your first ancestors and modern is your parents.

Who were our first ancestors?
The first man and the first woman.

Who were they?
The Bible calls them Adam and Eve, but every culture has its own Adam and Eve story of Genesis. Each race has its own master cell, its own first man and woman.

Who came first? The man or the woman?
The woman gave birth to man spontaneously through a dream. That was the Immaculate Conception, as it has come to be known in Christianity. Mary had a dream and she conceived through the power of God. There are other cultural interpretations of this same concept in your world. Recently, a Komodo dragon female who had never experienced a male dragon gave birth to six little dragons in captivity. It was spontaneous conception.

It can happen through energy. There doesn't have to be any physical contact for reproduction to occur. It's like what you call "spontaneous combustion."

Are there some worlds, then, where there is reproduction completely without physical contact?
Yes. The worlds of angels.

Angels have their own worlds?

Yes. But they are hard to get into, not as easy as your world to get into. They have many energy force fields that are impenetrable to us.

Why?
They are of higher technology than we are. They do not need space ships to go around. They go wherever they wish. Their wish is their spacecraft. They are pure energy.

Are they in our world?
Yes. They are in every world of their choice. They have earned this place in the Universe because they are complete pacifists. They can be completely trusted not to breach any world's laws. They have ambassadorship everywhere. They can materialize if they want to. You have probably seen many, many of them in your lifetime without ever knowing that it was an angel that you saw. They take on many forms. Some of them are the bag men and women that you see, or the alcoholics in the bars or the kids running in the park. Angels carry the Universal energy of God like the rings around the planet you call Saturn. They are the closest concentric circles to God's pure light of energy.

Can I communicate with the angels?
Yes. Anyone can. All you have to do is ask them to communicate with you.

I have and nothing happened.
It's not that nothing happened, it's that you didn't understand what DID happen, like when you were abducted for a couple of seconds

of earth time and you didn't even know what happened. Like that. Sometimes, an angel can just leave you with a feeling or a blessing and you won't feel any different because your perception is clouded by the expectation of something else.

Can I say, "Hi" to Andy? I mean the real Andy? Can I carry on a conversation with him? What is he doing now? Where is the real he?
He says, "Hi" back. He wants you to tell all his kids that he can't wait to see them again. He has done a lot in his life. It is his right alone to tell you about it when he gets around to it. You will have a chance to meet and a place to meet when God wills.

Why are some aliens conducting awful experiments on people?
Some aliens are bad and some are good. It is like this all over the universe. (The universe never stops expanding, you know, the old math formula, a limit does not exist.). The universe is limitless. It keeps expanding into infinity.

Who are the bad aliens and how can we protect ourselves against them?
The bad aliens are an evolutionary mix of good and bad DNA and the bad DNA is dominant and therefore gets carried through to the next generation. They have not genetically eliminated their reptilian heritage. It is still very much in their genes.

Why is everything reptilian bad even in aliens?
Reptilian anything is bad because they are the carriers of negative genetic characteristics. They are the containers of it, like your oil is carried in a barrel, the same thing. They are the carriers of bad traits, the eyes, the skin, the webbed fingers … they are also carriers of negative intelligence. That is why they bring pain to those they abduct. You can protect yourself against them by putting yourself in God's light and praying for protection. The same God that protects you from them is the same God that exists everywhere. There is only one God and His power is infinite in His universe. He created it and is still creating it. The reptilians think they are smarter than Him. They are "Lucifer's angels" in your world. They are called "demons" in your world. That is why they bring you harm and pain. Angels are the opposite. They bring you peace and love and

enlightenment and God's power. They give it away freely because it is free for everyone who asks for it. That's why all you have to do is ask the angels to be a part of your life and they will be.

★

How did you get here?

Through time / space warps. At that time, we knew that your people would call them "wormholes." They are bridges in space where you compress space and time based on a mathematical formula. Some are new and some are old, some are better than others, like your bridges on earth, not every bridge is going to be as good as the San Francisco bridge or look the same. Wormholes are like that. They have signs like you have yield signs and stop signs here. It takes a lot of technology to navigate some of them. Some wormholes are only to be used by higher intelligences because only those beings can read the meaning of the signs left by others. Some of them are superior technology, some are inferior ... like the difference in your world between a foot bridge and a foot escalator at an airport. Some of the signs cannot be even read by those who do not have the intelligence to navigate. The signs are not posted on board signs. You have to read them in the star system as you go by and you have to know where to look for them. If you do not know where to look and how to read, you're going to be totally lost.

What are the signs?

Like images or mirages of clouds around a star or star cluster or planet. You can read how long it's been there and what it says by the colours and the shapes that are left behind by others. The Inuit people had this same idea with their inukshooks. Our computers (we do not call them computers) also get messages in mathematical equations sometimes and the messages are contained therein.

What do you call your computers?

We call them after the name of the two people who designed them. They earned this name by designing them and creating them. Many generations later, they still have the same name, but the models have evolved many times over. They are the pioneers of this creation.

What are the computer's names?
Thorens and Therans. Thorens are the males and Therans are the females.

You mean, computers have a male and female?
Yes. The males contain the seeds of information and Therans give birth to new generations, in a manner of speaking. Your culture has not evolved yet to having male and female computers, but this time is coming for you.

★

P.S. In a subsequent communication, dated 19 August 2007, I learned the following: "Please do not write my name anywhere. Just write that we are both from a Plains Indian tribe … I do not go to my mountainside cave to make money. I go there to receive info (I am a receptor, they say) and to pass it on as freely as I received it. This attitude will take me far in the universe when I die here on earth."

EXPERIENCED MANY DIFFERENT THINGS

The following email I received on 12 August 2007. The email's subject-line appeared like this: "Reading your book."

The text read as follows:

I am reading one of your Canadian Ghost Stories. I am fascinated by all that I am reading.

Throughout my life, since childhood up until now when I am 47 years old. I have experienced many different things. I have never wanted to share them with anyone. I have recently started to talk to my partner about what I have experienced. Although he hasn't experienced anything at all he believes everything that I have told him.

Recently, while I was reading your book an acquaintance had come over and for some reason I felt free to tell her of some of the things that I have witness or been a part of.

I would be more than happy to share my stories with you. There are so many of them and so different. From knowing about deaths

> and births before being told of them. From having conversations with my phone when I am in need of company.
>
> There is a list of things I could tell you. And for the first time in my life I am ready to share them. Both of my parents have passed on. They would tell me not to tell anyone of what was happening as they were scared that someone would take their only daughter away from them. When I got older I was so afraid that if I said anything at all they would claim that I was unfit to bring up my sons.
>
> I am not afraid any longer. Please let me know if you are at all interested in hearing any of the many things I have experienced.

The email was signed "Jacqueline B." (I have the author's full name in my files.)

As soon as I could, I replied to Jacqueline in these words: "Please send me detailed accounts of your experiences. I would love to read them and presumably share them with my readers. I will respond quickly. I did not respond quickly to your email because I was in Montreal and only now received it."

Over the next two weeks, Jacqueline B. and I exchanged interesting emails, as I encouraged her to "take the plunge" and as she readied herself to begin to write up at least one of her experiences.

On 6 September 2007, I received the following, interesting account, which I am reproducing in full with a minimum of copy-editing. It holds the reader.

Psychologists and parapsychologists are familiar with the fact that young children often interact with imaginary playmates. These so-called playmates gradually fade away, the victims of the years. Indeed, young children are often felt to be deeply psychic, or at least intuitive, for they seem to sense danger and they react to it quickly.

In the account of a childhood experience that is so vividly described here, Jacqueline B. is able to enter into the emotions she felt when she was ten or eleven years old. Who can account for her fear of a canine? Who can dismiss as a mere coincidence the fact that she was bitten by a dog, just as she feared? This is a probable explanation for what happened, yet animals too are said to be psychic and unreasonably able to "sniff out" people who are frightened by them and people who have a ready kinship with them.

I will coax Jacqueline B. to share with us descriptions of other odd or eerie episodes from her life. I have decided to write about one of my experiences. I have many stories I could share, but they all seems to be linked to each other. It would not do the experience justice by leaving out details:

> I have picked this incident, because it stands alone and needs no background. This happened when I was 10 or 11 years old, on a

warm afternoon in June 1970–1971.

We lived in Ajax at the time and frequently visited my parents' long-time friends, who lived on King St. in Toronto, near the racetrack. They lived on the north side of the road, past a school that always had a black iron fence around it. They lived above a store that they owned. This store is where Mrs. Van Horne sewed curtains and dresses.

I remember the day so well. It was sunny and breezy. Perfect spring weather.

I was the kind of child who was shy and hardly spoke unless I was spoken to and even then it was sometimes difficult for me to find my voice as I was afraid of what I might hear myself say. I was an only child with all my relatives in Holland. My mother always tried to keep me by her side. When my parents went out visiting, I sat beside or behind my mother and listened and daydreamed. I spent many hours like this. It was the norm for me.

The Van Horne's had a daughter 4 years older than I was. I knew Maria all of my life. Maria never paid that much attention to me. Four years do make a big difference when you're a child. I would often watch her from afar and wish I were grown up like her. At the time, Maria was in high school. For some reason she had to go to her school to pick up something. (It could have been a report card.)

Maria asked both of our parents if she was allowed to take me along. I was so excited that she wanted me to go along. In the past no one had ever wanted to include me in anything. I looked into my mother's eyes and begged her to let me go. I promised to be good and to listen to Maria. I thought it was going to be so much fun going with her to her school. Our parents talked it over and decided that I could. That day I felt more grown up than I ever had.

We quickly started getting ready to go. I was getting my shoes on and tying the laces when Maria asked her mother if she could have money for the subway.

I stopped in my tracks. My heart was pounding, I started to sweat, and I swear I was shaking. I had this awful feeling and didn't know why. I wanted Maria's mother to say no, but she handed her the money.

I went to my mother's side and told her that I didn't want to go now. Mom assured me that I would like to go on the subway. It was just a fast train underground. She assured me that I had nothing to be afraid of.

Words flowed out of my mouth before I knew what I was saying. This had happened a few times before in other instances but nothing like this. I whispered in my mother's ear that I was afraid of a small black dog biting me.

The Van Horne's already had a small black poodle that used to be ours. I loved Mickey and didn't want my parents to give him away. I had missed him so much. I thought he was my only friend and I was losing him. My parents told me we would visit often.

Mom assured me that there were no dogs in the subway, only people, and I was being silly because I loved dogs. She got me to agree to go. I still thought the idea of Maria and me going out by ourselves was going to be exciting, so I didn't make too big fuss. I really did want to go.

Maria told me there was nothing to be afraid of and she would hold my hand the whole time. That made me feel better and secure.

We walked to the city bus stop, got on a bus, and walked to a subway station. I kept looking around me to make sure there were no dogs. Maria kept giggling and told me to relax because she wasn't going to let anything hurt me.

We went down the stairs and soon the subway train arrived. She warned me that the subway goes very fast, faster than any train. I wanted to be grown up and didn't tell her of my fear of going that fast. The subway zoomed and made quick stops to let a few people off and some others on. I enjoyed the ride but I also enjoyed watching all the different people around me. I was trying to forget my fear of the dog, but it was still nagging at me, no matter how hard I tried to think of other things. I couldn't see any dogs around anywhere.

The subway went over the Don Valley under Bloor St. It was exciting to see the traffic down below. The cars and trucks were so much smaller. I told myself I would never forget that bridge.

After a few stops, we halted and got out. Holding hands, we walked to her school and into her classroom and then to her locker. Maria seemed so much more grown up than I was. I didn't have a locker at my school. I wondered what I would put in my locker when I was older. The hallways were quiet and long. We did see a few other students, but Maria didn't stop to talk to anyone.

When closing her locker door, she said, "See, there is nothing to be afraid of! Aren't you glad you came?" I was glad and I tried to relax. All we had to do now was retrace our steps. Surely I could do that. Maybe it was the idea of being out without my parents that got me thinking of excuses not to come.

Still no dog in sight. I was feeling foolish, but couldn't stop looking around. We took the subway home. This would be my second ride on the subway and I wasn't scared about the speed. I was thrilled that I had finally got to ride the subway. I would tell my best friend, Diana, all about my trip the next time I saw her. On the way off the subway, there were so many people around, it was hard to believe. Where were all these people coming from? I felt as if I was being crushed. I was so short that I thought they didn't see me walking among them. They stepped on my feet and pushed me one way and then the other. I held onto Maria's hand tightly. Sometimes she had to pull me toward her. I didn't want to become separated in all this commotion. Now that would be really scary! My fear of the dog was not as prominent as that!

After all, I was almost back to her house. Slowly we climbed the stairs to go to level ground. It seemed to take forever. Everyone was trying to do the same thing we were doing. In front of me, all I could see where the backs of strangers and the sunlight above their heads. I was thankful that we would be back on the street again where it shouldn't be as crowded. I looked up and saw the subway sign. I was getting closer to the top of the stairs. I was four steps from the top, when all of a sudden, out of nowhere, something bit me, just under my bottom, on my right thigh. I was wearing my favourite purple shorts and could really feel the dog's teeth. I screamed in panic. I turned around. There behind me was a small black dog. This dog looked like the dog that was always on the Coppertone commercials, where the dog was pulling on the girl's red bathing-suit bottoms. An older woman, I think an Italian woman, was holding the leash. I don't think that she realized what her dog had done.

I went into hysterics. Maria had to pick me up, carry me the rest of the way up the stairs, and out onto the street, until the dog was out of sight.

The wound didn't draw blood, but the animal's teeth left marks imbedded in my flesh.

On the way back, we walked slowly from the subway to the city bus stop and then back to her house. I was walking on my toes because when my heel touched the cement it would hurt my wound. It took us longer to get back to Maria's house because of my slow limping.

Maria asked me how I knew about the dog. I said nothing. There was nothing to tell. My mother always warned me not to talk about "our secret." I told her it was a guess.

After walking up the stairs to where Maria lived, Maria yelled out that I was bitten by a little black dog. My mother gave me "the look." I went over and hugged her and told her that I was sorry. I didn't mean to be afraid of this dog. I didn't mean to know about this dog biting me.

Mr. And Mrs. Van Horne were interested in how I knew about this dog. I don't know what my parents told them. I sat on the middle on the living-room floor and played with Mickey.

I had never been afraid of small dogs. At times I could not explain my fears or how I knew it was going to happen. There were no thoughts before the words escaped my lips. There was no effort to form the words. No knowledge of what I was about to say until after I said it. Many times I wished I hadn't uttered a sound and there were times I didn't mean to say what I did.

My years were filled with such occurrences, including other premonitions, an apparition. and many visitations.

One day, I might find the time to tell the whole story of these.

Jacqueline B.

I SERIOUSLY BELIEVE SHE WAS AN ANGEL

It is not often that I receive an email that is like the one that appears here. It came on 15 October 2007, and it appeared on my screen in magenta rather than black and it was headed "Eerie experience … or *what was it?*" The long block of copy below certainly describes an experience that is eerie, one shared by mother and son. The vision that at first appears only to the son but which then appears to both mother and son is laden with meaning. Is "the lady in white" a spirit, a harbinger of bad or good news, or indeed a Guardian Angel? Is it as directly connected with the son's health, as the correspondent, Mrs. Allen, believes? There are no answers to these questions, but they must be asked, and having asked them, I will allow the reader the opportunity to answer them.

> My name is Melanie Allen. Last November, my son came down sick with what the doctor's call Fatty Liver Disease. This illness has affected his health for quite a few years now and he always got seriously ill with fever, vomiting, etc. Anyway, one night, I put him in our bed so I could keep an eye on him during the night. He was facing the big dresser on the right hand side of the room where there is a huge mirror on top of the dresser and he said to me, "Mom, do you see her?" When I looked I didn't see anything and he told me there was a lady in white watching him from the mirror. I told him it was probably his Guardian Angel, even though I couldn't see her. We left it at that. The next night, I again put him in our bed and he once again turned towards the mirror and said, "There she is again, mom. Do you see her now?" Upon turning to the mirror, to my surprise, I saw a lady in what looked like a white robe/dress with huge wings behind her! She looked like she was smiling at us. I, to my regret, immediately grabbed my son by the hand, and with tears flowing from my eyes we bolted from the room! The funny thing about this is that since that visit and vision, my son has not been ill with the F.L.D. And he always came down with this illness at least two or three times a year and would be sick for up to a month at a time. I do believe in ghosts, spirits, angels, etc., and am shocked and regretful of my fearful reaction to this visit. I seriously believe she was an angel sent to watch over my son, and by appearing to us she was giving us a sign that his F.L.D. was at an end. I don't know if you believe me or not, but this is true, and my son, now 15 years old, will verify what I have told you. Thanx for taking the time to read my letter.
>
> Sincerely,
>
> Mrs. Melanie Allen

AFTERWORD

Feel free to contact me if you have witnessed an odd event or had an unusual experience and are willing to share accounts of these with me and with my readers.

You may do so in one of three ways. You may write to me care of the Editorial Department of the publishing company whose address appears on the copyright page.

You may email me at *jrc@ca.inter.net*.

Or you may contact me through my website *www.colombo.ca*.

In the meantime, don't look over your shoulder!